MW01620813

American Abstract and Figurative Expressionism Style is Timely Art is Timeless

An Illustrated Survey with
Artists' Statements, Artwork and Biographies.

Edited by Marika Herskovic

NEW YORK SCHOOL PRESS New York, New Jersey

Published by the New York School Press
P.O. Box 305, Franklin Lakes
New Jersey, 07417-0305
708 Ashmont Road, Franklin Lakes
New Jersey, 07417
U.S.A.
www.nyschoolpress.com

First Published 2009

Telephone: 201 891 2063
Fax 201 891 8385
Printed in Germany by Cantz

Library of Congress Number: 2008944164

Cataloguing-in-Publication Data:

American abstract and figurative expressionism style is timely art is timeless an illustrated survey with artists' statements, artworks, and biographies/ edited by Marika Herskovic.
p. cm.
includes index

ISBN: 978-0-9677994-2-1 (alk. paper)
1. Abstract expressionism–United States. 2. Expressionism–United States. 3. Figurative expressionism–United States. 4. Arts, Modern -20th century. 5. Art, American-20th century. 6. Title. I. Herskovic, Marika

**TO MY HUSBAND
THOMAS HERSKOVIC
WHOSE BELIEF AND CONSTANT
ENCOURAGEMENT,
MADE IT POSSIBLE TO CARRY
OUT THIS PROJECT.**

CONTENTS

ACKNOWLEDGEMENT

It has been a difficult yet rewarding task to undertake an illustrated survey of the American abstract and figurative expressionism of the post-World War II era. In this volume we set out to demonstrate that a great number of the American expressionists refused to subordinate their work to formalistic restrictions. The artists created works of art both in representational and nonrepresentational expressionism. We will show the finest works of art by great artists who will convince the viewer that style is timely while art is timeless.

Artists, collectors, estates of artists, foundations, and a great number of photographic and permission services of museums and dealers were quick to respond.

Collectors, whether named or not, in the book allowed their treasured art works to be reproduced. I would like to express my gratitude for their contribution.

The professional staff of the photographic and permission departments of the following participating museums helped me to obtain the works in this book in an efficient and reliable fashion:

The Art Institute of Chicago, IL;
Aimee L. Marshall.

Crocker Art Museum, Sacramento, CA;
Erin Aitali.

The Detroit Institute of Arts, MI;
Sylvia Inwood.

Iris & B. Gerald Cantor Center for Visual Arts, Stanford University; Allison Akbay Associate Registrar.

Greenville Museum of Art, Greenville, SC;
Martha Severens, curator.

The Metropolitan Museum of Art, New York; Jeri Wagne.

Oakland Museum of California, Oakland, CA;
Robin Doolin.

Smithsonian American Art Museum, Washington, D.C.;
Leslie Green

Whitney Museum of American Art, New York;
Anita Duquette

I would like to express my gratitude to the artists' estates, foundations and dealers credited in the book who provided me with permission for statements and transparencies along with biographies for reproduction:

Robert Henri Adams Fine Art, Inc., Chicago, IL.;
Ken Probst, Peter Blair.

Ameringer &Yohe Fine Art, New York, NY; James Yohe, Mary Joan Waid.

Lori Bookstein Fine Art, New York, NY; Lauren Bakoin, director; Christina Lau.

Jerald Melberg Gallery, Charlotte, NC;
Jerald Melberg, Gaybe Johnson.

DC Moore Gallery, New York, NY;
Sandra Paci.

Tibor de Nagy Gallery, New York;

Lore Degenstein Gallery, Susquehanna University, Selinsgrove, PA;
Dan Olivetti, director.

Willem de Kooning Conservatory;
Amy Schichtel.

Hackett–Freedman Gallery, San Francisco, CA;
Michael Hackett, Susan McDonough.

Grace Hartigan — Studio;
Rex Stevens, Manager.

The Hans Moller Studios;
Larry Miley proprietor.

Kenkeleba Gallery, New York, NY;
Corrine Jennings.

Mitchell–Innes & Nash , New York, NY;
Jack Rutberg Gallery, Los Angeles, CA;
Jack Rutberg, Fabiola Munoz.

Anita Shapolsky Gallery, New York, NY;
Anita Shapolsky, Petra Valentova.

Estate of Jack Tworkov;
Jason Andrew, Archivist/Curator.

Spanierman Gallery, New York;
Ira Spanierman, Director; Gina Greer Associate Director; Bethany Dobson.

Greenberg Van Doren Gallery, New York, NY;
Georgia Franklin, Allison Alter.

Westbrook Galleries, Carmel, CA;
Brian and Christine Westbrook, Jim Clark.

Winfield Gallery, Carmel CA;
Christopher Winfield, Mary Corey.

Artists Rights Society (ARS);
Maggie Fleming.

I would like to thank the following individuals:

Bettina Goldschmidt from Dr. Cantz'sche Druckerei, Ostfildern, Germany, for the high quality printing of this book.

INSPIRATION

At an unspecified moment, from a source that today remains concealed from us, and yet inevitably, the work of art comes into the world.

Cold calculation, random spots of color, mathematically exact construction (clearly apparent or concealed), silent, screaming drawing, meticulous working out, fanfares of colors, their violin *pianissimo*, great, calm, heavy, disintegrating surfaces.

Is this not form?

Is this not *the means*?

Suffering, searching, tormented souls, with a deep rift, caused by the collision of the spiritual with the material. That which has been found. The living element of living and 'dead' nature. The consolation in the appearances of the world—external, internal. Premonitions of joy. The call. Speaking of the hidden by means of the hidden.

Is this not content?

Is this not the conscious and unconscious *purpose* of the compulsive urge to create

Shame upon him who has the power to put the necessary words into the mouth of art, but does not do so.

Shame upon him who turns his spiritual ear away from the mouth of art.

Human being speaks to human being about that which is superhuman—the *language* of art.

Murnau, (Oberbayern), August 1910

WASSILY KANDINSKY in the catalogue of the second exhibition held by the *NEUE KÜNSTLER-VEREINIGUNG*, Munich

INSPIRATION

.... It would be so easy to see that basically there are neither modern nor old-fashioned artists, because all new art is neither better nor worse than all genuine, already existing art—totally regardless of time and country. To divide artists according to country or time can be of purely cultural-historical interest, but in no case has any value for art.

.... When will the question of form no longer replace the question of art? When will it really be understood that art does not derive from form, but form from art? How many thousands of years are yet needed (nothing was learned from the previous thousands) for man to realize that each new content demands its own form, and that form without content is a sin against the spirit?

WASSILY KANDINSKY
On the Artist [Om Konstnären] *(Stockholm)*, February, 1916..

INTRODUCTION

This book is the third in the series of reference books published by the New York School Press, dealing with the American art and artists of the post-World War II era.

While New York by the end of the 20th century became "the new center of modernism,[1]" with the emergence of the New York School Abstract Expressionism, surveys on the American art of the post-World War II era avoided any inclusive discussion of American art's mainstream. Historians focused only on the works of a few artists as if their unique, disparate, non-representational *signature style* would qualify them to represent the entire movement of *American Abstract and Figurative Expressionism* of the post-World War II era.[2, 3, 4]

In spite of the critics and historians of the time there were a significant number of artists living in the East Coast, New York City, and the West Coast, especially in the San Francisco Bay Area who "sought to infuse fresh meaning into the style of abstract expressionism by introducing recognizable imagery."[5]

Historians and critics have documented the works of representational ("figurative") expressionists as a separate group of American expressionists. This resulted in further separation of art and artists based on formalistic grounds.[6]

This survey (a follow-up to the earlier volumes: *New York School Abstract Expressionists: Artists Choice by Artists;*[7] *American Abstract Expressionism of the 1950s An Illustrated Survey.*[8]) intends to present a significantly different approach. Fifty eight American painters and sculptors of the post-World War II era, are represented, each by one *abstract* and one *figurative* work.

The book intends to show that the most engaged mainstream creative work in New York and across the USA was not restricted to non-representational or representational expressionism but rather to the creative power of the individual expressionist artist.

The artists are represented in alphabetical order. The usual convention of critical analysis is replaced by statements written by the artists themselves. The statements may serve to enlighten the readers as to the artists' relation to their creative process.

The biographical information for each artist is presented in a standardized, uniform fashion.

It is critical that a reference book of this sort would provide excellent, large format reproductions. The books were printed by the world renowned Dr. Cantz'sche Druckerei in Ostfildern, Germany,

What distinguishes each and every reproduction that is presented in this book is the artist's creative expressionistic rendering of his or her work. As Wassily Kandinsky remarked, "Human being speaks to human being about that which is superhuman—the language of art."[9]

This editor firmly believes that the time has come to transcend the compulsion of a few individuals for notoriety, power and immortality at the expense of undermining the scope of the greatest American art movement of the 20th century: *American Abstract and Figurative Expressionism*.

In this book as in the previous one[8] all the American expressionist artists are seen together in the context of the post-World War II era regardless of gender, race or ethnic origin.

Some artists have been excluded from this book because adequate information was either not available or not obtained in a timely fashion. In other cases, difficulties with reproduction rights made inclusion impossible.

Ultimately, there is only so much room in any book and the editor must take responsibility for the final list of artists to be profiled. With the passage of time a more complete documentation of all the active members of the American avant–garde of the post-World War II era will become a published reality.

May the documentation presented in this book help to reevaluate art's mainstream and to shed new light on American art of our time.

Marika Herskovic, PhD, Editor

1. *Art History*; Revised Edition.
Harry N. Abrams, Inc.
Volume II, 1999, p. 1109.
2. *The Triumph of American Painting: A History of Abstract Expressionism*, by Irving Sandler. Harper & Row, Publishers, 1989. ISBN: 0-06-430075-7
3. *Abstract Expressionism*: The Critical Development, organized by Michael Auping, with essays by: Michael Auping, Ann Gibson, Donald Kuspit, Michael Leja, Marcelin Pleynet, Richard Shiff, David Sylvester and an interview with Lawrence Alloway. Harry N. Abrams, Inc., New York in association with the Albright–Knox Art Gallery, Buffalo, New York, 1987. ISBN: 0-914782-62-2 (pbk); ISBN: 0-8109-1866-8 (hc)
4. *The San Francisco School of Abstract Expressionism*, by Susan Landauer, with introduction by Dore Ashton. Laguna Art Museum. University of California Press, 1996.
5. *Bay Area Figurative Art 1950-1965*, by Caroline A. Jones. San Francisco Museum of Modern Art, University of California Press, 1990. ISBN: 978-0-520-06842-1
6. *The Figurative Fifties: New York Figurative Expressionism*. Exhibition organized by Paul Schimmel, Chief Curator of the Newport Harbor Art Museum and Judith E. Stein, Associate Curator of Pennsylvania Academy of Fine Arts. Rizzoli, New York, 1988. ISBN: 0-8478-0942-0 (Rizzoli); ISBN: 0-917439-12-5 (pbk.: NHAM)
7. *New York School Abstract Expressionists: Artists Choice* by Artists, by Marika Herskovic. New York School Press, 2000. ISBN: 0967799406
8. *American Abstract Expressionism of the 1950s: An Illustrated Survey*, by Marika Herskovic. New York School Press, 2003. ISBN: 0967799414
9. *WASSILY KANDINSKY in the catalogue of the second exhibition held by the 'NEUE KÜNSTLERVEREINIGUNG'* Murnau, August 1910

ARTWORK PHOTOCREDITS

It is the publisher's intention to take note of the special role of the photographers without whom the high quality reproduction of fine art would not be possible.

Special thanks to individual photographers:

Name of Photographer	Reproduction	page number
Roz Akin	Jan Müller	174
Christian Carone	Nicolas Carone	65, 66
	Sonia Gechtoff	105
	James Kelly	134
Sheldan C. Collins	Conrad Marca-Relli	220
Christopher Clamp	James Rosati	206
M. Lee Fatherree	Elmer Nelson Bischoff	45
Charles Fields	John Grillo	113, 114
Greg Hicks	Robert Nathans	178
Philip Hofstetter	Julius Hatofsky	125, 126
Aristidis Kyriazis	Peter Agostini	21
	Leo Amino	28, 29
	Rosemarie Beck	34
	Adelie Landis Bischoff	42
	William Brice	49
	Ernest Briggs	53
	Elaine de Kooning	73, 74
	Perle Fine	93, 94
	Sideo Fromboluti	101, 102
	Sonia Gechtoff	106
	Robert Goodnough	109, 110
	Buffie Johnson	129
	James Kelly	135
	Earl Kerkam	137
	Albert Kotin	141, 142
	Irving Kriesberg	149, 150
	Ezio Martinelli	162
	Hans Moller	169, 170

Name of Photographer	Reproduction	Page number
Aristidis Kyriazis	Jan Müller	175
	Robert Nathans	177
	George Ortman	180
	Felix Pasilis	189, 190
	James Rosati	205
	George Spaventa	217, 218
	Nora Speyer	221, 222
	Karl Zerbe	245, 246
Phocasso/J.W. White	Paul Wonner	238
Steven Sloman	Willem de Kooning	77
	Jackson Pollock	197
Philips/Schwab	Lee Krasner	145
Rex Stevens	Grace Hartigan	121, 122
Petra Valentova	Ernest Briggs	54
	Amaranth Ehrenhalt	89, 90
	Joe Fiore	97, 98
	Buffie Johnson	130
	Jeanne Reynal	201, 202
	Ethel Schwabacher	213, 214
Dennis Wyszynski	Joan Savo	210
James Zimmerman	Nanno de Groot	69, 70

We are privileged to provide extended documentation for Aristidis Kyriazis who is a distinguished creative photographer and responsible for the color management and most of the images in this book.

ARISTIDIS KYRIAZIS

In photography the artist encounters the task of subjectively discerning an already existing composition. In visual terms he questions and decides which elements are important and which must be omitted. By seeing and creating, the photographer unveils his own perception of reality by exposing the subject in a fraction of time when it stands revealed in its most evocative form. To see is to become sensitized to the particular subject matter in its decisive moment. To create is to convey the vision of the artist through the photograph as a means of communication with the audience.

I seek to strengthen my intuitive understanding of light and shadow by means of experience, study and observation. My continuous research into alternative processes reflects my respect for the history of the medium. The goal is to obtain images that sensitize us to those aspects of life and human experience that sometimes escape our attention.

Aristidis Kyriazis

Aristidis Kyriazis, Statement: provided to the editor
December 5, 2008

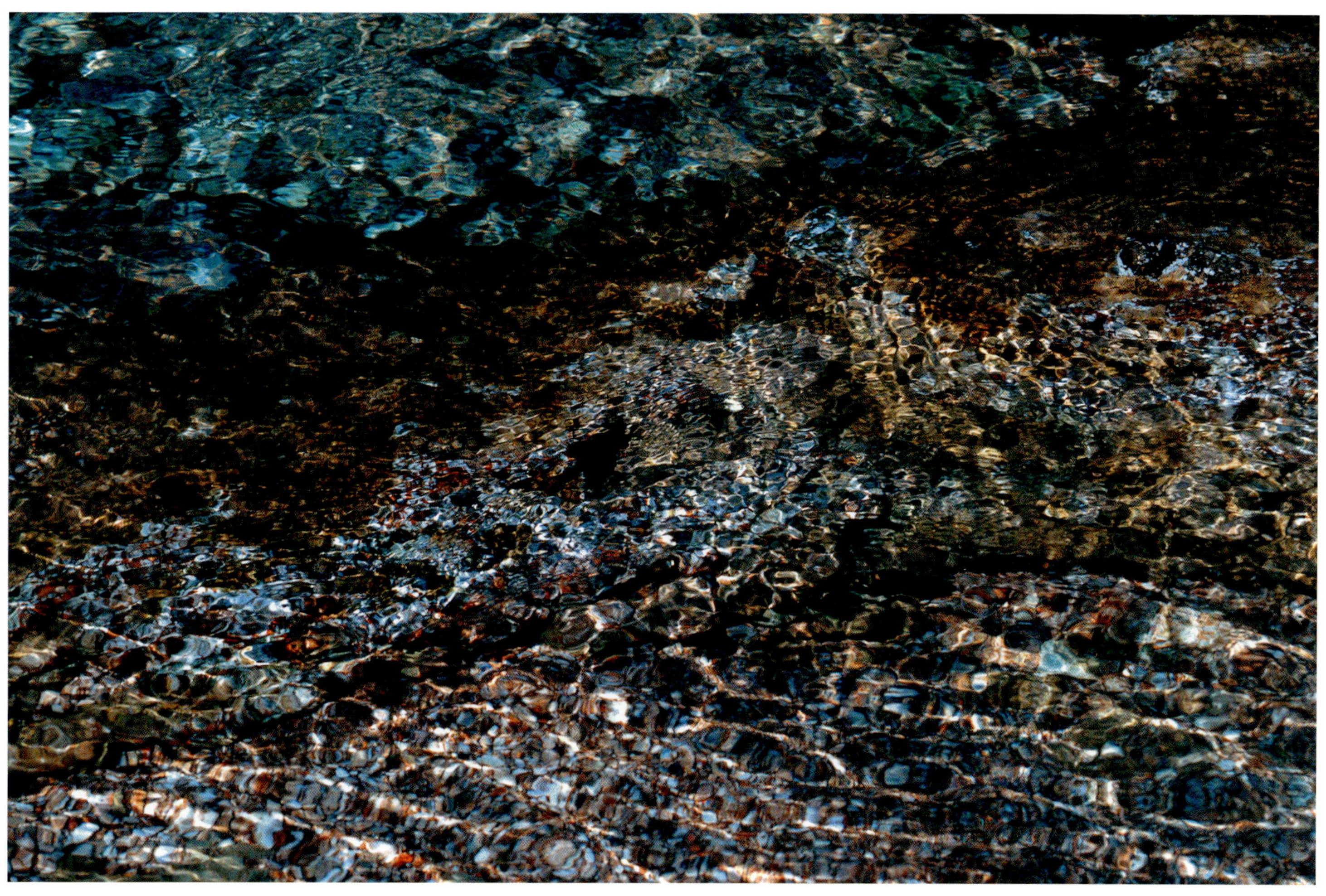

ARISTIDIS KYRIAZIS, *Water #2*, 1985
Pigment print, 14 x 21 inches
© Aristidis Kyriazis

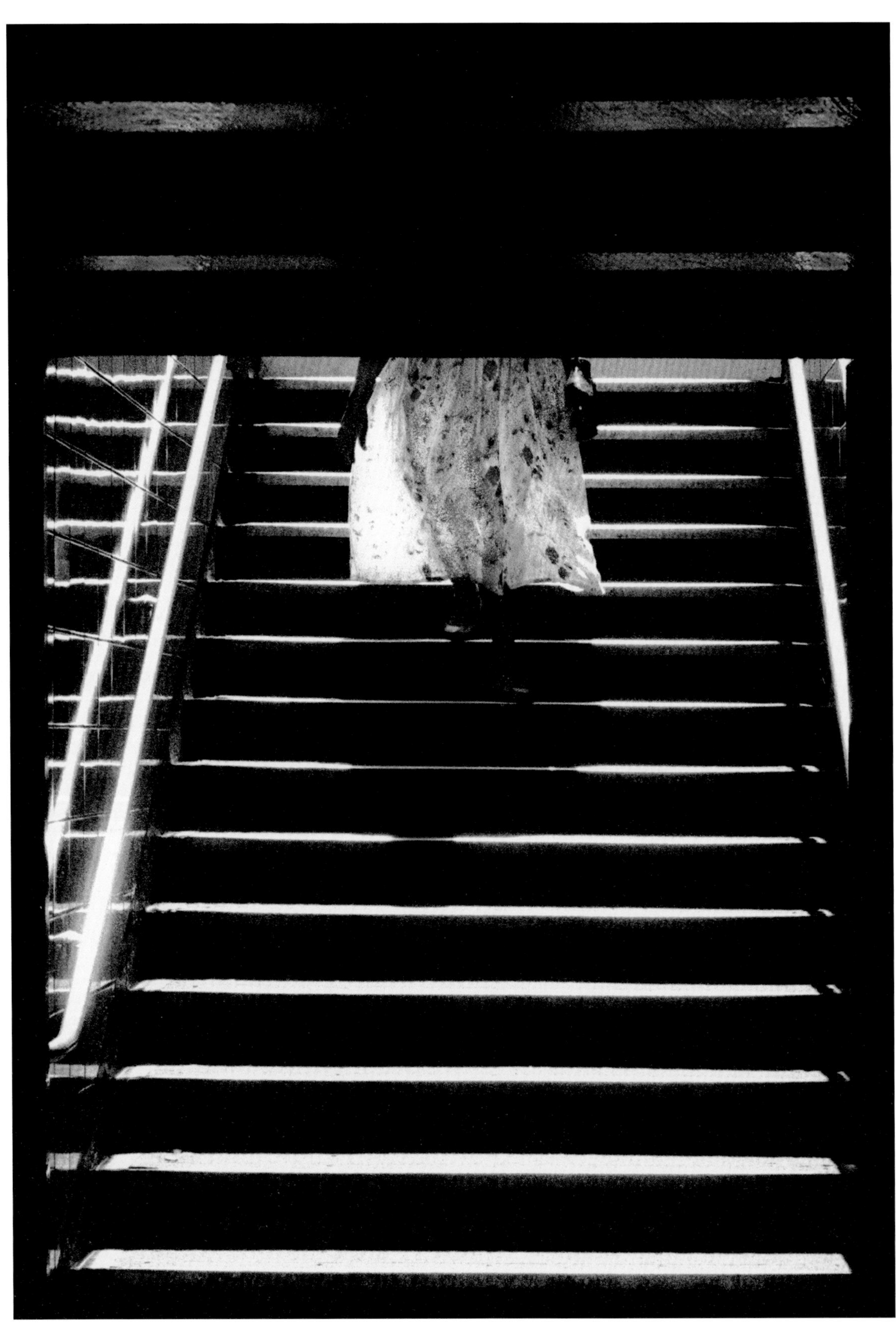

ARISTIDIS KYRIAZIS, *Untitled*, NY, 1997
Carbro print on paper, 14 3/4 x 9 7/8 in. (37.5 x 25.1 cm.)
Smithsonian American Art Museum
Gift of the Perkins Center for the Arts made possible by the Bogen Photo Corporation 1999.31

ARISTIDIS KYRIAZIS. [1949-]

Born May 20, 1949 in Thessalonica, Greece.

Studied 1967–1970: Toronto City College. Toronto, Canada;
1972–1974: Germaine School of Photography, NYC;
1974–1976: The New School for Social Research. NYC.

Teaching Positions 1992–2002: Photography workshops in Greece and New York.

Selected Solo Exhibitions
1989: *Range of Light*, circ., Creative Center for Photography Gallery, San Juan Capistrano, CA; 1992: *Retrospective*, Light Writing Gallery. Santa Ana, CA; 1997: *Singular Vision*, New York University, Alexander Onassis Center Art Gallery, NYC; *Palies Sinies*, New Fortress Museum. Corfu, Greece; 1998: *Sticks and Stones*, circ., Atelier Alternative Gallery. Hoboken, NJ; *Singular Vision*, Cypress College Photography Gallery, CA; 1999: *New York State of Mind*, Young & Rubicam Communications Gallery, NYC; Two Fifteen Gallery, Santa Ana, CA; 2000: *Phototechtronics: A Study of Process*, Kouros Gallery, NYC; 2001: *Retrospective*, Atelier Alternative Gallery. Hoboken, NJ; *Images of America*, Rocky Mountain School of Photography Gallery, Missoula, MT; 2002: 53 x 53: *Highlights of a Visual Journey*, Benefit for the Cathedral of St. John the Theologian, NJ; *After 9/11: Reconstructing the Image*, circ., Kouros Gallery, NYC; Andipa Gallery, London, England; 2005: *Corfu Images*, New Fortress Museum, Corfu, Greece; 2007: *The Environment and the Human Effect*, Museum of Corfu Municipal, Gallery. Corfu, Greece.

Selected Group Exhibitions
1982: *Europalia*, Group Exhibition representing Greece in the medium of Photography, Galerie Du Musee de la Photographie. Brussels, Belgium; 1987: *Southern California Artists*, Creative Center for Photography Gallery. San Juan Capistrano, CA; 1994: *New Photography*, Irvine Center for the Arts, Irvine, CA; 1995: *Two Person Exhibition*, Center for Photograph, Athens, Greece; 1999: *Untitled*, Albright Knox Museum Art Gallery, Buffalo, NY; *1st Anniversary Group Exhibition*, Two Fifteen Gallery. Santa Ana, CA; *Unrelated Subjects,* Atelier Alternative Gallery, Hoboken, NJ; *Photography 18*, Perkin's Center for the Arts. Moorestown, NJ; 2000: Light Writing Gallery, Santa Ana, CA; 2001: *Tribute to 9/11*, Jersey City Art Gallery, Jersey City, NJ; 2002: 9/11: *Remembering and Healing*, City Hall, Hoboken Cultural Affairs, Hoboken NJ; *Off the Wall*, Benefit Exhibit for the Jersey City Museum. Jersey City, NJ.

AMERICAN ABSTRACT AND FIGURATIVE EXPRESSIONISM STATEMENTS, ARTWORK AND BIOGRAPHIES

PETER SALVATORE AGOSTINI

Sculpture in a sense, cannot mean the facades of the past, or the half – facade of the present; it means instead a new language and new findings.

Many things pop up, such as toast, the facade of breakfast...as silence, the facade of inactive moment...the wonderment of possibilities: how heavy too much is, how speed + space + time + ? = possibilities, that form is time, heredity and passages a mood of time...or how many catch – phrases can catch a meaning...or what is sculpture when it is, or is sculpture sculpture – frontal or round or when it's hanging ...or houses, are they houses because they're housing...

To me, sculpture happens, names itself and it is.

Peter Agostini, Statement:
It is. No. 4, Autumn, 1959. A Magazine for Abstract Art. Second Half Publishing Co., Inc, NYC.

To me an accident is like a sweet nostalgia.

It leads me to a sense of where I can be free for a second.

The accident for me has a kind of inevitability leading to another action.

I find I am thinking about something I didn't consider before.

I don't ever get involved with my materials; any force that comes out of these comes from my manipulation of them.

If I am working with something, it leads to something else and this way I start rejections; and on these points of rejection I find other possibilities.

The only way I can find truth to anything is through accidents.

Peter Agostini, Statement:
from the archives of the Estate.

(I've done horses all my life as an artist because)...I love horses, that's all. I don't look at them when I sculpt or draw them, but I *know* them. They capture an essence of form and movement. When I make a horse, I don't give it much of a tail. The tail is a decorative element, like hair on a head. You notice my heads are basically bald...because I want to tighten up the skull. the form is the essence, not the surface decoration. I don't put much of a mane on the horse either, I just suggest it. The horse doesn't need a tail or mane, and a head doesn't need hair. I'm more interested in large volumes. Like the flanks.

Peter Agostini, Statement:
Homer Yost, dialog with Peter Agostini, The Coraddi University of North Carolina at Greensboro, NC. Spring 1984.

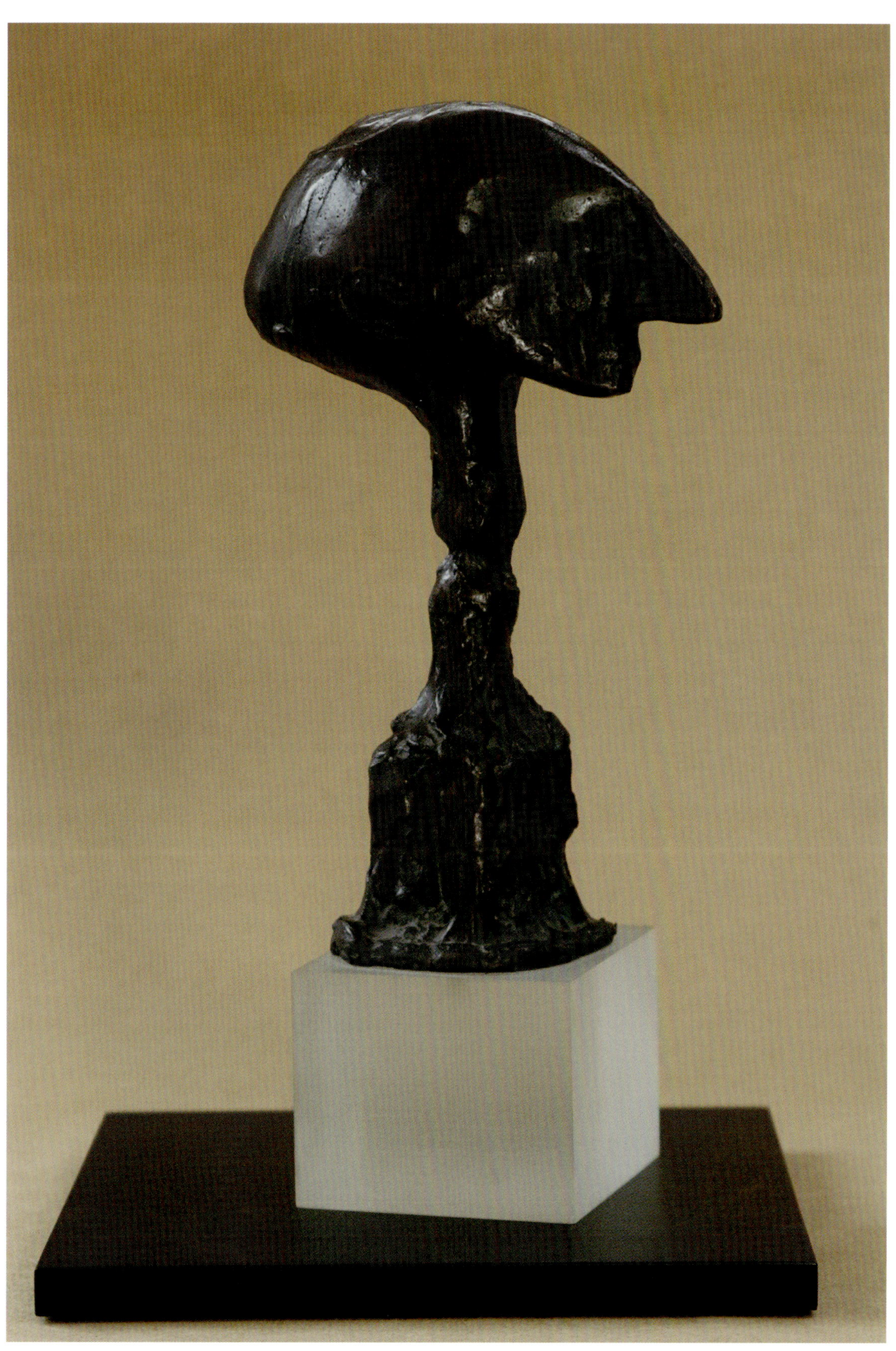

PETER AGOSTINI, *HEAD II (atoner series)*, 1955
Bronze, Ed., 2/7, brown patina. H: 9 inches on a 2 3/4 inch plexi cube
Private Collection

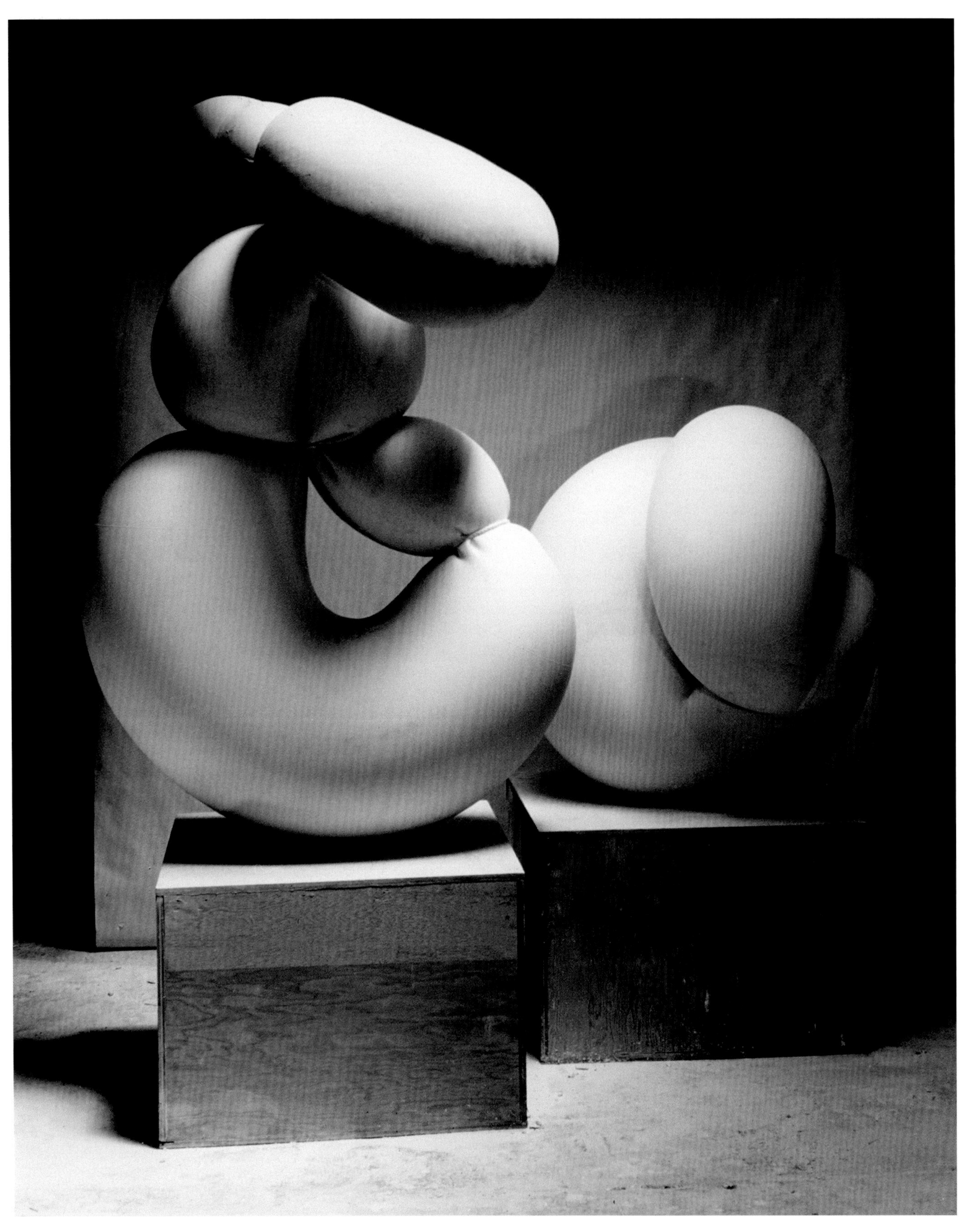

PETER AGOSTINI, *BURLESQUE QUEEN*, 1965
Plaster, H: 7 feet; W: 6 feet
Collection of the estate

PETER AGOSTINI, [1913-1993]

Born 1913, New York City, NY.
Died April 27, 1993, New York City, NY.

Studied Leonardo da Vinci Art School, NYC.

Teaching Positions 1967–1984: University of North Carolina, Greensboro; New York Studio School.

Selected Solo Exhibitions 1959 (first): Galerie Grimaud, NYC; 1960, 62-65, 67, 68: Stephen Radich Gallery; 1965: Richard Gray Gallery; 1969: University of North Carolina; 1971, 73, 76: The Zabriskie Gallery, NYC; 1977: Artists' Choice Museum, NYC; 1981, 83: New York Studio School; 1985, 86: Bernice Steinbaum Gallery, Ltd., NYC; 1991: Anita Shapolsky Gallery, NYC.

Selected Group Exhibitions 1960: Whitney Museum of American Art, NYC; Museum of Modern Art, NYC; Claude Bernard, Paris; 1962: The Art Institute of Chicago; The Wadsworth Athenium, Hartford, CT; 1963: *International Sculpture Exhibition*, Battersea Park, London; São Paulo Biennial, VII; 1964: New School for Social Research; *Recent American Sculpture*, Jewish Museum; 1964, 66, 68, 70: *Annuals*, Whitney Museum of American Art, NYC; 1967: *American Sculpture of the 60's*, Los Angeles County Museum of Art, Los Angeles, CA; 1970: Foundation Maeght, L'Art Vivant aux Etats-Unis; 1981: *Art on Paper*, University of North Carolina; 1984: *The Third Dimension*, Whitney Museum of American Art, NYC; University of North Carolina.

CHARLES HENRY ALSTON

January 4, 1971
Mr. Robert Doty, Curator
Whitney Museum of American Art
945 Madison Avenue
New York, N.Y. 10021

Dear Mr. Doty:
I must decline your invitation to participate in the Museum's projected exhibition of Black artists. The idea of separating artists on the basis of color is a repulsive affirmation of the racism and bigotry which permeate American society. The fact that such an exhibition is endorsed by, even insisted upon, by a number of Black artists, understandably outraged at the lack of opportunity to show their work, does not exempt the museum from the responsibility of foreseeing the implications of such an exhibition. Certainly, the last group I would expect to champion polarization and separatism in our society is an art institution. The Supreme Court of these United States has long since ruled that separate is not equal in the field of education. It is no more equal in the field of art.

I do not question the good intentions of the museum in attempting to rectify the unfair, unjust neglect of Black artists. However, I do question the value of a segregated show, and I do fear the long term harm it may do,– particularly to young and potentially important American artists who happen to be Black. Unless the Black artist is given the opportunity to exhibit with his peers of any race, color, nationality, creed or religion, he is being denied his right to be part of the mainstream of American art. The museum's role is not to mount an exhibition for Black artists only, but to seek out and find the talented Black as he has the talented White artist, and place him in the mainstream of American art, where he must be tested in the some crucible of quality as any other artist.

As for myself, albeit proudly Black, I would hate to think that I was in an exhibition because I'm Black, rather than because I am a good painter.

Finally, let me say to you and to others who advocate such a project, that separate exhibitions lead to separate standards and separate, I repeat, is by nature unequal in a democratic society.

Arthur Ashe and Muhammed Ali are Champions– not Black champions. These men, in spite of the bigotry, in spite of the racism, have proven their excellence against all comers, and have emerged in the dignity of their superiority. The Black artists in America cannot aspire to less.

Sincerely yours,
Charles Alston

Letter by Charles Alston: provided by the Estate of Charles Alston.

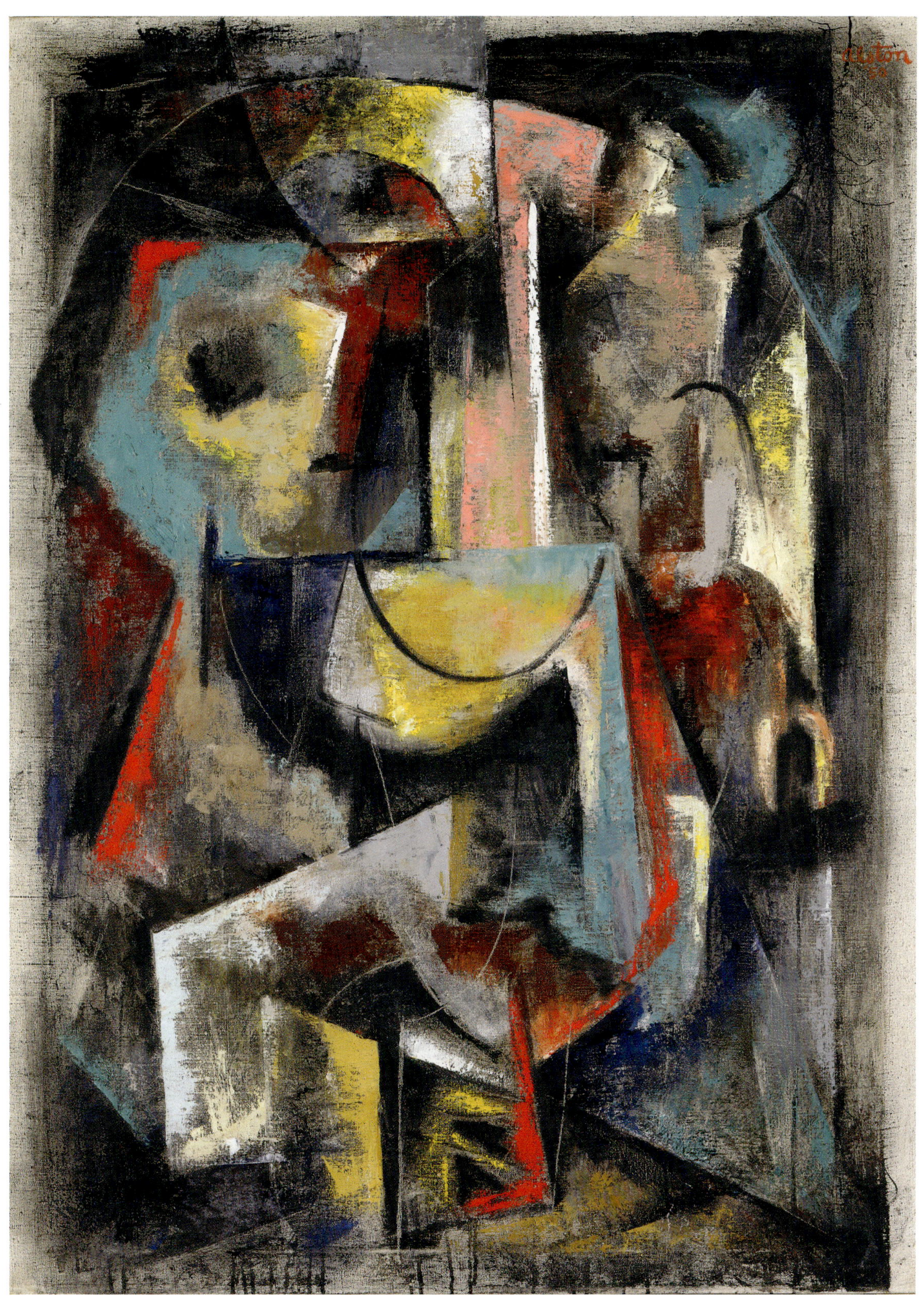

CHARLES HENRY ALSTON, *Painting*, 1950
Oil on canvas, 50 x 36 inches (127 x 91.4 cm)
The Metropolitan Museum of Art, Arthur Hoppock Hearn Fund, 1951. (51.18)
Photograph © 2009 The Metropolitan Museum of Art
© Estate of Charles Henry Alston, Courtesy of Kenkeleba Gallery, New York

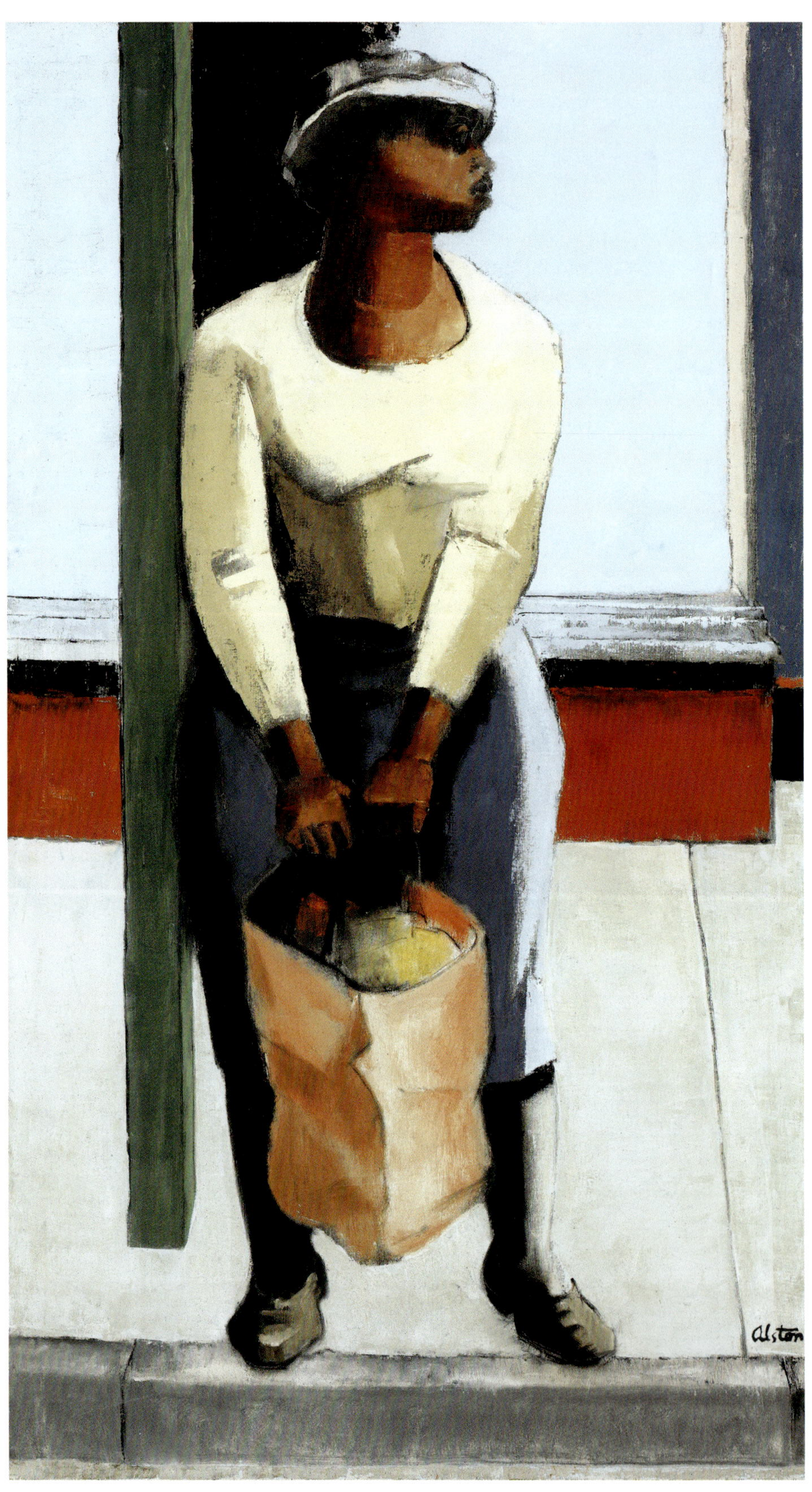

CHARLES ALSTON 1907 - 1977, *Woman with Shopping Bag*, circa 1955
Oil on canvas, 50 x 28 inches
Collection of the Greenville County Museum of Art, Museum purchase from the Arthur and Holly Magill Fund

CHARLES HENRY ALSTON, [1907-1977]

Born November 28, 1907, Charlotte, NC
Died 1977

Studied Columbia U., BA; 1931, MA; Pratt Institute (with Alexander Kostellow).

Federal Art Project 1935–1940: Mural and Lithography Supervisor; murals for Harlem Hospital, NY; Golden State Mutual Life Insurance Co.

Military Service in World War II
1941–1945: US Army.

Teaching Positions 1949–1957: Joe and Emily Lowe Art School, NY; 1950– : Art Students League, New York; City College; The Museum of Modern Art School, NY; New School for Social Research, NY.

Selected Solo Exhibitions 1950 (first): Seymour Oppenheimer Gallery, Chicago; 1953–1957: John Heller Gallery, NY; 1959: Dunbarton Gallery, Boston, MA; 1960: Feingarten Gallery, NY. Selective Retrospective, 1950–63: New York Cultural Center.

Selected Group Exhibitions 1936: *New Horizon in American Art*, The Museum of Modern Art, NYC; 1937: Baltimore Museum of Art, Baltimore, MD; 1945: RoKo Gallery, NY; 1950: *American Painting Today*, The Metropolitan Museum of Art, NY; 1951, 52, 54: The Whitney Museum of American Art Annuals and Biennials, NY; Museum of Fine Arts, Boston, MA; 1967: University of California; 1969: New York Cultural Center.

LEO AMINO

Polyester Resin Casting
Leo Amino, February, 1982.
Introduction

For over thirty-five years I have been involved with plastic, especially the use of its transparency for my work in sculpture. Transparency has been used, in such materials as glass and crystal, from the earliest times. However, due to technical difficulties involved in using these substances, modern sculptors have not made much use of transparency. The advent of World War II with its accompanying shortage of materials gave great impetus to the development of plastic as we know of it today.

The shimmering colors of red or white wine in cut crystal glasses under candlelight never ceases to give great pleasure. The flickering of candle light is not uniform, so that its effects are changeable and variable. Ordinarily, we take light for granted as something constant and unchanging, but there can be very many kinds of light, such as spotlight, floodlight and diffused light. Light also varies as to its density and its angle on the illuminated object. Dealing with transparency, one becomes very conscious of the effects of different kinds of light.

I was interested in the use of color for sculpture, so I started painting sculpture with oil, but the result was not to my satisfaction due to the painted quality of the surface.

By 1946 transparent plastics such as acrylic sheets, polystyrene resin and polyvinyl acetate emulsion were already on the market. Therefore, I began to experiment with polyvinyl acetate emulsion (mixed with pigments and filler into a paste form) applying it over armatures in the plaster direct method. This approach still did not answer the question of transparency. Plastic emulsion is a suspension of plastic particles with catalyst in water (as in the acrylic or vinyl paint of today)--and the mixture of filler and pigment made the suspension opaque. My next step was to proceed with the casting of acrylic and styrene resin, as they had better transparency. Here, I found that even with a thermostatically controlled oven, curing was slow and tricky, and bubbles often formed in the cast. Around 1947, polyester resin became available. Even though the resin itself was brownish in color, at least I was able to experiment with transparency, since the handling of the casting was easier. My first all-plastic sculpture show was held in 1948.

Today's polyester casting resin is a far cry from the old in that clarity and ease of handling have both been greatly improved. For still better clarity, polyester resin modified with acrylic resin is now also available.

Leo Amino, Statement: for exhibition held at the Zimmerli Art Museum, NJ, 1985.

It is interesting to speculate upon the effects of consensual attitude such as 'right things to do,' 'go with the crowds,' 'me-tooism,' etc., will have on the kind of art work produced by the individual who was brought up in any society. If the art is to be the expression of an individual one must question the validity of his consensual attitude even though he may be totally unaware. After all, consensual attitude is a kind of blind acceptance and is an enemy of individual creativity which is one of few avenues Modern Man has today.

Sept. 9, 1976.

Leo Amino, Statement: from the artist's diary provided by his wife, Mrs. Julie Amino.

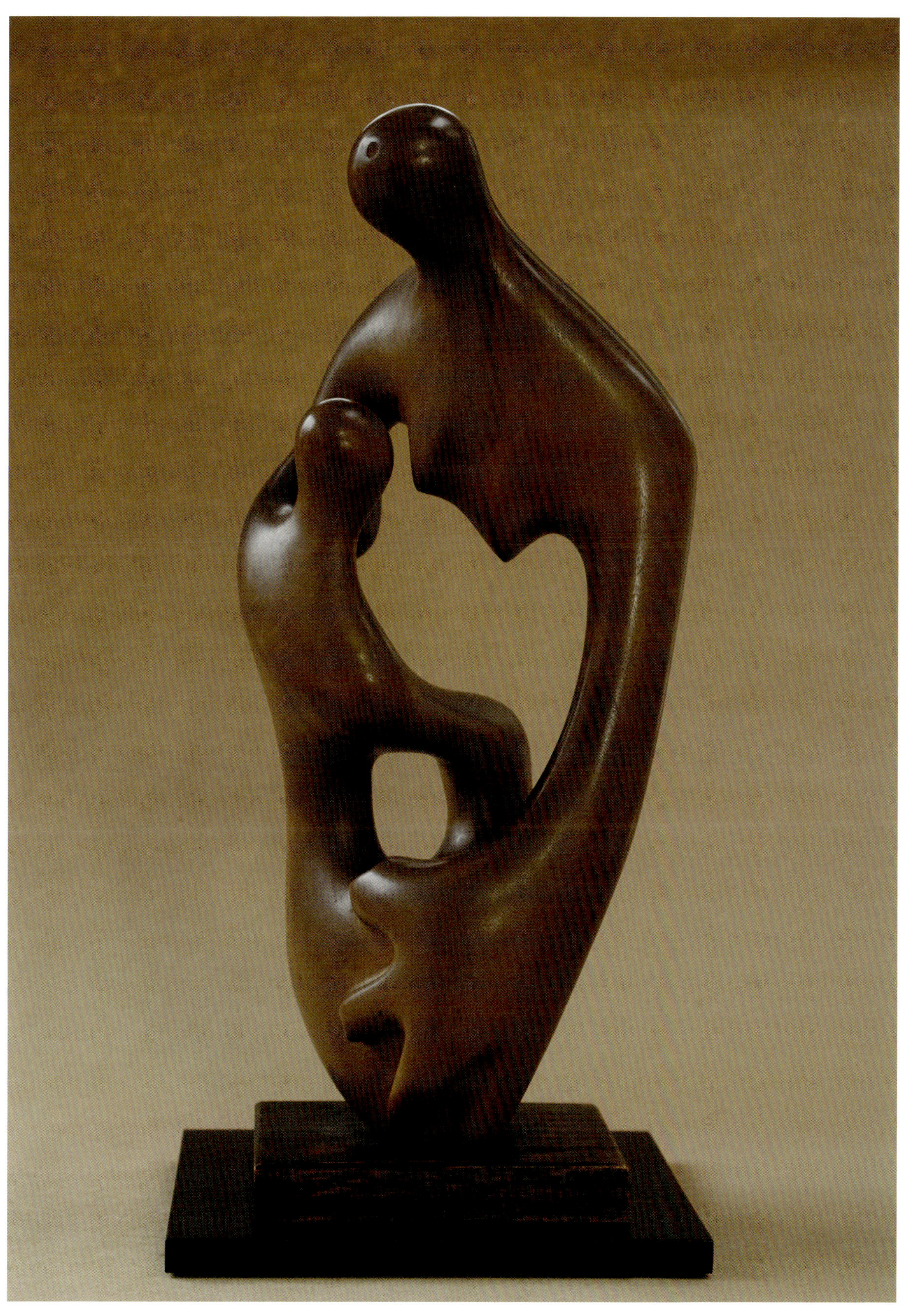

LEO AMINO, *Mother and Child*, 1946
Mahagony, 16 1/4 x 7 1/2 x 6 1/4 inches
Private collection

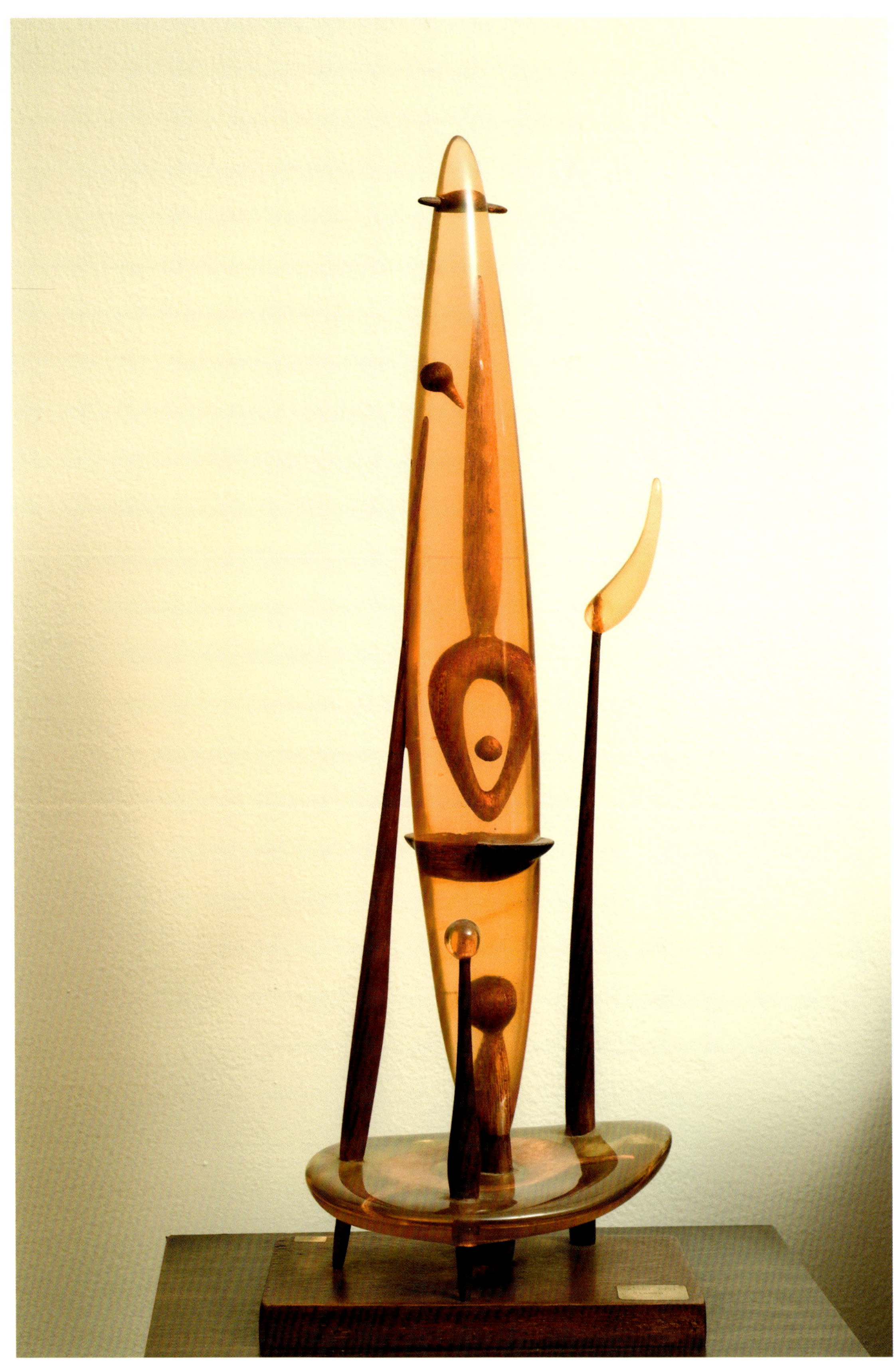

LEO AMINO, *Stamen 2,* 1951
Polyester with wood, 21 3/4 x 7 x 6 inches
Collection of Julie and Eriko Amino

LEO AMINO, [1911-1989]

Born June 26, 1911, in Taiwan (formerly Formosa of Japanese parentage). Emigrated to USA 1929. US citizen 1958. **Died** December 1, 1989, New York City.

Studied c. 1929–1933: San Mateo Junior College, CA;
c. 1936–37: New York University;
c. 1938: American Artists School, under tutelage of Chaim Gross.

Military Service in World War II
1943–45: Translator for the US Navy.

Teaching Positions 1946-1950: Black Mountain College;
1952–1977: Cooper Union.

Selected Solo Exhibitions 1940: Montross Gallery NYC; 1940, 43: Artists' Gallery NYC; 1941, 1946–1952, 54, 71, 73: Clay Club Gallery (re-named) Sculptors' Gallery (re-named) Sculpture Center Gallery NYC; 1945: Boneståll Gallery NYC; 1948: Grand Rapids Art Museum, MI; 1949: University of North Carolina, Person Hall Gallery; 1950: State Teachers College (Ball State University Art Gallery) IN; 1951: Philadelphia Art Alliance; 1953: Ben-Moore Gallery MA; 1957: DeCordova Museum MA; 1969, 70: East Hampton Gallery NYC; 1985: Rutgers State University of New Jersey, Zimmerli Art Museum; 1994: Berman Daferner Gallery NYC.

Selected Group Exhibitions 1939: American Art Today, New York Worlds Fair; 1950: *Carvers, Modelers and Welders*, Museum of Modern Art NYC; 1951: *American Sculpture*, Metropolitan Museum of Art NYC; *The New Decade*, (1955); *Nature in Abstraction*, (1958); *Decade of Transition*: *1940–1950*, (1981), Whitney Museum of American Art NYC; 1956: *Sculpture Today*, Montclair Museum of Art NJ; 1970: *A Plastic Presence*, Jewish Museum NYC; 1987: *Sculpture of the American Scene*, Philadelphia Art Alliance PA; *The Arts at Black Mountain College*: *1933–1957*, circ., Bard College, Edith Blum Art Institute; *2001: Vital Forms: American Art and Design in the Atomic Age, 1940–1960*, circ., Brooklyn Museum of Art, NY.

ROSEMARIE BECK

The eternal question: do we reveal more when we use the object or when we put it aside? One of the temptations of painting is simultaneity; this which I see/this which I make. The tussle and its pervasive rhythm reveal us.

Rosemarie Beck, Statement: from [unpublished Journal, 1-19-60] Rosemarie Beck *(1923-2003)*
ABSTRACTION INTO FIGURATION: PAINTINGS 1952-1966, October 16- December 1, 2007.
Lori Bookstein Fine Art, New York

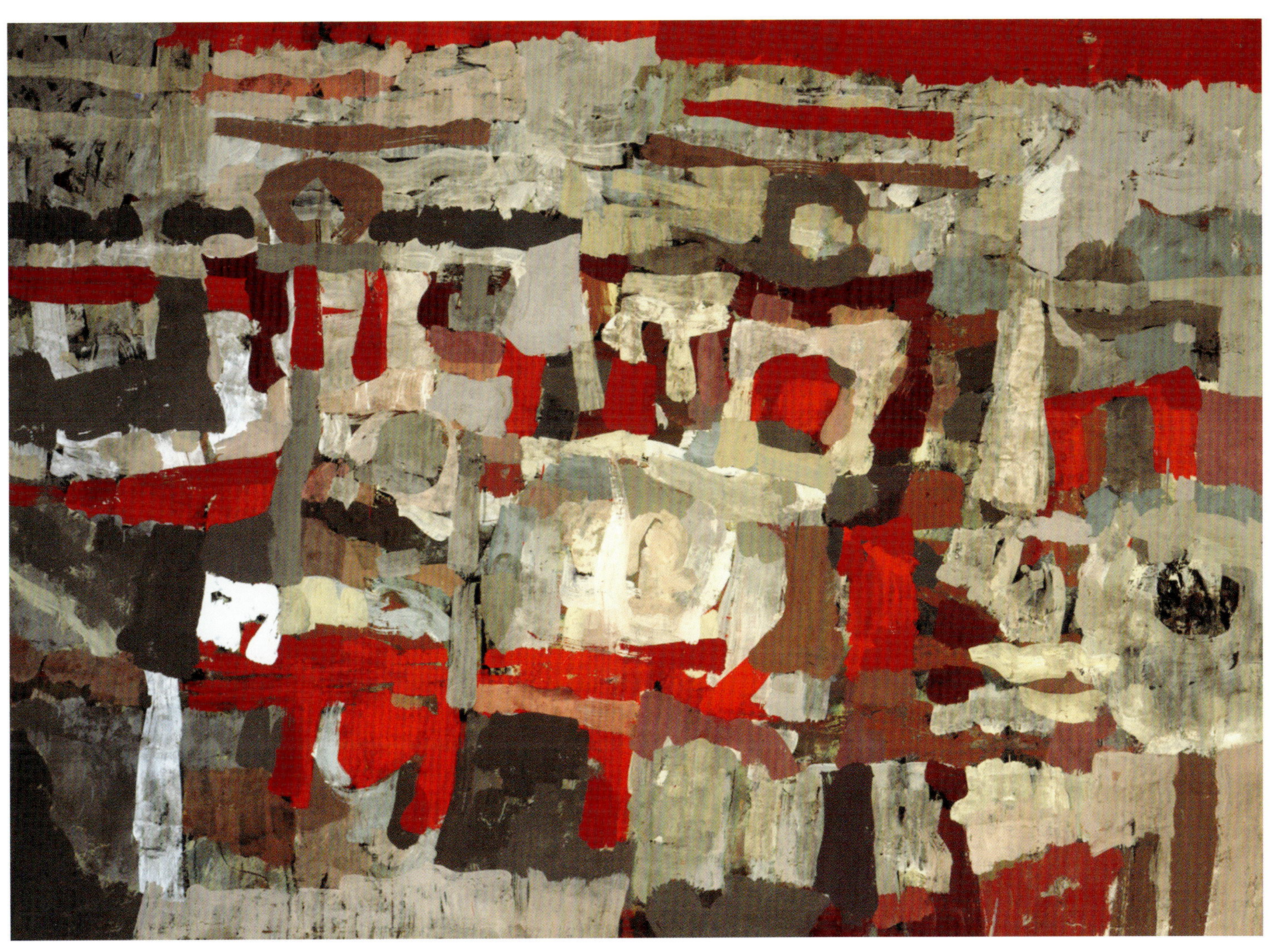

ROSEMARIE BECK, *Untitled*, 1952
Oil on masonite 46 x 62 inches
© Rosemarie Beck Foundation. Courtesy of Lori Bookstein Fine Art, New York

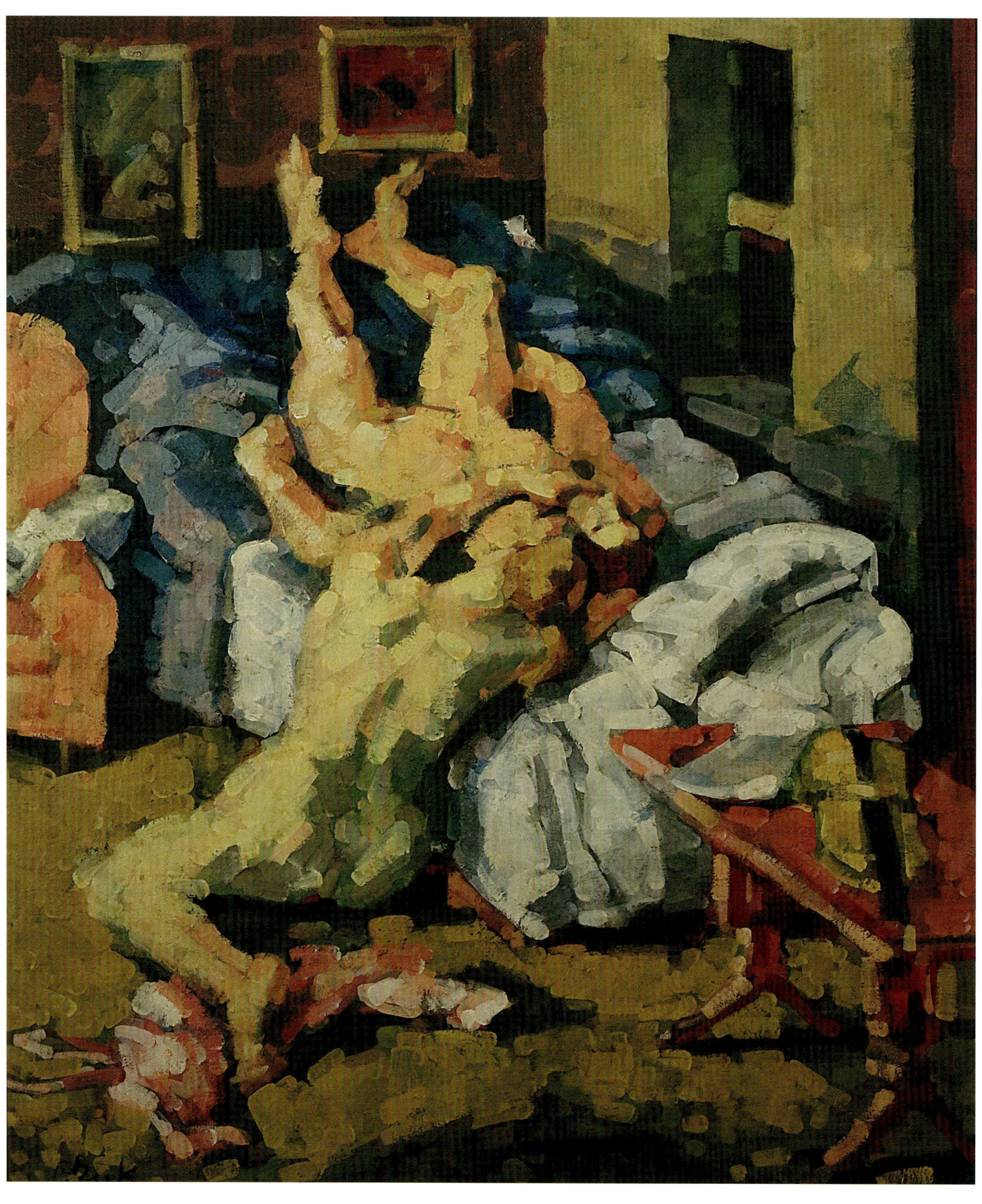

ROSEMARIE BECK, *Zina Room VI*, 1967
Oil on canvas, 34 1/4 x 28 inches
Private collection

ROSEMARIE BECK, [1923-2003]

Born July 8, 1923 in New York City.
Died July, 2003 in New York City.

Studied Oberlin College, BA; Columbia University, New York, NY; New York University, NY.

Teaching Positions 1957–1958, 61–62, 64–65: Vassar College, Poughkeepsie, NY; 1958, 59, 63: Middlebury College, VT; 1965–1968: Parsons School of Design, NY; 1968–1991: Queens College, NY.

Selected Solo Exhibitions 1944: Allen Art Museum, Oberlin, OH; 1948: Woodstock Artists Association; Maverick Concert Hall, Woodstock, NY; 1949: Copper Shop, Woodstock, NY; 1952: Copper Shop, Woodstock, NY; 1953, 55, 56, 59, 60, 63, 65, 66, 68, 70, 75: Peridot Gallery, New York, NY; 1957, 61: Vassar College Art Gallery, Poughkeepsie, NY; 1960: *12 Year Retrospective*, Wesleyan University, Middletown, CT; 1962: State University at New Paltz, NY; 1971: Zachary Waller Gallery, Los Angeles, CA; Duke University Museum, Chapel Hill, NC; Kirkland College, Clinton, NY; 1972: Peridot-Washburn Gallery, New York, NY; 1975, 80: Poindexter Gallery, New York, NY; 1975: *Travel Sketches*, Paul Klapper Library, Queens College, NY; 1979: Middlebury College, Middlebury, VT; Marl Galleries of Westchester, NY; 1980, 85, 89: Ingber Gallery, New York, NY; 1980: Cornell University, Ithaca, NY; Weatherspoon Gallery, Greensboro, NC; 1985: New York Museum Annex, Brooklyn, NY; 1992: Dartmouth College, Hanover, NH; 1999: *Retrospective Exhibition* Queens College, New York, NY; Smith College Museum of Art, Northampton, MA; Swathmore College, Swarthmore, PA; Ralph Greene Gallery, Albuquerque, NM; 2002: University Galleries, Wright State University, Dayton, OH; 2003: Belk Gallery, Western Carolina University, Cullowhee, NC; Knox College, Galesburg, IL; Jaffe-Friede & Strauss Galleries, Dartmouth College, Hanover, NH; Rider University Art Gallery, Rider University, Lawrenceville, NJ; 2004: New York Studio School of Painting, Drawing and Sculpture, New York, NY.

Selected Group Exhibitions 1951: *Young Talent Show*, Kootz Gallery, NYC; 1953, 55, 56: Stable Gallery Painting and Sculpture Annual, NYC; 1953: Pennsylvania Academy; 1946–53, 56, 57: Woodstock Artists Association NY; 1955: *Contemporary American Painting*, Whitney Museum of American Art, NYC; 1955, 57, 60, 61: Art Institute of Chicago, IL; 1956: *New Talent in the USA*, Martha Jackson Gallery, NY; *66th Annual Exhibition of Contemporary Art*, Nebraska Art Association; *American Exhibition*, University of Wisconsin, NE; 1957, 65: Walters Art Gallery, Baltimore, MD; 1957: *Young America*, Whitney Museum, NY; *Trends in Watercolor Today*, Brooklyn Museum, NY; 1958: *Nature in Abstraction*, Whitney Museum of American Art, NYC (traveled to Tate Gallery, London and the University of Nottingham); *Inauguration Exhibition*, Seagrams Building, NY; 1960: Nebraska Art Association, NE; *American Still Life Painting*, Peridot Gallery, NYC; 1962: The Arts Club of Chicago, IL; *The Figure*, Felix Landau Gallery, Los Angeles, CA; 1963: Kansas City Art Institute, KS; Wadsworth Atheneum, Hartford, CT; 1965: *65 Self-Portraits*, The School of Visual Arts, NY; 1966: Pennsylvania Academy, Philadelphia, PA; *Landscape Exhibition*, School of Visual Arts, NYC; 1968, 69, 72, 73, 78, 79, 96, 99: National Institute of Arts and Letters, NYC; 1970: *Painterly Realism*, circ., American Federation of Arts, NYC; Bowery Gallery, New York, NY; *Contemporary Women Artists*, National Arts Club, NYC; 1972, 80, 82, 83, 85, 86, 89, 91, 92, 94, 96, 97, 98, 2000, 01: National Academy of Design, NYC; 1975: Poindexter Gallery, NYC; Landmark Gallery, NYC; 1978, 79, 85: Ingber Gallery, NYC; 1983: Queens Museum, NY; 1987, 88: Joel Becker Gallery, Provincetown, MA; 1994, 97, 98: New York Studio School, NYC; 2004: *Women by Women*, Butler Gallery, Marymount College of Fordham University, Tarrytown, NY; Lovers, (drawings from 1968-69) with Paul Resika, Lori Bookstein Fine Art, New York, NY.

JANICE BIALA

Painting has become like a mistress whom one has to go through fire and water to meet.

Janice Biala Statement: from letter to Jack Tworkov, September 13, 1965.

[...] The very first spot of paint that you put on your canvas sets the note for everything that must follow. Just as in writing a novel, and no doubt in music and the other arts, every word you write must lead up to your climax, and no word or phrase must be there just because you happen to like it, so each spot of paint in your picture must lead up to some definite movement and must connect with every other spot of paint in the picture. Because red is not red by itself, its full quality of redness only becomes apparent when it has green beside it or the full quality of green is brought out only when it has purple beside it and so forth. Then against the color you play your forms, lines and texture. [...] The more intricate your design the more expert you must be, the more mind you must put on it and the less time you have to think of the laws that govern the real hunt. In the world that the picture has become, the rules of the real hunt have no importance and must give way to the rules of the picture

Janice Biala Statement: Excerpt from *A Talk About Painting*, delivered by the artist to the Colony Club, Detroit, MI, October 29, 1937.

I've always had Matisse in my belly.

Janice Biala Statement: from letter to Jack Tworkov, December 22,, 1966.

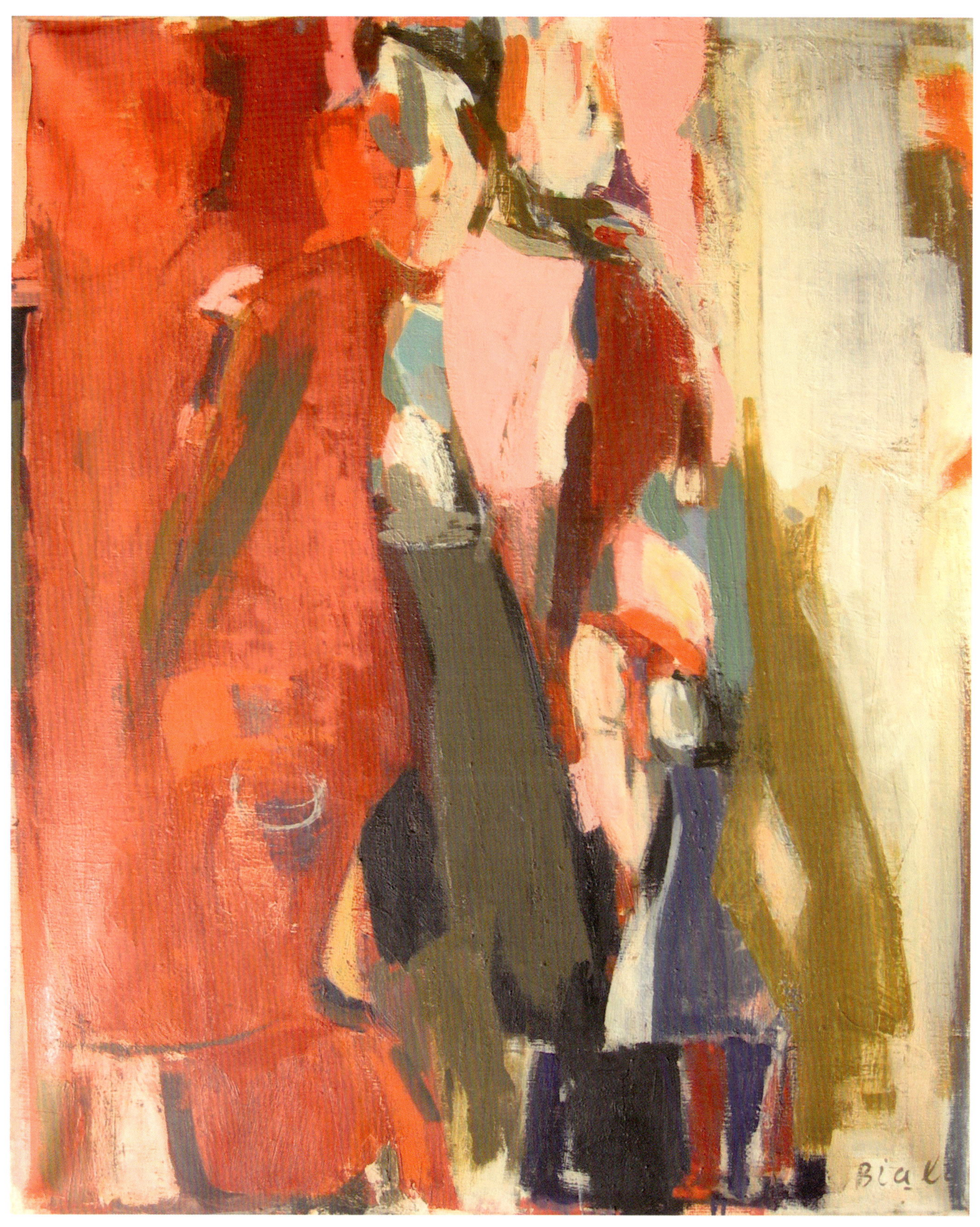

JANICE BIALA, *Marie Lorraine & Nicole*, 1958
Oil on canvas 36 x 28 1/2 inches

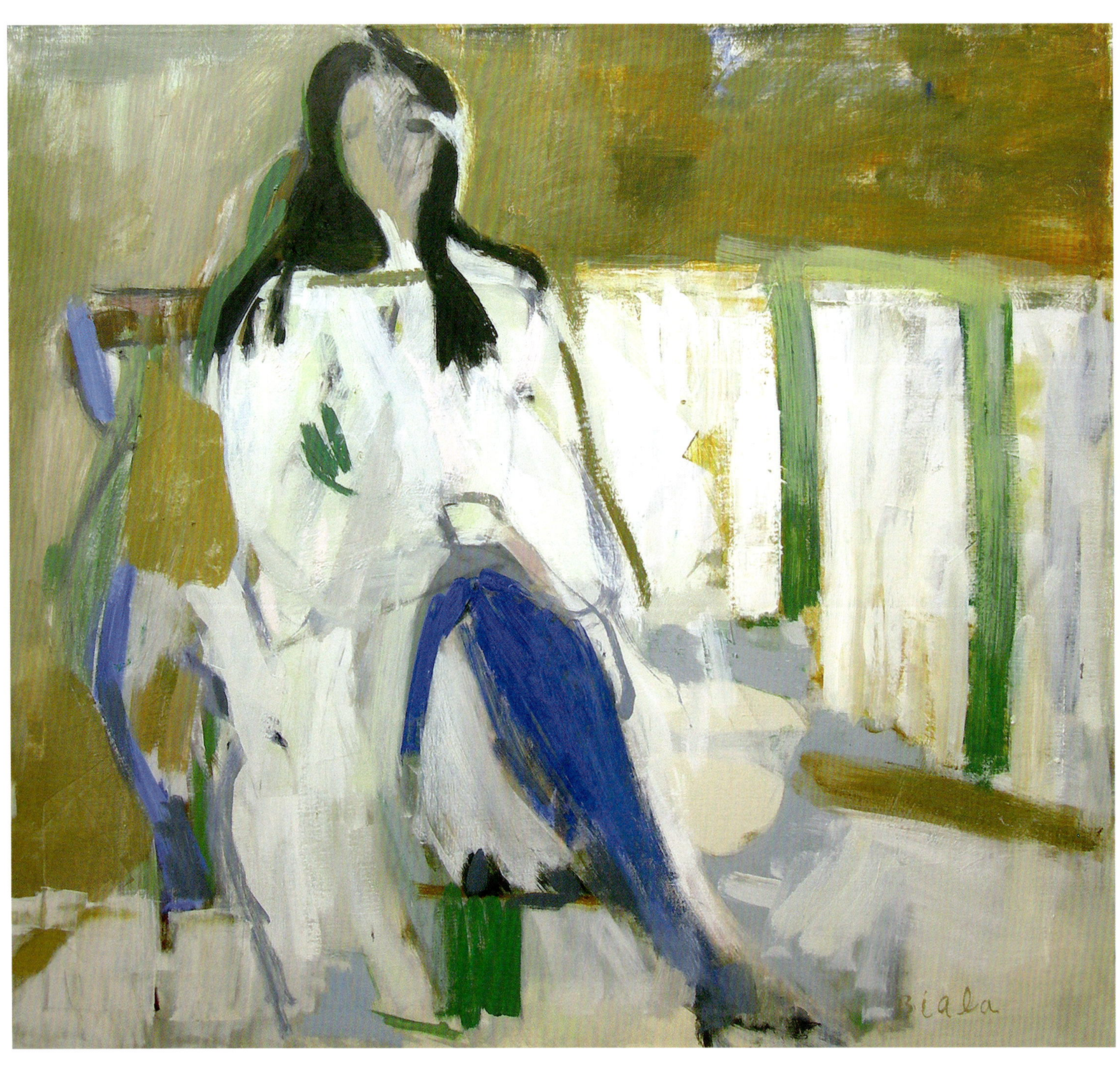

JANICE BIALA, *Untitled (61-24)*, 1961
Oil on canvas 39 3/4 x 43 inches
© Estate of Janice Biala. Courtesy of Tibor de Nagy Gallery, New York

JANICE BIALA, [1903-2000]

Born 1903 in Biala, Poland
To USA 1913. **USA citizen** 1923
Died September 24, 2000, Paris, France.

Studied 1923: National Academy of Design, NY; 1929: Art Students League, NY; 1929: Provincetown, MA, with Edwin Dickinson.

Selected Solo Exhibitions 1935, 37: Galerie Passedoit, NY; 1937: Denver Art Museum, Denver, CO; Olivet College, Olivet, MI; 1938, 39: Galerie Zack, Paris; 1941, 42, 43, 45, 47: Bignou Gallery, NY; 1947: Milwaukee Museum of Art, Milwaukee, WI; 1948, 49, 51, 54, 56, 57, 58, 60: Galerie Jeanne Bucher, Paris, France; 1950, 53: Carstair Gallery, NY; 1953, 55, 57, 59, 61, 63: Stable Gallery, NY; 1959: Galerie de Seine, Paris, France; 1962: Rina Gallery, Jerusalem, Israel; 1962, 70: Musee de beaux-arts, Rennes, France; 1962, 63: Galerie Point Cardinal, Paris; 1963: Andrew Dickson White Museum, Cornell University, Ithaca, NY; 1967, 87: Galerie Jacob, Paris; 1977: Livingston-Learmonth Gallery, New York, NY; 1978, 80, 81, 83, 85, 87: Gruenebaum Gallery, NY; 1989: Musee Tavet de Pontoise, Paris; 1990, 92, 93, 94, 96, 97, 98, 99: Kouros Gallery, NY; 1991: Louis Newman Galleries, Beverly Hills, CA; 2006, 07: Tibor de Nagy Gallery, New York, NY.

Selected Group Exhibitions
1944: *American Painting: 37th Annual Exhibition*, City Art Museum, St. Louis, MO; 1946, 55, 56, 59, 61: *Whitney Museum of American Art Annuals and Biennials*, NY; 1947: *Twentieth Biennial Exhibition*, The Corcoran Gallery of Art, Washington, D.C.; 1952: *Biala, Viera da Silva and Vera Pagava*, National Museum, Oslo, Norway; *Formes et Couleurs*, Musee Catonale, Lausanne, Switzerland; 1953: *Le Mouvement*, Musee Catonale, Lausanne, Switzerland; 1953, 54, 55, 56: *New York Painting and Sculpture Annuals*, Stable Gallery, New York, NY; 1962: *Three American Painters*, Musee de Rennes, France; 1964: *Collectors Graphics*, Peridot Gallery, NY; 1965: *Portraits*, New School Art Center, NY; 1968: *Contemporary Portraits*, Museum of Modern Art, NY; 1977: Some Americans in Paris, Centre George Pompidou, Paris, also in 1978; 1979: *Homage to Chardin*, Galerie Jacob, Paris; 1999: *In honor of Alan Groh '49: The Buzz Miller Collection of American Art*, Bayly Art Museum, The University of Virginia, Charlottesville; 1999: *The Artist's Eye: Jack Pierson Selects From The Collection*, The Provincetown Art Association and Museum, Provincetown, MA; 2004: *Abstract Expressionism: Second to None*, Thomas McCormick Gallery, Chicago, IL; 2006: *Picasso and the School of Paris*, Nassau County Museum of Art, Roslyn Harbor, NY; 2007: *Suitcase Paintings: Small Scale Abstract Expressionism*, Georgia Museum of Art, Athens, GA; *Americans in Paris: Paintings in the Fifties*, Tibor de Nagy Gallery, New York, NY.

ADELIE LANDIS BISCHOFF

Abstraction and figuration have been the two aspects of my painting career. The themes: landscape, still life, figures, are romantic.

Managing the problems of art making has always been in concert with expressing the outside and inner world; the world as seen and the world as felt. This inner, felt world found an outlet in my watercolor, pen & ink drawings. They start with spontaneous marks on paper. The process allows my imagination to take flight, often resulting in frequently bizarre, sometimes erotic, sometimes scary images. Black is often used as a formal and dominant motif in my recent drawings and paintings. Perhaps as an emotional element but also as a reductive simplification, an organizing principle.

Social inequalities and commentaries on war have been insistent, long time concerns, concerns that emerged during my high school years. It has been my committed focus to embrace these concerns, to find a visual language that can convey the specificity and intensity of which expressive figuration is capable and still be able to accomplish this in non–literal, abstract form.

In so doing, I would be establishing a union of sorts, a bringing together of the two strains of my painting career, imagined and as yet, unrealized.

Adelie Landis Bischoff, Statement: sent to the editor on 11/17/2008.

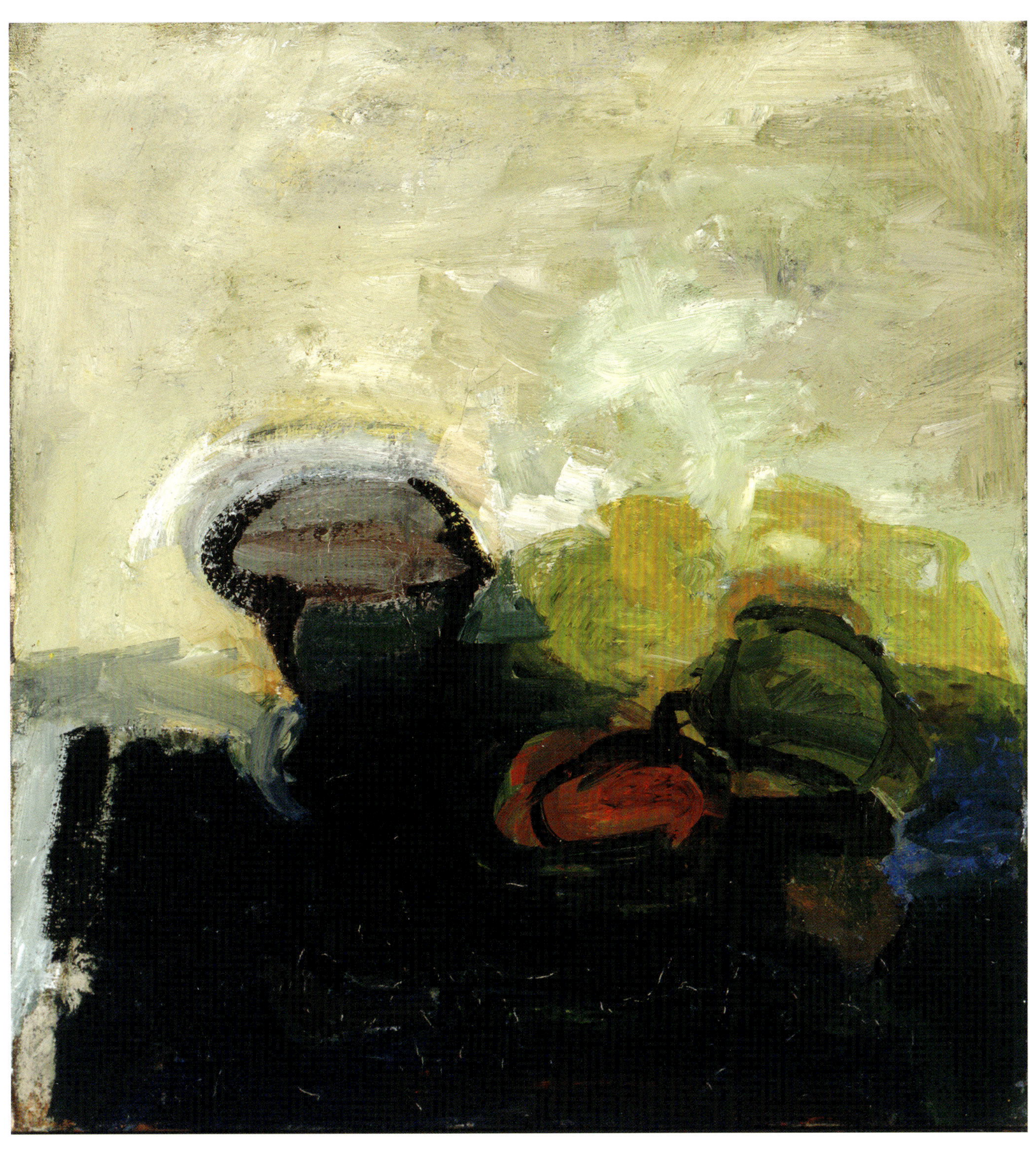

ADELIE LANDIS BISCHOFF, *Abstract Still Life*, 1958
Oil on canvas, 26 x 24 inches

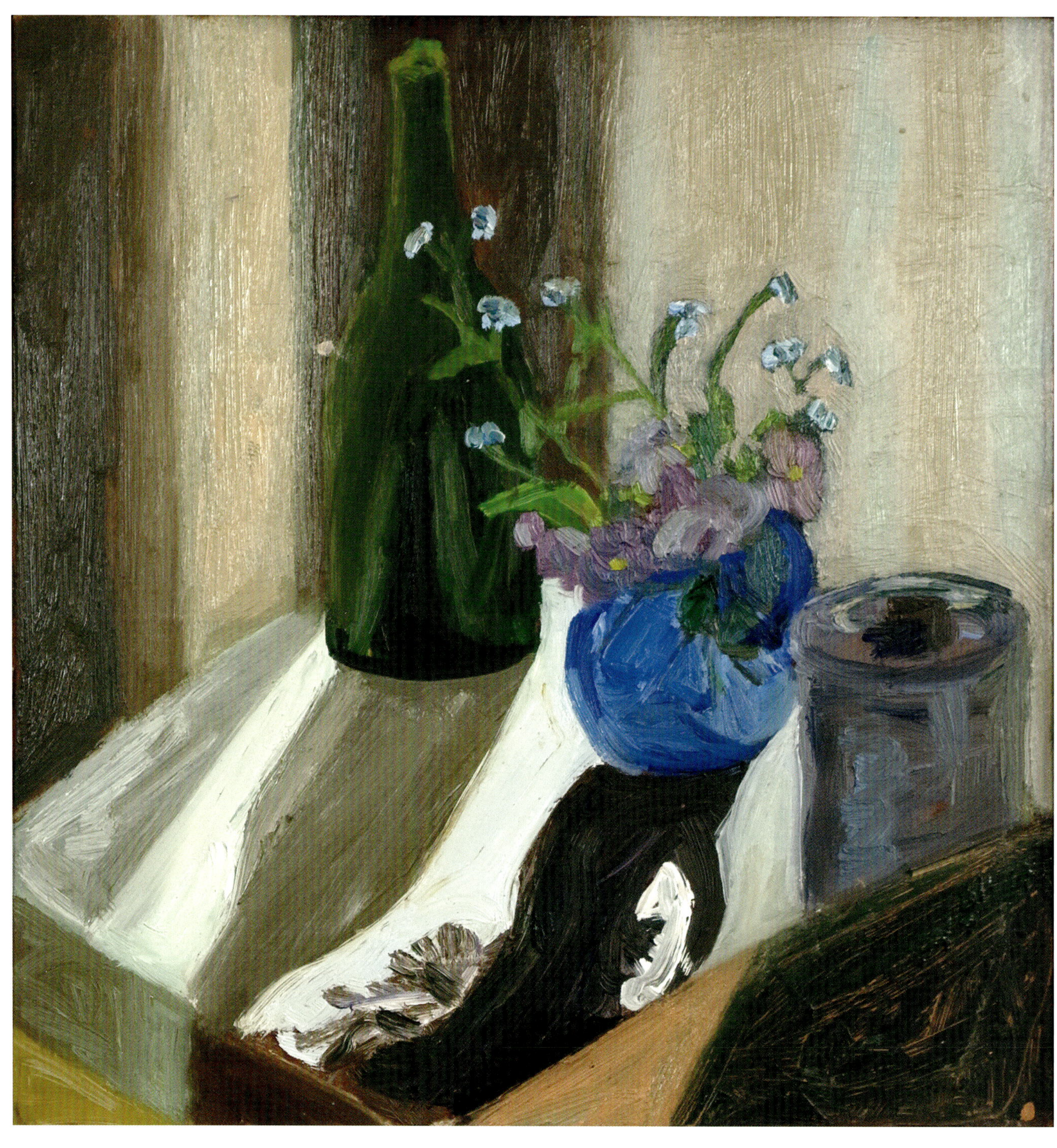

ADELIE LANDIS BISCHOFF, *Still Life*, 1967
Oil on masonite, 15 x 14 inches
Private collection

ADELIE LANDIS BISCHOFF, [1926-]

Born February 12, 1926 in Brooklyn, NY

Studied
1944: Brooklyn College, New York, NY;
1949: City College, New York, NY;
1949–1951: Art Students League, New York, NY;
1951–1953: California School of Fine Arts, San Francisco, CA;
1958: B.A., University of California, Berkeley, CA;
1959: M.A., University of California, Berkeley, CA;
1994: Santa Fe Institute of Fine Arts, workshop with Susan Rothenberg.

Selected Solo Exhibitions 1987, 97: 871 Fine Arts, San Francisco, CA; 1993: Kennedy Art Center, College of Holy Name, Oakland, CA; 2002: Salender–O'Reilly Galleries, NYC.

Selected Group Exhibitions 1953, 54: *Print Annual*, San Francisco Museum of Modern Art, San Francisco, CA; 1953: King Ubu Gallery, San Francisco, CA; 1954, 60, 64: *Annual*, Richmond Art Center, Richmond, CA; 1954: YMHA, NYC; 1955: Lucien Labaudt, Gallery, San Francisco, CA; *Merry–Go–Round Show*, Santa Monica Pier, Santa Monica, CA; 1963: Berkeley Gallery, Berkeley, CA; 1973: Artists' Cooperative Gallery, Berkeley CA; 1975: *Introduction '75*, Charles Campbell Gallery, San Francisco, CA; 1978: Dana Reich Gallery, San Francisco, CA; 1983: *Elegant Miniatures from San Francisco and Kyoto*, San Francisco Museum of Modern Art, San Francisco, CA & Belea House, Kyoto, Japan; 1986: *Works on Paper: Adelie Landis & Louise Smith*, Mondavi Winery Gallery, Oakville, CA; 1989: *Right Foot Forward*, San Francisco International Airport, San Francisco, CA; 1989: The *King Ubu Gallery Show,* Natsoulas Novelozo Gallery, Davis, CA; *Rags: Clothing as Allegory*, San Francisco Art Commission Gallery, San Francisco, CA; 1992: *New Work: June Felter and Adelie Landis*, 871 Fine Arts, San Francisco, CA; *The Art of June Felter, Adelie Landis and Louise Smith,* Wiegand Gallery, College of Notre Dame, Belmont, CA; 1996: *San Francisco Abstract Expressionism, 1940's – 60's*, Ted Mendenhall Gallery, Pasadena, CA; 1997: *Two Berkeley Artists: Robert Kehlmann and Adelie Landis*, Moochnek Gallery, Berkeley, CA; *The Shoe Show,* The Bedford Gallery, Walnut Creek, CA; 2000: *Scrambled Edge*, Hollis Street Project, Emeryville, CA.

ELMER BISCHOFF

I believe the best artists in this country will be working in various directions, as they are now. I don't know what trend most artists will be following. Direction is a matter of personal choice, simplified and strengthened by an element of personal necessity. While the dust is still thick the more talk about mass tendencies the more sanction for work that is merely facing the approved way.

Elmer Bischoff, Statement: *Contemporary American Painting and Sculpture*, University of Illinois, catalogue, 1961. p.65

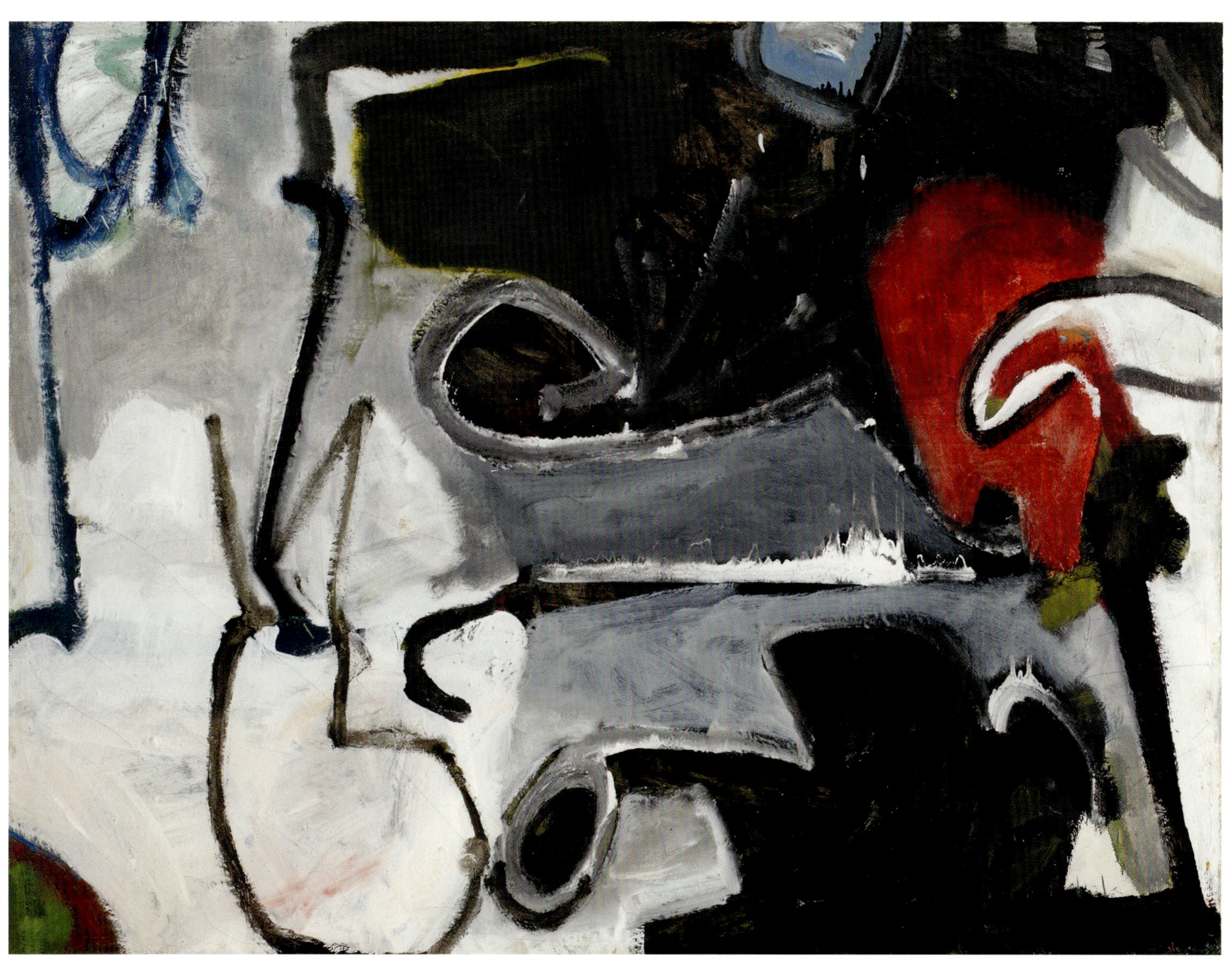

ELMER NELSON BISCHOFF, *Untitled (Scene with "X")*, c.1950
Oil on canvas, 42 1/2 X 54 5/8 inches
Collection of Iris & Gerald Cantor Center for Visual Arts, Stanford University. gift of Adelie Bischoff. 2006.115

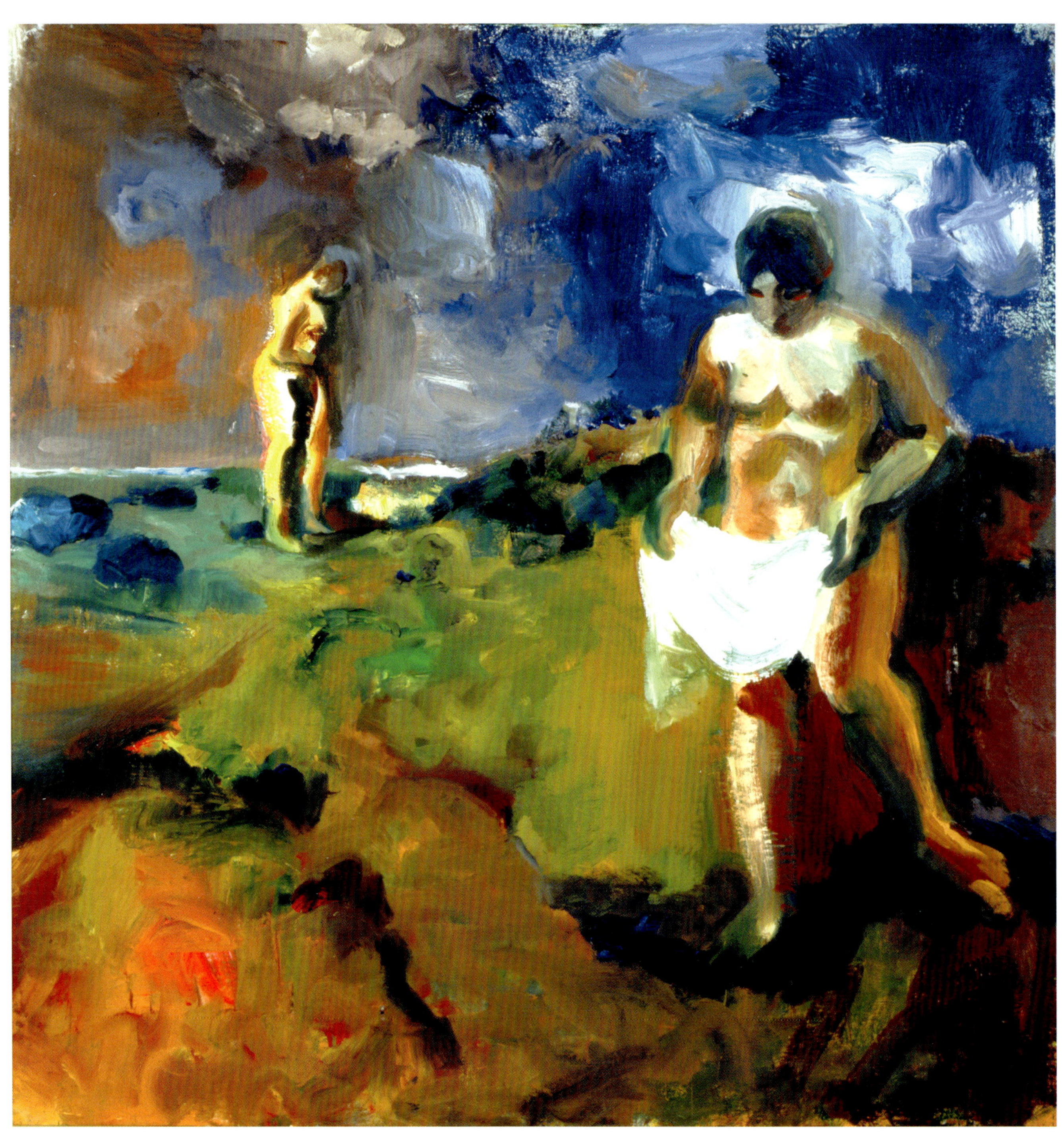

ELMER NELSON BISCHOFF, *Two Bathers*, 1960
Oil on canvas, 68 x 64 5/8 in. (172.7 x 164.2 cm.)
Smithsonian American Art Museum Gift of S.C. Johnson & Son, Inc. Accession number 1968.52.7

ELMER NELSON BISCHOFF, [1916-1991]

Born July 9, 1916, Berkeley, CA; **Died** March 2, 1991, Berkeley, CA.

Studied 1939: University of California, Berkeley, with Margaret Peterson, Erle Loran, John Haley, MA.

Military Service World War II 1942–1946 US Air Force.

Teaching Position 1946–52: California School of Fine Arts, San Francisco, CA; 1953–56: Yuba College, Marysville, CA; 1956–63: San Francisco Art Institute, San Francisco, CA; 1963–85: University of California, Berkeley, CA;

Selected Solo Exhibitions 1947: (first) California Palace of the Legion of Honor, San Francisco, CA; 1953: King Ubu Gallery, San Francisco, CA; 1955: Paul Kantor Gallery, Los Angeles, CA; 1956: San Francisco Art Association Gallery, San Francisco, CA; 1960, 62, 64, 69: Staempfli Gallery, NYC; 1961: M.H. de Young Memorial Museum, San Francisco, CA; 1964, 81: E.B. Crocker Art Gallery, Sacramento, CA; 1968: Henry Gallery, University of Washington, Seattle, WA; 1969: Richmond Art Center, Richmond, CA; 1971: San Francisco Museum of Art, San Francisco, CA; 1974: Boston University Art Gallery (with Richard Diebenkorn), Boston, MA; 1975: San Francisco Art Institute, San Francisco, CA; University Art Museum, University of California, Berkeley, CA; Oakland Museum, Oakland, CA; Charles Campbell Gallery, San Francisco, CA; Art Academy of Cincinatti, OH; 1979, 83, 88, 89, 90: John Berggruen Gallery, San Francisco, CA; 1979: San Jose Museum of Art, San Jose, CA; 1980: Arts Club of Chicago, Chicago, IL; 1982: *Matrix 55: Elmer Bischoff*, University Art Museum, Berkeley, CA; 1984: University of Arkansas, AK.
Retrospective: 1985–86: circ., San Francisco Museum of Modern Art, San Francisco, CA.

Selected Group Exhibitions 1942, 46, 52, 57, 59, 63: San Francisco Art Association Annuals; 1947, 59, 64: The Art Institute of Chicago; 1948, 50, 1960–63: California Palace; 1951: Los Angeles County Museum of Art, Los Angeles, CA; 1955, 56: Richmond Art Center, Richmond, CA; 1957: Oakland Art Museum, Oakland, CA; 1957: *American Painting, 1945-57*, Minneapolis Institute of Art, Minneapolis, MN; 1958: circ., *New Talent*, American Federation of Arts, NYC; 1959: ART: USA:59, NY; 1959, 61: University of Illinois; 1959, 61, 63, 65: Whitney Museum of Art Annuals and Biennials, NYC; 1959-60: circ., West Coast Artists, American Federation of Arts, NYC; 1960: Denver Art Museum, Denver, CO; Butler Institute of American Art, Youngstown, OH; 1961: *Painting from the Pacific*, Auckland, New Zealand; 1962: The Pennsylvania Academy of the Fine Arts, PA; *The Artist's Environment: The West Coast*, Fort Worth, TX; *Fifty California Artists*, circ., San Francisco Museum of Modern Art, CA; 1962–63: *Recent Painting USA, The Figure*, circ., Museum of Modern Art, NYC; 1962–67: Art: USA: *Now*, circ.; 1963: National Institute of Arts and Letters, NYC; Corcoran Gallery, Washington, D.C.; Achenbach Foundation (three-man drawing show); 1967: Carnegie, Pittsburgh, PA; 1973: University of Nebraska; 1974: University of Illinois; 1979: *American Paintings of the 1970's*, circ., Albright-Knox Art Gallery, Buffalo, NY; 1980: *The Human Form*, Corcoran Gallery, Washington, D.C.

WILLIAM BRICE

...I am involved with formal values and I always have been. In fact, if you ask what I work toward, I would answer synthesis. Some of the most memorable works for me are those that call to a composite of our responses–mental, emotional, physical, psychological.

...I think there was a recognition during the period of Abstract Expressionism of a difference between West and East Coast painting. I'm saying it rather indirectly, but New York painting reflected the energy, the congestion, the tension of the city. The paintings of the same period painted here–and I'm thinking in particular of earlier Diebenkorn paintings–were more expansive. I don't want to say they were painted with that conscious intention, but I see reflected a different physical environment.

...visual experience is complex. We respond to texture, substance, color, light, form, space and dimensionality simultaneously, and artists are selective in the priorities of their responses.

...there is also the need to create work which confirms the reality of one's existence, permits discovery and revelation. We are always working in a changing context and attitudes change about what we make. Someone attributed to Titian a comment about a red robe he had painted. He said that the red was as good as he could make it, but it would really be right in thirty years. Now, I don't think you would find many of us thinking that way, and perhaps artists today are more valued for their involvement in the creative process than for their ability to perfect an object.

William Brice, Statement: *View* Interview: Part I by Wendy Diamond, Constance Lowallen. Edited by Constance Lowallen. Published irregularly (six issues in Volume IV) by Point Publications,Vol. IV No. 6. Spring 1988

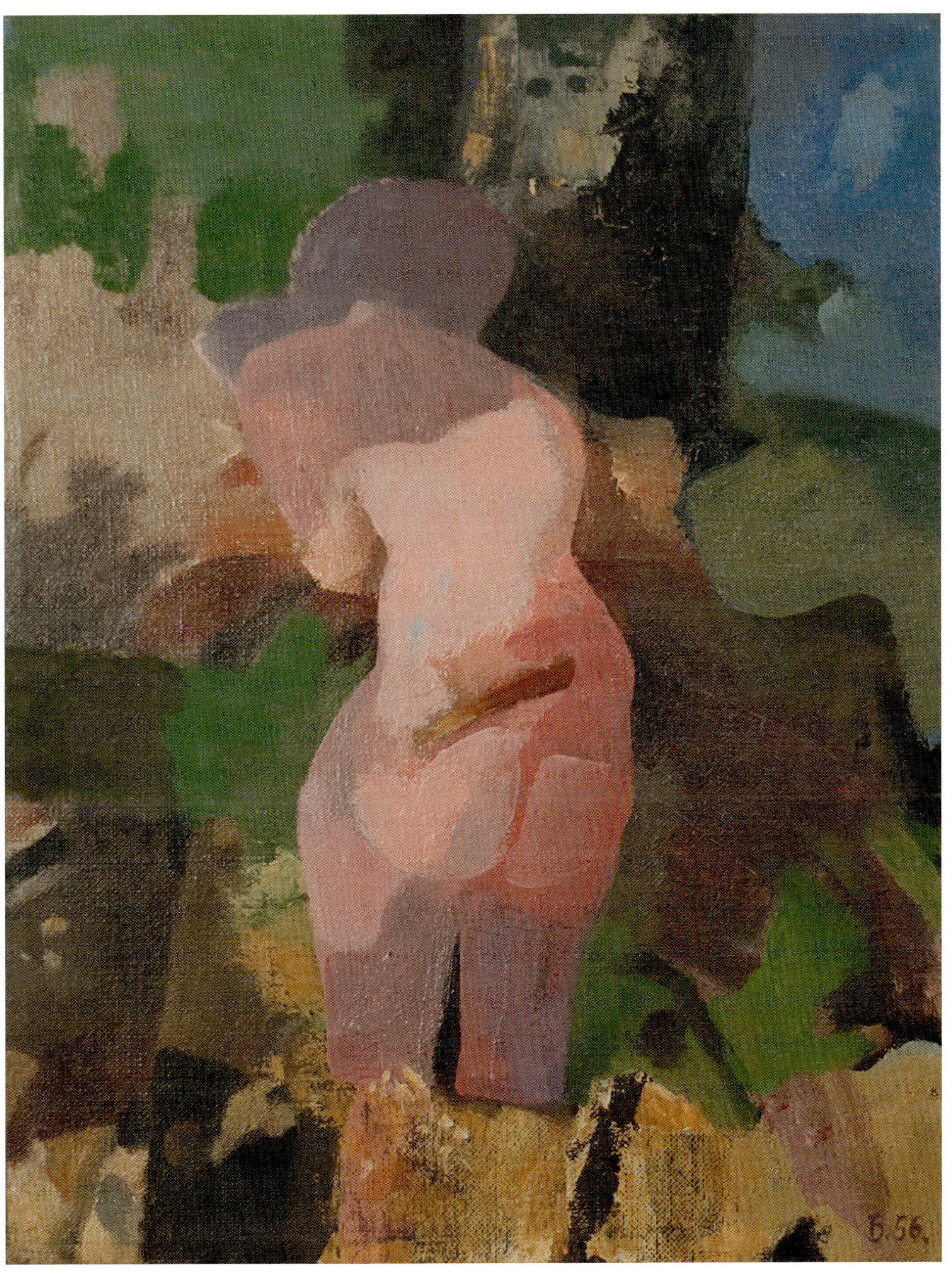

WILLIAM BRICE, *Figure and Landscape Study III*, 1956
Oil on canvas, inches
Private collection

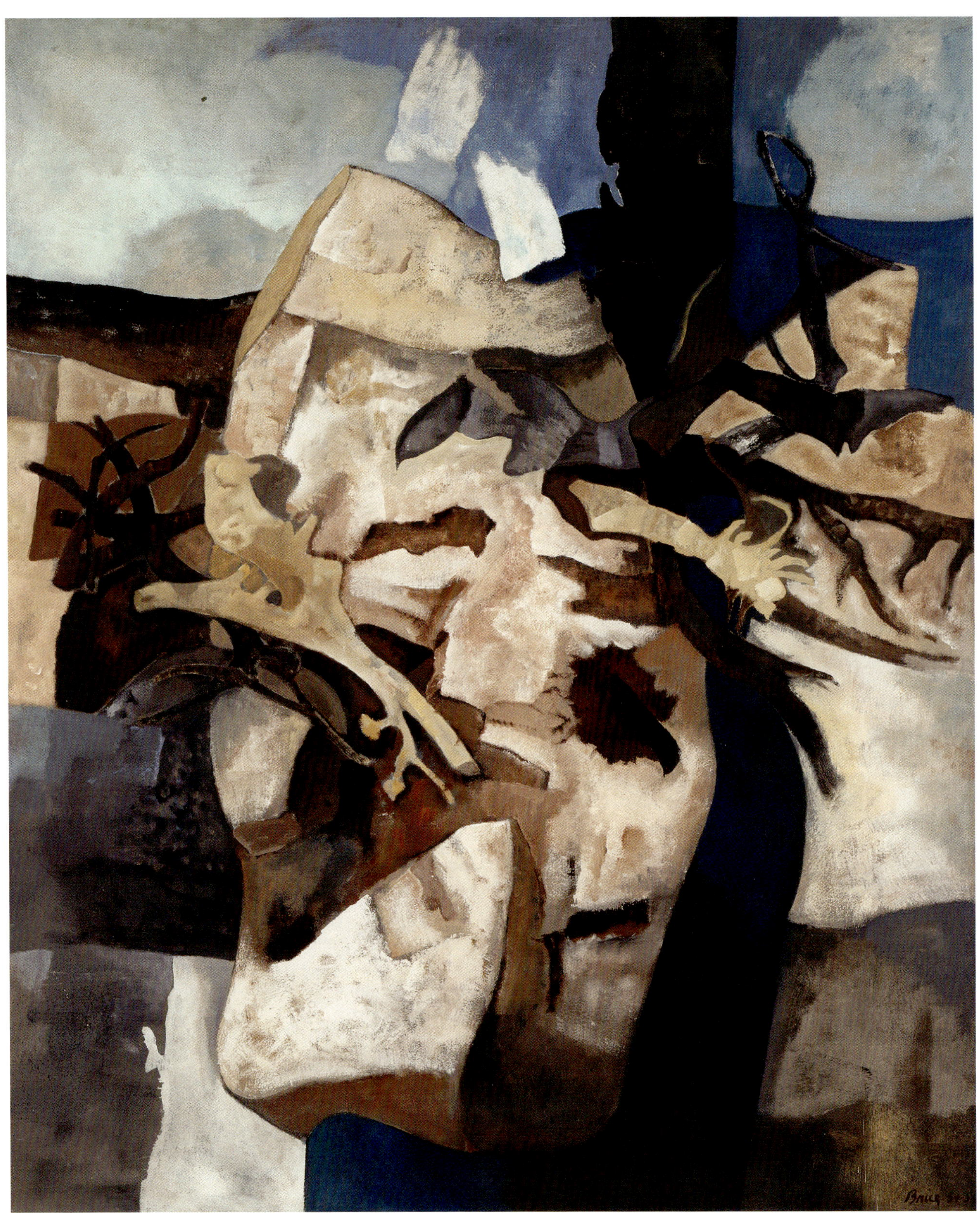

WILLIAM BRICE, *Land Fracture*, 1954–55
Oil and sand on board, 96 x 78 inches
Collection University of California, Los Angeles,
CLA Hammer Museum, Gift of Mr. and Mrs. Ray Stark
© Estate of William Brice

WILLIAM BRICE, [1921-2008]

Born April 23, 1921, New York City.
Died March 3, 2008, Los Angeles, CA.

Studied 1937, 1940–1942: Chouinard Art Institute, Los Angeles; 1939: Art Students League, New York;

Military Service in World War II
1942–1944: US Air Force.

Taught 1948–1952: Jepson Art Institute, Los Angeles; 1953–1991: University of California, Los Angeles, CA.

Selected Solo Exhibitions 1947 (first), 1958: Santa Barbara Museum of Art, Santa Barbara CA; 1949: The Downtown Gallery; 1952, 55, 56, 62: Frank Perls Gallery; 1955, 56, 64: The Alan Gallery, NY; 1967: University of California, San Diego; Colorado Springs Fine Arts Center; Dallas Museum of Fine Arts, Dallas, TX; San Francisco Museum of Modern Arts, CA; 1968: The Landau-Alan Gallery, NY; 1975: Hancock College, Santa Maria, CA; Orange Coast College; 1976: Charles Campbell Gallery, San Francisco; 1978: Institute of Contemporary Art, Los Angeles, CA.; University Nicholas Wilder Gallery, Los Angeles, CA; 1980, 84: Robert Miller Gallery, NY; Mary Porter Sesnon Gallery, Santa Cruz, CA; 1981: California State University, Dominquez Hills; 1983: Smith-Anderson Gallery, Paolo Alto; 1984: L.A. Louver Gallery, Venice, CA; Temple University; 1989, 90, 98: L. A. Louver Gallery, Venice, CA; 1990: Los Angeles County Museum of Art, CA; 1993: Gruenwald Center for the Graphic Arts, University of California, CA.
Retrospective: 1986: Museum of Contemporary Art, Los Angeles, CA; Grey Art Gallery and Study Center, New York University, NY.

Selected Group Exhibitions 1945: Santa Barbara Museum of Art, CA; 1948, 49, 50, 51, 52, 54, 56, 58, 60, 63: Whitney Museum of American Art, NY, *Annual and Biennial*; 1947–50: Los Angeles County Museum of Art, CA; 1948, 49, 54: Carnegie; 1950: *Americans Under 36*, Metropolitan Museum of Art, NY; 1951, 52: California Palace; *III Bienal*, Museu de Arte Moderna, Sao Paulo, Brazil; 1952, 56: Museum of Modern Art, NY; 1963: *Fifty California Artists*, Whitney Museum of American Art, NY; 1965: *A Decade of American Drawings*, Whitney Museum of American Art, NY; 1966: *American Painting 1966,* Virginia Museum of Fine Arts, Richmond; *Selected Artists-'67*, Des Moines Art Center, Iowa; 1976: *Private Images*, Los Angeles County Museum of Art, CA; 1977: *Artists at Work*, Los Angeles County Museum of Art, CA; 1981: *Drawings and Illustrations by Southern California Artists before 1950*, Laguna Beach, Museum of Art, CA; 1982: *Drawings by Painters*, Long Beach Museum of Art, CA; 1983: *Twentieth Century American Drawings: The Figure in Context*, circ., International Exhibitions Foundation, Washington, D.C.; 1985: *Sunshine and Shadows,* University of Southern California, CA.

ERNEST BRIGGS

The discipline to free one's image from the conventional aspects without surrendering the affirmative drama of human insight to the sterility of decoration or simple design problems has been, and I believe will be, my continuing direction.

For me the challenge of painting lies implicit in the act– to penetrate inherited conceptual deposits and attempt the possible impingement of spirit, the personal image, remains the enduring command of conscience.

Ernest Briggs, Statement: from the artists' notes 1950's provided by his widow, the sculptor Ann Arnold.

Ernest Briggs, Statement: *12 Americans, catalogue*, The Museum of Modern Art, New York, 1956.

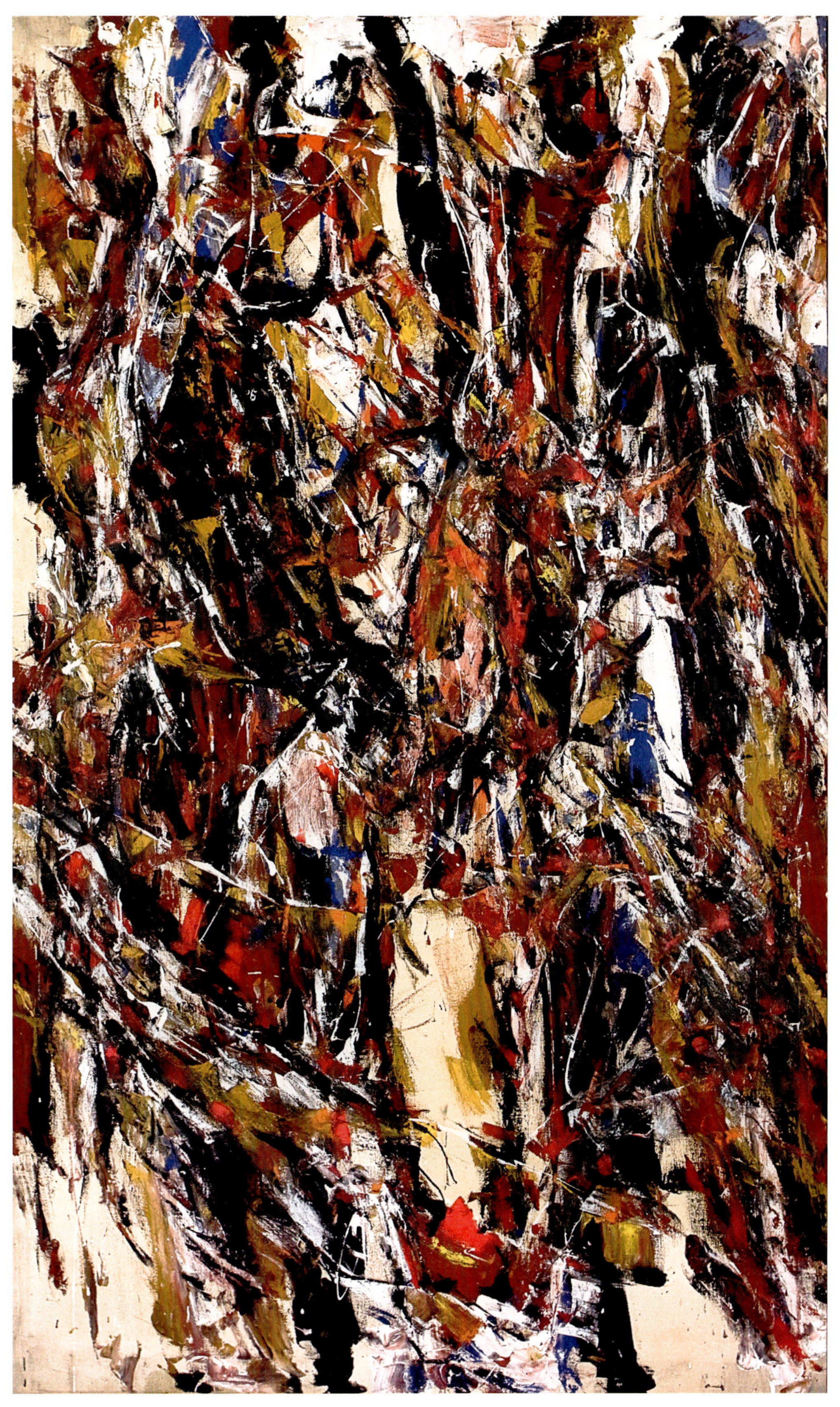

ERNEST BRIGGS, *#4, Feb.* 1954
Oil on canvas, 70 x 42 inches
Private collection

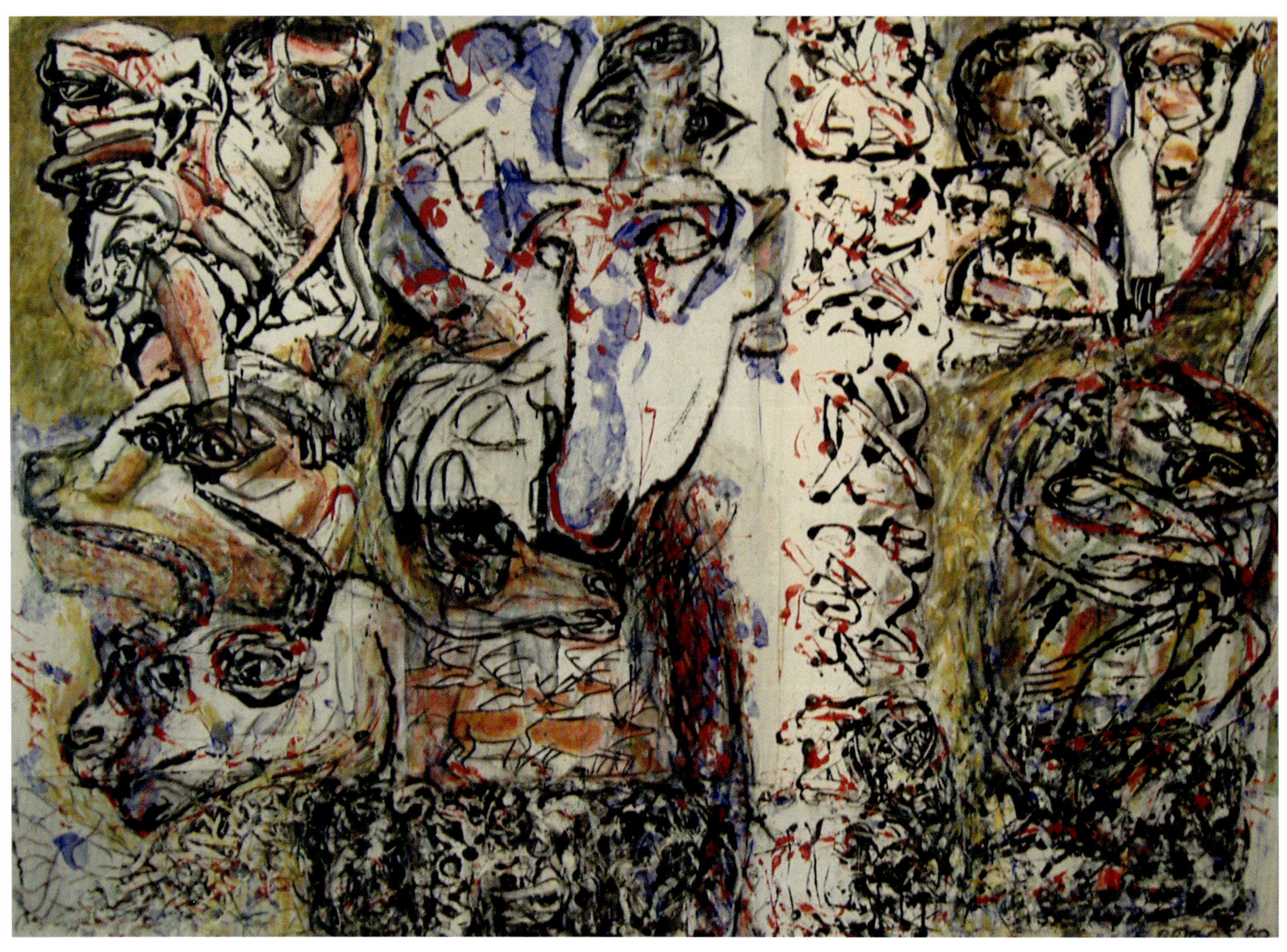

ERNEST BRIGGS, *Untitled I, II and III*, 1954
Oil on canvas, 96 x 150 inches
Collection of the Estate

ERNEST BRIGGS, [1923–1984]

Born 1923, San Diego, CA.
Died June 12, 1984.

Studied 1947–1951: California School of Fine Arts, San Francisco, with Clifford Still, David Park, Mark Rothko.

Military Service in World War II 1943–1946: US Army Signal Corps, with year 1945–46 in India.

Taught 1958: University of Florida; 1961–84: Pratt Institute; 1967–68: Yale University, New Haven, CT.

Selected Solo Exhibitions 1949: (first) Metart Gallery, San Francisco, CA; 1954, 55: Stable Gallery, New York; 1956: San Francisco Art Association Gallery, CA; 1960, 62, 63: The Howard Wise Gallery, NY; 1968: Yale University, New Haven, CT; 1969: Alonzo Gallery, NY; 1973: Green Mountain Gallery, NY; 1975: Susan Caldwell, Inc., NY; 1977: Aaron Berman Gallery, NY; 1980: Landmark Gallery, NY; 1980, 82: Gruenebaum Gallery, NY; 1984: *Memorial Exhibition*, Gruenebaum Gallery, NY; 2001: Anita Shapolsky Gallery, NYC; 2002: Mishkin Gallery, Baruch College, City University New York.

Selected Group Exhibitions 1948, 49, 53: San Francisco Art Association Annuals; 1955, 56, 61: *Annuals and Biennials*, Whitney Museum of American Art, NYC; 1953: *Five Bay Area Artists*, California Palace of the Legion of Honor, San Francisco, CA; 1956: *12 Americans*, circ., Museum of Modern Art, NYC; 1961: Corcoran Gallery of Art, Washington, D.C.; Carnegie Institute of Technology, Pittsburgh, PA; 1962: 1961, Dallas Museum of Fine Arts, Dallas, TX; 1962: *Contemporary Art Exhibition*, San Francisco Museum of Modern Art, CA; 1963: *Directions-Painting-USA*, San Francisco Museum of Modern Art, San Francisco, CA; 1967: *Large-Scale American Painting*, Jewish Museum, NY; Johnson Museum, Cornell University, Ithaca, NY; 1969, 70: American Academy of Arts and Letters, NY; 1970: Proctor Art Center, Bard College, Annandale-on-Hudson, NY; *San Francisco 1945–1950*, Oakland Art Museum, CA; 1976: *California Painting and Sculpture: The Modern Era*, San Francisco Museum of Modern Art, CA; 1977: *Bay Area Update*, Huntsville Museum of Art, Alabama; 1978: Cape Split Place, Addison, ME; 1984: *Underknown, Institute for Art & Urban Resources,* P.S. 1, Long Island City, NY; 1989: Anne Weber Gallery, Georgetown, ME; Portland Museum of Art, ME; 1991: *The Prevailing Fifties,* also with Edward Dugmore, Anita Shapolsky Gallery, NYC; 1992: *The Tradition*, also with Ibram Lassaw, Anita Shapolsky Gallery, NY; 1994*: New York–Provincetown: A 50s Connection*, Provincetown Museum, MA; Maryland Art Institute, MD; 1994, 96: Josiah White Exhibition Center, Jim Thorpe, PA; 1995: *The Fifties*, Anita Shapolsky Gallery, NYC; 1996: *Other Artists of the 50s*, Kendall Campus Art Gallery; Miami–Dade Community College, FL; *The San Francisco School of Abstract Expressionism*, San Francisco Museum of Art, CA; 1997: *Artists of the 1950s*, Part 1 and 2, Anita Shapolsky Gallery, NYC; 1998: *Paper Works*, Anita Shapolsky Gallery, NY; 1998–99: *Artists of the 50s; The Development of Abstraction,* Anita Shapolsky Gallery, NY; 1999: *Abstract Expressionist Tradition*, Anita Shapolsky Gallery, NY; 2000: Art *For Art's Sake–Credo of the Fifties,* Anita Shapolsky Gallery, NYC.

JOAN BROWN

Throughout the twenty five years that I've been painting, my work has dealt with introspection...I strongly feel the need to put this introspection in the form of pictures. I then become the 'student' and consciously 'study' the content of the pictures I've painted...Looking in a mirror, becoming a spectator, literally describing myself, is a very graphic way of being introspective...I strive for that delicate balance between reason and feeling, knowing that sometimes the pictures will lean one way or the other. I'm constantly trying to pull out new information from my intuitive self, which results in the surprises that I discover in my work, and which keeps me ever stimulated.

Joan Brown, Statement: from Archives of American Art, Smithsonian Institution, Washington, D.C., Paul J. Karlstrom interview with Joan Brown. Transcribed manuscript, 1 San Francisco, July 15, 1975, p.10.

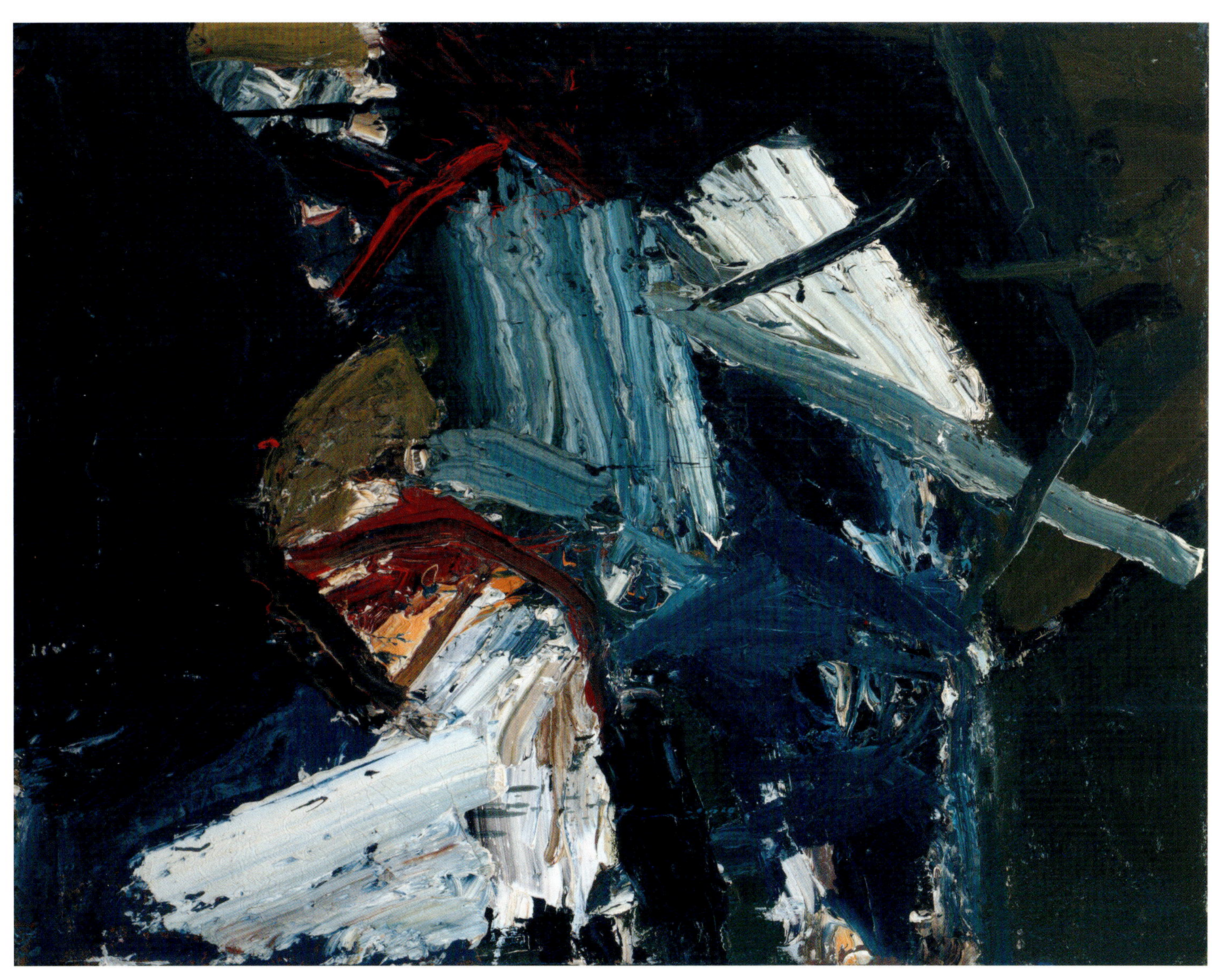

JOAN BROWN, *Brambles*, 1957
Oil on canvas, 46 x 36 1/2 inches
Oakland Museum of California; gift of Robert J. Steinhart in memory of Barbara B. Steinhart.

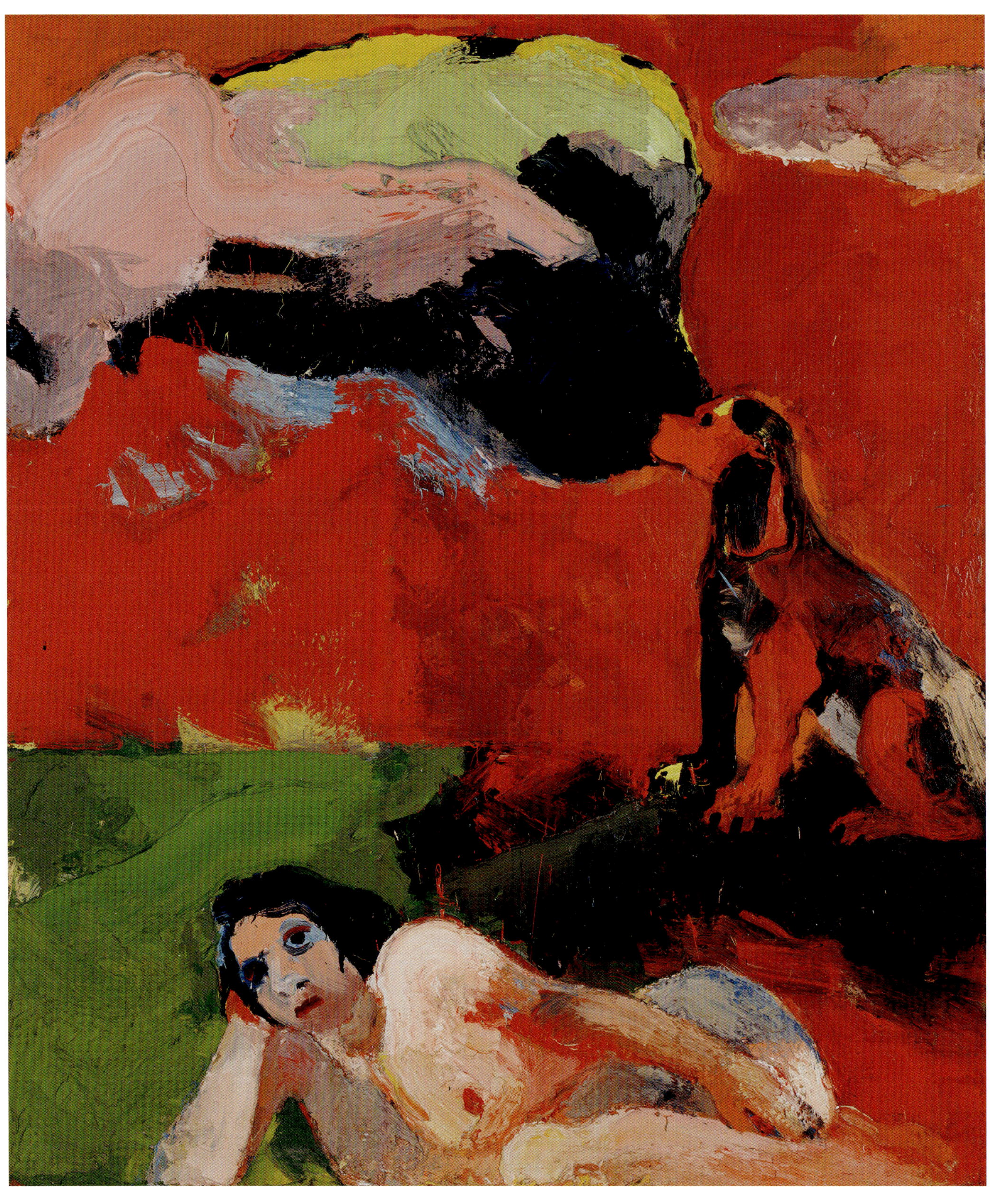

JOAN BROWN, *Nude, Dog, Clouds*, 1963
Oil on canvas, 72 x 60 inches (182.9 x 152.4 cm.)
Smithsonian American Art Museum, Bequest of Edith S. and
Arthur J. Levin. Accession number: 2005.5.11

JOAN BROWN, [1938-1990]

Born 1938 in San Francisco, CA.
Died 1990 during work on an installation in Proddatur, India.

Studied 1955: Graduated from High School, 1955–1960: California School of Fine Arts (now called the San Francisco Art Institute), 1959 received BFA; 1960 received MFA.

Selected Solo Exhibitions 1957: Six Gallery; 1958: The Cellar Foyer, San Francisco, CA; 1959, 1961: Batman Gallery, San Francisco,CA; 1959: Spatsa Gallery, San Francisco, CA; 1960, 61, 64: Staempfli Gallery, New York; 1961, 62: Primus-Stuart Gallery, Los Angeles, CA; 1971: San Francisco Museum of Art, San Francisco, CA; 1973: San Francisco Art Institute, San Francisco, CA; 1974, 75: Charles Campbell Gallery, San Francisco, CA; 1974: University Art Museum, Berkeley, CA; 1974, 76, 79, 81, 82: Allan Frumkin Gallery, New York; Retrospective, September 1998–January 1999: The Oakland Museum and University Art Museum, CA.

Selected Group Exhibitions 1958, 63: *Annual Painting and Sculpture Exhibition of the San Francisco Art Association*, San Francisco Museum of Art, CA; 1973: *A Period of Exploration: San Francisco 1945–1950*, The Oakland Museum, CA; 1976: *Painting and Sculpture in California: The Modern Era,* San Francisco Museum of Art, CA; 1990: *Bay Area Figurative Art*, San Francisco Museum of Modern Art, CA; Hirschhorn Museum and Sculpture Garden, Smithsonian Institution, Washington, D.C.; Pennsylvania Academy of the Fine Art, Philadelphia, PA.

HANS BURKHARDT

I live in a life where there's nothing but war–the first World War, the second one, then Korea, then Vietnam, Lebanon, Central America and now Kuwait. And I say it's wrong. There must be other ways to settle things.

Hans Burkhardt, Statement: Hans Burkhardt Desert Storms by Peter Selz. Published by Jack Rutberg Fine Arts Inc., Los Angeles, CA, 1991, pp. 18.

My ideas for painting come from nature–the figure, landscapes, tortured nails or rusty wires of a city dump, the happy play as well as the sad faces of children, the seeds of a tree falling on the grave of an unknown. And from social and political upheaval.

I have to make a painting the moment something happens; I cannot go back to a subject years later with the same power.

Look how the world has changed in fifty years. You can't do one painting and make the same thing over and over.

I feel whenever I accomplish something that I have to be satisfied, even if it doesn't please anyone else. I paint the way I live.

Hans Burkhardt, Statement: Still Working, Edited by Stuart Shedletsky. Published by Parsons School of Design, New York, in association with University of Washington Press, Seattle and London, 1994, p. 34.

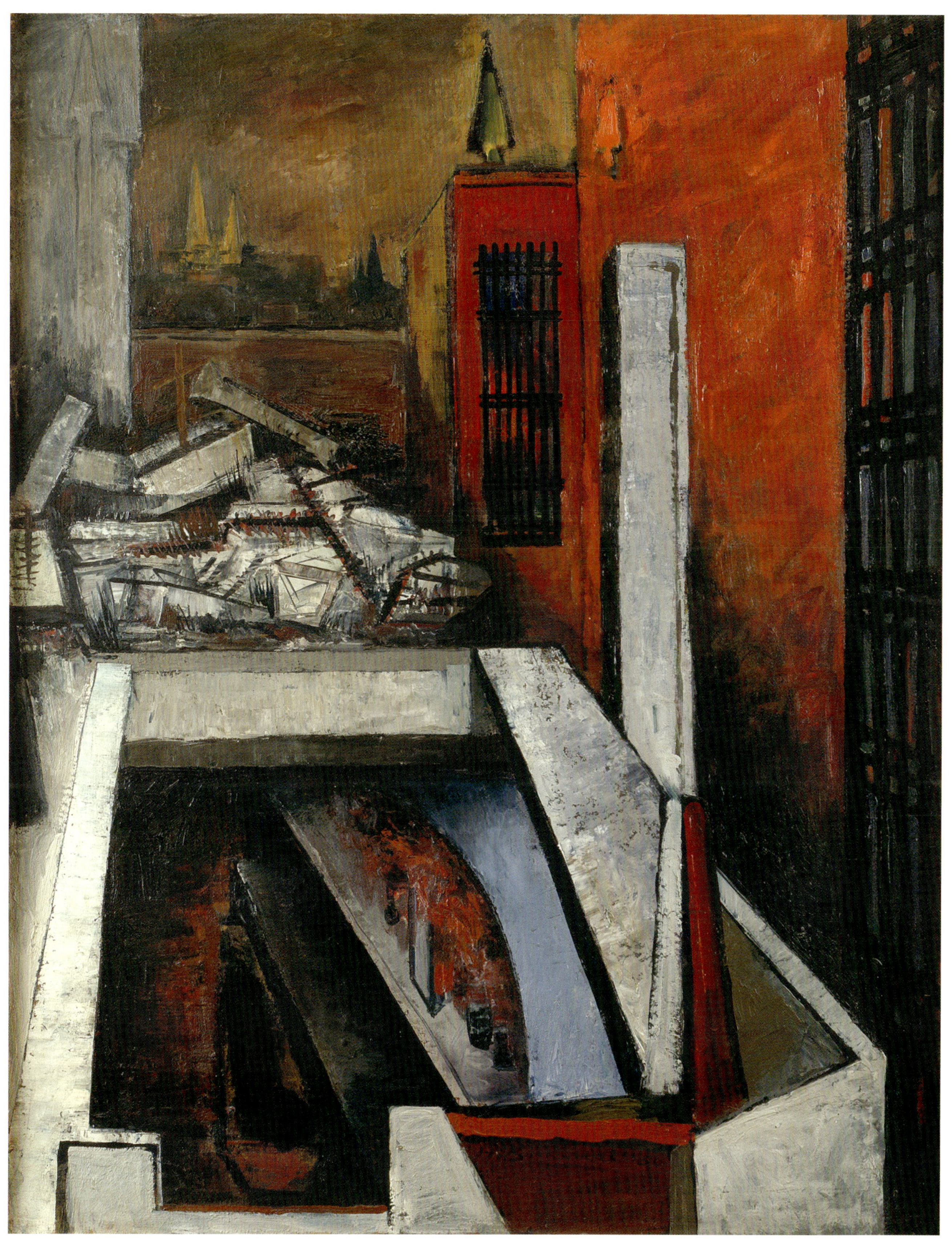

HANS BURKHARDT, *BURIAL GROUND*, 1950
Oil on canvas, 42 x 32 inches

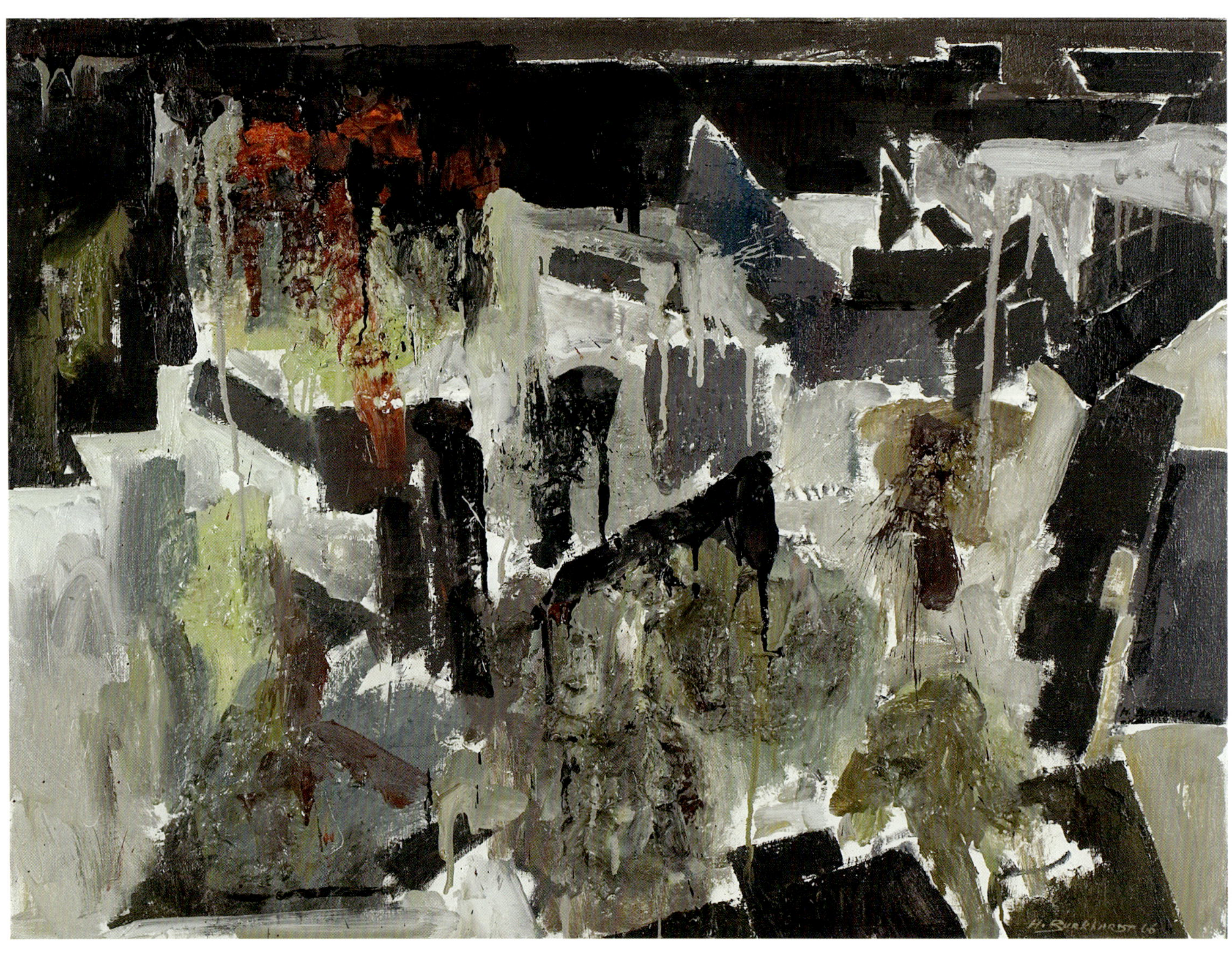

HANS BURKHARDT, *MOTHER'S TEARS*, 1966
Oil on canvas, 32 x 42 inches

HANS BURKHARDT, [1904-1994]

Born December 20, 1904, Basel, Switzerland. To USA 1924.
Died April 22, 1994, Los Angeles, CA.

Studied Cooper Union, 1925–27; Grand Central School, NY, 1927–28, with Arshile Gorky, and privately with Gorky, 1928–37.

Military Service in World War II 1943: U.S. Army, Camp Walters, TX.

Teaching Positions 1959: Long Beach State College; 1959: University of Southern California; 1961–63: University of California, Los Angeles; 1962–63: University of California, Los Angeles; 1962: Otis Art Institute; 1962–63: Choninard Art Institute, Los Angeles; 1962–64: California Institute of the Arts; School of Art and Design, Laguna Beach, CA; 1963–73: San Fernando Valley State College (now California State University at Northridge).

Selected Solo Exhibitions 1939: (first) Stendahl Gallery, Los Angeles; 1940–45: Open Circle Gallery, Los Angeles; 1945: Los Angeles County Museum of Art; 1947: University of Oregon; 1951: Musco de Bellas Artes, Guadalajara; 1952: Paul Kantor Gallery, Los Angeles; 1953, 60: University of Southern California, Los Angeles; 1956, 58, 60: Instituto Allende, San Miguel Allende, Mexico; 1957: Pasadena Museum of Art, CA; 1961–62: *Thirty Year Retrospective*, circ., Santa Barbara Museum of Art, Palace of the Legion of Honor, San Francisco; 1963, 65, 73, 75: California State University, Northridge; 1964, 79: Palm Springs Desert Museum; 1965: Freie Schule, Basel, Switzerland; 1966: *Forty Year Retrospective*, San Diego Art Institute; 1968: *Vietnam Paintings*, Fine Arts Gallery of San Diego, CA; 1972: *Retrospective*: *1950–1972,* Long Beach Museum of Art, CA; 1977, 94: Santa Barbara Museum; 1978, 90, 94: Laguna Beach Museum of Art, CA; 1979: Robert Schoelkopf Gallery, NY; 1987: Oakland Museum, Oakland, CA; 1990–95: Galway Art Festival, Ireland; 1990–91: *Mark Tobey and Hans Burkhardt from the Permanent Collection*, Portland Art Museum, OR; 1993: *Hans Burkhardt: Desert Storms*, Graduate Theological Union, Berkeley; *Burkhardt: Pastels*, Galerie Hesselbach, Berlin; 1996: *Hans Burkhardt: Drawings: 1932–1989*, Arkansas Art Center; 1982–85, 87–91, 93, 94, 98, 2003, 08: Jack Rutberg Fine Arts, Los Angeles, CA; 2008: *Hans Burkhardt – In The University Collection*, California State University Northridge, CA.

Selected Group Exhibitions 1940, 45–48, 53, 54, 57, 59 Los Angeles County Museum of Art Annuals; 1947, 51, 82, 83: Corcoran Gallery of Art, Biennial Exhibitions, Washington, D.C.; 1947, 48, 52: Art Institute of Chicago, IL; 1947, 48, 57: Palace Legion of Honor, San Francisco, CA; 1950: *American Painting Today*, Metropolitan Museum of Art, NYC; 1951–52, 55, 58: *Whitney Museum of American Art Annuals and Biennials*, NYC; 1955: III Sao Paulo Biennial, Brazil; 1957–58, 61, 92: Santa Barbara Museum of Art, CA; 1960–61: Fifty Paintings by Thirty-Seven Painters, circ., Dallas Museum of Contemporary Art, TX; 1964: Kunsthalle, Basel, Switzerland; 1976–77: *Painting and Sculpture in California: The Modern Era*, circ., San Francisco Museum of Modern Art, CA; 1984–85: The Hirshhorn Museum and Sculpture Garden, Smithsonian Institution, Washington, D.C.; 1987: *Artists of Union Square*, Associated American Artists, NY; 1988: *Unique Visions*, ACE Gallery, Los Angeles, CA; 1990: *Turning the Tide: Early Los Angeles Modernists 1920–1956*, circ., Santa Barbara Museum of Art, CA; 1992: American Academy Institute of Arts and Letters; *American Abstract Drawing*, Claremont College; 1994: *Still Working*, Corcoran Gallery of Art, Washington, D.C.; *Old Glory: The American Flag in Contemporary Art*, circ., Phoenix Art Museum, AZ; 1996: *On the Edge of America: California Modernist Art 1900–1950*, Jack Rutberg, Fine Arts, Los Angeles, CA; *Recent Acquisitions*, The British Museum, London, England; 1998: *Gold Rush to Pop: 200 Years of California Art*, Orange County Museum of Art, Newport Beach, CA; 2000: *Made in California 1900–2000*, Los Angeles County Museum of Art, Los Angeles, CA; 2001: *The Stamp of Impulse: Abstract Expressionist Print*, Worchester Art Museum, Worchester, MA; 2008: *The American Scene Hopper to Pollock 1905–1960*, The British Museum, London, England.

NICOLAS CARONE

In art, the image is the sensation of an internal experience that does not rely on optics. Image is the spiritual sense of being in the realm of imagination. The image is the elusive form that is revealed by the light of the mind.

When the figure goes abstract it deals with the medium that the artist works with. The musician plays the violin which has its own range of music. Painting has the same thing. The plane can be multiplied. When it is analyzed it is a constant addition and subtraction of planes. It is a constant give and take.

The content is very important in a painting. You cannot paint an abstract painting without the figurative emotion being involved. It has a narrative but the narrative comes out of the conscious and of the unconscious dialogue. This is a very important factor as the painting develops in scale, dimension and content.

Finally, the painting has to breathe. It doesn't matter whether the painting is abstract or figurative. For me, the painting has to be art and art is abstract.

Nicolas Carone, Statement:
Interview with the editor.
September 4, 2008

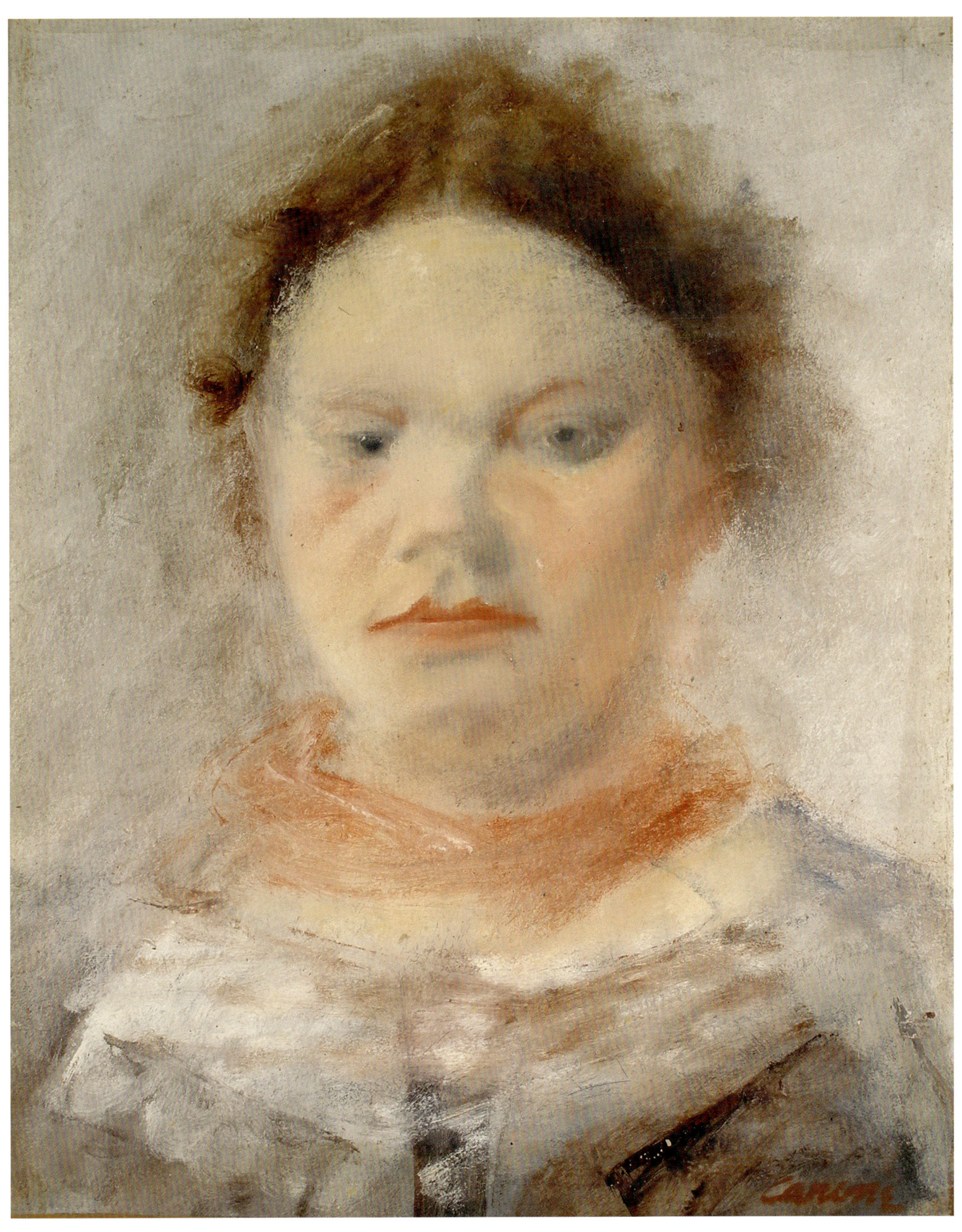

NICOLAS CARONE, *Irish Girl*, 1989
Oil on paper, 22 1/2 x 18 inches
Collection of Emily Cheng, New York

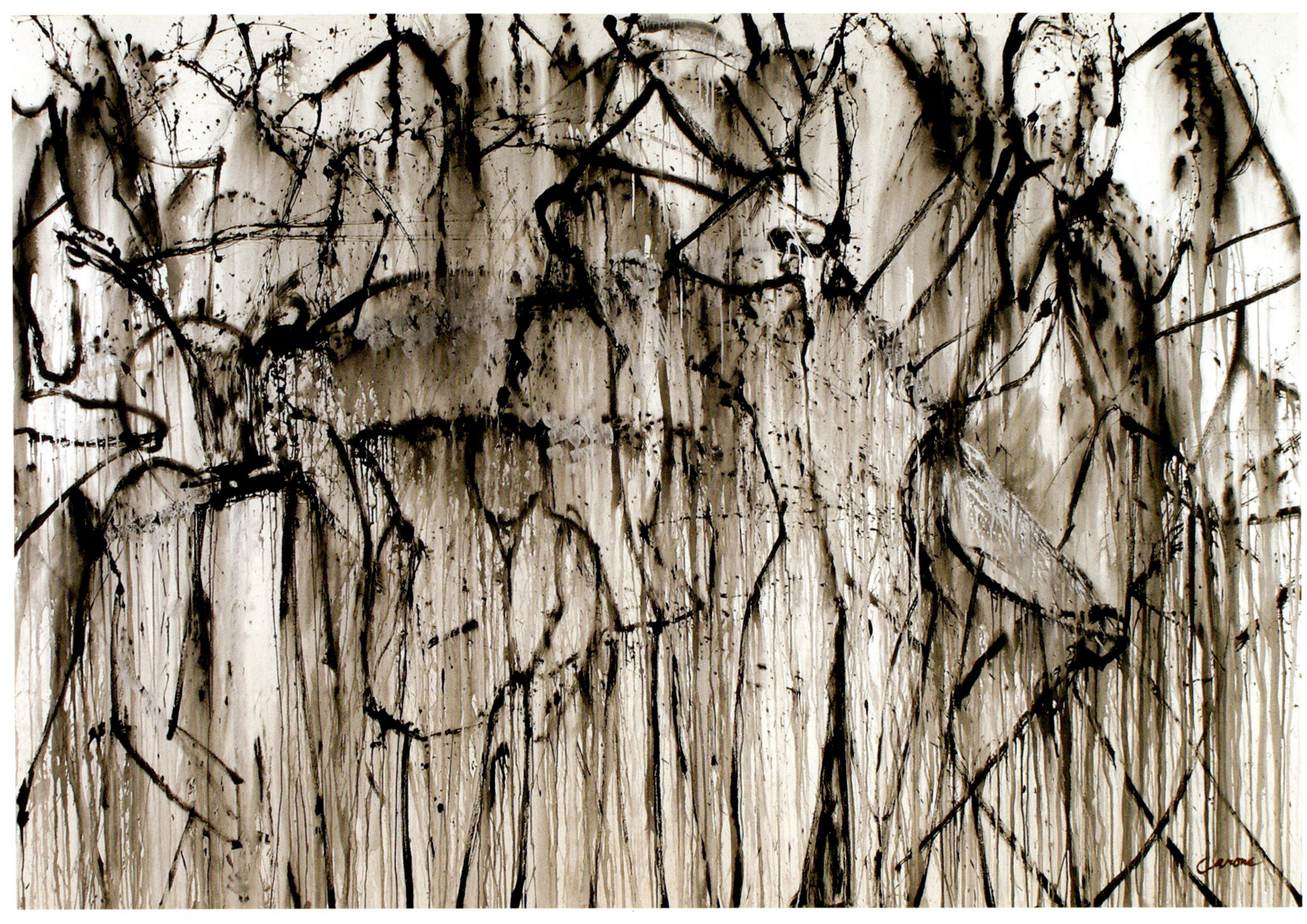

NICOLAS CARONE, *Shadow Dance*, 2007
Acrylic on canvas, 84 x 119 3/4 inches
Collection of the artist
© Nicolas Carone. Courtesy of the Washburn Gallery, New York

NICOLAS CARONE, [1917-]

Born June 4, 1917, New York City, NY.

Studied 1928: Leonardo da Vinci Art School, St.Mark's Place, NYC; 1929: National Academy of Design, NYC; 1934: Art Students League, NYC; 1946–47: Hans Hofmann School of Art in New York City.

Military Service in World War II 1942–1945 U.S. Air Force.

Teaching positions 1957–63: Cooper Union, NYC; 1959–60, 1963–65: Yale University, New Haven, CT; 1963–64: Columbia University, NYC; 1963 (summer): Skowhegan, Maine; 1964 (summer): Cornell University, Ithaca, NY; 1967: Maryland Institute of Art, Baltimore, MD; 1968–69: Brandeis University, Waltham, MA; 1964–1988: New York Studio School, NYC; 1989–2000: International School of Art, Umbria, Italy.

Selected Solo Exhibitions 1949: Cortile Galleria, Rome, Italy; 1951: Galleria Nazionale d'Arte Moderna, Rome; 1952: Frumkin Gallery, Chicago, IL; 1954, 1956: Stable Gallery, New York City; 1958: Stadler Gallery, Paris, France; 1958, 1959, 1962: Staempfli Gallery, New York City; 1978, 93: Carone Gallery, Fort Lauderdale, FL; 2003: Butler Institute of American Art, Youngstown, OH; 2005, 07: Lohin Geduld Gallery, NYC; 2008: Washburn Gallery, NYC.

Selected Group Exhibitions 1948: Modern Museum, Rome, Italy; American Foundation, Rome; Rome Quadriennale; 1951, 1953-1957: *The 9th St.* Show, the first New York Painting and Sculpture Annual Exhibition and subsequent 5 *New York Artists' Annual Exhibitions*, Stable Gallery, NYC; 1957: Brussels Universal and International Exhibition, Belgium; 1958: *American Artists Paint The City*, XXVIIIth Venice Biennial; Stadler Gallery, Paris; 1957, 61: The Whitney Museum of American Art Annual & Biennial Exhibitions, NYC; 1961: *60 American Painters, 1960*, Walker Art Center, Minneapolis, MN; 1961: *American Abstract Expressionists and Imagists*, The Solomon R. Guggenheim Museum, NYC; *Contemporary Painting and Sculpture*, Krannert Art Museum, University of Illinois, Urbana; 1962: *65th American Exhibition*, Chicago Art Institute, Chicago, IL; *American Abstract Artists*, Museum of Modern Art, Sao Paulo, Brazil; 1963-1964: *Hans Hofmann and His Students,* circ., Museum of Modern Art, NYC; 1964: Internationale Der Zeichnung, Zurich, Switzerland; 1969: *Artists Abroad*, Institute of International Education, NY; 1970: Brandeis University Museum, Waltham, MA; 1973: *Ciba Geigy Collection Exhibition*, University of Austin, TX; 1980: *17 Abstract Artists of East Hampton: The Pollock Years, 1946-56*, The Parrish Art Museum, Southampton, NY; 1981: *Ciba Geigy Collection Exhibition,* Sewall Art Gallery, Rice University, Houston, TX; 1990: *East Hampton Avant-Garde, A Salute to the Signa Gallery*, Guild Hall Museum, East Hampton, NY; 1992: *American Vanguard*, Stuart Levy Gallery, NYC; 1993: *Memory and Metaphor*, Andre Zarre Gallery, NYC; 1994: *Reclaiming Artists of the New York School. Toward a more inclusive view of the 1950's,* Baruch College, City University, NY; *New York-Provincetown: A 50's Connection*, Provincetown Art Association and Museum, MA; *American Choice, Muriel Kallis Steinberg Newman Collection*, The Metropolitan Museum of Art, NYC; 1995: *Italian American Artists: 1945–68*, Hunter College, NYC; 1999: Corcoran Gallery of Fine Arts, Washington, D.C.; Lowe Art Museum, Coral Gabels; Tate Modern, London, England; 2006: *Artisti 'stranieri' in Umbria*, Chiesa–Museo di San Francesco, Corciano, Italy; *American Academy Invitational Exhibition of Painting and Sculpture*, American Academy of Painting and Sculpture, NY; 2007: *Breaking the Mold: Selections from the Washington Gallery of Modern Art, 1961–1968*, Oklahoma City Museum of Art.

NANNO DE GROOT

As a child I didn't want to be anything. I later learned that small boys want to become engine drivers, soldiers, firemen, cowboys; but such aspirations were alien to me. I did not, however, actively want to be nothing when I grew up. The whole thing merely never occurred to me at all. People were, a house was, the canal was, the bridge was, the sky was and I was. Not becoming, not having been—anything, or something else. In moments of clarity of thought I can sustain the idea that everything on earth is nature, including that which springs forth from a man's mind, and hand. A Franz Kline is nature as much as a zinnia. Once that idea is thought it becomes clouded by the idea that this would include a paper flower or a plaster Jesus.

I have now painted nearly 30 vases full of flowers and am still discovering many new things. It is strange how completely abstract a completely true to nature painting becomes. It is probably that one is so little used to looking closely enough at the color of things that it has escaped one that a red flower, for instance, has about a dozen colors haphazardly put together—one color next to the other. Every red flower (of the samered) has different reds in it and they are distributed differently and very crudely. Painted that way, reality is approached much more closely than trying to imitate the subtleties a flower contains. Those subtleties are there in the end, wonder of wonders, in the painting, and even the delicacies of texture.

Nanno de Groot, Statement: Nanno de Groot's work books, written c.1958. Property of Mrs. Pat de Groot.

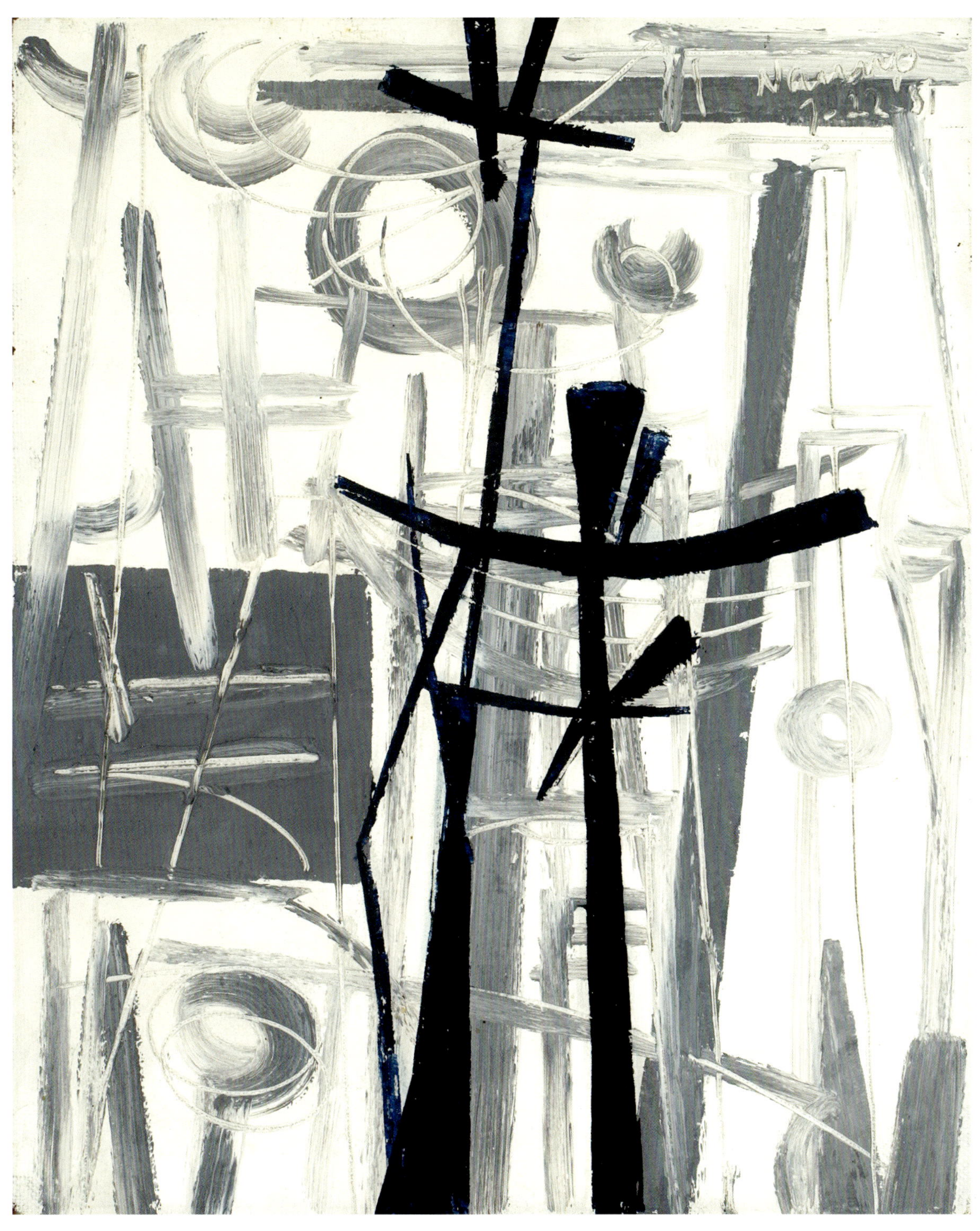

NANNO DE GROOT, *The Roebuck*, 1951
Oil on canvas, 20 x 16 inches
Collection of the Estate of Nanno de Groot

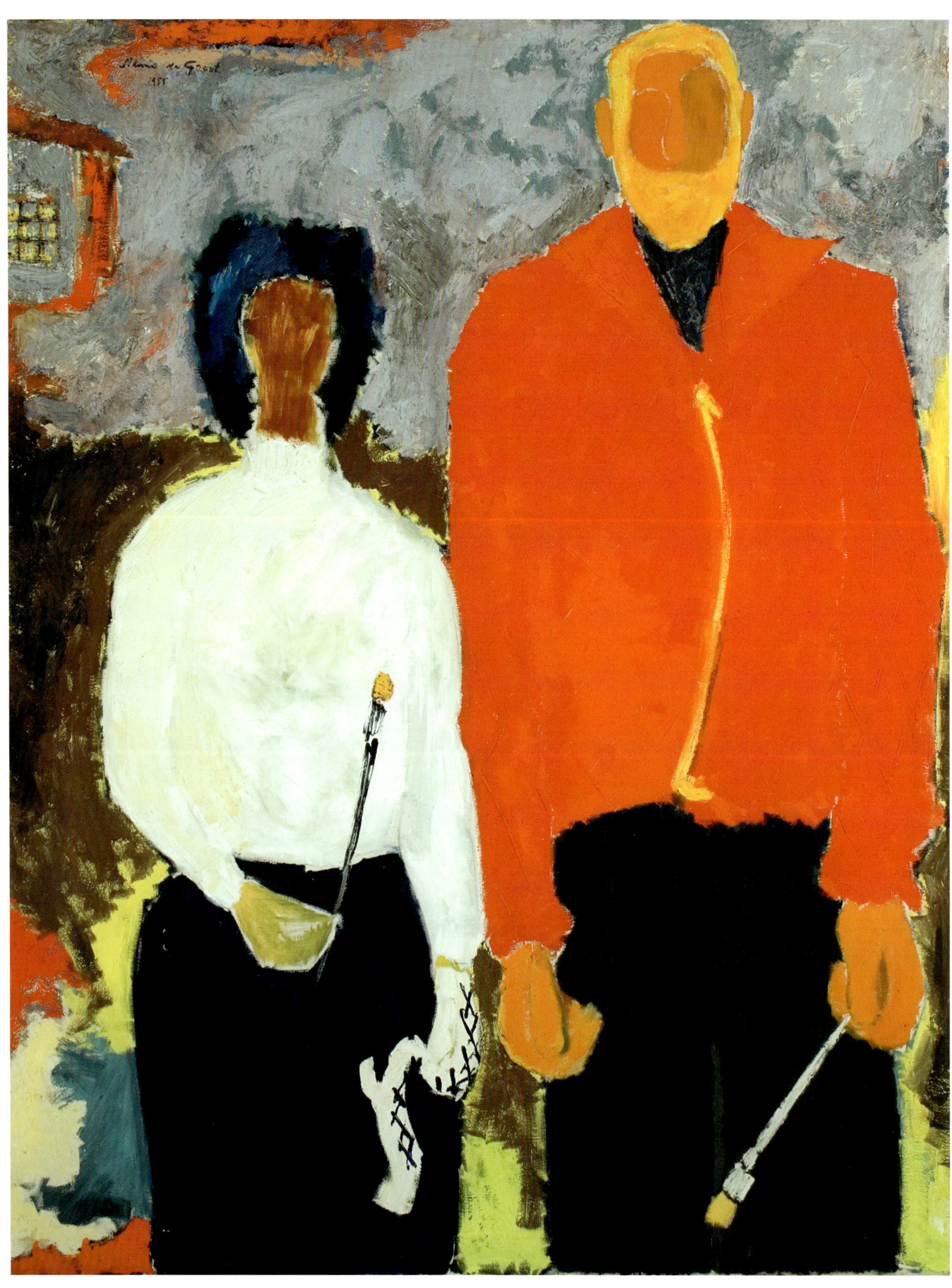

NANNO DE GROOT, *Alain and Biala*, 1955
Oil on canvas, 70 x 52 1/2 inches
Collection of the Provincetown Art Association and Museum, Provincetown, MA; Gift of Marguerite and Dan Stevens

NANNO DE GROOT, [1913-1963]

Born March 23, 1913 in Balkbrug, Holland. **To USA** 1941. **USA Citizen** 1954. **Died** December 26, 1963 in Provincetown, MA.

Military Service in World War II 1941: Dutch Navy; 1942–1946: Lieutenant Commander in charge of the Dutch Port Authority in San Francisco.

Selected Solo Exhibitions 1952 : Saidenberg Gallery, NYC; 1954, 55: Bertha Schaefer Gallery, NYC; 1956, 59, 60, 61, 64 (memorial): HCE Gallery, Provincetown, MA; 1957, 58, 59, 61: Parma Gallery, NYC; 1960: October, Stamford Museum, CT; 1971: Jack Gregory Gallery, Provincetowns, MA; 1982: *Retrospective Exhibition*, Provincetown Art Association and Museum, Provincetown, MA; 2004: *Nanon de Groot: The New York Years*, ACME Fine Art, Boston, MA; 2007: *Nanon de Groot: Earth, Sea & Sky*, ACME Fine Art, Boston, MA.

Selected Group Exhibitions 1953 Saidenberg Gallery, NYC; 1953 Hansa Gallery, NYC; 1954, 55: Tanager Gallery, NYC; 1954, 55, 56, 57: *New York Painting and Sculpture Annuals*, Stable Gallery, NYC; 1962, 63: HCE Provincetown, MA; 1953–1964: Provincetown Art Association and Museum, Provincetown, MA; 1982: *Provincetown Painters*, Everson Museum, principal collections; 1994: *Reclaiming Artists of the New York School. Toward a More Inclusive View of the 1950's*, Baruch College, City University, NY; *New York-Provincetown: A 50's Connection*, Provincetown Art Association and Museum, MA; Anita Shapolsky Gallery, NYC; 2003: *The New York School*, ACME Fine Art, Boston, MA; *Provincetown Painters*, ACME Fine Art, Boston, MA; *Summer Salon*, ACME Fine Art, Boston, MA; 2004: *Beyond Likeness*, ACME Fine Art, Boston, MA; *Summer Salon*, ACME Fine Art, Boston, MA; *Reuniting an Era: Abstract Expressionists of the 1950s*, Rockford Art Museum, Rockford, IL.

ELAINE DE KOONING

...I don't choose my subjects or my style or my colors, they choose me and I'm grateful to them. Nor do I ever decide to abandon them; I'm torn away from them.

There are conflicts. The excessive liberality of idea struggles with the illiberality of desire, and desires contradict each other, but the strongest desire always wins. I inform the painting of my ideas; the painting informs me of my desires.

Elaine de Kooning, Statement (1959): From *Elaine de Kooning The Spirit of Abstract Expressionism.* Selected writings. Publisher: George Braziller, New York, 1993. p. 175

For me the most important thing about the words "painting" and "drawing" is that they end in ing. A painting to me is primarily a verb, not a noun, an event first and only secondarily an image.

...For years these events occurred for me in vertical space. Now they interact in horizontal areas. ...For one thing, I want gesture, of any kind of gesture, all kinds of gesture, gentle or brutal, joyous or tragic, the gesture of space soaring, sinking, streaming, whirling, the gestures of light flowing or spurting through color. I see everything as possessing or possessed by gesture. I've often thought of my paintings as having an axis around which everything revolves.

Elaine de Kooning, Statement: It Is. No.4, Autumn, 1959. Magazine for Abstract Art, Second Half Publishing Co., NY. pp. 29, 30

...When I painted my seated men, I saw them as gyroscopes. Portraiture has always fascinated me because I love the particular gesture of a particular expression or stance. I'm enthralled by the gesture of the silhouette (for portraits or anything else), the instantaneous illumination that enables you to recognize your father or a friend three blocks away or, sitting in the bleachers, to recognize the man at bat. Working on the figure, I wanted paint to sweep through as feelings sweep through. Then I wanted the paint to sweep the figure along with it — and got involved with men in action — abstract action, action for its own sake — the game. And finally, I wanted the paint to sweep through, around, over and past, to hack away at contours and engulf silhouettes.

Elaine de Kooning, Statement: It Is. No.4, Autumn, 1959. Magazine for Abstract Art, Second Half Publishing Co., NY. p.30

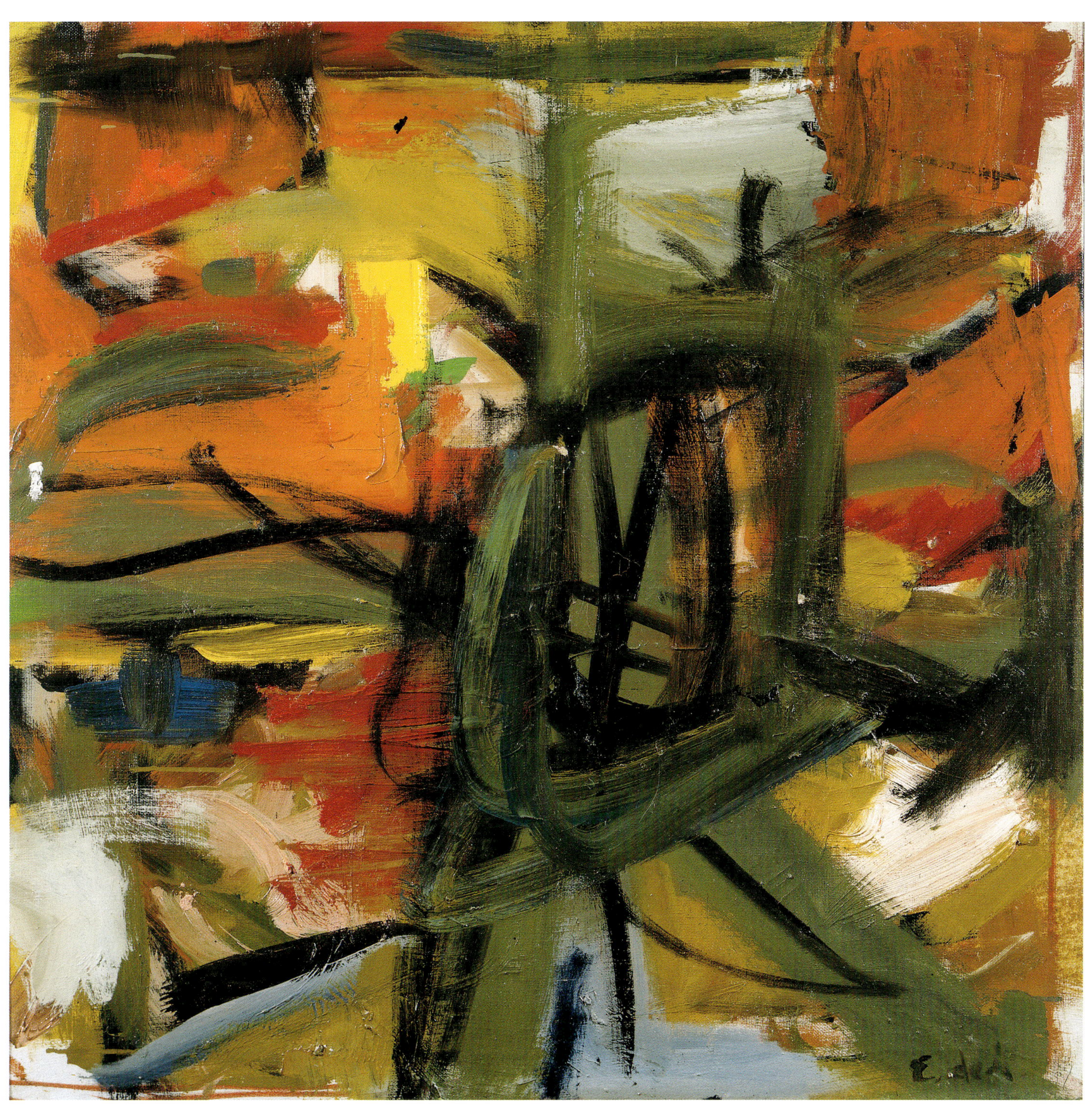

ELAINE DE KOONING, *Untitled*, 1957
Oil on canvas, 30 x 30 inches
Private collection

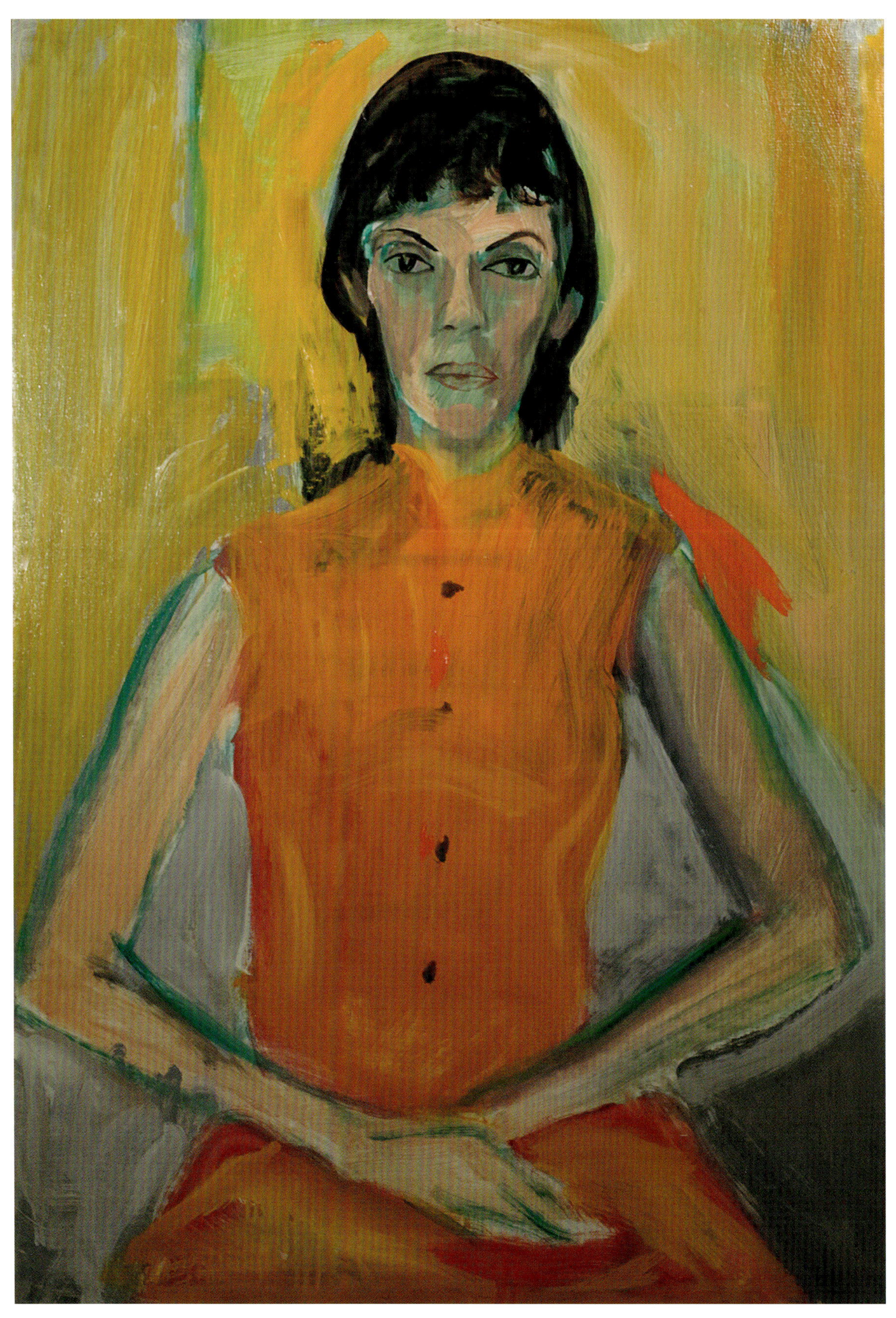

ELAINE DE KOONING, *Sheila Rosenstein*, c. 1962
Oil on canvas 47 3/4 x 32 3/8 inches
Private collection

ELAINE MARIE (CATHERINE) DE KOONING, [1918-1989]

Born in New York City, in 1918.
Died in New York, in 1989.

Studied 1937 at the Leonardo Da Vinci Art School, Hoboken, NJ; 1938 at the American Artists School. 1948: Editorial Associate for the Art News magazine.

Teaching Positions 1959: University of New Mexico; 1960: The Pennsylvania State University; 1963–64: University of California, Davis; 1967: Yale University; 1968: Pratt Institute; 1968–70: Carnegie-Mellon University; 1971–72: University of Pennsylvania; 1971: Wagner College; 1974: NY Studio School, Paris; 1974–75: Parsons School of Design, NYC; 1976–79: University of Georgia.

Selected Solo Exhibitions 1952, 1954, 1956: Stable Gallery, NYC; 1957: Tibor de Nagy Gallery, NYC; 1959: Lyman Allen Art Museum, New London, CT; 1960: Ellison Gallery, Fort Worth, TX; 1960, 1963, 1965, 1975: Graham Gallery, NYC; 1964: *25 Portraits of J.F.K.*, Peale House Gallery, The Pennsylvania Academy of Fine Art, Philadelphia, PA; 1979: *Bacchus, Works on Paper*, Lauren Rogers Library and Museum, Laurel, Mississippi; 1982, 86: Gruenebaum Gallery; 1983: *Elaine de Kooning and the Bacchus Motif*, The Arts Club of Chicago; 1991: *Black Mountain Paintings from 1948*, Joan T. Washburn Gallery, NYC.

Selected Group Exhibitions 1951, 1953-1957: *The 9th St. Show*, the first New York Painters and Sculptors Annual Exhibition and subsequent 5 *New York Artists' Annual Exhibitions*, Stable Gallery, NYC; 1956: *Abstract Expressionism*, circ., by the Walker Art Center, Minneapolis, MN.; *Young American Painters*, circ., The Museum of Modern Art, NYC; *Pittsburgh International*, Carnegie Institute, Pittsburgh; 1958: *Action Painting, 1958*, Dallas Museum of Contemporary Arts; 1960: *Abstract Expressionists Painting of the Fifties*, The Walker Art Center, Minneapolis, MN; 1961: The Whitney Museum of American Art Annuals and Biennials, NYC; 1964: *67th Annual American Exhibition: Directions in Contemporary Painting and Sculpture*, The Art Institute of Chicago; 1980: *The Fifties: Aspects Painting in New York*, Hirshhorn Museum and Sculpture Garden, Washington, D.C.; 1990: *East Hampton Avant-Garde, A Salute to the Signa Gallery*, Guild Hall Museum, East Hampton, NY.

WILLEM DE KOONING

Spiritually I am wherever my spirit allows me to be, and that is not necessarily in the future. I have no nostalgia, however. If I am confronted with one of those small Mesopotamian figures, I have no nostalgia for it but, instead, I may get into a state of anxiety. Art never seems to me peaceful or pure. I always seem to be wrapped in the melodrama of vulgarity. I do not think of inside or outside—or of art in general—as a situation of comfort. I know there is a terrific idea there somewhere, but whenever I want to get into it, I get a feeling of apathy and want to lie down and go to sleep. Some painters, including myself, do not care what chair they are sitting on. It does not even have to be a comfortable one. They are too nervous to find out where they ought to sit. They do not want to 'sit in style.' Rather, they have found that painting—any kind of painting, any style of painting—to be painting at all, in fact—is a way of living today, a style of living, so to speak. That is where the form of it lies. It is exactly in its uselessness that it is free. Those artists do not want to conform. They only want to be inspired.

Willem de Kooning, excerpts from "What Abstract Art Means to Me," *Bulletin of the Museum of Modern Art* (New York), Vol. XVIII, No. 3 (Spring, 1951), p. 7.

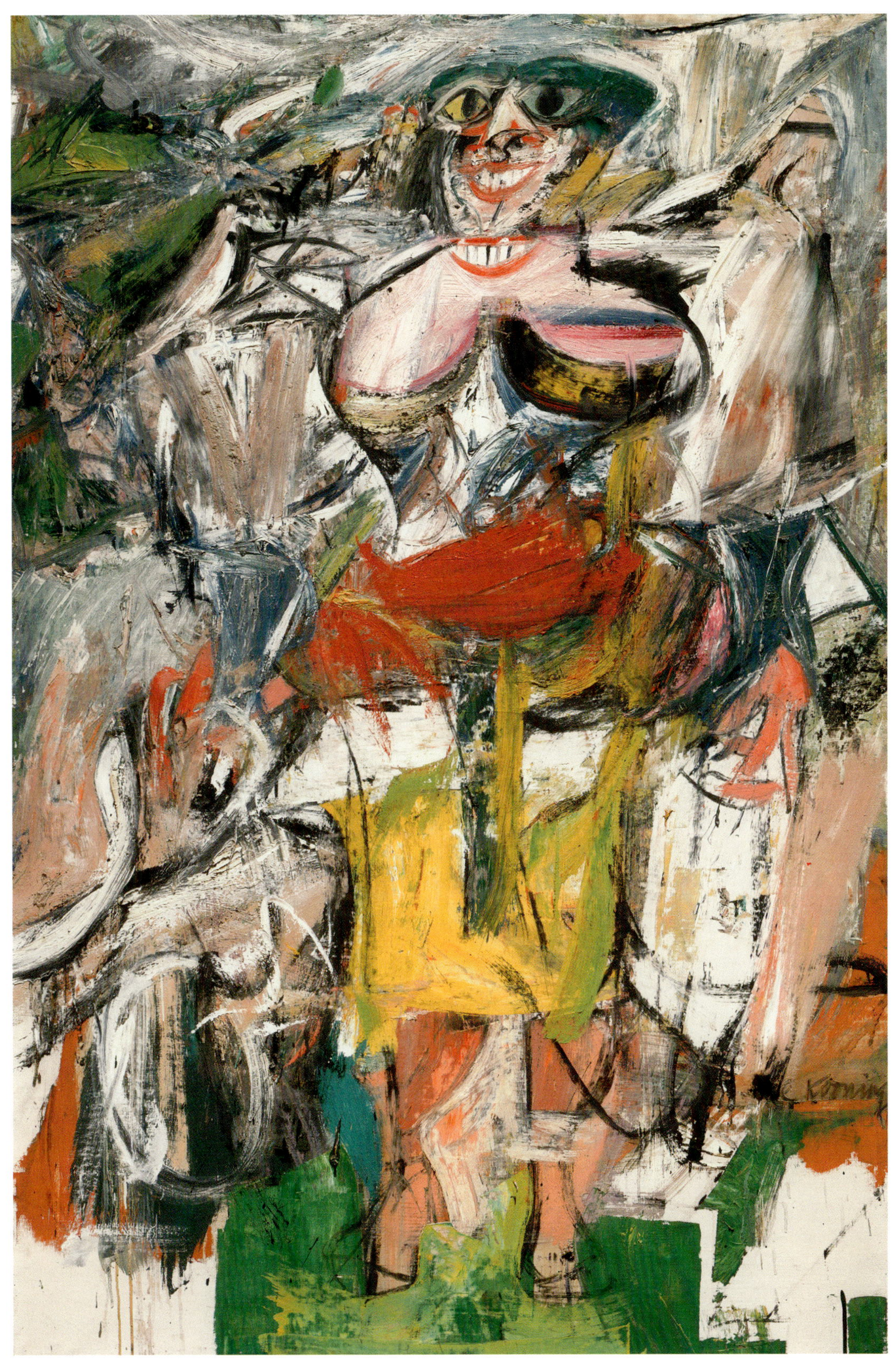

WILLEM DE KOONING, *Woman and Bicycle,* 1952-53
Oil on canvas, 76 1/2 x 49 inches (194.3 x 124.46 cm)
Whitney Museum of American Art, New York; purchase 55.35

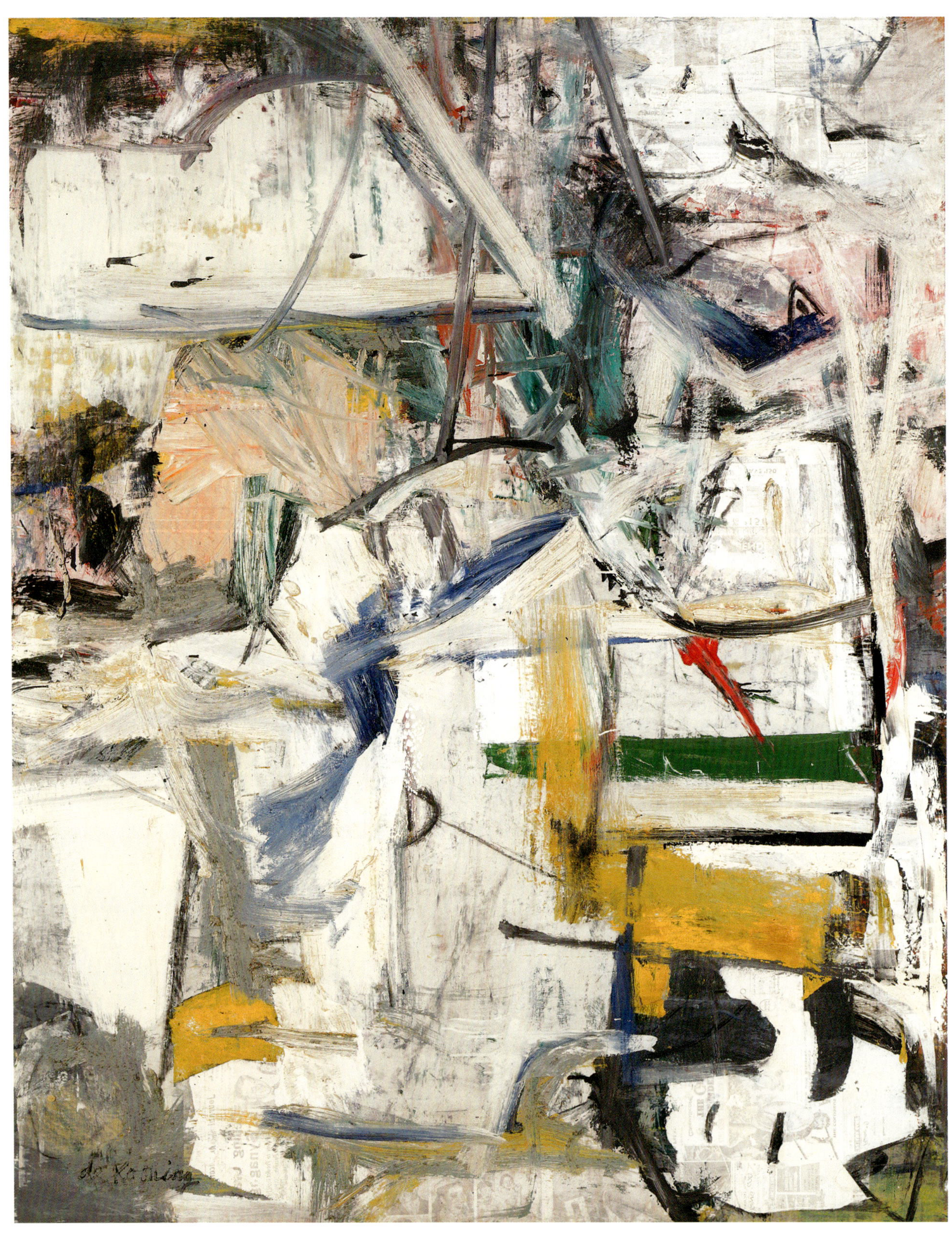

WILLEM DE KOONING, *Easter Monday*, 1955–56
Oil and newspaper transfer on canvas, 96 x 74 inches (134.9 x 101.6 cm)
Collection of The Metropolitan Museum of Art, Rogers Fund, 1956. (56.205.2)
Photograph © 1983 The Metropolitan Museum of Art
© 2009 The Willem de Kooning Foundationt / Artists Rights Society (ARS), New York

WILLEM DE KOONING, [1904-1997]

Born April 24, 1904, Rotterdam, Holland. **To USA**, 1926 illegally. **US citizen** 1962. **Died** March 19, 1997, East Hampton, Long Island, NY.

Studied 1917–21: Attended night classes in fine arts and gilding at Rotterdam Academy of Fine Arts and Techniques.

Teaching Positions 1948 summer: Black Mountain College, NC; 1950–51: Yale University.

Selected Solo Exhibitions 1948 (first), 1951: Charles Egan Gallery; 1951: Arts Club of Chicago; 1953, 56, 59, 62, 72 : Sidney Janis Gallery; 1955: Martha Jackson Gallery, NYC; 1961, 65: Paul Kantor Gallery, Beverly Hills, Calif.; 1962 (two man), 1964, 66, 71, 72: Allan Stone Gallery, NYC; 1967, 69, 71, Paris, 1968, 71: M. Knoedler & Co, NYC; 1974: Walker; 1975: Fourcade, Droll Inc., NY; 1975: Norton Gallery, West Palm Beach, FL.; 1976: Seattle Art Museum, Seattle, Wash.; 1976, 83: Stedelijk Museum Amsterdam; 1976, 77: Corcoran Gallery, Los Angeles; 1977, 84: Galerie Daniel Templon, Paris; 1976: University of Houston; 1978: The Solomon R. Guggenheim Museum, NY; 1979: Carnegie; 1980: Richard Gray Gallery, Chicago; 1981, 94: Guild Hall, East Hampton, NY;1983: Galerie Maeght Lelong, NYC; 1985: Studio Marconi, Milan; 1990, 93: Salander-O'Reilly Galleries, NYC; 1993: *Willem de Kooning from the Hirshhorn Museum Collection*, circ., Hirshhorn Museum and Sculpture Garden, Washington, D.C.
Retrospectives: 1953: *de Kooning: 1935–1953*, circ., School of the Museum of Fine Arts, Boston, MA; 1965: *Willem de Kooning*, circ., Smith College Museum of Art, Northampton, MA; 1968: *Willem de Kooning*, circ., Stedelijk Museum, Amsterdam, Holland; 1983–84: *Willem de Kooning: Drawings, Paintings, Sculpture*, circ., Whitney Museum of American Art, NYC; 1994: *Willem de Kooning: Paintings*, circ., National Gallery of Art, Washington, D.C.; 1995: *Willem de Kooning: The Late Paintings, The 1980's*, circ., San Francisco Museum of Modern Art, CA.

Selected Group Exhibitions 1936: *New Horizons in American Art*, Museum of Modern Art, NYC; 1951, 1953–57: *9th St.* Show, the first New York Painters and Sculptors Annual Exhibition and subsequent 5 *New York Painting and Sculpture Annual*, Stable Gallery, NYC; 1948–54, 56, 59, 63, 65, 67, 69, 72, 81, 87: The Whitney Museum of American Art Annuals and
Biennials, NYC; 1958: *Nature in Abstraction*, circ. The Whitney Museum of American Art, NYC; 1950, 54, 56: XXV, XXVII, & XXVIII Venice Biennials; 1951: *Abstract Painting and Sculpture in America*, Museum of Modern Art, NYC; 1958: Brussels World's Fair; 1958–59: *The New American Painting*, circ., Europe, Museum of Modern Art, NY; 1964: *Painting and Sculpture of a Decade, 1954–64*, The Tate Gallery, London; 1965: *New York School*, Los Angeles County Museum of Art; 1967: *Two Decades of American Painting and Sculpture*, National Gallery of Victoria, Melbourne, Australia; 1969: *The New American Painting and Sculpture*, Museum of Modern Art, NY; 1978: *American Art Mid-Century*, The National Gallery, Washington, DC.

RICHARD DIEBENKORN

Your questions concern groups of artists and their changing attitudes, which I take for granted and about which I'm not very interested. What interests me is that a few strong painters are at work, some of whom, incidentally, will remain 'non-representative' while others will 'return.' Others yet will not have to return, having never departed. 'Out-moded' will mean as little to them as it meant to Monet.

I don't mean to try to belittle your questions. The concerns they reflect produce information about the past that makes a position such as I take possible.

Richard Diebenkorn, Statement: *Contemporary Painting and Sculpture*, University of Illinois, Urbana, 1961. Catalogue, p. 91.

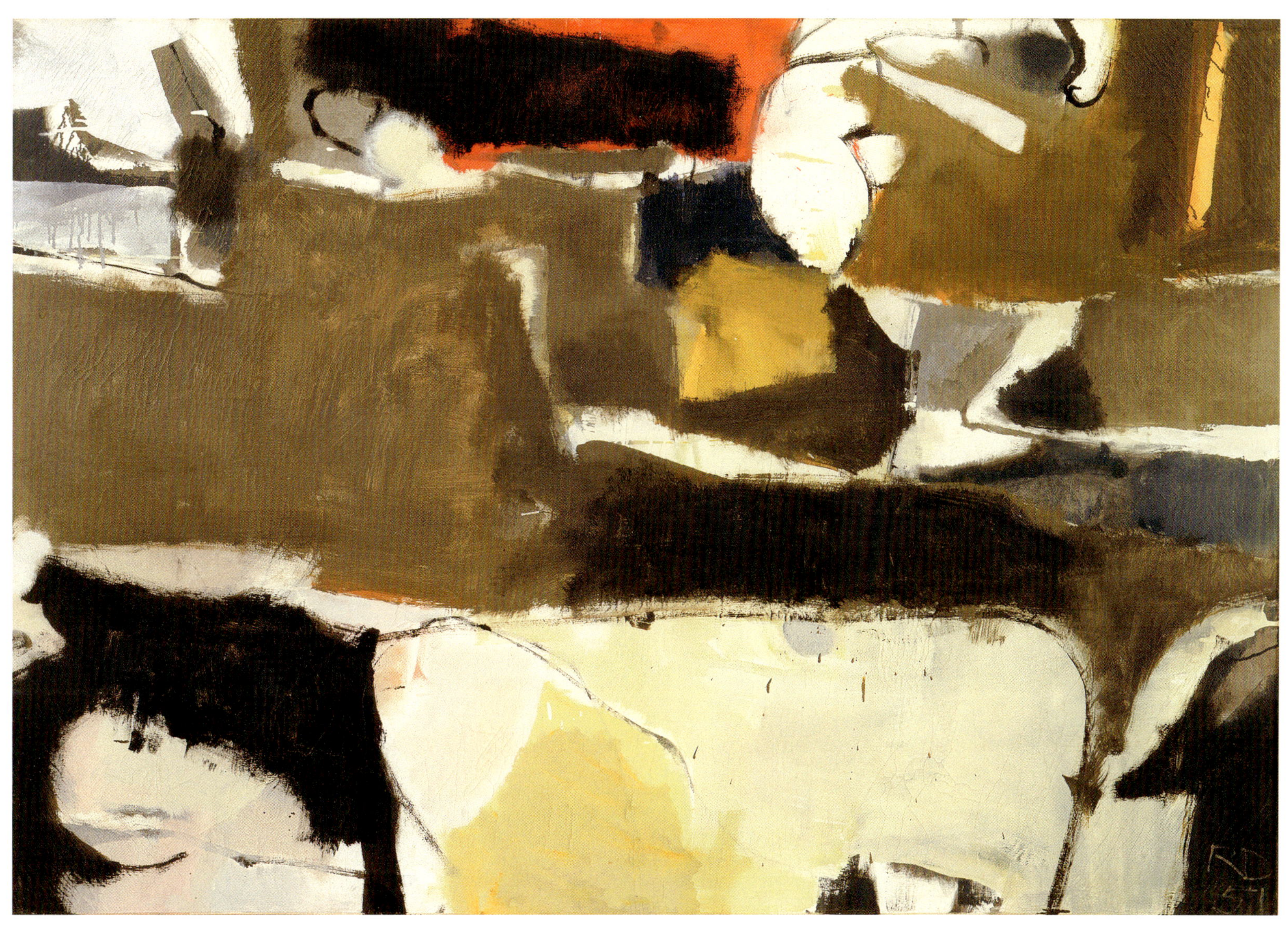

RICHARD DIEBENKORN, *Untitled*, 1951
Oil on canvas, 39 3/4 x 55 1/2 inches (RD 2376)

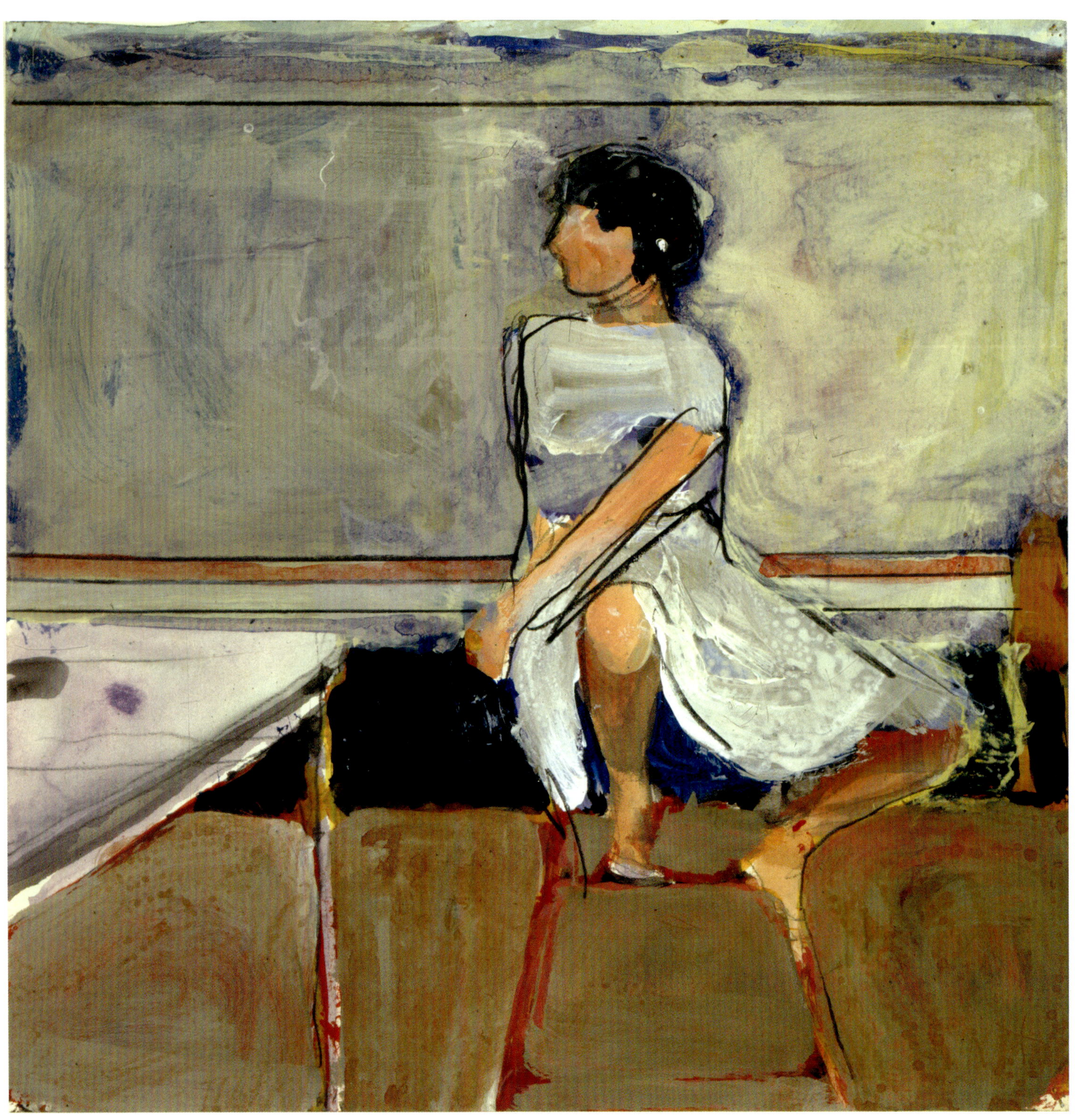

RICHARD DIEBENKORN, *Woman on Stool*, 1965
Gouache and pencil on paper, 12 3/8 x 12 1/16 inches (31.4 x 30.6 cm)
(Catalogue Raisonné #2174)

RICHARD CLIFFORD DIEBENKORN, [1922- 1993]

Born April 22, 1922, Portland, OR.
Died March 30, 1993, Berkeley, CA.

Studied 1940–43: Stanford University; 1943–44: University of California, Berkeley, CA; 1946: California School of Fine Arts; 1949: Stanford University, BA; 1951–52: University of New Mexico, MFA.

Military Service in World War II
1943–45: US Marine Corps.

Teaching Positions 1947–50: California School of Fine Arts; 1952–53: University of Illinois; 1955–59: California College of Arts and Crafts, Oakland; CA; 1959–63: San Francisco Art Institute, CA; 1963–64: Stanford University; 1966–73: University of California, Los Angeles.

Selected Solo Exhibitions 1948 (first), 60: California Palace of the Legion of the Honor, San Francisco, CA; 1951: University Art Museum of New Mexico, Albuquerque, NM; 1954, 73: San Francisco Museum of Modern Art, CA; 1955, 58, 61, 63, 66, 68: Poindexter Gallery, NYC; 1958, 61: The Phillips Gallery, Washington, D.C.; 1963, 94: M.H. de Young Memorial Museum, San Francisco; 1964: Stanford University, CA; 1968: Richmond Art Center, CA; 1969: Los Angeles County Museum of Art, CA; 1971, 74: Marlborough Gallery, Inc., NYC; 1975: *Early Abstract Works*, 1948–1955, circ., James Corcoran Gallery, Los Angeles, CA; *The Ocean Park Series: Recent Work*, Marlborough Gallery, NYC; 1976: *Monotypes*, Frederick S. Wight Gallery, University of California, Los Angeles, CA; *Paintings and Drawings 1943–1976*, circ., Albright-Knox Art Gallery, Buffalo, NY; 1977–80, 82, 84, 85, 87, 91, 94: M. Knoedler & Co. Inc., NYC; 1978: *From Nature to Art, from Art to Nature*, (Richard Diebenkorn), American Pavilion, XXXVIIIth Venice Biennale; 1981: *Matrix! Berkeley 40*, University of California, Berkeley; 1983, 95, 96: John Berggruen Gallery, San Francisco, CA; 1985: University of Nebraska, Lincoln; 1989: *Graphics 1981–1988*, circ., Yellowstone Art Center, Billings, Montana; 1992: *Ocean Park Paintings*, Gagosian Gallery, NYC; 1999, 2000: Lawrence Rubin Greenberg Van Doren Fine Art, NYC; 2002: *Figurative Drawings, Gouaches, and Oil Paintings*, Artemis Greenberg Van Doren Fine Art, NYC; 2004: *Richard Diebenkorn: Prints 1948–1993*, Katonah Museum of Art, Katonah, NY; *Richard Diebenkorn Works on Paper: Ocean Park, Clubs and Spades*, Artemis Greenberg Van Doren Gallery, NYC; 2005: *Richard Diebenkorn: Unseen Santa Barbara Works*, Santa Cruz Island Foundation (producer), Reynolds Gallery, Westmont College, Santa Barbara, CA; 2006: *Richard Diebenkorn: Paintings and Drawings on Paper*, Greenberg Van Doren Gallery, NYC; 2007: *Diebenkorn in New Mexico, 1950–1952*, circ., Harwood Museum of Art, University of New Mexico, Taos, NM; *Richard Diebenkorn: The Female Form*, Thomas Gibson Fine Art Ltd, London; 2008: *Richard Diebenkorn, Artist, and Carey Stanton, Collector: Their Stanford Connection*, Cantor Arts Center, Stanford University, CA.
Retrospectives: 1960: Norton Simon Museum, Pasadena, CA; 1964: Washington Gallery of Modern Art, Washington, D.C.; Jewish Museum; 1976: University of California, Los Angeles, circ.; 1981: Minneapolis Institute of Art, MN, circ.; 1983: San Francisco Museum of Modern Art, CA; 1988: *The Drawings of Richard Diebenkorn*, circ., Museum of Modern Art, NYC; 1997–98: *The Art of Richard Diebenkorn*, The Whitney Museum of American Art, NYC.

Selected Group Exhibitions 1954: *Younger American Painters*, Solomon R. Guggenheim Museum, NY; 1955, 58, 61, 63, 65, 67, 69, 72, 81: *Annuals and Biennials*, Whitney Museum of American Art; 1955, 58, 61, 70: Carnegie; 1957: IV Sao Paulo Biennial; 1958: Brussels World's Fair; 1959: *New Images of Man*, Museum of Modern Art, NY; 1964: *Paintings and Sculpture of a Decade*, Tate Gallery, London, England; 1965: *Two American Painters: Sam Francis and Richard Diebenkorn*, National Gallery of Scotland, Edinburgh; 1968, 78: XXIV Venice Biennial; 1974: *Drawings: Elmer Bischoff and Richard Diebenkorn*, Boston University; 1975: *California Landscape*, Oakland Art Museum, CA; 1978: *American Paintings of the 1970's*, Albright-Knox Art Gallery, Buffalo, NY; 1981: Corcoran Biennial; 1983: *American Still Life, 1945–1983*, Contemporary Art Museum, Houston, TX; 1985: *Art in the San Francisco Bay Area, 1945–1980*, Oakland Art Museum, CA; *Contrasts of Form: Geometric Abstract Art 1910–1980*, Museum of Modern Art, NYC.

AMARANTH EHRENHALT

Some are born with a silver spoon in their mouth; I arrived with a paint brush in my hand and have painted steadily since the age of four. My work is abstract expressionist. "Unexpected" and "radiating energy" are often used to describe my art. I try to create that which does not sleep, but rather looks like it is constantly in motion: dancing, vibrating, gyrating, shimmering, stretching, jumping. My paintings often follow in series.

There is a persistent idea that keeps me frustrated until I paint it. Then the theme begins to change and suggests to me new concepts for another series. In so much as they fulfill my expectations, my painting attempts to stimulate the viewer: to excite, to relax, to entice, to seduce, to pleasure. Like a favorite piece of music, art should enrich one's life.

Amaranth Ehrenhalt, Statement: Provided to the editor, Jun, 2005

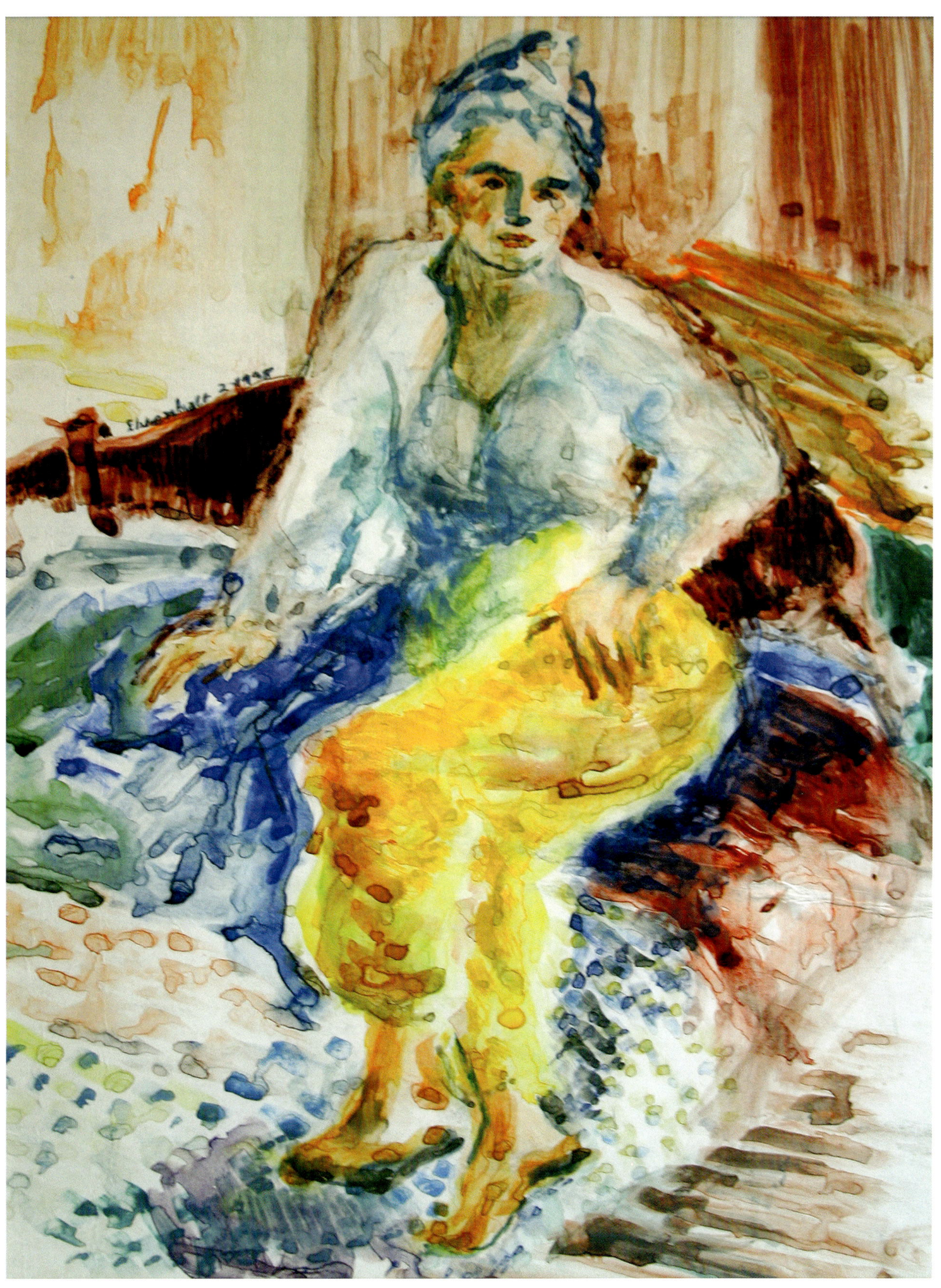

AMARANTH EHRENHALT, *Mother*, 1951
Oil on canvas, 15 x 11 inches
Collection of Edwin S. Ehrenhalt

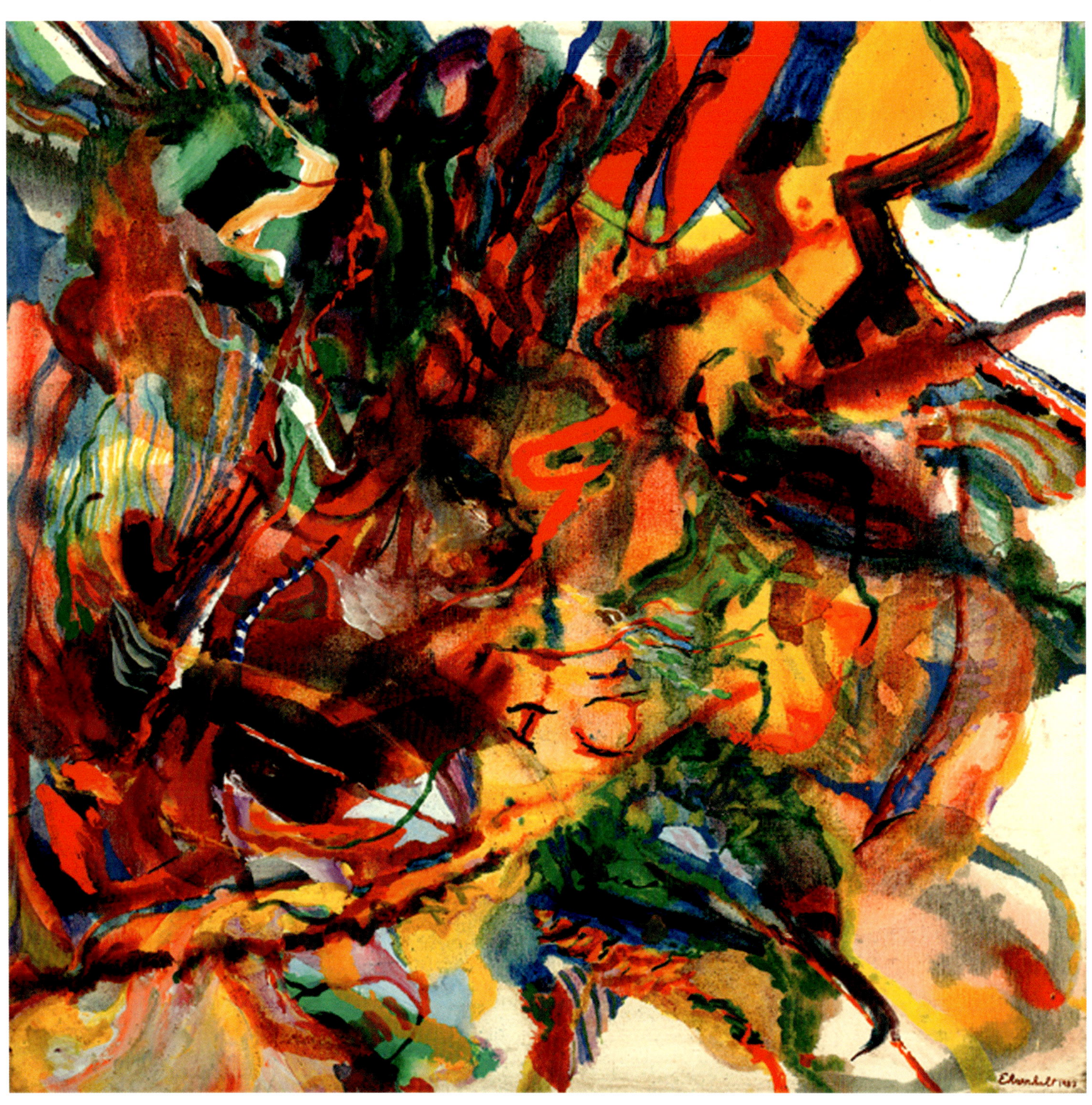

AMARANTH EHRENHALT, *Carmona*, 1957
Oil on canvas, 40 x 40 inches
Collection of the artist

AMARANTH ROSLYN EHRENHALT, [1928-]

Born January 15, 1928, Newark, New Jersey.

Studied Pennsylvania Academy of the Fine Arts, Honors Scholarship; B.F.A. University of Pennsylvania; The Barnes Foundation, Marion, PA, M.A; Atelier Saint-Cyr. Chateau de Montvillargennes (Tapestry study).

Teaching Positions/Lectures American Cultural Center, Paris, France; Bagneux Cultural Center, France; Chatillon, Cultural Center, France; National School of Engineering, Metz, France; Robert American College, Istanbul, Turkey.

Selected Solo Exhibitions 1960; Rhodes Cultural Center, Rhodes, Greece, 1962: Galerie Zunini, Paris, France; 1963: Galerie Murs Blancs, Ostende, Belgium; 1966, 67, 69: American Cultural Center, Paris, France; 1970: Downey Museum of Art, Downey, CA., USA; 1971: Chatillon Cultural Center, Chatillon, France; School of Architecture, City College of New York City, NY; Anderson Gallery, University Commonwealth of Virginia, VA; 1973: Bagneux Cultural Center, Bagneux, France; 1975: Albany Art Gallery, State University of New York, NY; Esther Robles Gallery, Los Angeles, CA; 1976: Tapestry Exhibition, Chateau de Montvillargenne; 1979: Cramer Gallery, Washington D.C.; 1991: Public Commission of a Ceramic Mural,- Bagneux, France; 1992-93: Musee d'Art d'Aujourd'hui, Bagneux, France; 1994: Gallery Pascal Odile, Paris, France; 1995: Schiller International University, Paris, France; 1999: Palazzo Cisterna, Turin, Italy; 2001: Zeneta Kertisz, Venice, CA; Atelier Portes Ouvertes, Bagneux; 2002, 03: Artolant, Paris, France; 2002: Jordan Contemporary Art Gallery, Greenville, SC; 2004: Atelier Yves & Lynn Pennec, Montrouge; Expo International Itinerante.

Selected Group Exhibitions 1961: Traveling Exhibition: Museums of Amiens, Avignon, Bourges, Montpellier and Nancy, France; 1964: Modern Europe Gallery, Occidental College, Los Angeles, CA; 1970: Long Beach and La Jolla Museum of Art, CA; 1977: Fresno Art Center, Fresno, CA; 1979: Museum of Richmond Virginia, *American Painting*, Richmond, VA; 1981: Bibliotheque Nationale, *Contemporary Prints*, Paris, France; 1983: Sarah Rentschler Gallery, East Hampton, NY; Downey Museum, Downey, CA; Albright Knox Museum, Buffalo, NY; 1985: Reece Gallery, New York, NY; 1986: Unesco, Paris, *Arelis, Magie de la Tapisserie*, Paris, France; 1989: Museum Roy Adzak, *Hommage to Adzak*, Paris, France; 1990, 91, 92, 93: *Salon des Realites Nouvelles*, Museum of the Grand Palais, Paris, France.

PERLE FINE

Tell me, what do you think when you paint? Do you paint what you see? What is it related to? Through seeing, feeling, through feeling, seeing. Which comes first, the chicken or the egg? The better question, how deeply do you feel about what you see, and how did you get that way? One thing is certain, only when it came to expression in my own language, through my own verity of experiences, both subjective and cumulative, did it sharpen my perception and apperception.

Perle Fine, Statement: It Is, no. 2 Autumn, 1958. A Magazine for Abstract Art, Second Half Publishing Co., NY.

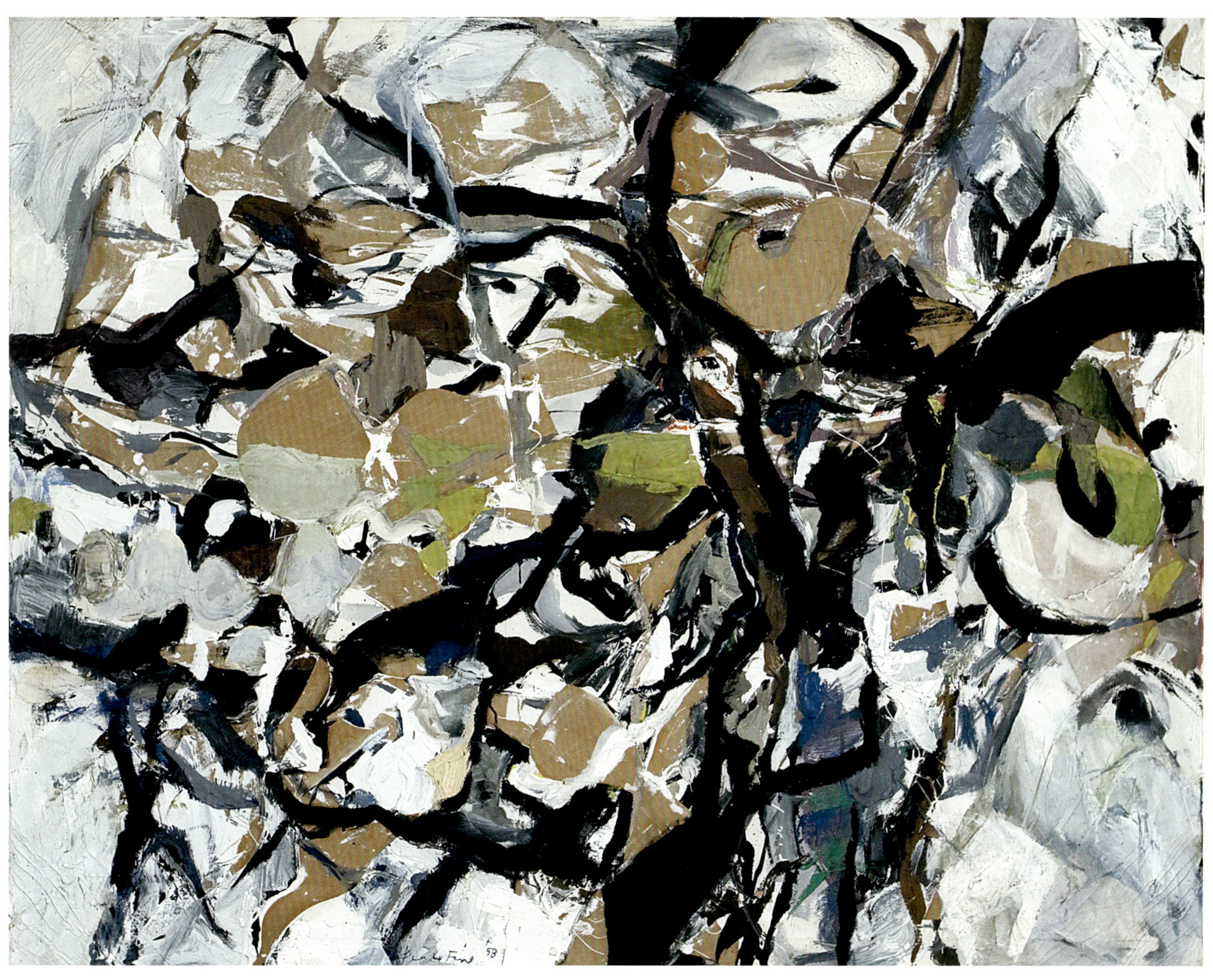

PERLE FINE, *Roaring Wind*, 1958
Oil collage on canvas with aluminum foil, 42 x 52 1/4 inches
Private collection
Courtesy of Anita Shapolsky Gallery, New York

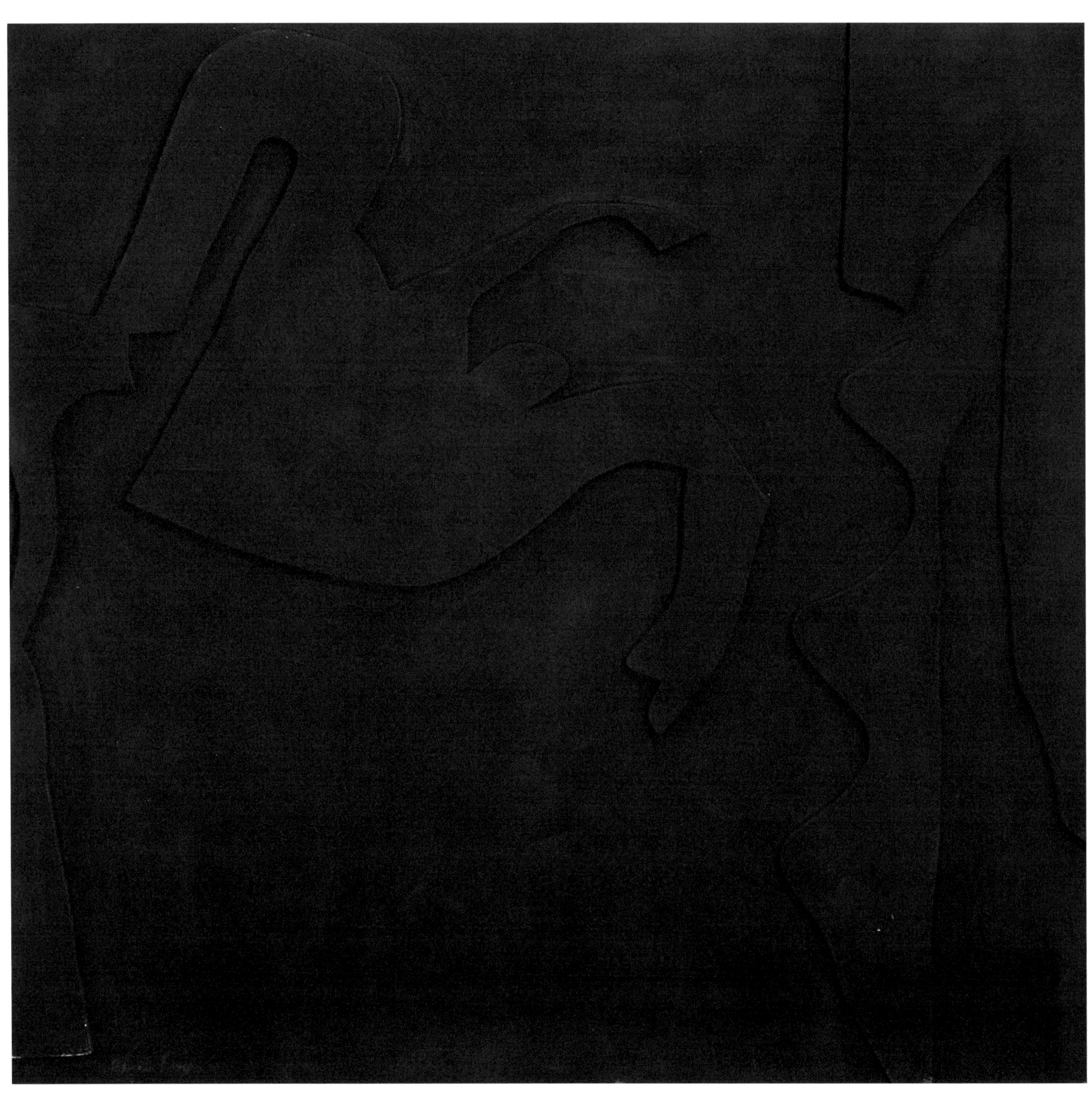

PERLE FINE, *Blue–Chip Blue #1*, c.1974
Acrylic polymer emulsion wood collage on masonite
Private collection
Courtesy of Anita Shapolsky Gallery, New York

PERLE FINE, [1908-1988]

Born 1908, in Boston, MA.
Died 1988, East Hampton, NY.

Studied 1920 at the Art Student League, NY, with Kimon Nicolaides; in the late 1930s with Hans Hofmann in New York City and in Provincetown, MA; at the Atelier 17 with Stanley William Hayter.

Teaching Position 1954–1966: Associate Professor of Art at Hofstra University Long Island, NY.

Selected Solo Exhibitions 1945: Marian Willard Gallery, NYC; 1946–47: Nierendorf Gallery, NYC; 1947: M.H. de Young Memorial Museum, San Francisco, Ca; 1949, 1951-53: Betty Parsons Gallery, NY; 1955, 58: Tanager Gallery, NYC; 1961, 63, 64, 67: Graham Gallery, NY; 1972: Joan Washburn Gallery, NY; 1978: *Major Works: 1954–1978: A Selection of Drawings, Paintings, and Collages*, Guild Hall Museum, East Hampton, NY.

Selected Group Exhibitions 1945: Art of This Century, Solomon R. Guggenheim Museum, NYC; 1950: *American Painting Today 1950*, The Metropolitan Museum of Art, NYC; 1951, 1953–57: *9th St.* Show, the first and subsequent 5 *New York Painting and Sculpture Annual*, Stable Gallery, NY; 1946, 47, 49, 51, 52, 54, 55, 58, 61, 72: The Whitney Museum of American Art Annuals and Biennials, NY; 1958: *Nature in Abstraction; The Relation of Abstract Painting and Sculpture to Nature in Twentieth-Century American Art*, circ.,The Whitney Museum of American Art, NYC; 1961–62: *The Art of Assemblage*, circ., Museum of Modern Art, NYC; 1963–64: *Hans Hofmann and His Students*, circ., Museum of Modern art, NYC; 1967: *Selection 1967: Recent Acquisitions in Modern Art*, University Art Museum, University of California, Berkeley, CA; 1984: *The Return of Abstraction,* Ingber Gallery, NYC; 1990: *East Hampton Avant-Garde; A Salute to the Signa Gallery*, Guild Hall Museum, East Hampton, NY; 1994: *Reclaiming Artists of the New York School. Toward a More Inclusive View of the 1950's*, Baruch College City University, NYC; *New York-Provincetown: A 50's Connection*, Provincetown Art Association and Museum, MA; 2001: *Abstract Expressionism: SECOND TO NONE*, Thomas McCormick Gallery, Chicago, IL.

JOE FIORE

The question of whether or not more American artists are today turning to figurative subject matter is to me irrelevant, and I don't think abstract art is dead, dying, or outmoded. The evidence is to the contrary. The situation is open, and vital. The artist states his position through his work, an individual act, intensified by his loneliness and his sense of tradition, which cuts across all false boundaries of categorization. Any other statement of position is at best merely a corollary to the work after the fact, and at worst acquiescence to the pigeon–holing of some writers–on–art, academicians, and museum officials who are essentially too lazy or perhaps incompetent to address themselves fully to the issue of the individual artist and his particular work. I reject all the black–and–white alternatives of abstract vs. figurative , forms vs. content, beat vs. square, etc., ad anuseam [sic].

Subject matter is not synonymous with content, and form, as a total concept, cannot be separated from content. Subject matter, or direct reference to nature, can be a springboard to form–content, but is it ever more? The artist can accept or reject such springboards, according to his own inner necessities. The content of any given work seems to me to be the revelation of its metaphysical basis, realized through the discipline to the artist's total engagement of form, his aesthetic. I believe that art can communicate values on a different (higher?) level of consciousness from that or ordinary verbal discourse, and Art in this sense includes all the arts.

Joseph Fiore, Statement: From *Contemporary American Painting and Sculpture*, University of Illinois, Urbana. February 26 through April 2, 1961, exhibition catalog. Krannert Art Museum. College of Fine and Applied Arts. p. 106.

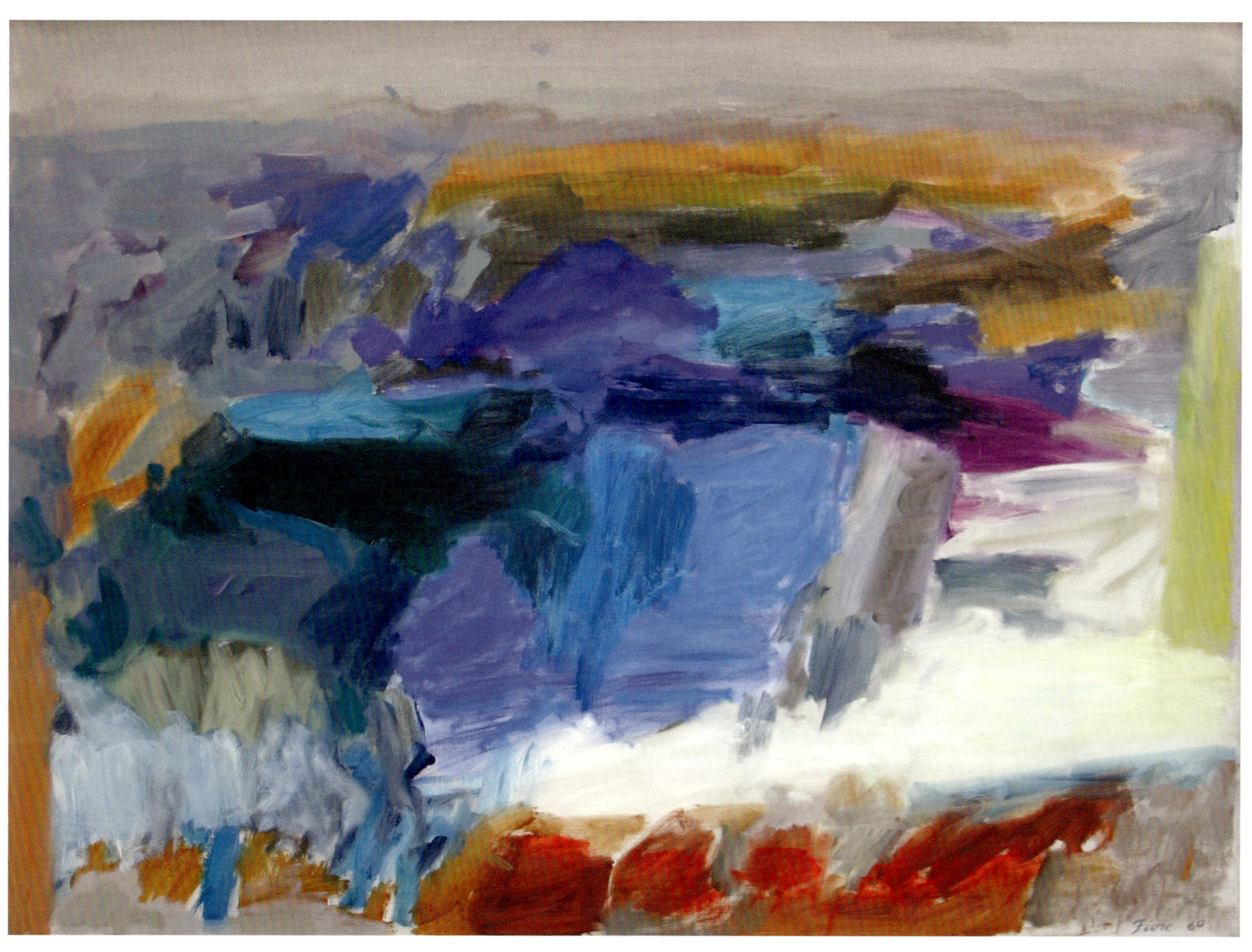

JOE FIORE, *Somerville Blue*, 1960
Oil on canvas, 30 x 40 inches
Private collection

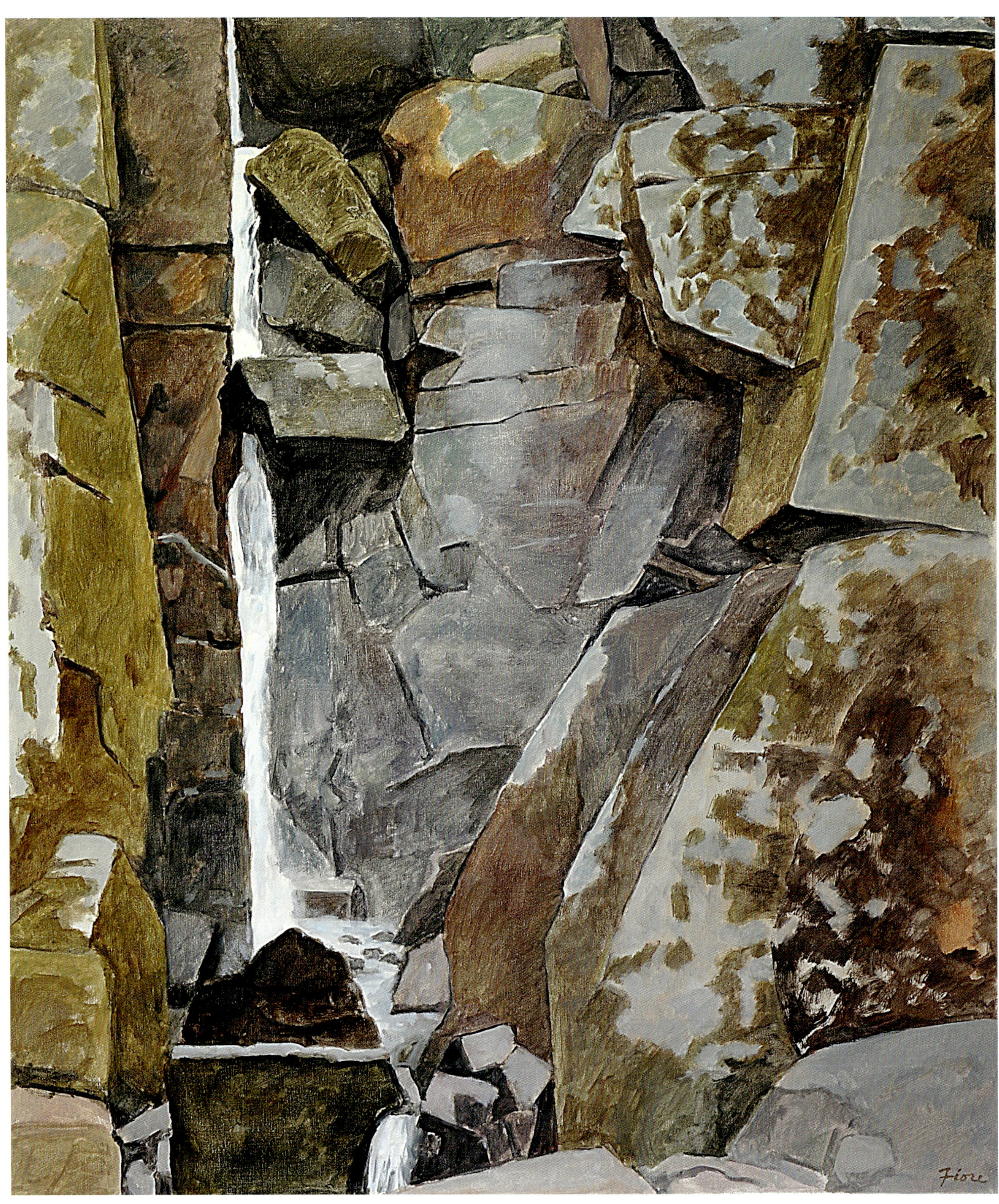

JOE FIORE, *Rock and Stream*, 1980
Oil on canvas, 50 x 38 inches
Collection of the Estate

JOE FIORE, [1925-2008]

Born February 3, 1925 in Cleveland, OH. **Died** September 18, 2008, in New York City.

Studied 1946–1948: Black Mountain College, North Caroline;
1948–1949; California School of Fine Arts, San Francisco, CA.

Teaching Positions 1949–1956; Black Mountain College, NC; 1962–1970; Philadelphia College of Art, Philadelphia, PA; 1970–1975: Maryland Institute College of Art, Baltimore, MD; 1972–1983: Visiting Artist/Critic, Artists for the Environment Foundation, Walpack, NJ; 1980: Program, Dordogne, France; 1987: Vermont Studio School, Johnson, VT.

Selected Solo Exhibition 1944, 48, 50: Ten-Thirty Gallery, Cleveland, OH; 1955: Gallerie Parnass, Wuppertal, Germany; 1960: Staempfli Gallery, NYC; 1965, 69: Robert Schoelkopf Gallery, NYC; 1973: Green Mountain Gallery, NYC; 1974: Bernard Myers Gallery, NYC; 1977, 81: Fischbach Gallery, NYC; 1988: Caldbeck Gallery, Rockland, ME; 1991: Le Va Tout Gallery. Waldoboro, ME; 1995, 96: *50 Year Retrospective*, Black Mountain College Museum & Arts Center, Asheville, NC; 1997, 2002: Round Top Center for the Arts, Damariscotta, ME; 1997: Cathedral of St. John the Divine, NYC; Eliza Sweet Gallery, Waldboro, ME; 2002: River Gallery, Damariscotta, ME.

Selected Group Exhibition 1954, 55: *New York Painting and Sculpture Annual*, Stable Gallery, NYC; 1959: *Annual*, Whitney Museum of American Art, NYC; 1961: *Contemporary American Painting and Sculpture*, University of Illinois, Urbana, IL; 1964: *Traveling Exhibition*, American Federation of Art, NYC; 1975: Corcoran Gallery of Art, Washington, D.C. 1976; State Museum, Augusta, GA; 1977: Cape Split Space, Addison, ME; 1981, 98; American Academy of Arts & Letters, NYC; 1982: *Painterly Landscape*, Jersey City Museum, NJ; 1983: Artists Choice Museum, Farnsworth Museum, Rockland, ME; 1987: Grey Art Center, New York University, NYC; North Carolina State Museum, Raleigh, NC; Bard College, NYC; The Visual Art at Black Mountain College Asheville, NC; Gilliam and Peden Gallery, Raleigh, NC; 1992: Snyder Fine Arts, NYC; 1997, 99, 2000, 07: *Artists of the 50's, The Development of Abstraction, Three from Maine*, Anita Shapolsky Gallery, NYC; 1998: Silvermine Guild Galleries, New Canaan, CT; 2001: Emily Lowe Gallery, Hofstra University, Long Island, NY.

SIDEO FROMBOLUTI

Explain! I can't. I cannot explain what I do in my painting, not before, not in the process, not afterwards. I distrust confident artists, stylists, trap pictures with no ideas, ideas with no soul. I believe in my instincts acquired with a life time of buried knowledge and experimental ideas. Both of which are intangibles you must learn to trust.

So what have we? Ideas as a tool to work with and our own inner poetry for inspiration, and I do not worry about contributing something new for everyone lives his own life, each one with his own truth, to reach understanding.

We don't make art, we are the art we make.

Sideo Fromboluti, Statement: Provided to the editor, October 14, 2008

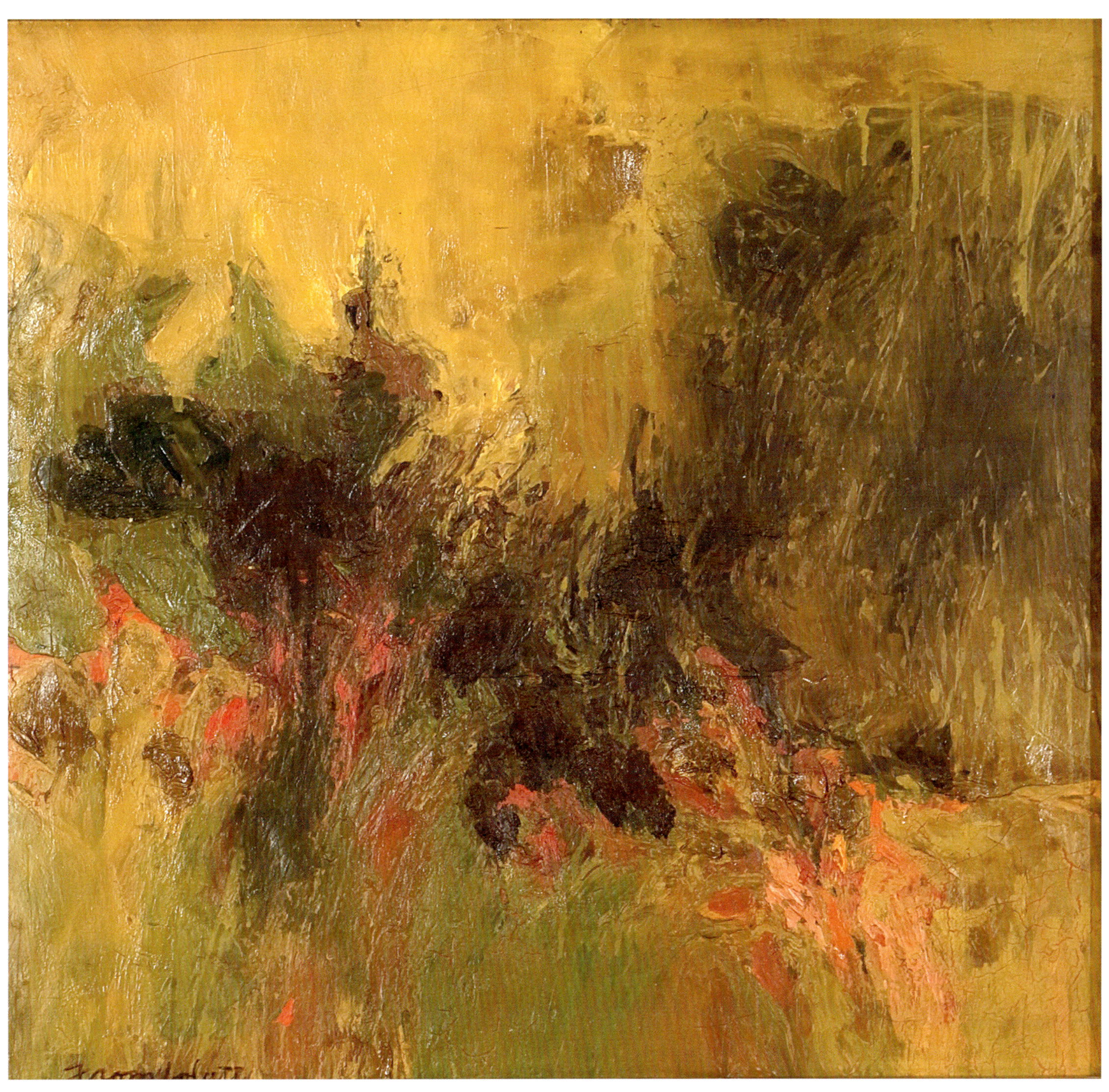

SIDEO FROMBOLUTI, *Thicke*t, 1959
Oil on canvas, 27 x 25 inches
Private collection

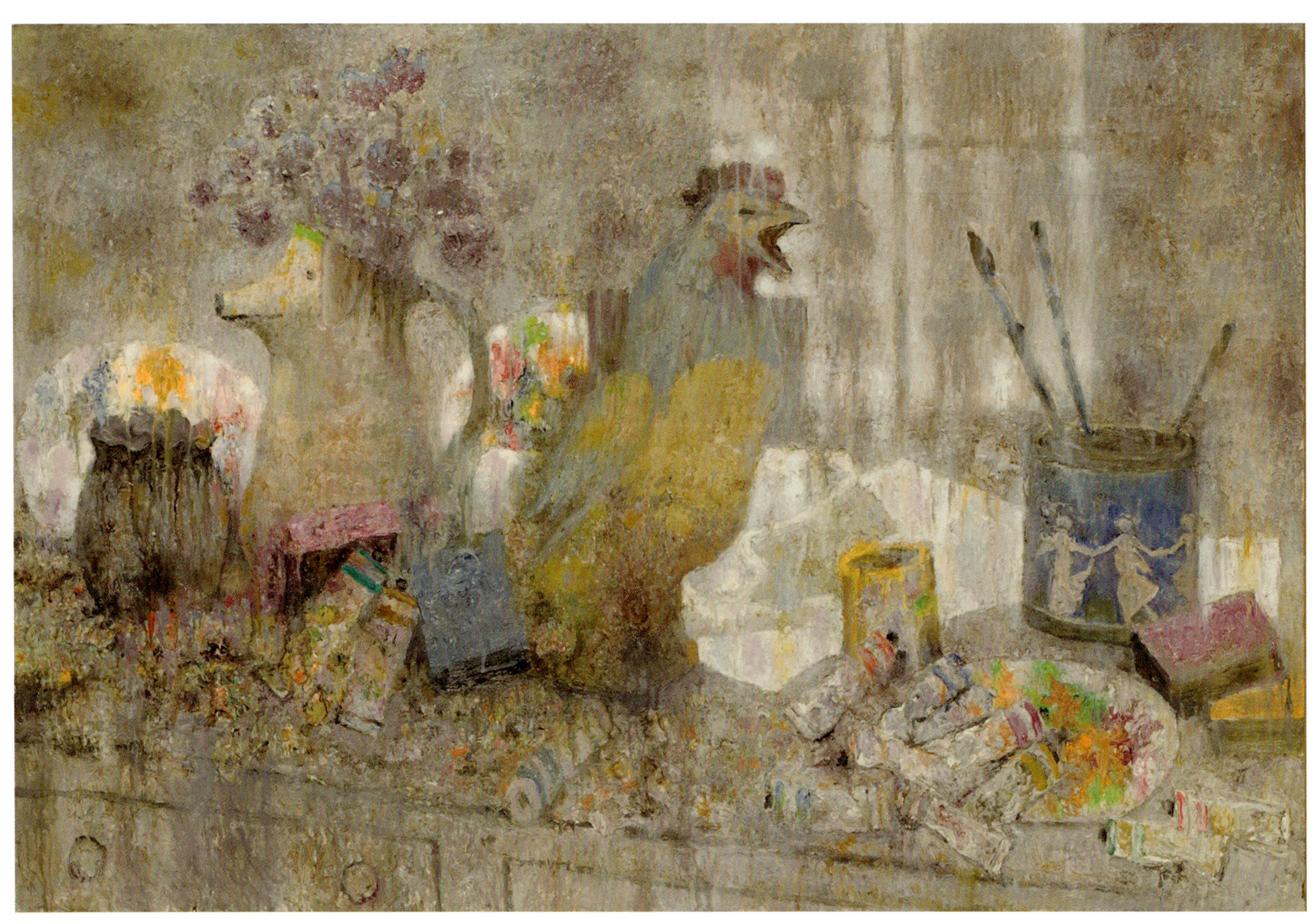

SIDEO FROMBOLUTI, *Still Life*, 2007
Oil on canvas, 50 x 80 inches
Collection of the artist

SIDEO FROMBOLUTI, [1920-]

Born 1920, Hershey, Pennsylvania.

Studied 1931: Graphic Sketch Club; 1938–1942: Tyler School of Art, Temple University, PA with Alexander Abels and Franklin Watkins; 1952–1957: New York University Institute of Fine Arts, NYC.

Military Service World War II
1943–1945: drafted into the army at Fort Riley, Kansas.

Selected Solo Exhibitions 1950: (first) Zena Gallery, Woodstock, NY; 1951, 53, 55: Artist Gallery, NYC; 1958, 60: Zabriskie Gallery, NYC; 1962: Osgood Gallery, NYC; 1965: Great Jones Gallery, NYC; 1968, 71: Terza Karlis Gallery, Provincetown, MA; 1969, 72, 75, 82, 93: Galerie Darthea Speyer, Paris, France; 1972, 74, 76, 78, 80: Landmark Gallery, NYC; 1977, 79, 81, 86. 89, 92, 95: Longpoint Gallery, Provincetown, MA; 1978: *Six Americans, National Drawing Invitational*, South Carolina Museum; 1984: Gross McCleaf Gallery, Philadelphia, PA; 1986: Century Club, NYC; 1987: Armstrong Gallery, NYC; 1988: Ingber Gallery, NYC; 1994: New York Studio School Gallery, NYC; 1998–2000: *Summer Paintings*, circ., Provincetown Art Association and Museum, MA; Carnegie Museum of Art, Pittsburgh, PA; 2001, 02, 05: Cherry Stone Gallery, Wellfleet, MA; 2006: Cape Cod Museum of Art, Dennis, MA.

Selected Group Exhibitions 1950: *Biennial Exhibition*, Whitney Museum of American Art, NYC; 1956, 57: *New York Painting and Sculpture Annual*, Stable Gallery, NYC; *Summer Exhibition*, Chrysler Museum, Provincetown, MA; 1959: U.S.A. New York Coliseum; *15 Americans*, St. Louis Art Museum, MO; *Biennial Exhibition*, University of Nebraska; 1984: *Emotional Impact, New York School, Figurative Expressionism*, circ., Philadelphia Museum of Art, PA; *Images and Imagery,* Pace University Art Gallery, NY; 1985: *Eight Americans*, Gross McCleaf Gallery, Philadelphia, PA; 1986: *Return of the Figure*, Southern Allegheny Museum of Art, Loretto, PA; 1987: *Four–man Show*, Kouros Gallery, NYC; 1994: *Italian Americans*, Hunter College, NYC.

SONIA GECHTOFF

Between abstraction and representation – an old and continuing quest. During the late 50's and early sixties figurative elements entered my paintings but very slyly. For many years now – since the late 70's – landscape has been an underlying part of my work. I consider myself to be an abstract expressionist basically with elements of the 'real' suggested.

Sonia Gechtoff, Statement:
Interview with the editor.
September 11, 2008.

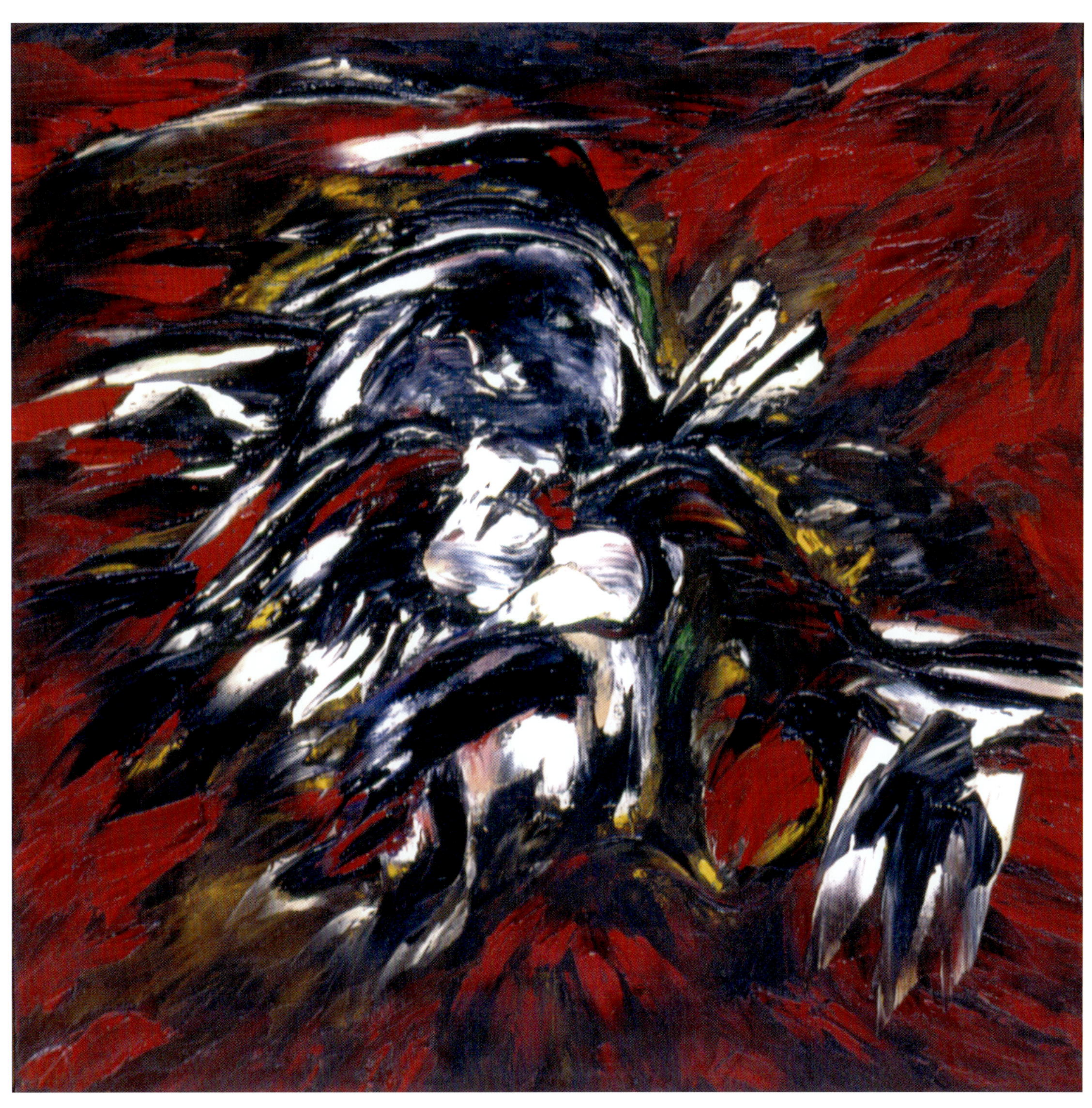

SONIA GECHTOFF, *THE VISITOR*, 1960-1961
Oil on canvas, 32 x 32 inches
Collection of the National Academy Museum, New York

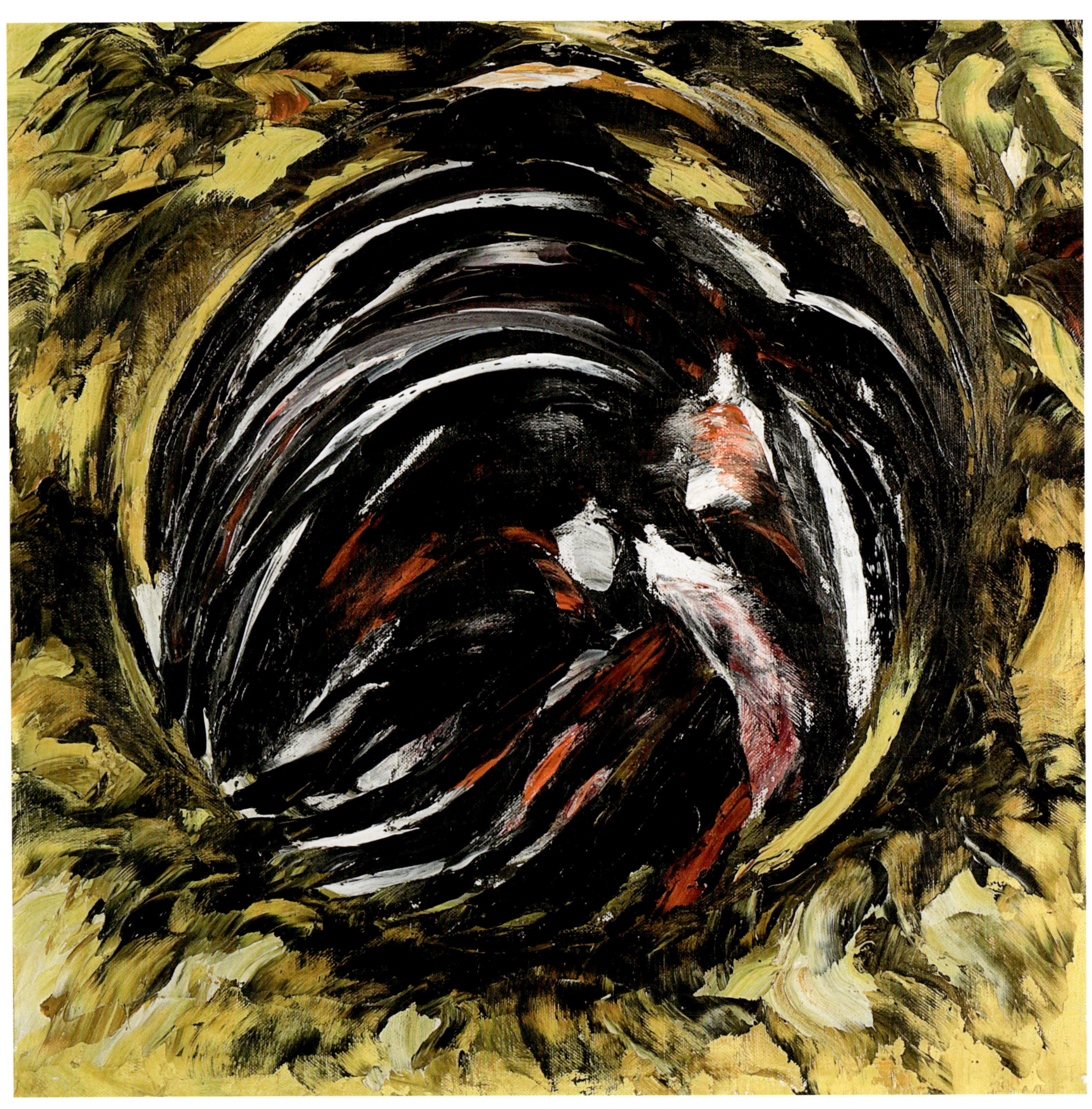

SONIA GECHTOFF, *Golden Corrie*, 1960
Oil on canvas, 20 1/8 x 20 1/8 inches
Private collection

SONIA GECHTOFF, [1926 -]

Born 1926 in Philadelphia, PA.

Studied 1950: Philadelphia Museum School of Art, PA.

Teaching Positions 1956–57: California School of Fine Art; 1960-70: New York University; 1970–74: Queens College, New York; 1974–75: University of New Mexico; 1988–1990 (summers): Painter in Residence, Skidmore College, New York; 1989: Visiting Artist, Art Institute of Chicago, IL; 1991 and 1993: Painter in Residence, Adelphi University, New York; 2000: National Academy School of Fine Art, NYC.

Selected Solo Exhibitions 1957: De Young Museum, San Francisco, CA; 1957, 59: Ferus Gallery, Los Angeles, CA; 1959, 60: Poindexter Gallery, NYC; 1963, 66: East Hampton Gallery, NYC; 1974: Gallery One, Montclair State College, NJ; 1976, 78: Gloria Cortella Gallery, NYC; 1979, 80, 82, 83, 85, 87: Gruenebaum Gallery, NYC; 1984, 89: Witkin Galleries, NYC; 1990, 92, 95, 98: Kraushaar Galleries, NYC; 1991, 93: University Center Gallery, Adelphi University, New York; 1995: *4 Decades Work on Paper*, Skidmore College, Saratoga Springs, NY.

Selected Group Exhibitions 1954: *Younger Americans*, Solomon R. Guggenheim Museum, NYC; 1958: *Painting Annual*, Whitney Museum of American Art, NYC; *1st Paris Bienale, American Section*, Paris, France; *17 American Painters*, circ., USA Pavilion, Brussels World Fair; Carnegie International, Carnegie Institute, Pittsburgh, PA; *American Painting*, Virginia Museum of Art; 1960: *60 American Painters*, Walker Art Center, Minneapolis, MN; *Young America*, Whitney Museum of American Art, NYC; 1961: VI Bienal do Museu de Arte Moderna, Sao Paolo, Brazil; 1962: *American Abstract Drawings & Watercolors*, Selected by Museum of Modern Art, New York, International Council, South America; 1966: *Drawing, National Exhibition*, University of Texas, Austin, TX; 1968: *East Coast-West Coast Painting*, University of Oklahoma & Philbrook Art Center; 1973: *Women Choose Women*, New York Cultural Center; 1975: Phoenix Art Museum Biennial, Phoenix, AZ; 1976: *Last Time I Saw Ferus*, Newport Harbor Art Museum, Newport Beach, CA; 1976–1977: *California Painting and Sculpture-Modern Era*, National Collection of Fine Arts, Smithsonian Institute, Washington, DC & San Francisco Museum of Modern Art, CA; 1977: *America Drawn & Matched*, Museum of Modern Art, NYC; *Extraordinary Women*, Museum of Modern Art, NYC; 1981: *New Dimensions in Drawing, 1950–1980,* Aldrich Museum of Contemporary Art, Ridgefield, CT; 1983: *Directions in Bay Area Painting-A Survey of Three Decades, 1940s–1960s*, Richard L. Nelson Gallery, Davis, CA; 1985: *Cross Overs*, Usdan Gallery, Bennington College, VT; 1985–1986: *American Art-American Women*, Organized by Stamford Museum, CT; 1987: *Paper Now,* Weatherspoon Gallery, University of North Carolina, NC; *Selections-Works on Paper*, California Palace of the Legion of Honor, San Francisco, CA; 1989: *Abstract Painting of the Fifties*, 871 Gallery, San Francisco, CA; 1990: *79th Annual Exhibition*, Maier Museum of Art, Randolph-Macon Woman's College, VA; 1991: *Sonia Gechtoff/James Kelly, Paintings from the 1950s and the 1980s*, 871 Fine Arts, San Francisco, CA; *Out of Abstract Expressionism*, Schick Art Gallery, Skidmore College, NY; 1996: *San Francisco School of Abstract Expressionism*, San Francisco Museum of Modern Art, CA; 2001: *Stamp of Impulse, Abstract Expressionist Prints*, Worcester Art Museum, MA; National Academy of Design, Annual Exhibition, NYC; 2006: *Recent Acquisitions*, Menil Collection, Houston, TX; *Abstract Expressionist Prints–Charles Dean Collection*, Pollack–Krasner House, East Hampton, NY; 2007–2008: *The abstract Impulse*, National Academy Museum, NYC.

ROBERT GOODNOUGH

...Once you've gotten down the idea of the energy and the emotional feeling you're after, that's the point to leave it. Why try to polish it too much?

...I tried to get the three dimensional feeling you get from nature, or from figures, then I started thinking of it as being completely abstract, developed to a point of not having any third dimension. I've heard people say they see this three-dimensionality—I don't. I think of the images as just shapes on canvas.

Robert Goodnough; Statement: From *GOODNOUGH* Text and interview by Martin Bush, Director, Edwin A Ulrich Museum of Art at Wichita state University. Published by Cross River Press, 1982. pp. 103, 108-110

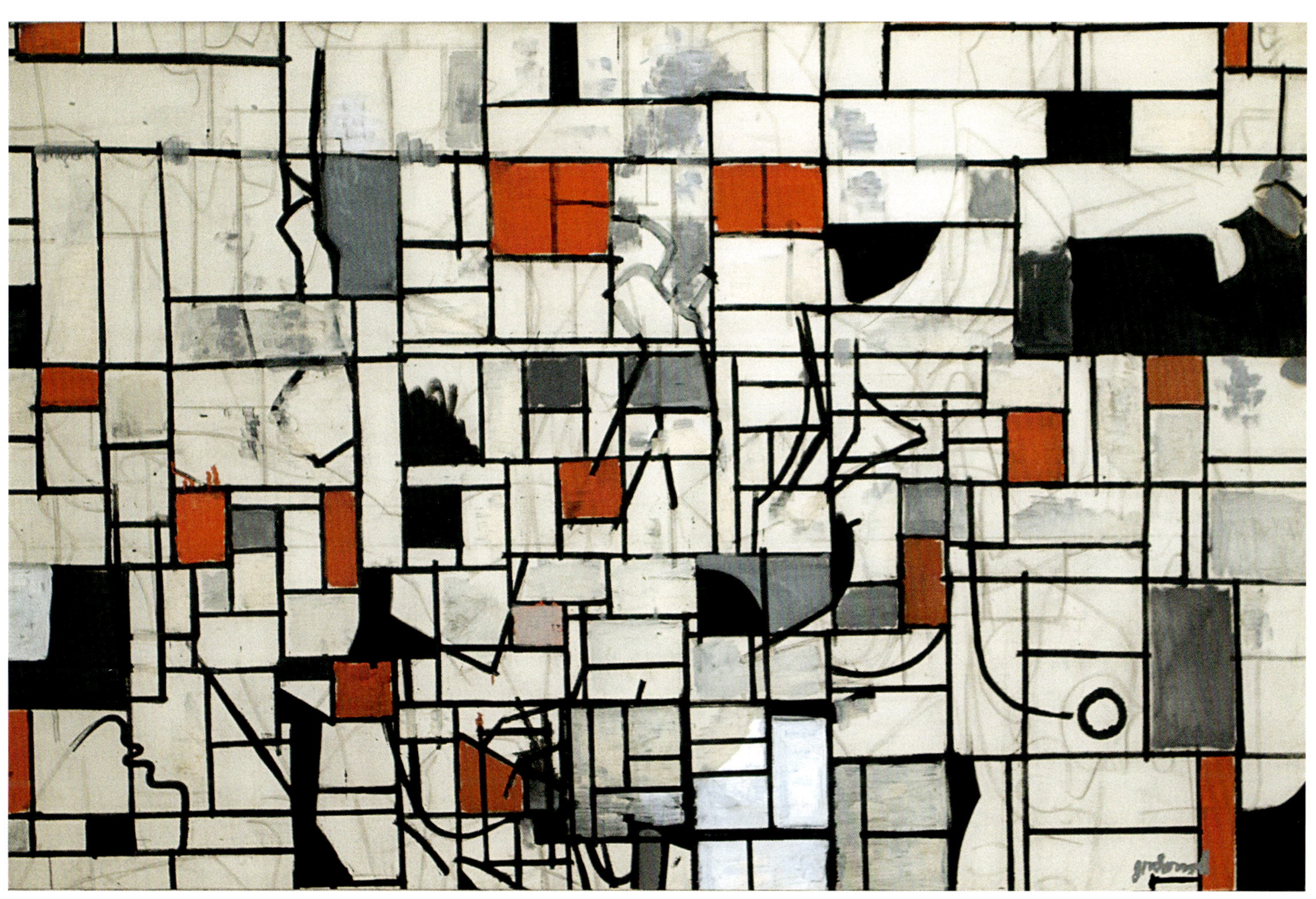

ROBERT GOODNOUGH, *Sheridan Square*, 1959
Oil on Board, 40 x 59 7/8 inches
Private Collection
© Robert Goodnough

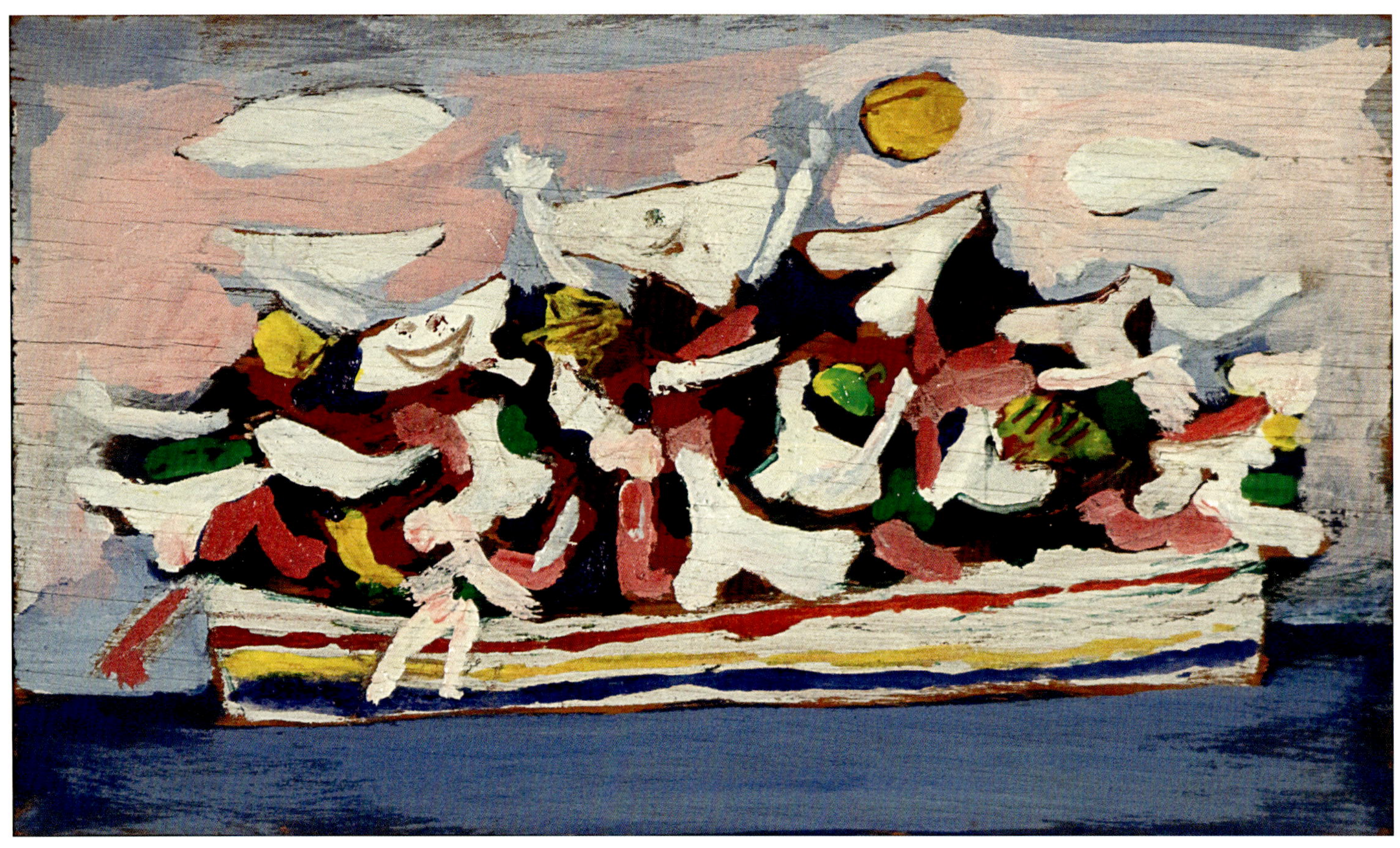

ROBERT GOODNOUGH, *Figures in a Boat* – A3, 1963
Oil on board, 5 ¾ x 9 ⅜
Private Collection

BOB GOODNOUGH, [1925 -]

Born October 23, 1925 in Cortland, NY.

Studied 1940: Syracuse University; 1946: Amèdèe Ozenfant School of Fine Arts; 1947: Hans Hofmann School of Art in Provincetown in the Summer; 1947–50: New York University, MA degree.; 1949: New School for Social Research.

Military Service World War II 1941–1945 at Fort Bragg, Pacific Theater.

Teaching Positions Cornell University; New York University; Fieldstone School, NYC.

Selected Solo Exhibitions 1950: Wittenborn Gallery, NYC; 1952–70, 1984–86: Tibor de Nagy Gallery, NYC; 1960, 61: Art Institute of Chicago, IL; 1964: University of Minnesota; University of Notre Dame; Arts Club of Chicago; New Vision Center Gallery, London; USIS American Embassy, London, England; 1969: Albright-Knox Art Gallery, Buffalo, New York; The Whitney Museum of American Art, NYC; 1969, 70: Galerie Simonne Stern, New Orleans, LA; 1972, 74, 75, 76, 78: Harcus Krakow Gallery, Boston, Mass.; 1972–74, 80, 82: Andre Emmerich Gallery, NYC; 1991: ACA Galleries, NYC; 1999: Neuberger Museum of Art, Purchase College, State University of New York;

Selected Group Exhibitions 1950: *New Talent*, The Kootz Gallery, NYC; 1956: *Four Younger Americans*, Sidney Janis Gallery, NYC; 1951, 1953–57: *9th St.*, Show, the first and subsequent 5 *New York Painting and Sculpture Annuals*, Stable Gallery, NYC; 1956, 57, 59–61, 63, 65, 67: *Annuals and Biennials*, The Whitney Museum of American Art NYC; 1958: *Nature in Abstraction; The Relation of Abstract Painting and Sculpture to Nature in Twentieth-Century American Art*, circ., The Whitney Museum of American Art, NYC; 1961–62: *The Art of Assemblage*, circ., Museum of Modern Art, NYC; 1963–64: *Hans Hofmann and His Students*, circ., Museum of Modern Art, NYC; 1964: Yale University; Carnegie, Art Institute of Chicago; 1969: *The New American Painting and Sculpture*, The Museum of Modern Art, NYC; University of Illinois; 1970: *XXV Venice Biennial*; 1982: *The Americans: The Collage*, Contemporary Art of Houston; 1994: *New York-Provincetown: A 50s Connection*, Provincetown Art Association and Museum, MA.

JOHN GRILLO

As a very young man, my first ambition was to be a portrait painter, inspired by the paintings in the Wadsworth Athenaeum.

I entered Hartford Art School in 1935. We began with the plaster cast. My early work was figurative; friends, family, the streets of Hartford.

I enlisted in the Navy in 1944, on the boat going to Okinawa; I drew portraits of my fellow sailors. It was during my time in Okinawa that I first began to experiment with abstraction.

After my discharge in 1946, I entered the San Francisco School of Fine Arts. After 18 months there, I returned to the East Coast and with the aid of the GI Bill, I began to study with Hans Hofmann, in New York City and in Provincetown.

While I was studying with Hofmann, in 1948 I had my first one man show in New York City of work that I had done in San Francisco. In 1951, Hofmann bought one of my paintings.

From 1946 until 1967 my creative effort was devoted exclusively to exploring abstraction.

When I began teaching drawing and painting at the University of Massachusetts at Amherst, being confronted daily with the nude model, I became intrigued with the figure and with representation again. From then until the present day, I go back and forth between abstraction and representation. My figurative work informs my abstraction and the reverse is also true. All figurative work is abstract colors and shapes on a flat surface.

Now that I'm 91 years old and look back over what has happened to the art world during this time, even during the abstract expressionist years, some artists have followed different trends.

Representation has never died. All the years of my creative life I have researched many directions, pure abstraction, figures, portraits, and no subject at all. Whether working abstractly, or figuratively, when I work rapidly, my energy is fully focused. I feel more alive and the creative urge is more fully realized on the surface of canvas or paper.

It's like playing the piano when one gets more expressive sound, there is more life!

John Grillo, Statement: Provided to the editor in Wellfleet, Massachusetts. August 5, 2008

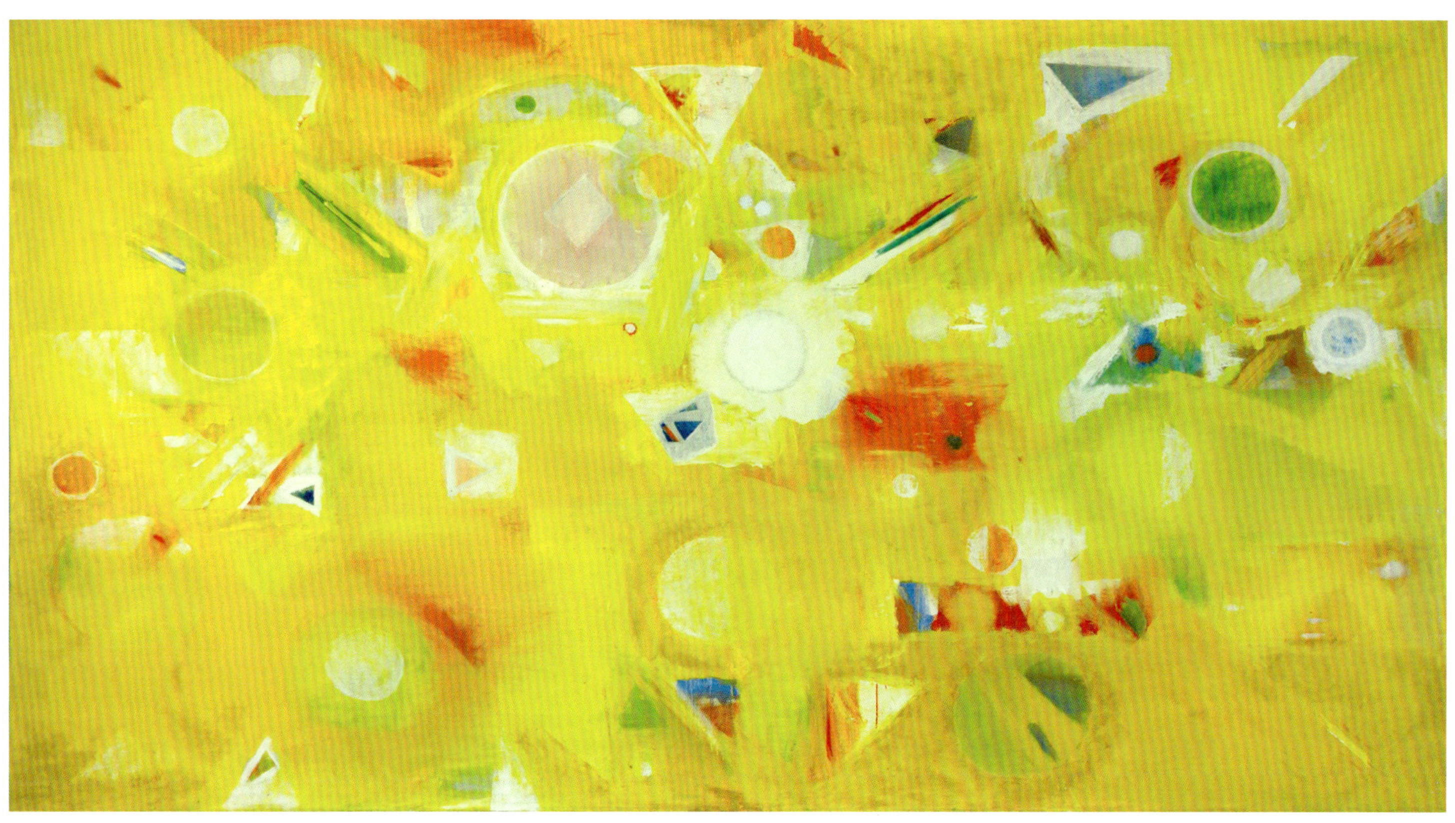

JOHN GRILLO, *UNTITLED*, 1963
Oil on canvas, 80 x 139 1/2 inches
Collection of the artist

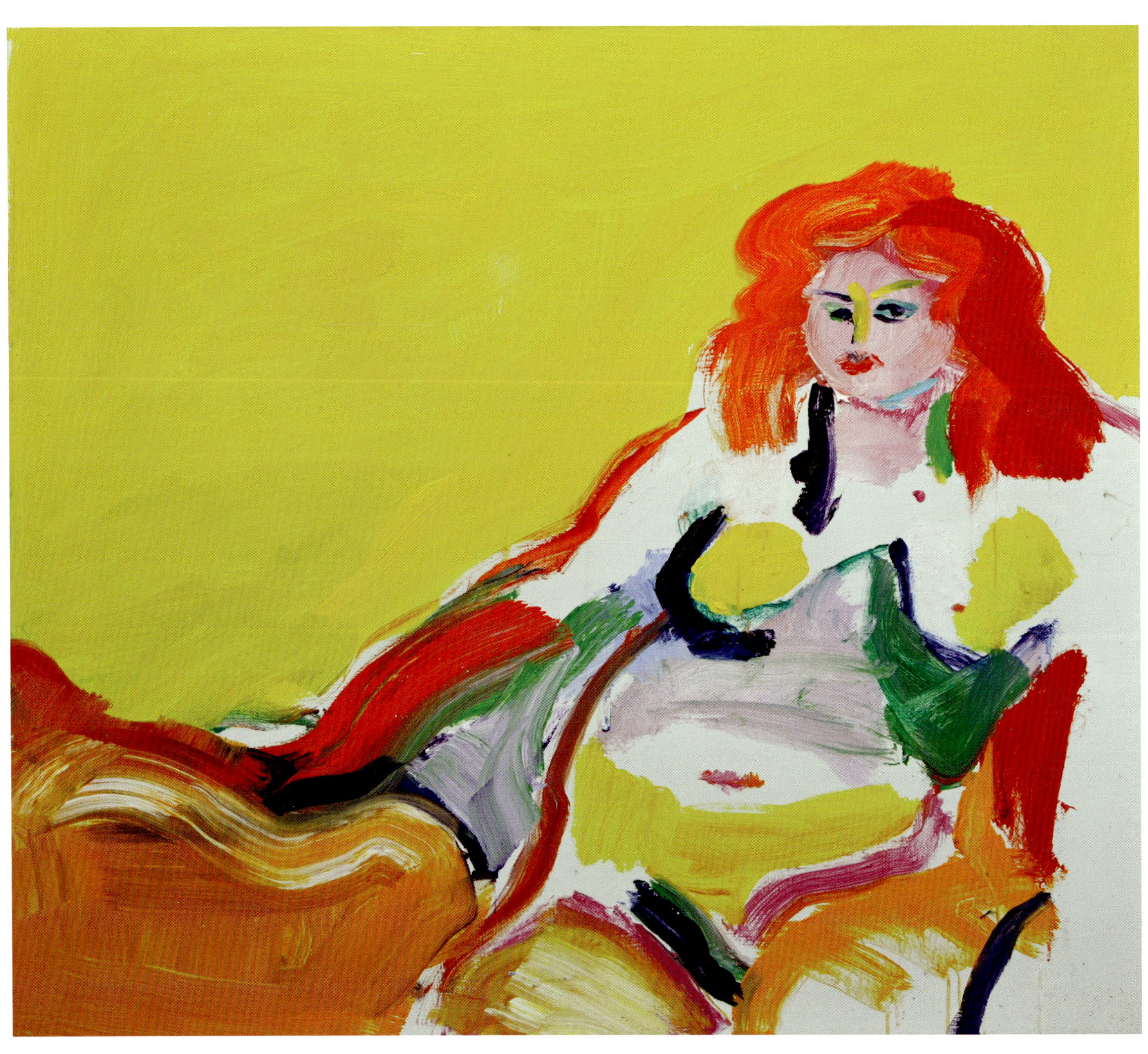

JOHN GRILLO, *Portrait of Rose at Cove Gallery*, 2003
Acrylic on canvas, 48 x 48 inches
Collection of the artist

JOHN GRILLO, [1917-]

Born July 4, 1917, Lawrence, MA.

Studied 1935–38: Hartford Art School; 1946: California School of Fine Arts; 1949–50: Hans Hofmann School, NYC.

Military Service in World War II 1944–46: US armed forces.

Teaching Positions 1960: Southern Illinois University; 1961: School of Visual Arts, NYC; 1962–63: University of California, Berkeley; 1964–66: New School for Social Research; 1965–66: Pratt Institute; 1967-: State University of lowa; 1967–91: University of Massachusetts.

Selected Solo Exhibitions 1947: Daliel Gallery, Berkeley; 1948: Artists' Gallery, NYC; 1952, 60: Tanager Gallery, NYC; 1953, 70: Tibor de Nagy Gallery, NYC; 1955, 57, 59: The Bertha Schaefer Gallery, NYC; 1959, 62: HCE Gallery, Provincetown, MA; 1961, 62, 63: The Howard Wise Gallery, NYC; 1962: Ankrum Gallery; University of California, Berkeley; 1963: East End Gallery, Provincetown; 1964: Butler Institute of American Art, Youngstown, OH; 1966: Waitsfield Bundy; 1967: New School for Social Research; 1967: State University of lowa; 1968: Simmons College; Eleanor Rigelhaupt Gallery, Boston; 1969: Benedict Art Center, St. Joseph, MN; Horizon Gallery, NYC; 1970: Robert Dain Gallery, NYC; 1973: Landmark Gallery Inc., NYC; 1975, 77, 78: Borgenicht Gallery, Inc., NYC; 1977: Pisces Gallery, Wellfleet, MA; Union College, Cranford, N.J.; 1979: Art Association of University Newport, R.I.; 1982, 83, 84: Jean Lumbard Fine Arts, NYC; 1983, 87, 88, 89, 90, 91: University of Massachusetts at Amherst; 1984: Museo de Arte Moderna, La Tertulia; 1989, 96, 98, 2001: Cove Gallery, Wellfleet, MA; 2000: Aaron Gallery, Chicago, IL.
Retrospective: 1956–60: The Olsen Foundation, Inc., circ., USA; 1988: Provincetown Art Association.

Selected Group Exhibitions 1950: *Fifteen Unknowns*, The Kootz Gallery, NYC; 1955: *Vanguard*, Walker Art Center, Minneapolis, MN; 1953, 59: *Annuals and Biennials*, Whitney Museum of American Art, NYC; 1960: *60 American Painters*, Walker Art Center, Minneapolis, MN; 1961: *Abstract Expressionists and Imagists*, Solomon R. Guggenheim Museum, NYC; 1961: *Contemporary Painting*, Yale University, CT; 1961, 62: Dallas Museum of Fine Arts, Dallas, TX; 1962: Seattle World's Fair; 1963–64: *Hans Hofmann and His Students*, circ., Museum of Modern Art, NYC ; 1963: *Directions–Painting U.S.A.*, San Francisco Museum of Modern Art, CA; 1964: Albright–Knox Art Gallery, Buffalo, NY; 1970: *Print Biennial*, Brooklyn Museum, NY; *Tanager (Gallery) Artists of the Fifties*, Roko Gallery, NY; 1973: *California Artists, 1944–1952*, Oakland Art Museum; 1977: *40 Post War Painters*, Solomon R. Guggenheim Museum, NYC; *Provincetown Painters, 1890s–1970s*, Everson Museum of Art, Syracuse, NY; 1979: *Hans Hofmann as Teacher: Drawings by His Students*, Metropolitan Museum of Art, NY; 1987–89: *Contemporary American Collage, 1960–1986*, circ., Herter Art Gallery, University of Massachusetts at Amherst; 1994: *Italian-American Artists, 1945–1968, a Limited Survey,* Hunter College, NY; 1996*: The San Francisco School of Abstract Expressionism*, The Laguna Beach Museum, CA.

PHILIP GUSTON

...For me the most relevant question and perhaps the only one is, 'When are you finished?' When do you stop? Or rather, why stop at all? But you have to rest somewhere.

Of course you can stay on one surface all your life, like Balzac's Frenhofer. And all of your life's work can be seen as one picture—but that is merely 'true.' There are places where you pause.

Thus it might be argued that when a painting is 'finished,' it is a compromise. But the conditions under which the compromise is made are what matters. Decisions to settle anywhere are intolerable. But you begin to feel as you go on working that unless painting proves its right to exist by being critical and self-judging, it has no reason to exist at all—or is not even possible.

The canvas is a court where the artist is prosecutor, defendant, jury and judge. Art without a trial disappears at a glance: it is too primitive or hopeful, or mere notions, or simply startling, or just another means to make life bearable. You cannot settle out of court. You are faced with what seems like an impossibility—fixing an image which you can tolerate.

What can be? Where? Erasures and destructions, criticisms and judgments of one's acts, even as they force change in oneself, are still preparations merely reflecting the mind's will and movement. There is a burden here, and it is the weight of the familiar. Yet this is the material of a working which from time to time needs to see itself, even though it is reluctant to appear.

To will a new form is inacceptable, because will builds distortion. Desire, too, is incomplete and arbitrary. These, strategies, however intimate they might become, must especially be removed to clear the way for something else—a condition somewhat unclear, but which in retrospect becomes a very precise act. This 'thing' is recognized only as it comes into existence. It resists analysis—and probably this is as it should be. Possibly the moral is that art cannot and should not be made.

Philip Guston, Statement: "FAITH, HOPE AND IMPOSSIBILITY," *Art News Annual*, 1966, vol. 31, p. 103.
Reprinted courtesy of the publisher.

....I do not see why the loss of faith in the known image and symbol in our time should be celebrated as a freedom. It is a loss from which we suffer, and this pathos motivates modern painting and poetry at its heart.

....I think the only pressing question in painting is: when are you through? For my own part it is when I know I've 'come out the other side.' This occasional and sudden awareness is the truest image for me. The clock-like path of this recognition suppresses a sense of victory; it is an ironic encounter and more of a mirror than a picture."

Philip Guston, Statements: *Nature in Abstraction*, Whitney Museum of American Art, New York, 1958. Quoted in catalogue assay by John I. H. Bauer.

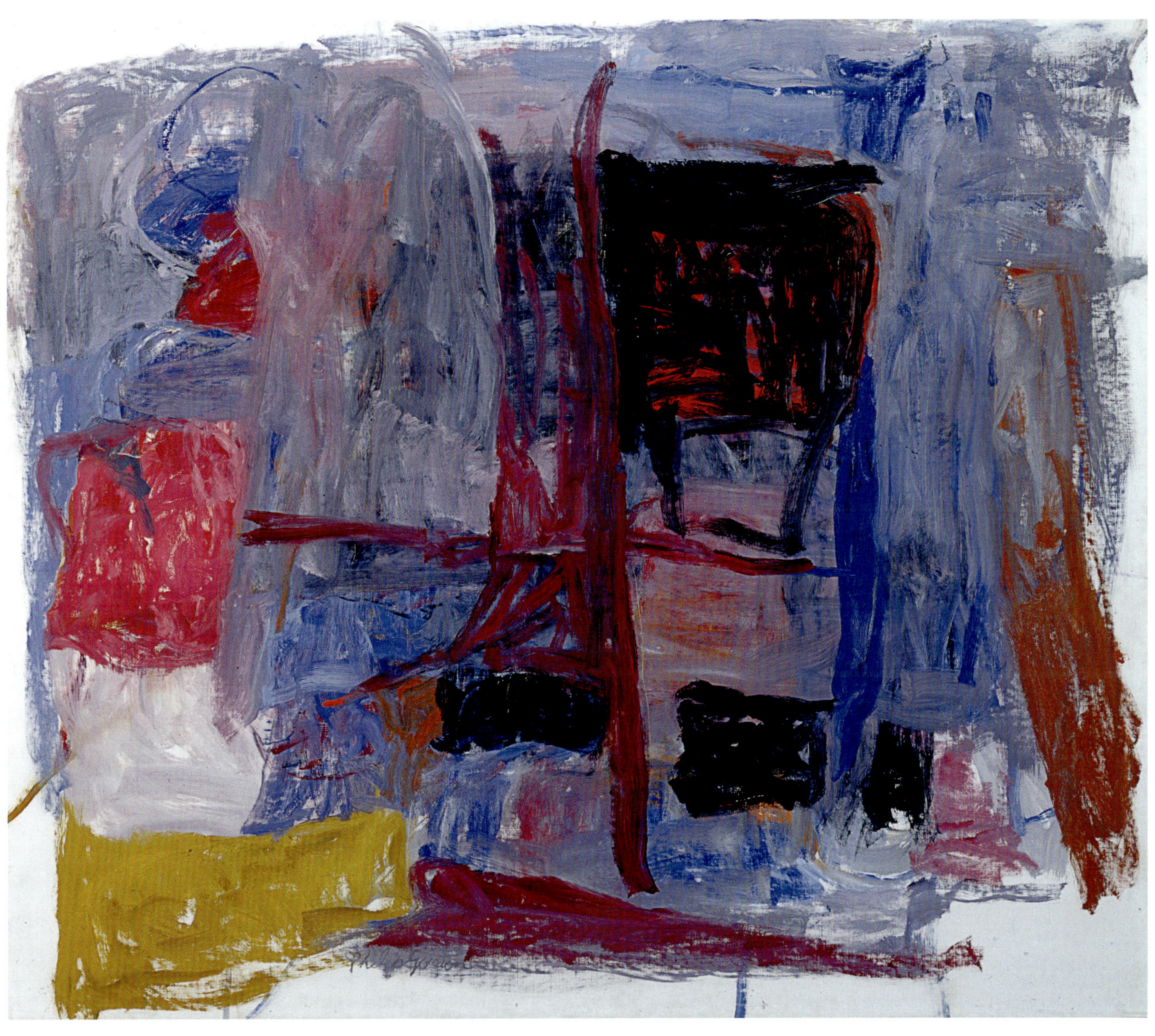

PHILIP GUSTON, *Painter III*, 1960
Oil on canvas, 60 5/8 x 68 in. (154.1 x 172.8 cm)
Smithsonian American Art Museum, Gift of S.C. Johnson & Son, Inc., Accession number: 1969.47.59

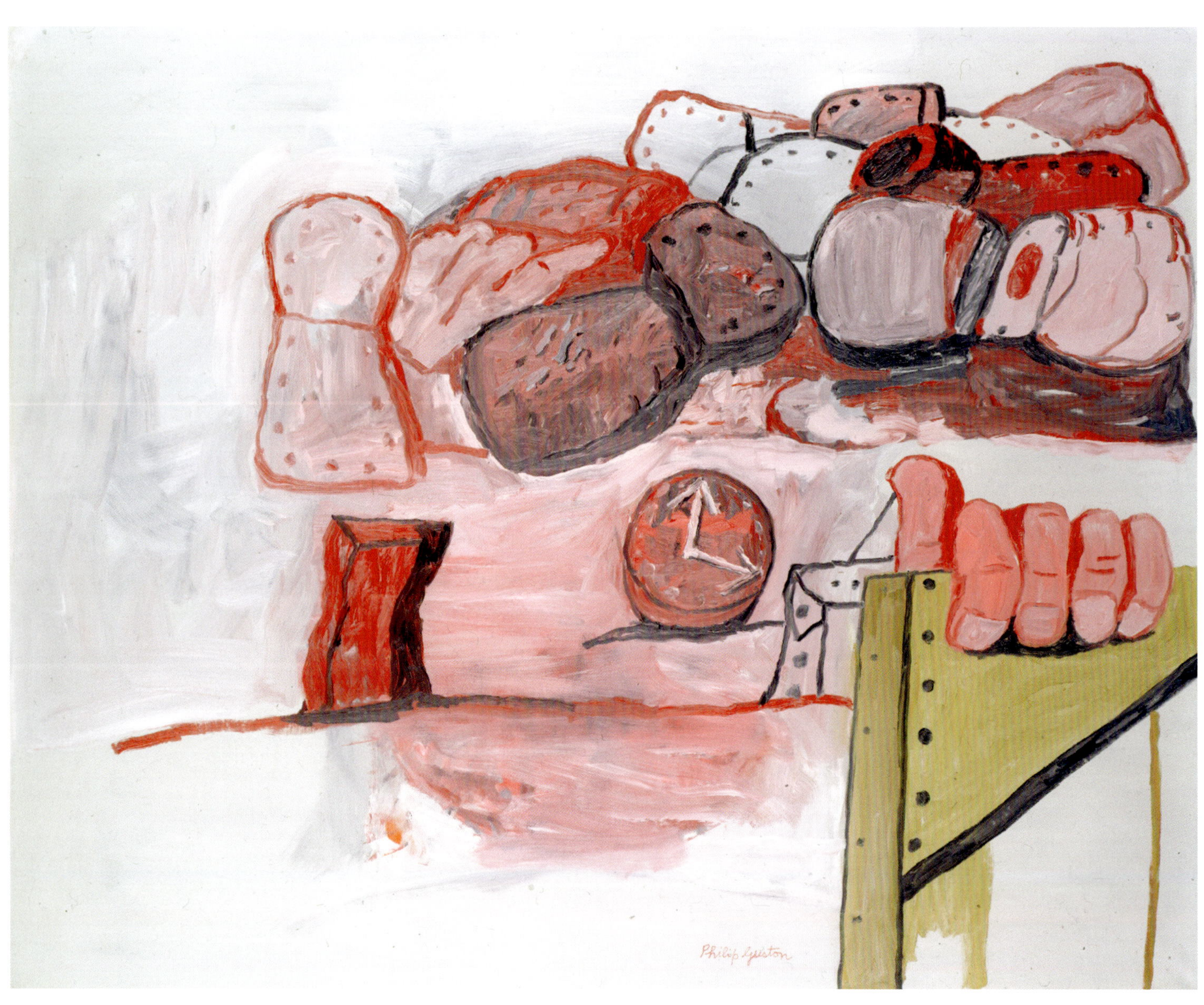

PHILIP GUSTON, *Transition*, 1975
Oil on canvas, 66 x 80 1/2 inches (167.6 x 204.5 cm)
Smithsonian American Art Museum, Bequest of Musa Guston. Accession number: 1992.89

PHILIP GUSTON, [1913-1980]

Born June 27, 1913 Montreal, Canada. **To USA** 1919.
Died June 7, 1980, Woodstock, NY.

Studied 1927: Manual Arts High School; 1930: Otis Art Institute, LA.

Federal Art Project (WPA/FAP) 1935–1939: Mural Division.

Teaching Positions 1941–45: Artist–in–Residence, State University of Iowa City; 1945–47: St. Louis School of Fine Arts, Washington University; 1950: University of Minnesota, MN; 1951–58: New York University, NYC; 1953–58: Pratt Institute, Brooklyn; 1961, 63, 71, 73, 74: Yale Summer School, Norfolk, CT; 1966: Brandeis University, Waltham, MA; 1967–73: New York Studio School, NYC; 1968: Skidmore College, Saratoga Springs, NY; 1969–70, 1972–73: Columbia University, Graduate School of Fine Arts; 1970–71: American Academy, Rome; 1973–78: Boston University, MA.

Selected Solo Exhibitions 1931: Stanley Rose Bookshop, LA; 1944: State University of Iowa City; 1945: Midtown Galleries NY; 1947: Munson-Williams-Proctor Institute, Utica, NY; School of the Museum of Fine Arts, Boston; 1952: Peridot Gallery, NY; 1953: Charles Egan Gallery, NY; 1956, 58, 59, 61: Sidney Janis Gallery, NYC; 1962: circ., Solomon R. Guggenheim Museum, NY; 1966: Jewish Museum, NYC; Brandeis University, Waltham, MA; 1967; Santa Barbara Museum of Art, CA; 1969, 73, 74: Gertrude Kasle Gallery, Detroit, MI; 1970: Marlborough Gallery, NYC; 1970, 74: Boston University, Boston, MA; 1973: *Philip Guston: Drawings, 1938-1972*, The Metropolitan Museum of Art, NYC; 1974, 1976–1980, 82, 83, 85, 90, 91, 95, 96 : David McKee Gallery, NYC; 1978 and 1980 circ.: San Francisco Museum of Modern Art, San Francisco, CA; 1981: Phillips Collection, Washington, DC; XVI Sao Paulo Bienal; 1984: Art Gallery of New South Wales, Sydney, Australia, circ.; 1988: *The Drawings of Philip Guston,* circ., Museum of Modern Art, NYC; *Philip Guston, Centro de Arte Moderna*, circ., Reina Sofia, Madrid, Barcelona; 1999: *Philip Guston, Gemalde 1947–1979*, circ., Kunstmuseum, Bonn, Stuttgart, National Gallery of Canada, Ottawa, Centre Pompidou, Paris.

Selected Group Exhibitions 1933, 34: Los Angeles Museum; 1937, 39: American Artists Congress, NYC; 1938, 40, 1942–48, 1950–53, 1955–58, 1961–63, 66, 79: *Annuals and Biennials*, Whitney Museum of American Art, NYC; 1941, 1943–45,1947–49, 50: Carnegie Institute, Department of Fine Arts, Pittsburgh, PA; 1942–46, 51, 59: *Annuals*, Art Institute of Chicago; 1943, 45, 49, 55: Corcoran Gallery of Art, Washington DC; *1951: Abstract Painting and Sculpture in America*, Museum of Modern Art, NYC; 1952: *Expressionism in American Painting*, Albright Art Gallery, Buffalo, NY; 1951, 53, 56, 57: The *9th St*. Show, the first and subsequent 3 *New York Painting and Sculpture Annuals*, Stable Gallery, NYC; 1956: *12 Americans*, Museum of Modern *Art, NYC; 1958: Nature in Abstraction: The Relation of Abstract Painting and Sculpture to Nature in Twentieth-Century American Art*, Whitney Museum of American Art, NY; 1960: *XXX Biennale Internazionale d'Arte, Venice*; 1961: *American Abstract Expressionists and Imagists*, Solomon R. Guggenheim Museum, NYC; 1963–64: *Hans Hofmann and His Students*, circ., Museum of Modern Art, NYC; 1964: *Painting and Sculpture of a Decade*: 1954-1964, Tate Gallery, London, England; 1969: *New York Painting and Sculpture*: *1940–1970*, Metropolitan Museum of Art, NYC; 1981: *A New Spirit in Painting*, Royal Academy of Arts, London, England; *Amerikanische Malerei, 1930–1980*, Haus der Kunst, Munich, Germany; 1990: *High and Low. Modern Art and Popular Culture*, Museum of Modern Art, NYC.

GRACE HARTIGAN

As soon as I left subject, I was able to go more deeply into content. Now I am trying to find my own internal world rather than the world that is across the street or down the stairs.

Gide said an artist should want only one thing and want it constantly. I want an art that is not 'abstract' and not 'realistic' - I cannot describe the look of this art, but I think I will know it when I see it. I no longer invite the spectator to walk into my canvases. I want a surface that resists, like a wall, not opens, like a gate. I have found my 'subject', it concerns that which is vulgar and vital in American modern life, and the possibilities of its transcendence into the beautiful. I do not wish to describe my subject matter, or to reflect upon it—I want to distill it until I have its essence. Then the rawness must be resolved into form and unity; without the 'rage for order' how can there be art?

Grace Hartigan, Statement: Provided to the editor by Rex Stevens-Hartigan Studio. October 24, 2008.

Grace Hartigan, Statement: *12 Americans*, The Museum of Modern Art, New York, 1956. Catalogue, p. 53.

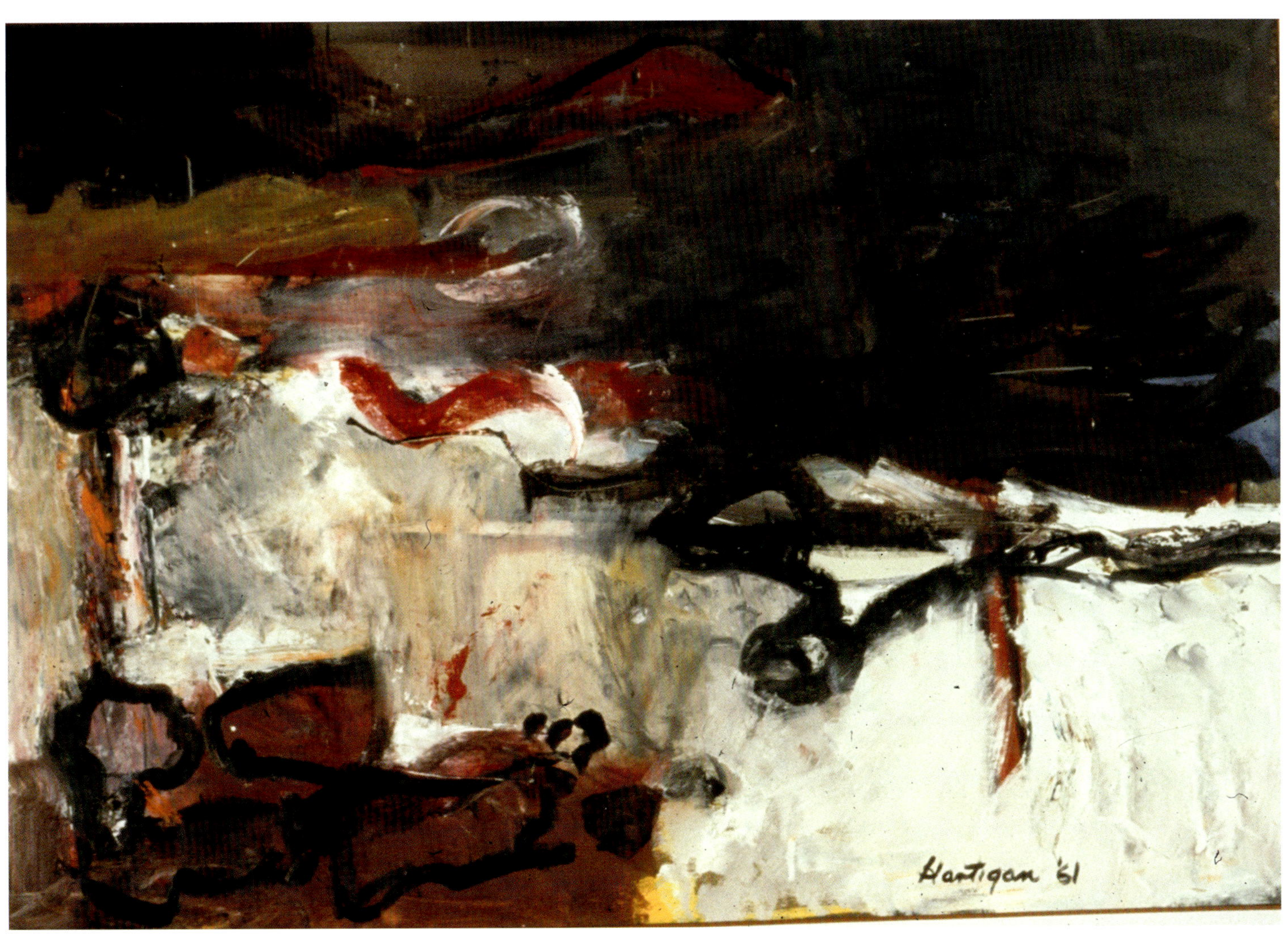

GRACE HARTIGAN, *Maryland*, 1951
Oil on canvas, 55 1/2 x 79 inches
Collection of the artist

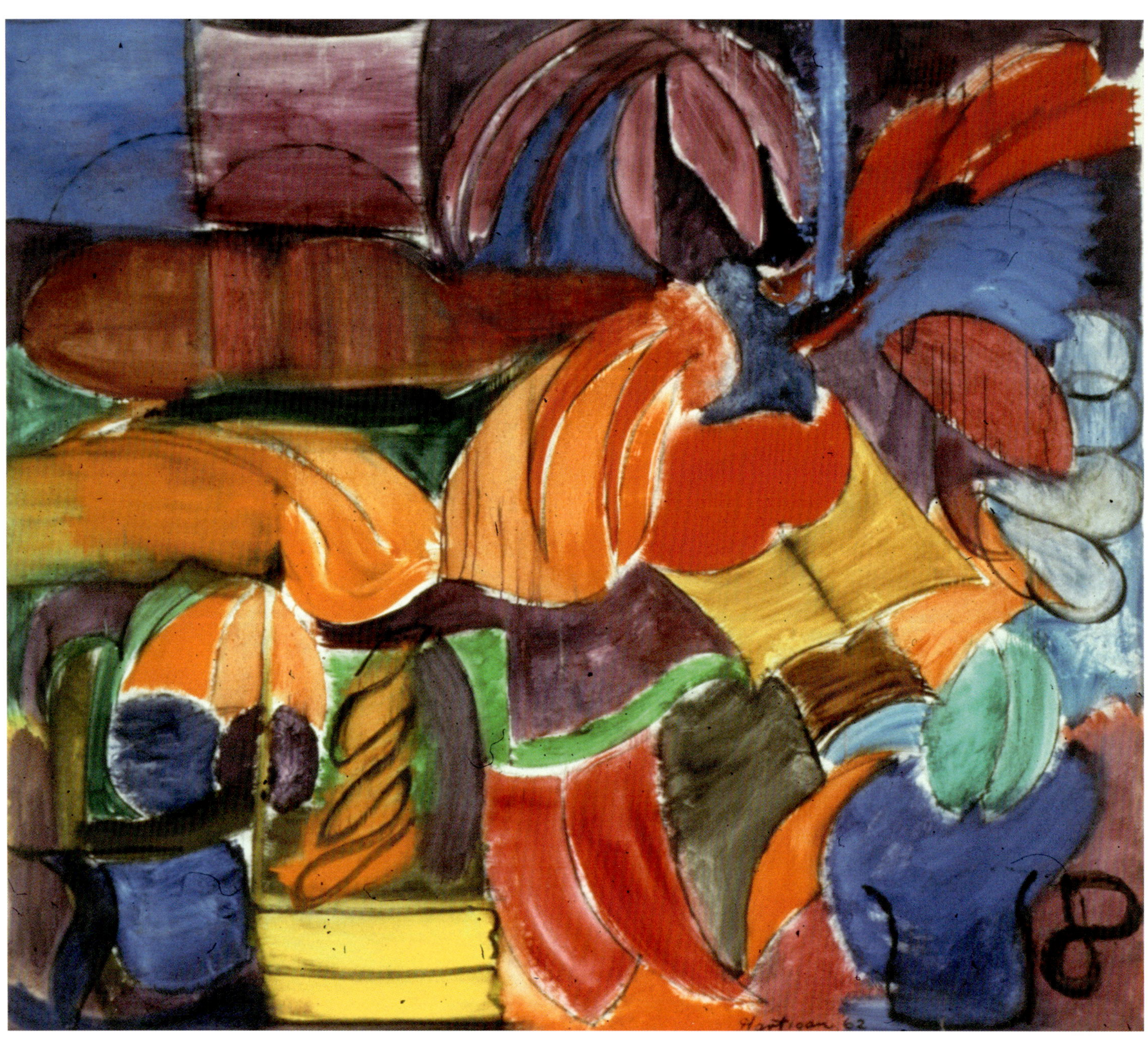

GRACE HARTIGAN, *The Phoenix*, 1962
Oil on canvas, 80 1/2 x 88 1/4 inches
Collection of the artist

GRACE HARTIGAN, [1922-2008]

Born March 28, 1922 in Newark, NJ.
Died November 15, 2008 in Baltimore MD.

Studied 1945–46: with Isaac Lane Muse, Newark, NJ.

Teaching Positions 1967-: Director Maryland Institute, Graduate School; 1983: Bard College, artist in residence.

Selected Solo Exhibitions 1951(first), 52, 53, 54, 55, 57, 59: Tibor de Nagy Gallery, NYC; 1955: Vassar College; 1967: University of Chicago, IL; Maryland Institute College of Art, Baltimore, MD; 1962, 64, 67, 70: Martha Jackson Gallery, NYC; 1969, 72, 74, 76: Gertrude Kasle Gallery, Detroit, MI; 1975: William Zierler Gallery, NYC; American University, Washington, D.C.; 1977, 78: Genesis Gallery, NYC; 1980: Baltimore Museum of Art, Baltimore, MD, Myers Gallery, State University of New York, Plattsburgh, NY; University of Maryland Art Gallery, University of Maryland, College Park, MD; 1981: Hamilton Gallery of Contemporary Art, NYC; Mint Museum of Art, Charlotte, NC; Georgia Museum of Art, Athens, GA; Fort Wayne Museum of Art, Fort Wayne, IN; 1983: Van Wickle Gallery, Lafayette College, Easton, PA; 1984: Dolly Fitterman Gallery, Minneapolis, MN; 1987: *Grace Hartigan, A Mini Retrospective, 1954–1984*, Watkins Gallery, The American University, Washington, D.C.; 1984, 86, 88: Gruenebaum Gallery, NYC; 1989: Kouros Gallery, NYC; 1993: *Grace Hartigan and the Poets*, Skidmore College, Saratoga Springs, NY; 1997: *Hartigan's Women*, The Robeson Center Art Gallery, Rutgers University, Newark, NJ; The Art Gallery at Brooklyn College, Brooklyn, NY; Allen Priebe Art Gallery, University of Wisconsin, Oshkosh, WI; *AB-EX Pointillism/ 1988–1993*, Loyola College Art Gallery, Baltimore, MD; Lawrence Gallery, Rosemont College, Rosemont, PA; 1991, 92, 94, 97, 2001: ACA Gallery, NYC; 1979, 81, 82, 84, 86, 87, 89, 90, 92, 93, 95, 97, 2000, 01: C. Grimaldis Gallery, Baltimore, MD; 2000: *Paintings from Popular Culture*, Sasquevehanna Museum, PA; 2001: *5 Decades of Large Scale Paintings*, Neuberger Museum, Purchase, NY.

Selected Group Exhibitions 1951, 1953–57: *9th St.*, Show, the first and subsequent 5 *New York Painting and Sculpture Annuals*, Stable Gallery, NYC; 1950: *Talent 1950*, Kootz Gallery, NYC; 1955–58, 61, 63: *Annuals and Biennials*, The Whitney Museum of American Art, NYC; 1955: *Rising Talent*, University of Minnesota; *Modern Art in the United States*, circ. in Europe, The Museum of Modern Art, NYC; 1956: *12 Americans*, The Museum of Modern Art, NYC; International Biennial Exhibition of Paintings, Tokyo; IV Sao Paulo Biennial; 1957: *Artists of the New York School, Second Generation*, The Jewish Museum, NYC; 1958: *The New American Painting*, circ, in Europe, The Museum of Modern Art, NYC; Brussel World's Fair; 1959: Documenta II, Kassel; 1960: *60 American Painters, 1960*, The Walker Art Center, Minneapolis, Minn.; 1961: *Abstract Expressionists and Imagists*, The Solomon R. Guggenheim Museum, NYC; *American Vanguard*, circ. in Europe, Solomon R. Guggenheim Museum and The United States Information Agency; 1965: White House Festival of Arts, Washington, D.C.; 1971: *Collages by American Artists*, Ball State University; *American Painting since World War II*, Delaware Art Museum; 1974: *A Poet Among Painters*, The Whitney Museum of American Art, NYC; 1980: *Poets and Painters*, National Collection of Fine Arts, Washington D.C.; *The Fifties Aspect of Painting in New York*, Hirshhorn Museum and Sculpture Garden, Smithsonian Institution, Washington, D.C.; *Modern American Painting*, The Baltimore Museum of Art, Baltimore, MD; 1982: *The Americans, The Collage*, Contemporary Arts Museum, Houston, TX; 1988–89: *The Figurative Fifties: New York Figurative Expressionism*, Pennsylvania Academy of Fine Arts, Philadelphia, PA; 1999–2000: *The American Century, 1950–2000*, The Whitney Museum of American Art, NYC.

JULIUS HATOFSKY

...Inventing imagery is the basis of my painting. Once involved, I concentrate on scale, inner light, drawing, surface, rhythm, color. Developing these painting concerns has helped to focus my emotional intensity and release my imagination. At age 83, I have a range and variety of expression and imagery and feel a command over the work that has taken over sixty years to acquire. I constantly try to reach deeper, to move beyond my limitations, to challenge myself and to learn. I feel I've made considerable progress in the last 25 years.

Julius Hatofsky, Statement: From the artist's archives. Provided by the Estate of Julius Hatofsky.

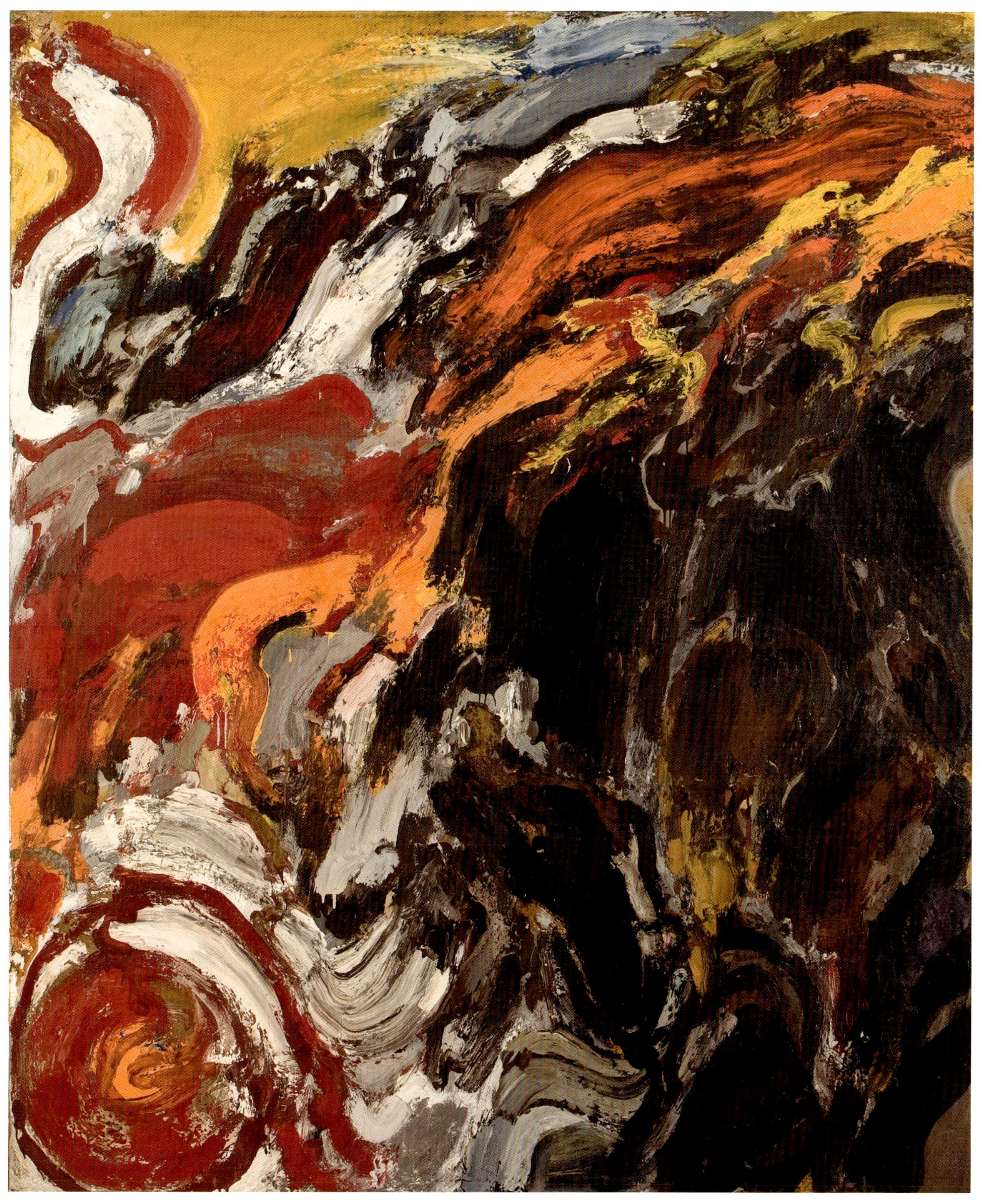

JULIUS HATOFSKY, *Untitled*, 1962
Oil on canvas, 83 x 63 inches
Collection of the Estate
© Estate Julius Hatofsky

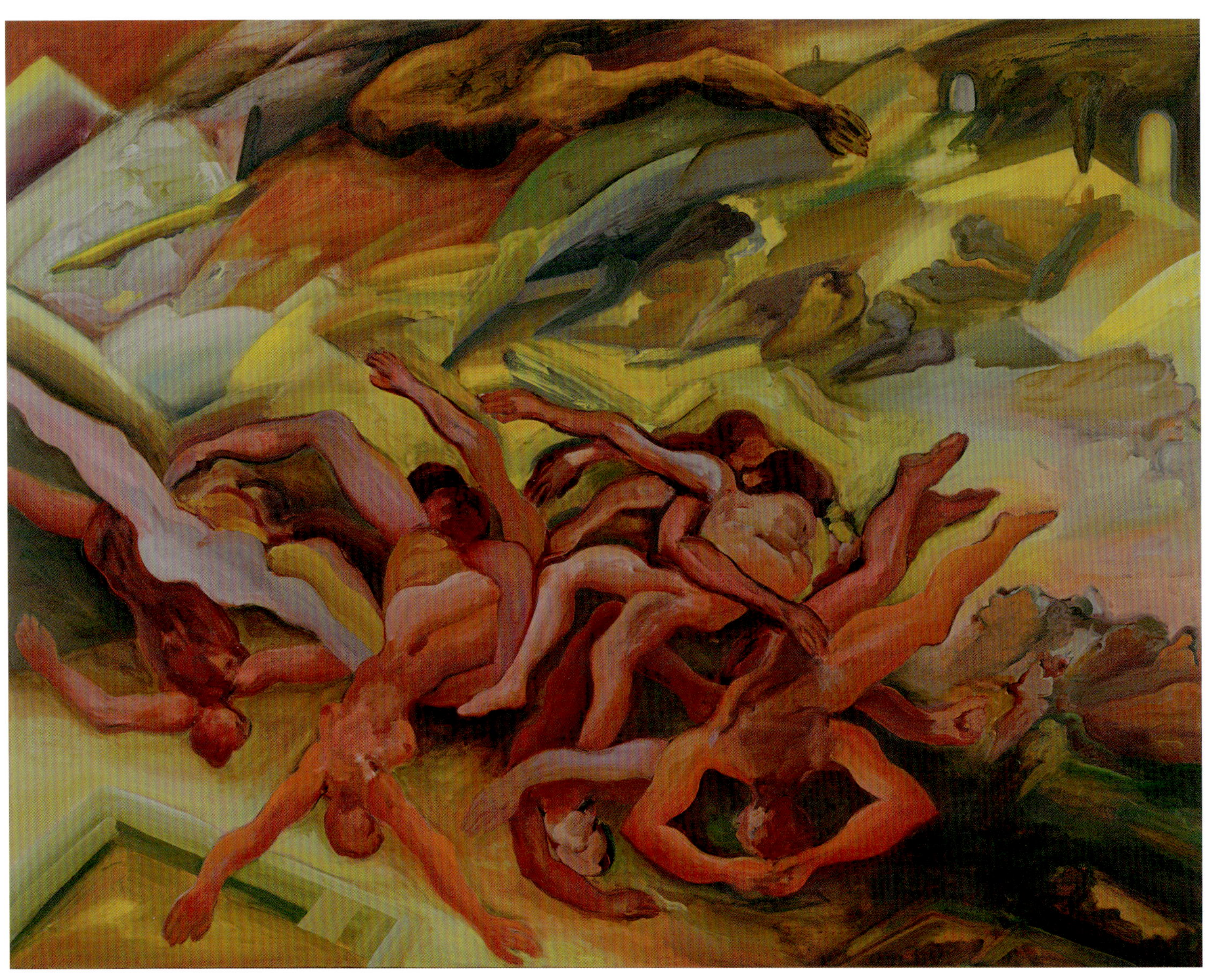

JULIUS HATOFSKY, *Fallen Fragments*, 1990
Oil on canvas, 90 x 114 inches
Collection of the Estate

JULIUS HATOFSKY, [1922-2006]

Born Ellenville, New York, 1922.
Died Vallejo, California, 2006.

Studied 1945–1950: Art Students League, NYC; 1950–1951: Grande Chaumière, Paris, France; 1952: Hans Hofmann's School New York, NY.

Military Service in World War II 1942, Julius Hatofsky was drafted into the 82nd Airborne and served in the Battle of the Bulge and the invasions of Holland and Normandy; later he participated in the liberation of a concentration camp.

Teaching Positions 1962–1995: Painting and Drawing Instructor, San Francisco Art Institute, San Francisco, CA.

Selected Solo Exhibitions 1958: Avant-Garde Gallery, New York, NY; 1959: Holland Goldowsky Gallery, Chicago IL; 1961, 63: Charles Egan Gallery, NYC; 1965, 66: Marylhurst College, Portland, OR; 1967: University of Kansas Art Museum, Lawrence, KS; 1968: Emmanuel Walters Gallery, San Francisco Art Institute, San Francisco, CA; 1974: Smith-Anderson Gallery, Palo Alto, CA; 1975: Smith-Anderson Gallery, San Francisco, CA; 1983, 85: Paule Anglim Gallery, San Francisco, CA; 1987, 89: Pier 23 Gallery, San Francisco, CA; 1988: Museum of Modern Art Rental Gallery, San Francisco, CA; 1993: Monterey Peninsula Museum of Art, Monterey, CA; 1994, 96: D.P.Fong Galleries, San Jose, CA; 2000: *Painting and Drawing*, Fresno Art Museum, Fresno, CA; 2003: *Drawings*, Carl Cherry Center for the Arts, Carmel, CA; 2005: *Painting and Drawing*, Triton Museum of Art, Santa Clara, CA; 2008: *Paintings*, The Bank of America, San Francisco, CA.

Selected Group Exhibitions 1958: Newark Museum Biennial, Newark, NJ; 1959: Whitney Museum Annual, New York, NY; 1968: University of Texas, Austin, TX; 1977: San Francisco Museum of Modern Art, San Francisco, CA; 1978: Kansas City Art Institute, Kansas, MO; 1979: Smith-Anderson Gallery, Palo Alto, CA; 1987: Mira Godard Gallery, Toronto, Canada; Jack Gallery, New York, NY; 1995: Museum of Modern Art Rental Gallery, San Francisco, CA; 1994–1996: *Still Working*, circ., United States.

HARRY JACKSON

All creative arts – including figurative and non-figurative abstract expressionism – are finite manifestations of one infinite and eternal dream.

Harry Jackson, Statement: Provided by the artist to the editor, December 17, 2008

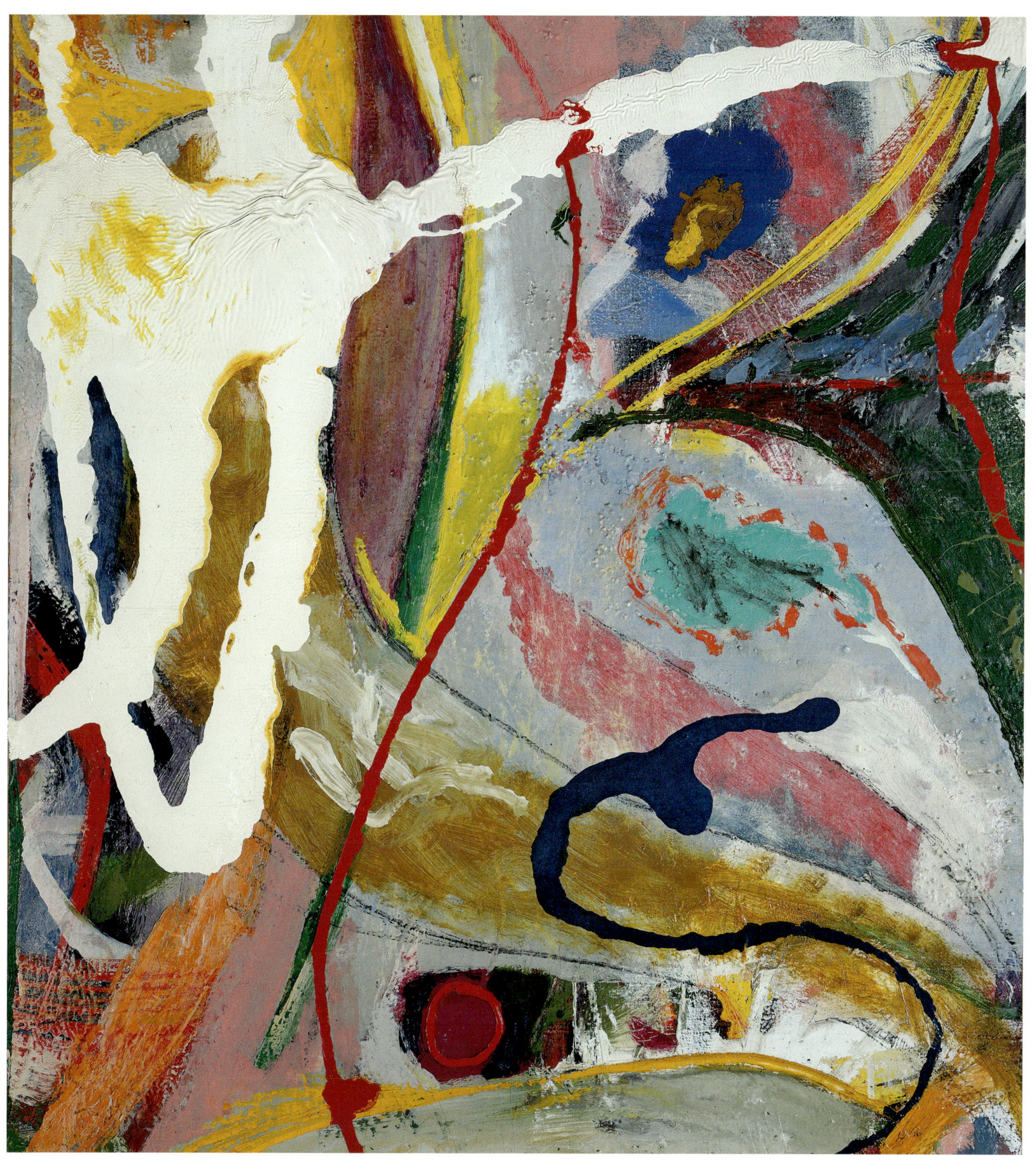

HARRY JACKSON, *Red, Yellow and Blue*, 1951
Oil and enamel on canvas, 31 1/2 x 28 inches

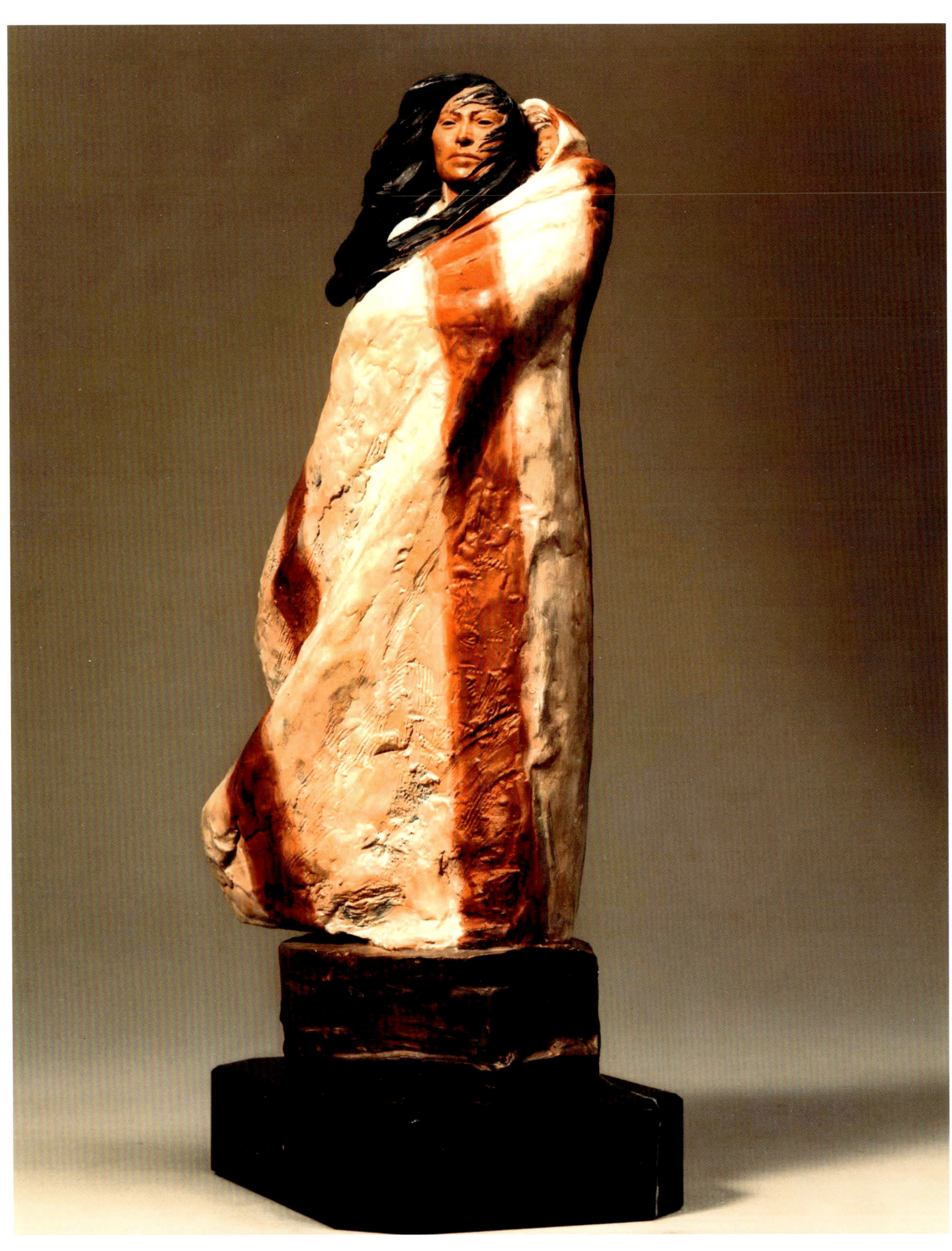

HARRY JACKSON, *Sacajawea II*, 1980
Polychrome bronze, H: 18 x W: 8 x D: 7 inches

HARRY JACKSON, [1924-]

Born April 18, 1924, in Chicago.

Studied 1932–37: Chicago Art Institue; 1938–41: Fredrick Mizen Academy, The Chicago Academy of Fine Arts, Chicago Art Institute; 1946–48: Moves to New York and studies with Jackson Pollock, Willem de Kooning, Ruffino Tamayo and Hans Hofmann.

Military Service in World War II
1942–45: United States Marine Corps. Twice wounded and decorated. Appointed USMC Combat Artist.

Selected Solo Exhibitions 1949: Brooklyn Museum Art School Gallery, NY; 1952: 53 Tibor de Nagy Gallery, NY; 1953: Bennington College, Vermont; 1956: Martha Jackson Gallery, NY; Buffalo Bill Museum, Cody, WY; 1960: M. Knoedler & Co., NY; 1961: Amon Carter Museum, Fort Worth, TX; 1964, 68, 69: Kennedy Galleries, NY; National Collection of Fine Arts, Washington, D.C.; Whitney Gallery of Western Art, Cody, WY; Montana Historical Society, Helena, MT; Wyoming Artists Association, Sheridan, WY; 1965: Mile-High Center, Denver, CO; 1966 National Cowboy Hall of Fame, Oklahoma City, OK; 1968: Cody County Art League, Cody, WY; Amon Carter Museum, Fort Worth, TX; 1970 American Library, USIS, Rome, Italy; Agra Gallery, Wash., D.C.; 1971 Fort Pitt Museum, Pittsburgh, PA; 1972, 73: Main Trail Galleries, Scottsdale, AZ and Jackson, WY; 1973: Buffalo Bill Historical Center, Plains Indian Museum, Cody, WY; Thomas Gilcrease Institute of American History and Art, Tulsa, OK; Hunter Gallery, San Francisco, CA; Altermann Gallery, Dallas, TX.
Retrospectives: 1985: Museums: Camaiore, Italy; Buffalo Bill, Cody, WY; Palm Springs, CA;
Minneapolis, MN; 1987: University of Wyoming, Laramie, WY.

Selected Group Exhibitions 1944: Stendhal Gallery, Los Angeles, CA; 1945: *Exhibition of USMC Combat Art*, circ., also in Europe, Corcoran Gallery of Art, Washington, D.C.; 1950: Jacques Seligmann Gallery, NYC; Kootz Gallery, NYC; 1951, 52, 53: Tibor de Nagy Gallery, NYC; 1951, 54: *9th St.*, Show, first and subsequent *New York Painting and Sculpture Annual*, Stable Gallery, NYC; 1959, 62: Whitney Gallery of Western Art, Cody, WY; 1959–63: M. Knoedler & Co., NY; 1961: Pennsylvania Academy of Fine Arts, Philadelphia; 1962: Hirschl & Adler, NY; Valley House Galleries, Dallas, TX; 1962–77: Kennedy Galleries, NY; 1964, 65, 67, 68: National Academy of Design, NY; 1966: XVII Mostra Internazionale d'Arte, Premio del Fiorino, Florence, Italy; 1967: Pennational Artists Annual, Pennsylvania; 1968: American Artists Professional League, New York Mostra di Arte Moderna, Convento de S. Lazzaro, Camaiore, Italy; 1968–74: Main Place Gallery, Dallas, TX; 1969: Tryon Gallery, London, England; 1971–76: Texas Art Gallery, Dallas, TX; 1971–78: Sandra Wilson Gallery, Santa Fe, NM; 1973: Trailside Galleries, Jackson, WY, and Scottsdale, AZ; 1976: Hunter Gallery, San Francisco, CA; 1980: Sanford Smith Gallery, NY.

BUFFIE JOHNSON

From the very beginning, from the first pictures that I painted as a young child, my work has been inspired by the mysterious forces of the natural world. For me, that world has always incorporated both the visible and the invisible realms.

My attempt, at the age of eight, to capture the "Spirits" of the Sun, the Moon, the Stars, the Winds, Sky, and Earth in a series of forty watercolors, was a serious endeavor whose purpose was to show the unity of those realities. Each of these "Spirits" was represented in female form, their long flowing hair and robes swirling in and out of space in undulating waves.

The dreamy aura that envelopes many of the female figures in some of my early representational paintings owes much to these cosmic goddesses. It was not until the mid 1940s, however, when I began to study esoteric symbolism and mythology and Jung's theories of the archetypes of the unconscious, that I became aware of the enormous significance of my "Spirits" of childhood. I had uncovered the very source and foundation of my life's work. From that point forward, I always held an image in my mind that each of my paintings was to be an altarpiece to the Great Goddesses. Although my painting styles have changed considerably over the years, this conscious intention has remained true throughout.

From the mid-forties until 1968, except for the many portraits that I painted during that time, my work was strictly abstract. The work that led up to and culminated in the 1959 murals for the Astor Theatre in New York, is, perhaps, best described by an art critic who reviewed the theater's murals. He compared the experience of the vast, continuous abstract images of a "New York Summer Night" that appeared to float on the curved theater walls, to the caves at Lascaux and Altamira.

The abstract periods that followed this celestially-scaled experience were characterized by an energy of movement, bold sweeping brushstrokes, glowing suns and moons, ancient glyphic sigils symbolic of the Goddess's powers, spirals and serpents, bulls and scorpions. As my work gradually evolved into metaphors for the cyclical mystery of life, I felt compelled to speak more directly of this mystery and so abandoned abstraction to return to a realistic style.

The single image frontal plant forms that I painted for the next twenty years were very large-scale monumental icons to the Goddess. The large, botanically-detailed images dwarfed the viewer, putting things in proper perspective. They demonstrated the overwhelming majesty and power of the cycles of life and death that are so immediately visible in the flower, the fruit, and the dying pod filled with seeds for the next generation.

When my eyesight began to fail and I could no longer see the minute detail of my subjects, I returned to abstraction. This was to be my final period, which I called "The Numbering Series." The apparent minimal austerity of the imagery emulates the geometric simplicity of sacred Tantric art whose meanings are complex. The red and black cosmic orbs that float on a very excited ground of blue are intended to show the power that arises from zero, or Chaos, at the beginning of creation. A drama of the sexes is played out between the black, which symbolizes the ancient feminine wisdom, and the red, which stands for the masculine driving power that plants the seed. The paintings are numbered from zero to twenty-two, a reflection of the cards in the major arcana of the Tarot deck, which is said to contain all of the wisdom of the world.

Buffie Johnson, Statement: From the artist's archives. Provided by Jenny Johnson Sykes.

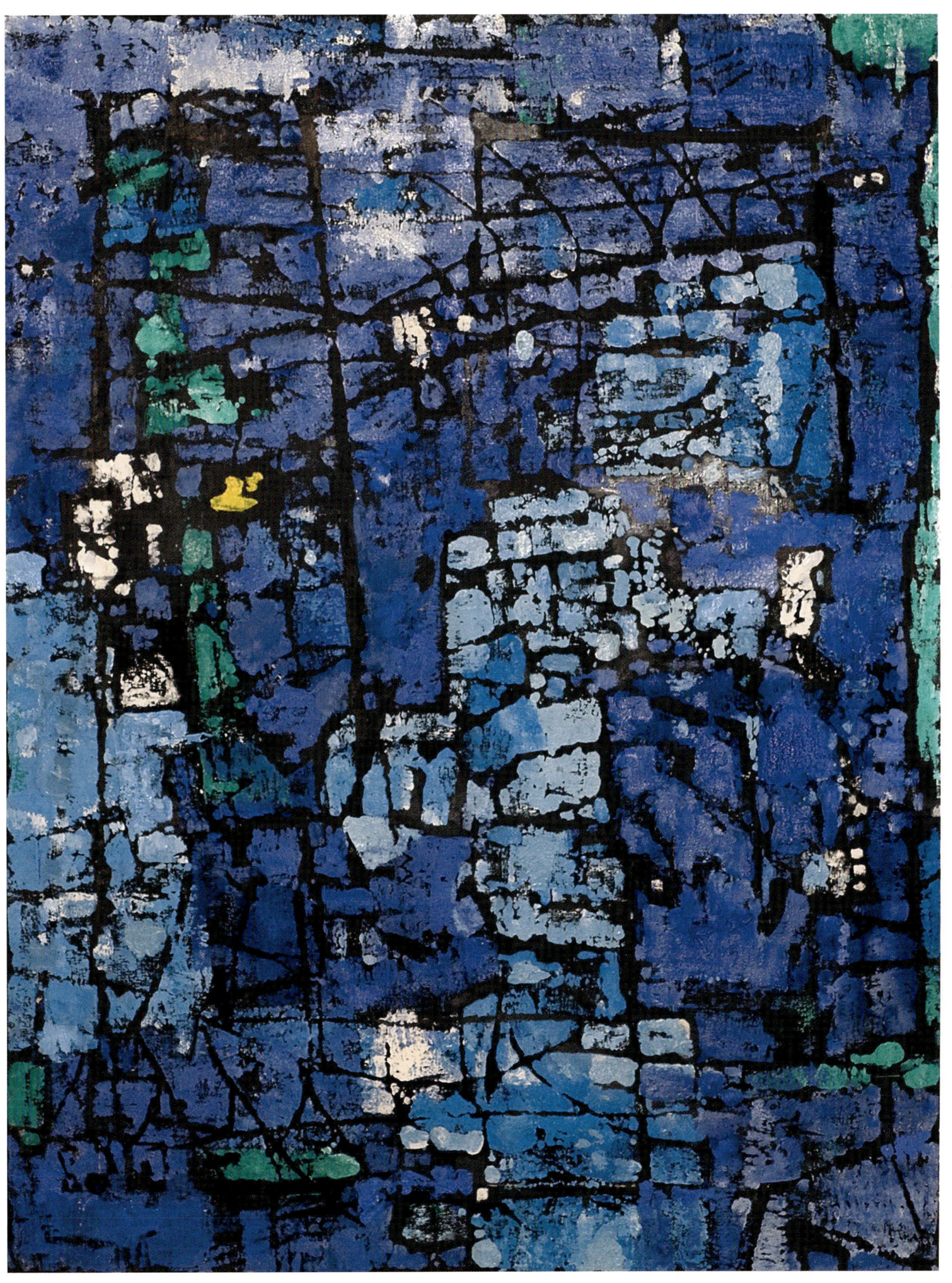

BUFFIE JOHNSON, *The Bridge-I*, 1952
Oil on canvas, 36 1/4 x 26 3/4 inches
Private collection

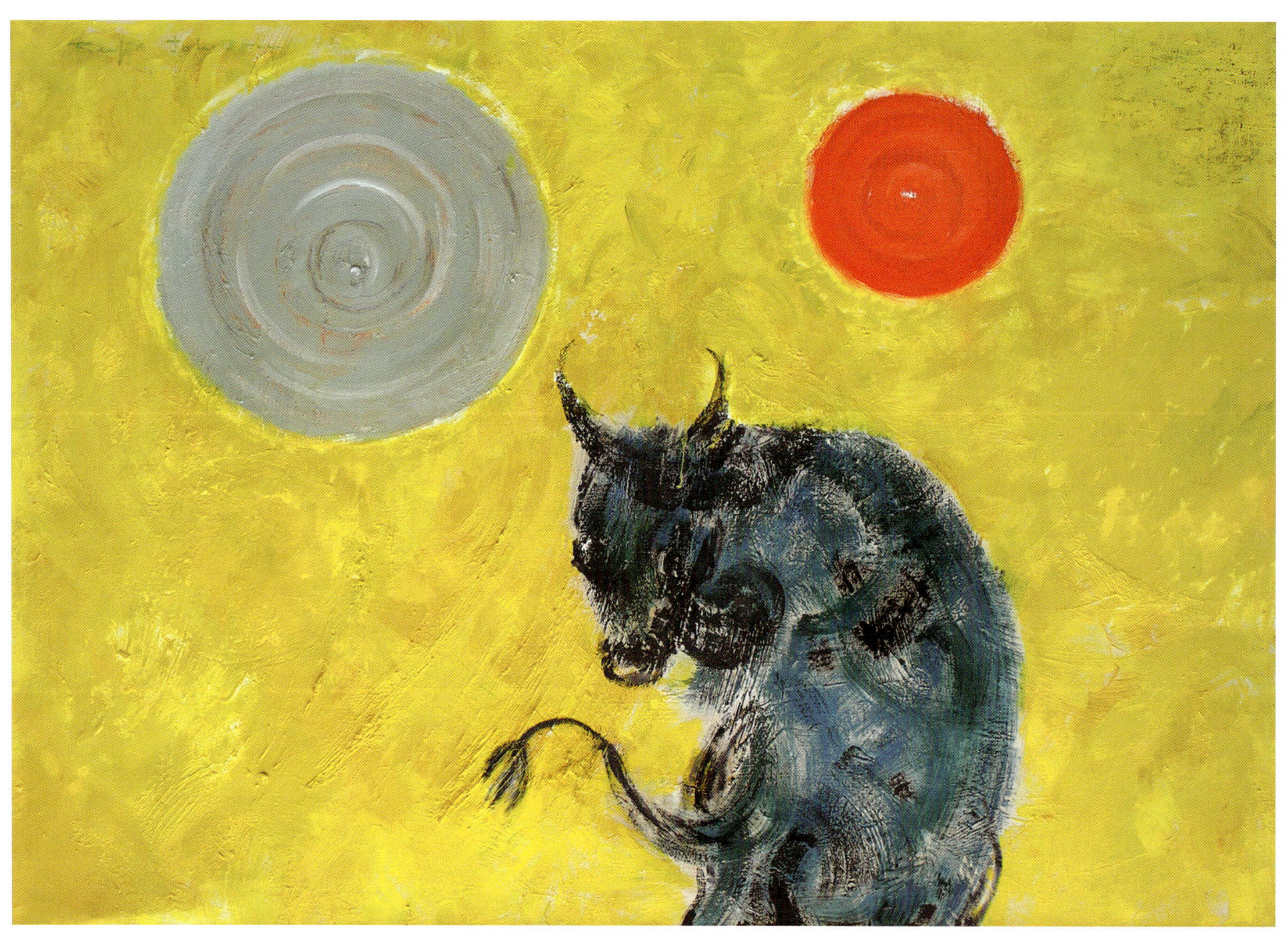

BUFFIE JOHNSON, *Hieros Gamos 13*, 1962
Oil on canvas, 45 x 62 inches
Collection of Jenny Johnson Sykes

BUFFIE JOHNSON, [1912-2006]

Born February 20,1912 New York City.
Died August 11, 2006, New York City.

Studied 1927-28: Art Students League of New York; 1931-36: University of California, Los Angeles (B.F.A.); 1938: Academie Julien, Paris; 1938–39: S.W. Hayter Atelier, Paris; Independent Study with Francis Picabia, Paris.

Teaching Positions 1935–36: University of California, Los Angeles; 1946-50: Parsons School of Design, NYC.

Selected Solo Exhibitions 1937: (first) Jake Zeitlin Gallery, Los Angeles; 1939: Galerie Rotge, Paris; Wakefield Gallery, NYC; 1942: Caresse Crosby's G Place Gallery, Washington, D.C.; 1945: Howard Putzel's 67 Gallery, NYC; 1948: Ringling Museum of Art, Sarasota; Galleria del Cavallino, Venice; 1949: Hanover Gallery, London; Gallery Collette Allendy, Paris; 1950: Betty Parsons Gallery, NYC; 1951, 56, 60: Galerie Bing, Paris; 1960: Bodley Gallery, NYC; 1961: Gallery Thibaut, NYC; 1963: World House Gallery, NYC; 1964, 66: Galeria Antonio Souza, Mexico City; 1964: Granville Gallery, NYC; 1969: New School, NYC; 1973: Max Hutchinson Gallery, NYC; 1975: Palm Beach Galleries; 1976: Andre Zarre Gallery, NYC; 1981: Ankrum Gallery, Los Angeles; 1981: *Retrospective*, Landmark Gallery, NYC; 1991: Cardiff House at University of California, Santa Cruz; 1992: PMW Gallery, Stamford; 1993: The Institute for Contemporary Art, P. S. 1 Museum, Long Island City; 1997: *Buffie Johnson: The Spirit of Plants*, Chuck Levitan Gallery, NYC, (Part I), 1998: (Part II); 2002: *Buffie Johnson: Transcendentalist*, 2007: *Buffie Johnson Memorial Exhibition*, Anita Shapolsky Gallery, NYC.

Selected Group Exhibitions 1941: *International Exhibition of Painting and Sculpture*, Carnegie Institute; 1943: *31 International Women Painters*, Peggy Guggenheim's Art of This Century, NYC; 1945: Howard Putzel's 67 Gallery, NYC; 1946: *136 Americans*, Walker Art Center, Minneapolis; 1948, 49: *Salon des Realites Nouvelles*, Paris; 1950: Betty Parsons Gallery, NYC; *Fourth Annual Print Show*, The Brooklyn Museum, NY; *Twelve Women Painters of the South Fork*, The Parrish Art Museum, Southampton, NY; 1953: *17 East Hampton Artists*, Guild Hall Museum, East Hampton, NY; 1954, 55: Stable Gallery, NYC; The Baltimore Museum; *International Watercolor Show*, The Brooklyn Museum, NY; *Eight Painters*, The Hampton Gallery Workshop, East Hampton, NY; 1956: *Junge Amerikanische Kunst*, Ljubljana Museum; *Group Espace*, Paris; 1957: *Second Exhibition*, Signa Gallery, East Hampton, NY; 1959: *Works by Gallery Artists*, Hirschl & Adler Galleries, NYC; 1960: *Monotypes and Prints*, Guild Hall Museum, East HamptonNY; *Business Buys American Art*, Whitney Museum of American Art, NYC; 1961: *Contemporay Collage*, Bertha Schaefer Gallery, NYC; 1964: *Long Island - Its Artists*, The Parrish Art Museum, Southampton, NY; 1971: Le Salon International de la Femme, Nice; *Penthouse Exhibition*, Museum of Modern Art, NYC; *American Art of Our Century*, Whitney Museum of American Art, NYC; 1972: *American Women Artists*, Kunsthaus Hamburg; 1973: *Women Choose Women*, The New York Cultural Center, NYC; 1973: *Biennial Exhibition: Contemporary American Art*, Whitney Museum of American Art, NYC; *Ciba-Geigy Collection of Contemporary Paintings*, University of Texas at Austin; A .I. R. Gallery, NYC; 1974: *Waves: An Artist Selects*, Cranbrook Academy of Art, Bloomfield Hills; 1975: *Color, Light & Image*, Women's Interart Center, NYC; *Women's Exchange Exhibitions*, Pratt Institute, Brooklyn; *Women Artists Here & Now*, Ashawagh Hall, Springs, NY; *A Change of View*, The Aldrich Museum of Contemporary Art, Ridgefield, CT; *Works on Paper: Women Artists*, The Brooklyn Museum, NY; 1976: *Artists and East Hampton: A 100 Year Perspective*, Guild Hall Museum, East Hampton, NY; *The Year of the Woman: Reprise*, The Bronx Museum of the Arts, NY; 1977: *Contemporary Women: Consciousness and Content*, The Brooklyn Museum, NY; 1981: *Paintings And Sculpture by Candidates for Art Awards*, American Academy and Institute of Arts and Letters, NYC; 1997: *Art of This Century: The Women*, Pollock-Krasner House, East Hampton, NY; 2001: *Abstract Expressionism, Then and Now*, Emily Lowe Gallery, Hofstra University, Hempstead, NY; 1997, 98, 2003, 04, 05, 07, 08: Anita Shapolsky Gallery, NYC.

JAMES KELLY

I had a nagging concern that something was missing in my work; either I'm keeping it out or I'm not capable of getting it in; a bridge to the audience... a feeling of humanness. I was painting at a time when I was between one kind of expression and another—from more diffuse to more precise. You can recognize a shape that asserts itself.

James Kelly, Statement: Letter to the editor, 2002. Previously unpublished.

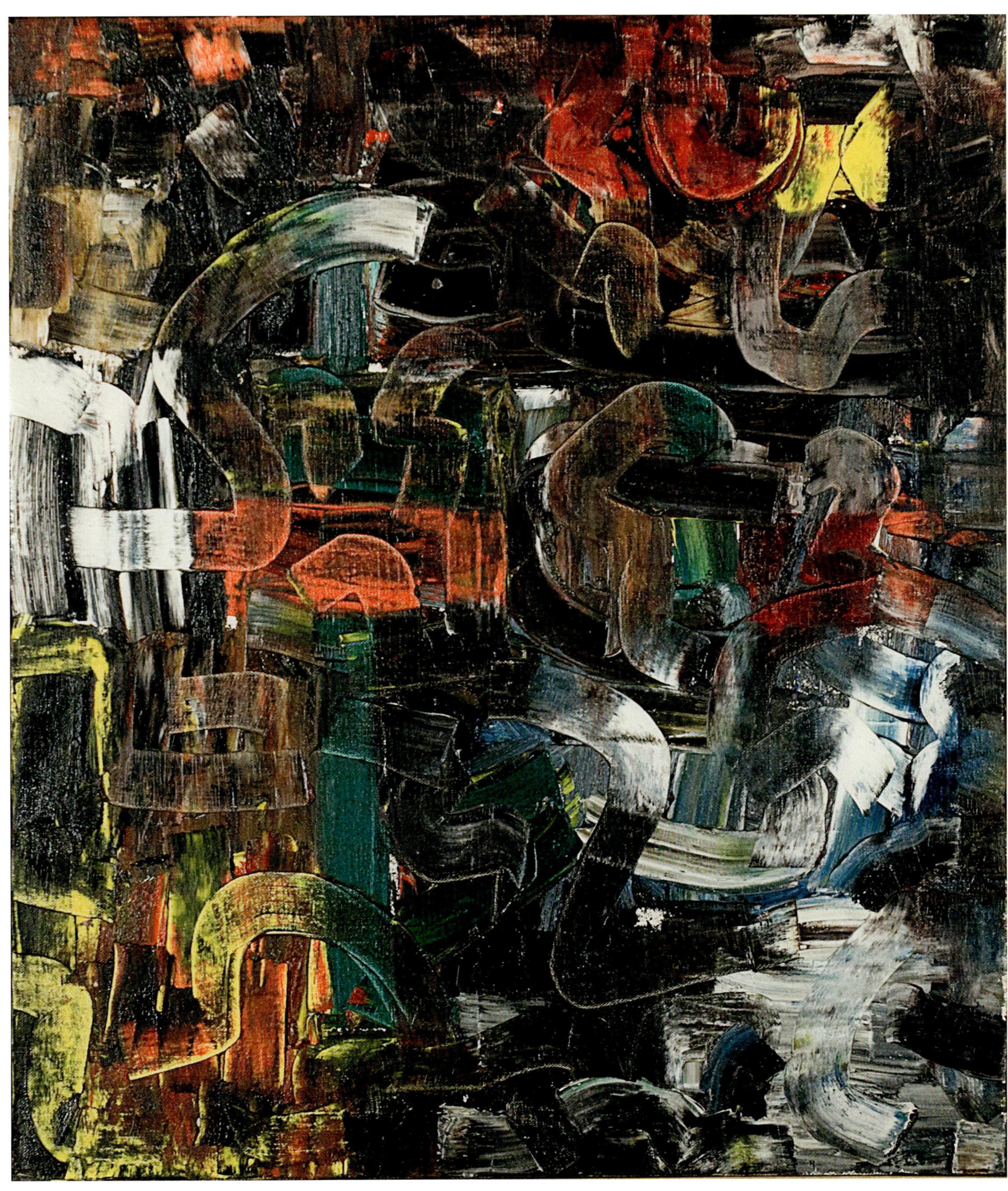

JAMES KELLY, *Embarcadero Three*, 1956
Oil on canvas 23 3/4 x 20 1/4 inches
Private collection

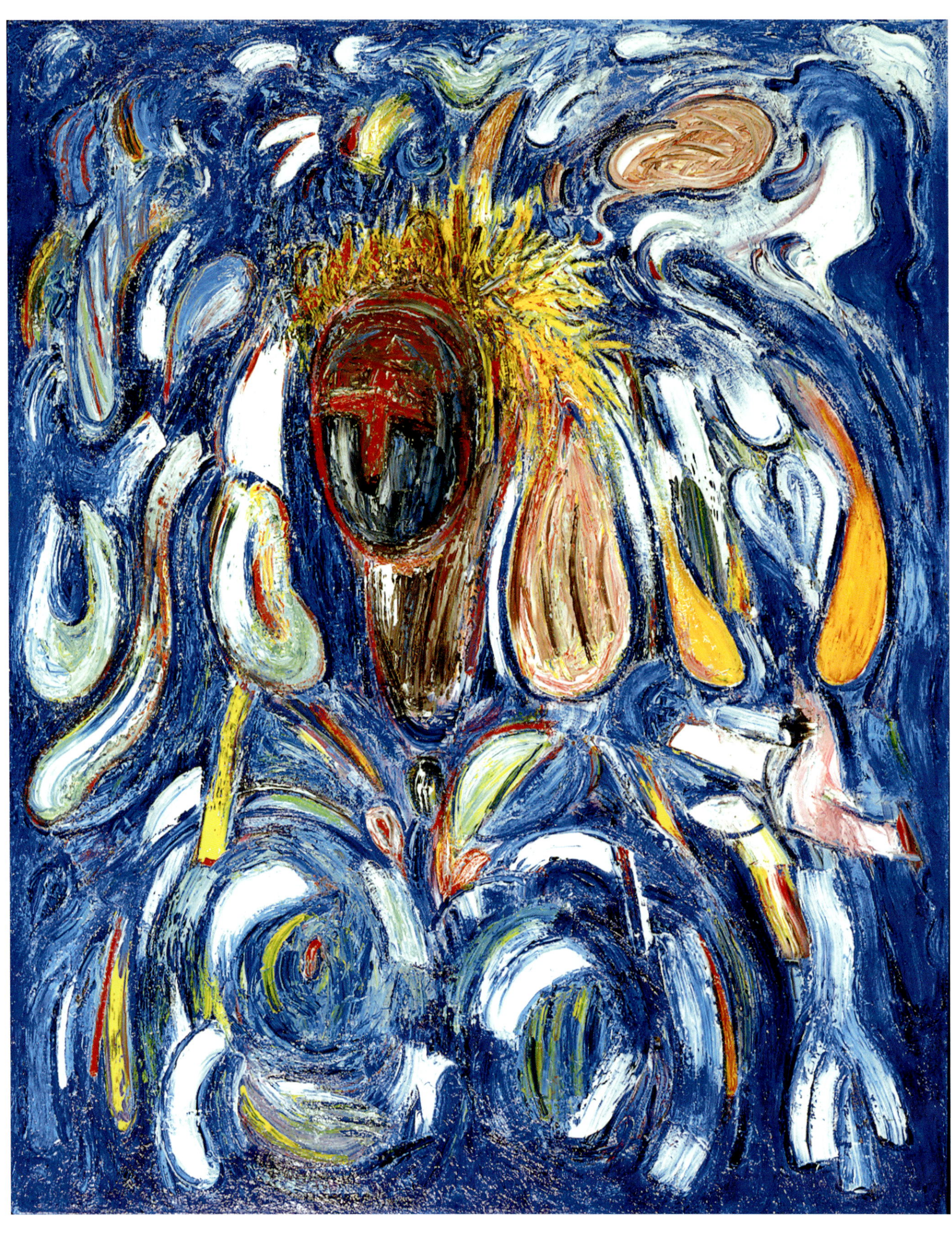

JAMES KELLY, *African Queen*, 1981
Oil on canvas 48 x 36
Collection of the Estate

JAMES KELLY, [1913-2003]

Born 1913, Philadelphia, PA.
Died 2003, New York City, NY.

Studied 1937: Philadelphia Museum School; 1938: Pennsylvania Academy of Fine Arts; 1941: Barnes Foundation; 1951-54: California School of Fine Arts.

Military Service in World War II
1941–45: 13th U.S. Air Force.

Selected Solo Exhibitions 1951: The Place, San Francisco, CA; 1956: San Francisco Art Association Gallery, CA; 1963: Stryke Gallery, NY; 1965, 69: East Hampton Gallery, NY; 1966: Albright College, Reading, PA; 1968: Long Island University, Brooklyn, NY; 1971, 72: Westbeth Gallery, NY; 1990: Wiegand Gallery, College of Notre Dame, Belmont, CA; 2006: *Paintings 1950's–1990's*, Katherina Rich Perlow Gallery, NYC.

Selected Group Exhibitions 1949: Contemporary Art Association, Philadelphia, PA; 1951: Pyramid Club, Philadelphia, PA; Pennsylvania Academy of Fine Arts; *Philadelphia–San Francisco Art Festival*, San Francisco, CA; 1952: *Mirror Five Group*, California School of Fine Arts Gallery, CA; 1953: King Ubu San Francisco, CA; 1954; *From San Francisco*, Kaufman Art Gallery, NY; 1955: *Action Painting of the West Coast*, Concert Hall Workshop, Santa Monica, CA; East and West Art Gallery, San Francisco, CA; 6 Gallery, San Francisco, CA; 1955, 56, 58: *Annual Drawing and Print Show*, San Francisco Museum of Art, CA; 1956: *California Painters Exhibit*, University of Minnesota, MN; *California School Yes or No*, The Oakland Museum, CA; *20th Annual Watercolor Exhibition*, San Francisco Museum of Art, CA; *6th Annual Oil and Sculpture Exhibition*, Richmond Art Center, Richmond, CA; 1956, 57, 58: *Painting and Sculpture Annuals*, San Francisco Museum of Art, CA; 1957: *California Painters Exhibition*, The Oakland Museum, CA; *American Paintings, 1945–1957*, Minneapolis Institute of Arts, MN; *Direction–Bay Area Paintings, 1957*, circ., Richmond Art Center, Richmond, CA; *Second Pacific Coast Biennial Exhibition*, circ., Santa Barbara, CA; 1957, 58, 59: Ferus, Gallery, Los Angeles, CA; 1958: *Bay Area Invitational Exhibition*, Gump's Gallery, San Francisco, CA; *Fresh Paint, 1958*, De Young Museum, San Francisco, CA; *West Coast Artists*, circ., American Federation of Arts, NYC; 1959: *West Coast Artists,* Time Life Building, NYC; 1961: *Invitational Show*, Camino Gallery, NY; 1962: *Contemporary Paintings and Sculptures*, Riverside Museum, NY; 1963, 64, 65, 66: East Hampton Gallery, NY; Berkeley Gallery, CA; *Art Present and Future*, Englewood Armory, NJ; 1964: *New Dimensions of Lithography*, University of Southern California; 1965: *Multiple Editions*, San Francisco Museum of Art, CA; 1966: Phoenix Gallery, NY; 1967: *National Lithography Exhibition*, Florida State University; 1968: *Late Fifties at the Ferus*, Los Angeles College Museum, CA; 1970: *Invitational Group*, Albright College, Reading, PA; 1973: *A Period of Exploration*, The Oakland Museum of Art, CA; 1975: *Four Corners State Biennial*, circ., Phoenix Art Museum, AZ; 1976: *The Last Time I Saw Ferus*, New Port Harbor Art Museum, CA; 1976–77: *California Painting and Sculpture: The Modern Era*, circ., San Francisco Museum of Modern Art, CA; 1985: *Art of the San Francisco Bay Area, 1945–1980*, The Oakland Museum, CA; 1996: *San Francisco School of Abstract Expressionism*, San Francisco Museum of Modern Art, CA.

EARL CAVIS KERKAM

Earl Kerkam enjoys a unique position in American painting for his example of wholehearted devotion to the evolution of his own art concepts. Beginning with an apprenticeship in French painting and an ardent admiration for Paul Cezanne, since the 1930's he pursued his own quiet development in the subtle modeling of the figure and still life. One of the most widely respected among his artist contemporaries, he remained unknown to the art market of New York, even at his death in 1965.

A painter of enormous poetic awareness, self-directed, almost totally without direct influence, he stands as an original American artist in the best sense. Patient, unconcerned with the problems of living or material possessions, he wished only to clarify his seeing, to express his emotional sensibility through paint.

.....A small group of his friends wrote a petition to the Museum of Modern Art, New York, in July of 1965, requesting that the institution consider an exhibition of Earl Kerkam's work. Signers included Willem de Kooning, Philip Guston, Mark Rothko, George Spaventa and Esteban Vicente. They wrote: 'Kerkam in our eyes is one of the finest painters to come out of America, and as working Artists, we could afford the stimulation such an exhibition would provide us, and the younger generation who have not had the opportunity to study his work."

Gerald Norland: Essay to: Earl Kerkam Memorial Exhibition, May 13 - June 26, 1966; Washington Gallery of Modern Art, Washington, D.C.

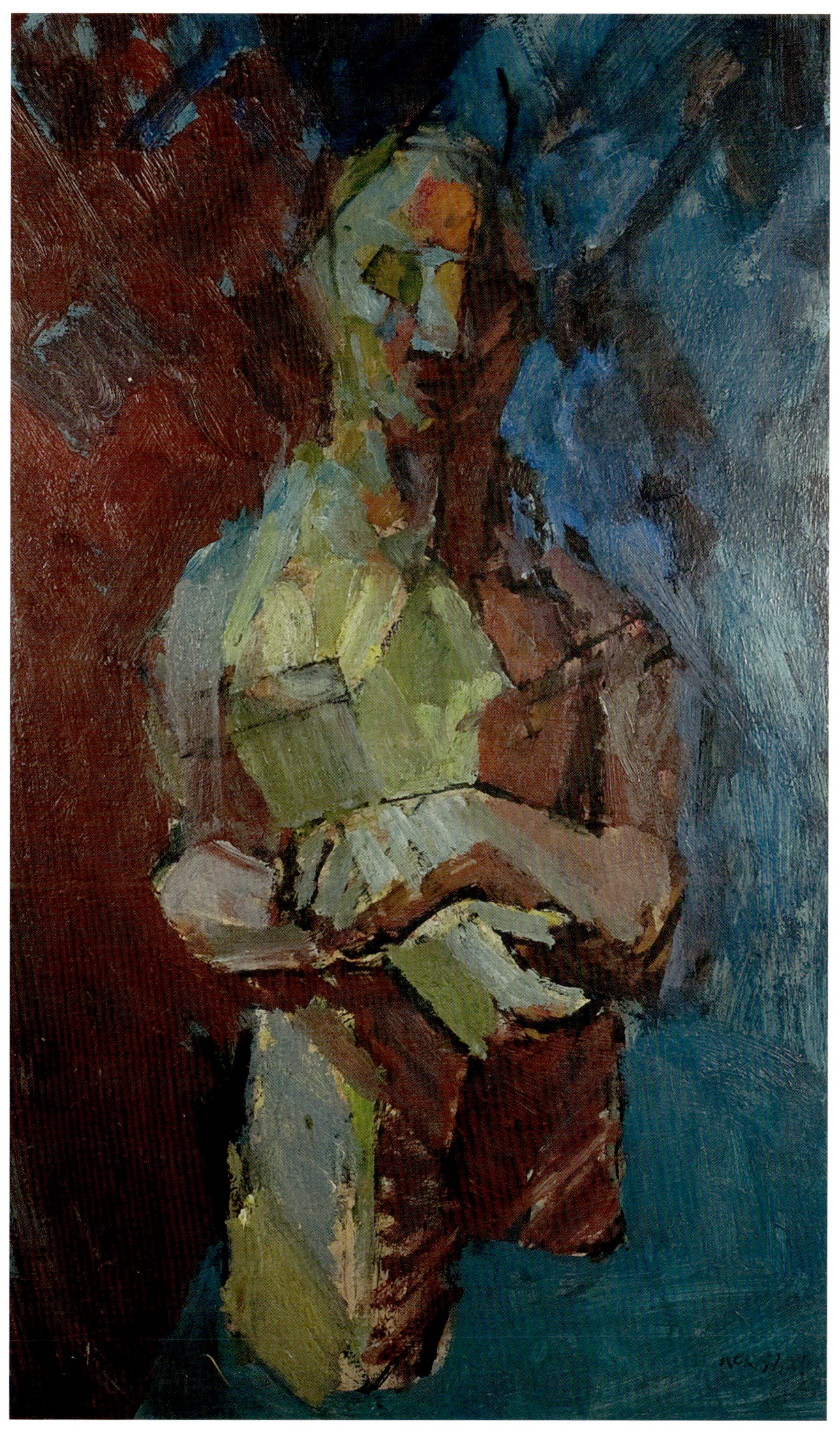

EARL KERKAM, *Torso*, 1955
Oil on masonite, 32 1/2 x 19 1/2
Private collection

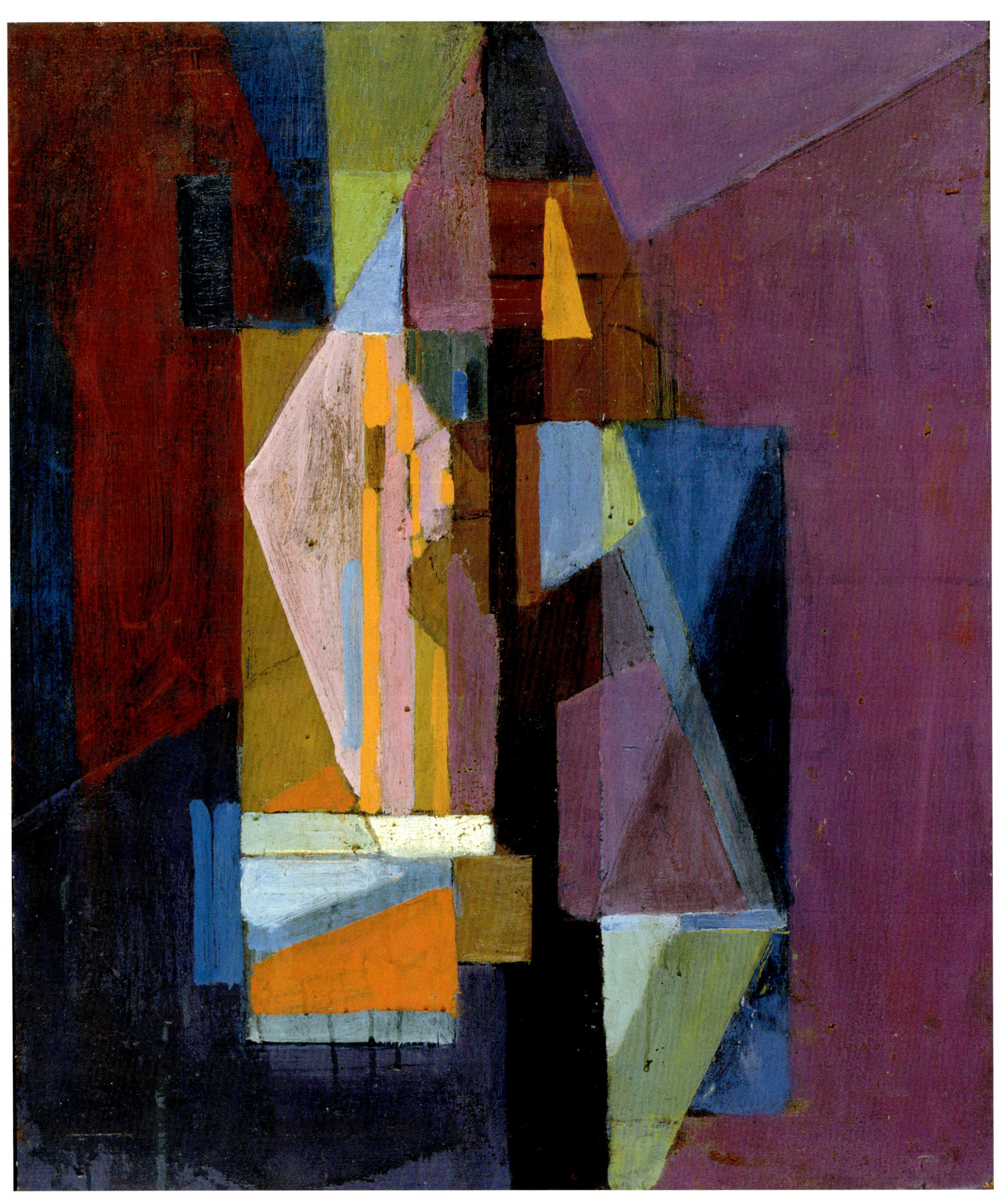

EARL KERKAM, *Head*, 1960
Oil on canvasboard, 29 3/4 x 24 3/4 in. (75.6 x 62.8 cm)
Smithsonian American Art Museum, Museum purchase, Accession number: 1978.32

EARL CAVIS KERKAM, [1891-1965]

Born October 7, 1891, the District of Columbia.
Died January 12, 1965, New York City.

Studied Rand School; Art Students League; the School of Design; at Robert Henri's men's class; the Pennsylvania Academy of Fine Arts; Institute of Art, Montreal. During World War I he was assigned as Art Editor of the official Tank Corps magazine: *Treat 'Em Rough*. He was movie poster designer at Warner Brothers Pictures. 1935

Selected Solo Exhibitions 1933(first) and the 1930s: Contemporary Arts Gallery; Babcock Gallery; J.B. Newmann Gallery; 1940, 42, 43, 44: Bonestell Gallery, NY; 1946, 48, 52, 53, 55: Charles Egan Gallery, NYC; 1947–49: Harold Wacker's Chinese Gallery; 1955, 56: Poindexter Gallery, NYC; 1960, 61, 63: World House Gallery, NYC; 1964: B.C. Holland Gallery, Chicago.

Selected Group Exhibitions 1951, 1953–57: *9th St.*, Show, the first and subsequent 5 *New York Painting and Sculpture Annuals*, Stable Gallery, NYC; 1949, 55: *Annuals and Biennials*, The Whitney Museum of American Art, NYC.

ALBERT KOTIN

OUTSIDER

At intervals
I leave my body
To go deep into a canvas
That I am painting
A painting which so often
Evokes a landscape
Not as it appears to the eye
But as if the surface
Had been peeled to permit
The turbulence of earth
To be glimpsed for a moment
By a tightly closed eye.
The shell I inhabit
Remains before the painting
Holding a brush a paint rag a
cigarette
Staring at my work from the outside
Whereas I am really deep
Deep inside
The two dimensional plane
Of painted linen
Weaving my unseen self
Into each brush stroke
Of a world
That is yet to be
Created.

THE PAINTER

Every day
He grinds up
A small piece
Of his umbilical cord
Mixes it with oil
With varnish
And with turps
To paint
A self-portrait
On a
Tightly
Stretched
Placenta.

Albert Kotin, Poems: Artist's Diary. Previously published: *American Abstract Expressionism of the 1950s; An Illustrated Survey*. New York School Press, 2000. p.190. Private collection

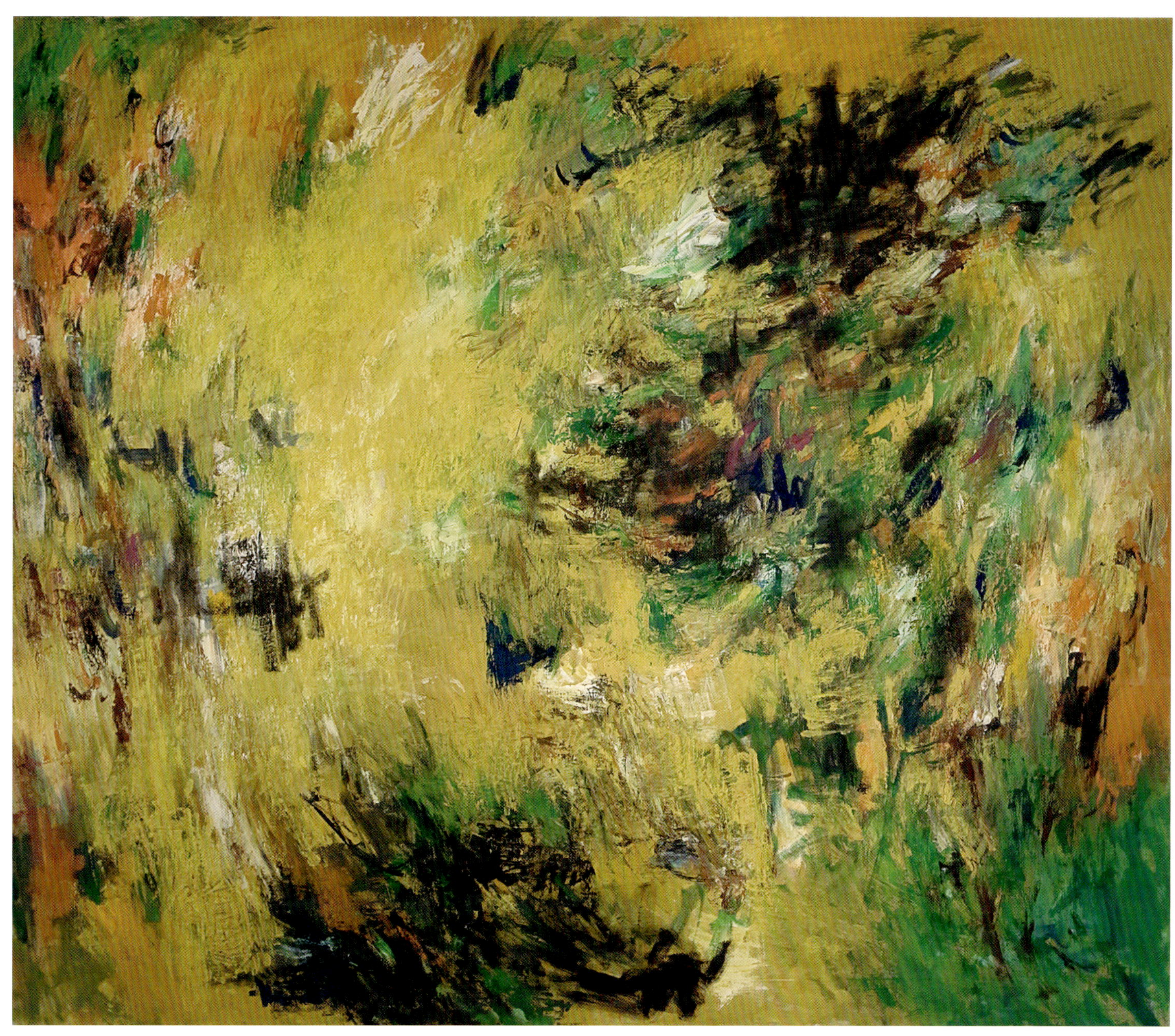

ALBERT KOTIN, *Westerly*, 1957
Oil on canvas, 69 x 79 inches
Private collection

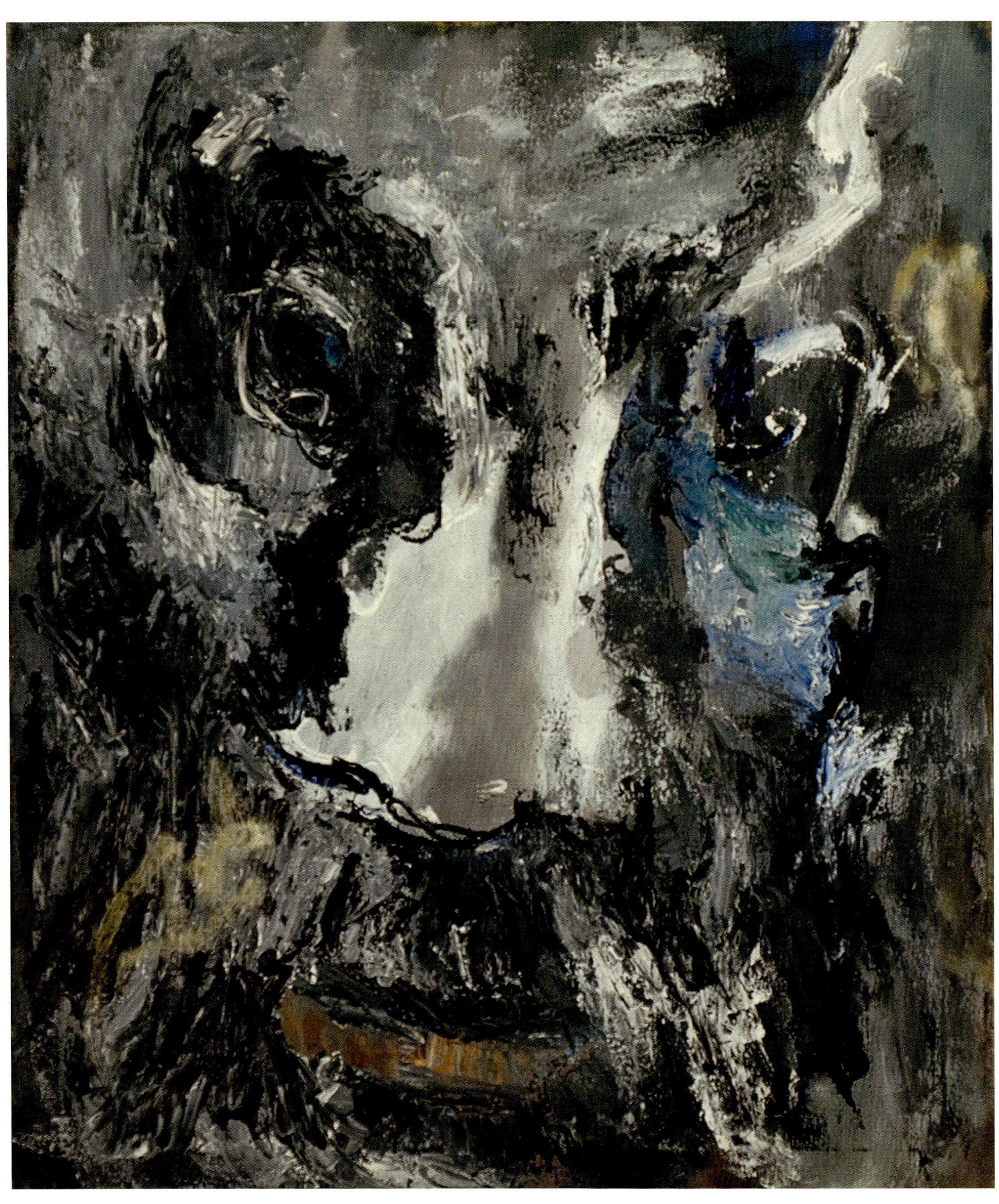

ALBERT KOTIN, *Head*, c. 1968
Oil on canvas, 29 ¾ x 36 inches
Private Collection

ALBERT KOTIN, [1907-1980]

Born August 7, 1907 in Minsk, Russia. **To USA** in 1908. **US citizen** 1923. **Died** 1980 in New York City.

Studied 1924–1929: National Academy of Design with Charles Hawthorne, Provincetown, MA; 1929-32: Academie Julian, Academie de la Grande Chaumiere, Atelier de Fresque and Colarossi, Paris; 1947–1951: Art Student League, NYC ; with Hans Hofmann in Provincetown, MA, and in New York City.

Federal Art Projects, (PWAP and WPA/FAP) 1933–34 and 1935–40;

Military Service World War II 1941–1945: US Army Engineering School.

Teaching Positions 1947-51 City College, NYC; 1952–61: Polytechnic Institute, Brooklyn, NY; 1961: Visiting Professor in Art, Southern Illinois University; 1964–65: Stout State University, Menomonie, WI; 1966–1975: Long Island University, NY.

Selected Solo Exhibitions 1951 (first) Hacker Gallery, NYC; 1958: Grand Central Moderns Gallery, NYC; 1959: Tanager Gallery, NYC; 1960: Galerie Iris Clert, Paris; Pollock Gallery, Toronto, Canada; 1964: Byron Gallery, Inc., NYC; 1968: Long Island University, Brooklyn, NY; Retrospectives 1968: *Ten Year Retrospective of Albert Kotin's Work*, Long Island University, Brooklyn, NY; 1982: *Albert Kotin, 1907–1980*, Memorial Exhibition, Barron Arts Center, Woodbridge, NJ; 1988: *Albert Kotin Retrospective: Paintings, Drawings*, Prints, Artfull Eye, Lambertville, NJ.

Selected Group Exhibitions 1935: *Exhibition of Oil Paintings*, WPA Federal Art Project, Federal Art Gallery, NYC; 1946: *First National Print Competition Exhibit*, Associated American Artists, NYC; 1947: *J&E.R. Pennell Exhibition of Prints*, Library of Congress, Washington, D.C.; 1948: *8 & 2 Exhibition*, The New School for Social Research, NYC; 1951, 1953–57: *9th St.*, Show the first and the subsequent 5 *New York Painting and Sculpture Annuals*, Stable Gallery, NYC; 1956–57: *Painters and Sculptors on 10th Street*, Tanager Gallery, NYC; 1957: *1st Spring Annual Exhibition*, March Gallery, NYC; 1958: *A to Z in American Arts*, circ., M. Knoedler & Co., NYC; Camino Gallery, NYC; 1959: *10th Street*, Contemporary Arts Museum, Houston, TX; *Annual Contemporary Painting Exhibition*, Broadway Congregational Church, NYC; 1960: *New York Artists: A Drawing Show*, Allyn Hall Gallery, Southern Illinois University, Carbondale IL; 1961: *15th Annual Art Exhibition of Contemporary Art*, Downtown Community School, NYC; 1962: *Multiples*, Graham Gallery, NYC; 1962, 67: *Faculty Exhibition*, Long Island University, Brooklyn, NY; 1963: *Invitational Show of Prints and Drawings*, The Agis Gallery, NYC; 1963–64: *Hans Hofmann and His Students*, circ. Museum of Modern Art, NYC; 1964: *Group Show of Gallery and Guest Artists,* Key Gallery, NYC; *One Hundred American Drawings*, Byron Gallery, Inc., NYC; 1965: *5 Works by 8 Faculty*, Stout State University, Menomonie, WI; 1966: New York '66: *A Collection of Drawings, Prints, and Paintings by New York Artists*, College Museum, Hampton Institute, Hampton, VA; 1971: *Homage to Tanager*: *1952–1962,* Roko Gallery, NYC; 1972: *The Witnesses*, Museum Universitario, Mexico City, Mexico; 1976: *118 Artists*, Landmark Gallery, Inc., NYC; 1987: *Abstract Expressionist Tendencies 1955–1965*, Princeton Gallery of Fine Art, Princeton, NJ; 1994: *Reclaiming Artists of the New York School. Toward a More Inclusive View of the 1950s,* Baruch College City University, NYC; *New York-Provincetown: A 50s Connection*, Provincetown Art Association and Museum, MA; 1995: *Early works: Albert Kotin, Ibram Lassaw, Kyle Morris*, Anita Shapolsky Gallery, NYC; 1995–96: *The Fifties*, Anita Shapolsky Gallery, NYC.

LEE KRASNER

Painting, for me, when it really 'happens' is as miraculous as any natural phenomenon–as, say, a lettuce leaf. By 'happens,' I mean the painting in which the inner aspect of man and his outer aspects interlock. One could go on forever as to whether the paint should be thick or thin, whether to paint the woman or the square, hard-edge or soft, but after a while such questions become a bore. They are merely problems in aesthetics, having only to do with the outer man. But the painting I have in mind, painting in which inner and outer are inseparable, transcends technique, transcends subject and moves into the realm of the inevitable–then you have the lettuce leaf.

Lee Krasner, Statement: *Lee Krasner: A Retrospective*, Barbara Rose, The Museum of Fine Arts, Houston, and the Museum of Modern Art, New York, 1983. Catalogue, p. 134.

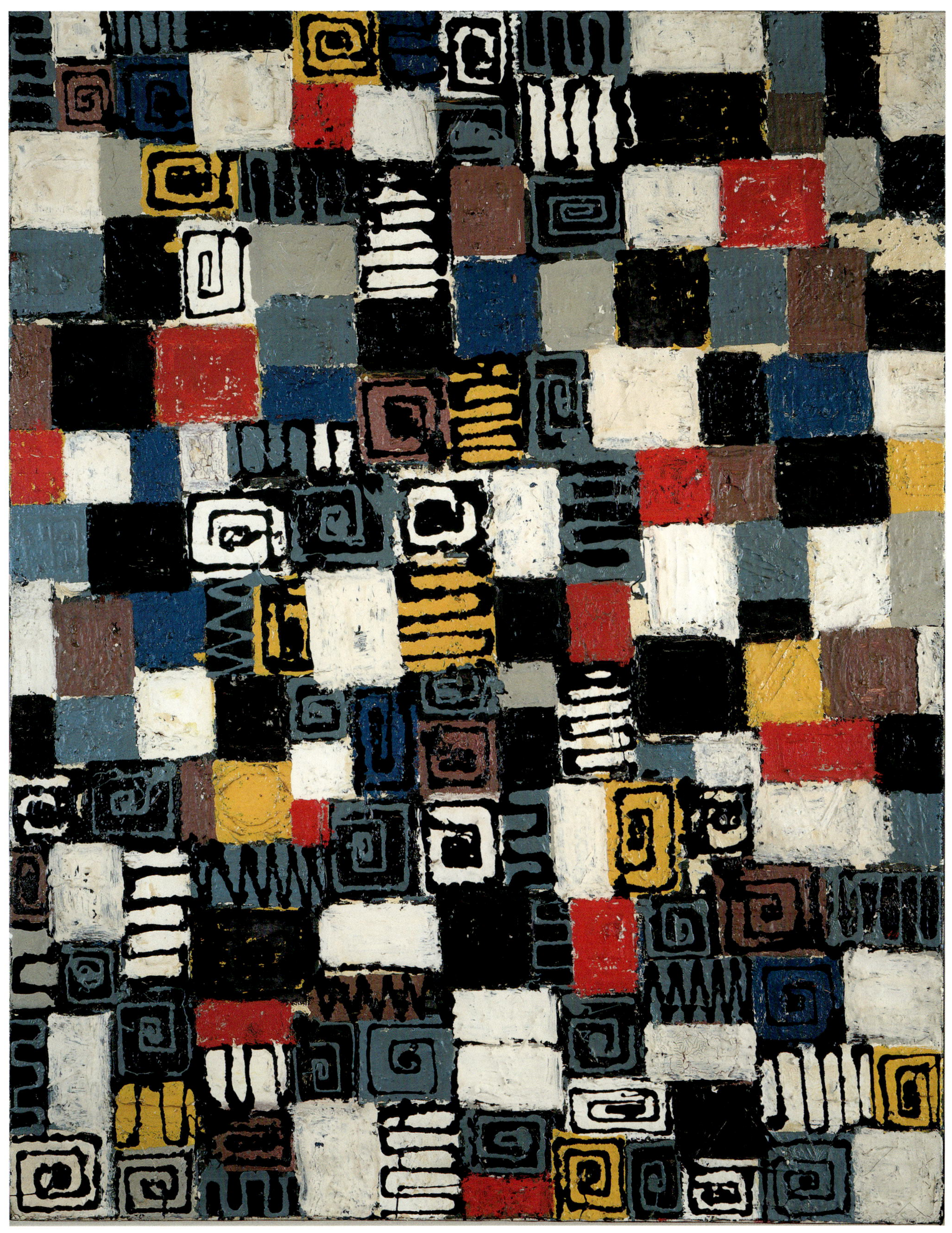

LEE KRASNER, *Untitled*, 1949
Oil on canvas, 38 x 30 inches (96.5 x 76.2 cm)
Photograph Courtesy Robert Miller Gallery, New York (KRAS–0037)

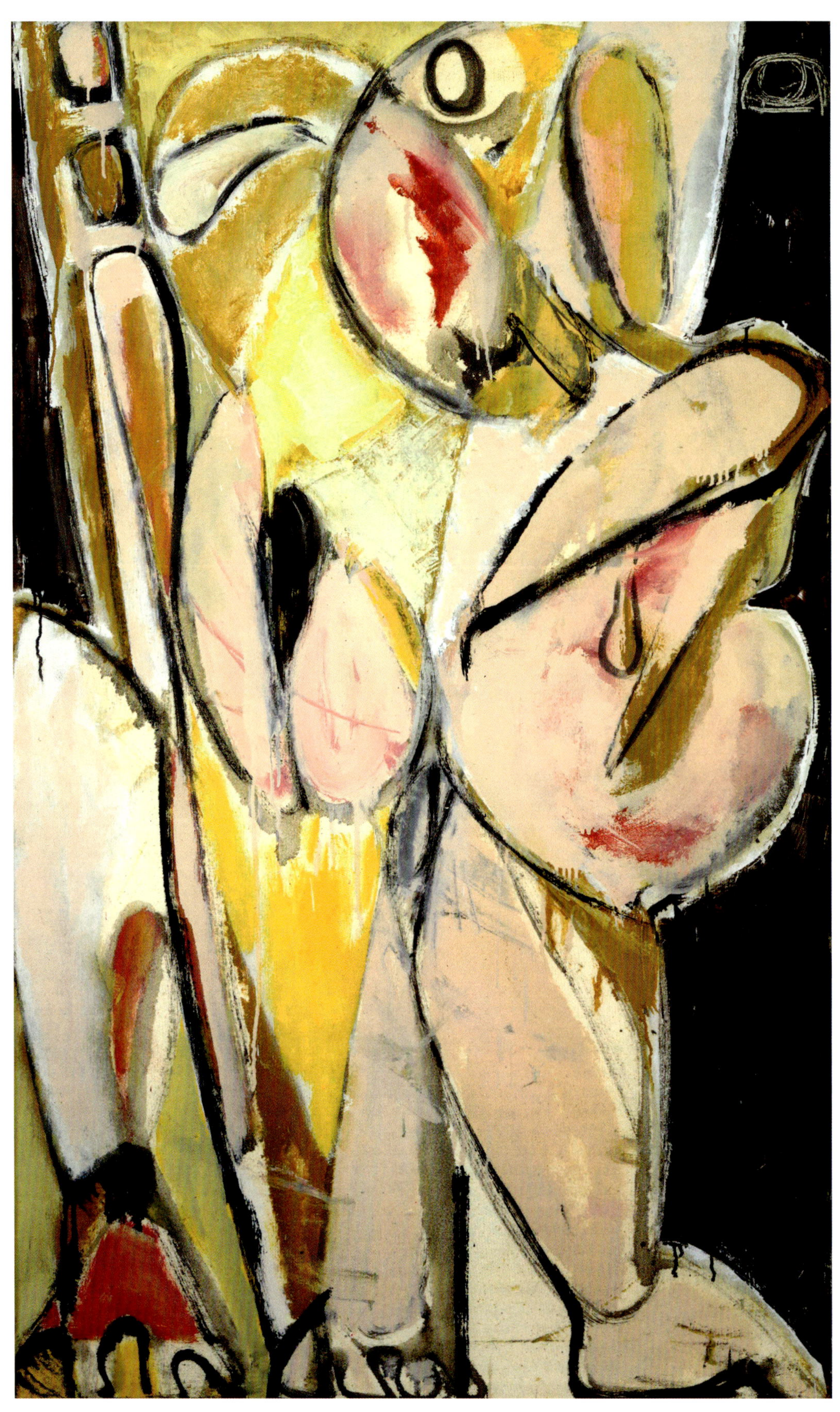

LEE KRASNER, *Prophecy*, 1956
Oil on cotton duck, 58 1/8 x 34 inches

LEE KRASNER, [1908-1984]

Born October 27, 1908 in Brooklyn, NY.
Died 1984, New York, NY.

Studied 1922–25: Washington Irving High School, Manhattan; 1926–1929: Women's Art School of Cooper Union; 1928: Art Students League, NYC; 1929–1932: National Academy of Design; 1933: City College and Greenwich House; 1937–1940: Hans Hofmann School of Fine Art.

Federal Art Projects Public Works of Art Project

(PWAP), 1934

WPA/FAP 1935–1941: Mural Division.

Selected Solo Exhibitions 1951:(first) *Paintings 1951, Lee Krasner*, Betty Parsons Gallery, NYC; 1954: *The House of Books and Music*, East Hampton; 1955: Stable Gallery, NY; 1958: *Lee Krasner, Recent Paintings*, Martha Jackson Gallery, NY; 1959: *Lee Krasner, Paintings 1947–59,* Signa Gallery, East Hampton, NY; 1960, 62; Howard Wise Gallery, NY; 1965: *Lee Krasner, Paintings , Drawings and Collages*, Whitechapel Art Gallery, London, circ.; 1967: University of Alabama, Tuscaloosa; 1968, 69, 73, 75: Marlborough Gallery, NY; 1974: Miami-Dade Community College, circ., Miami, FL; 1975: *Lee Krasner: Collages and Works on Paper, 1933–1974*, Corcoran Gallery of Art, Washington, D.C., circ.; 1977, 79, 81: Pace Gallery, NY; Susanne Hilberry Gallery, Birmingham , MI; 1978, 81: Janie C. Lee Gallery, Houston, TX; 1982: *The Late Fifties*, Robert Miller Gallery, NY; 1983: *Lee Krasner: A Retrospective*, The Museum of Fine Arts, Houston, and the Museum of Modern Art, New York.

Selected Group Exhibitions 1937: *Pink Slips over Culture*, Artists Union and Citizens Committee; 1940, 41, 43: *First Annual Exhibition of the American Modern Artists, Fifth- and Seventh Annual Exhibition of the American Abstract Artists*, Riverside Museum, NY; 1944: *Abstract and Surrealist Art in America*, Mortimer Brandt Gallery, NY; 1948: *The Modern Home Comes Alive-1948–49*, Bertha Schaefer Gallery, NYC; 1949: *Man and Wife*, Sidney Janis Gallery, NY; 1950, 53, 64, 70, 72, 73, 74: Guild Hall, East Hampton, NY; 1951, 55, 56, 57: *9th St.*, Show, the first and subsequent 3 *New York Painting and Sculpture Annuals*, Stable Gallery, NYC; 1955: *Pacific Coast Art*, circ., United States Representation at the III Biennial of Sao Paulo, Brazil; 1956: *Art in the 20th Century*, San Francisco Museum of Modern Art, CA; 1958: *Three: Walter Kuhlman, Clare Falkenstein, James Budd Dixon*, San Francisco Museum of Modern Art, CA; *Fresh Paint*, Stanford Art Gallery, Palo Alto, CA; *American Painting*, Virginia Museum of Art; 1956, 60: California Palace of the Legion of Honor, San Francisco, CA; *Period of Exploration*, Oakland Museum, CA; 1976: *Painting and Sculpture in California: The Modern Era*, circ., San Francisco Museum of Modern Art, CA; 1978: *Period of Exploration: 1945–50*, Oakland Museum, CA; 1983: *A Survey of Three Decades on Bay Area Painting,* Nelson Gallery, University of California, Davis, CA; 1996: *The San Francisco School of Abstract Expressionism*, circ., Laguna Art Museum, Laguna Beach, CA; 2001: *The Stamp of Impulse*, Worcester Art Museum, MA; *Pioneers of the 20th Century*, Robert Green Fine Art, Mill Valley, CA; 2002: *San Francisco Abstract Expressionism 1948–62*, Hacett–Freedman, Gallery, San Francisco, CA.

IRVING KRIESBERG

Technically my paintings are depictions with a fluid focal point. The objects in them are shown not as taken from a fixed point in space nor at a single instant of time. Traditionally we expect a picture to show a scene taken a given point in space and time. How can a single fixed depiction impart many points of view and many moments of time? Well, how can a depiction on a flat surface impart a sense of depth and space? It can, it does. We daily see such pictures: we look at a flat piece of paper, we see a spacious vista, and we sense nothing illogical. The idea is contradictory, but it works. It works because we want it to.

The medieval man saw his icon simply as it was. Of course it symbolized something else, but his Madonna had little optical reference to a specific woman. The Renaissance man saw his Madonna as a woman: what the artist painted blue was not only a symbol, it was the depiction of a robe, a real garment a real person might wear. Together the artist and the observer altered the meaning of the colored panel: from being a symbolic object it became also a depiction of natural objects. The optical means employed were arbitrary conventions but they gave to painting an unsurpassed richness and scope. We are still within this tradition. We admire medieval art and borrow from it, but we still seek to depict natural objects with all the richness and vitality we perceive in them. If a flat surface can show the depth and space of nature then a single fixed surface can show the change and motion of nature. I see that nature is motion and change and that is what I paint. True, it is illogical, but then art is illogical. How can patches of color transmit to one man the passions felt by another? It is impossible. It is utterly marvelous.

Irving Kriesberg, Statement: From 15 americans, The museum of modern art, new york, edited by Dorothy C. Miller. With Statements by the artists and others. p. 36

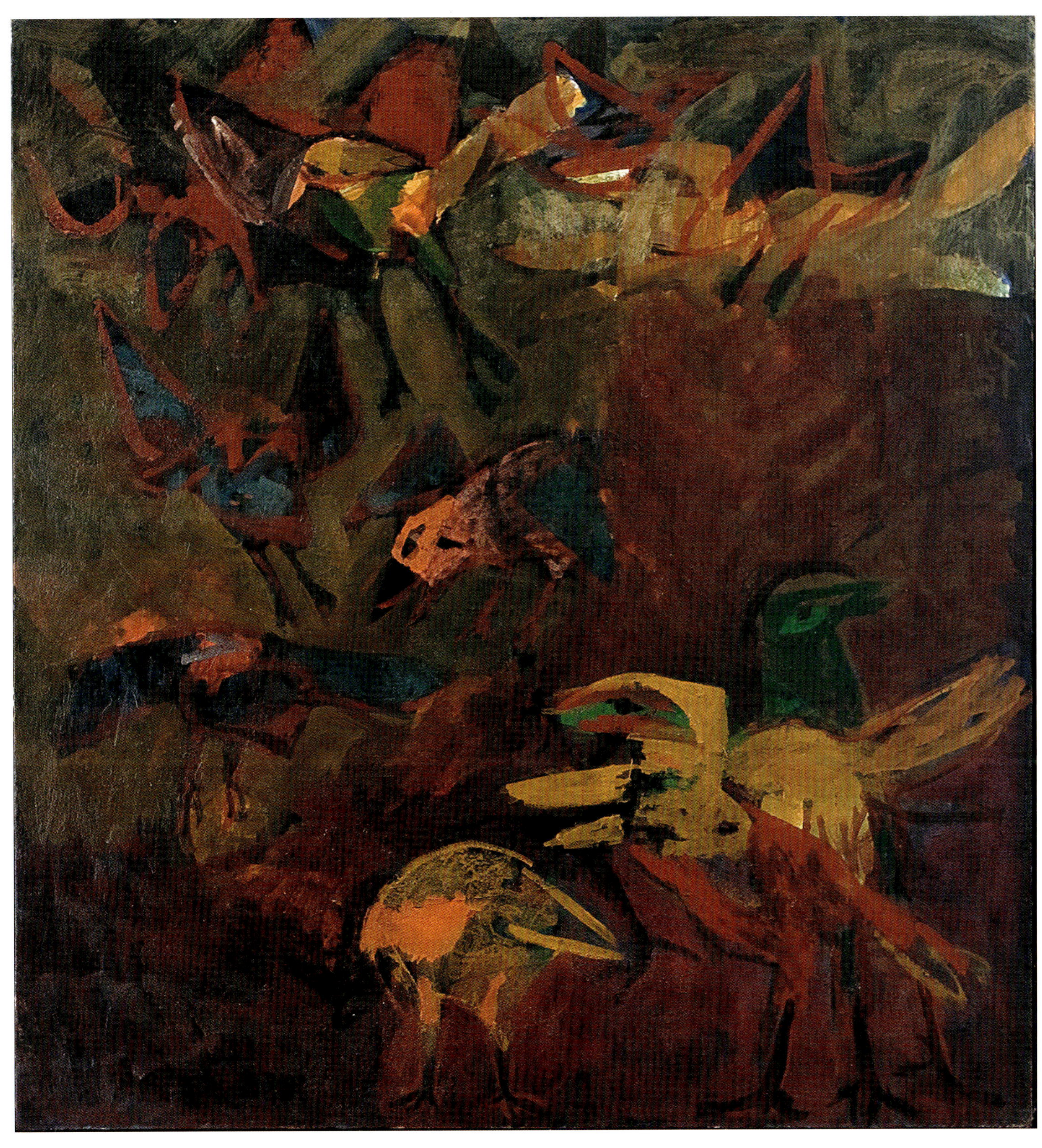

IRVING KRIESBERG, *Birds Alighting*, 1951
Tempera on board, 32 ¾ x 30 inches
Private collection
© Irving Kriesberg

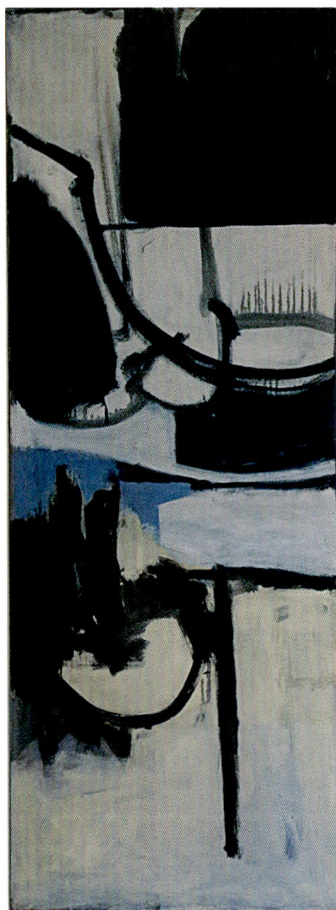
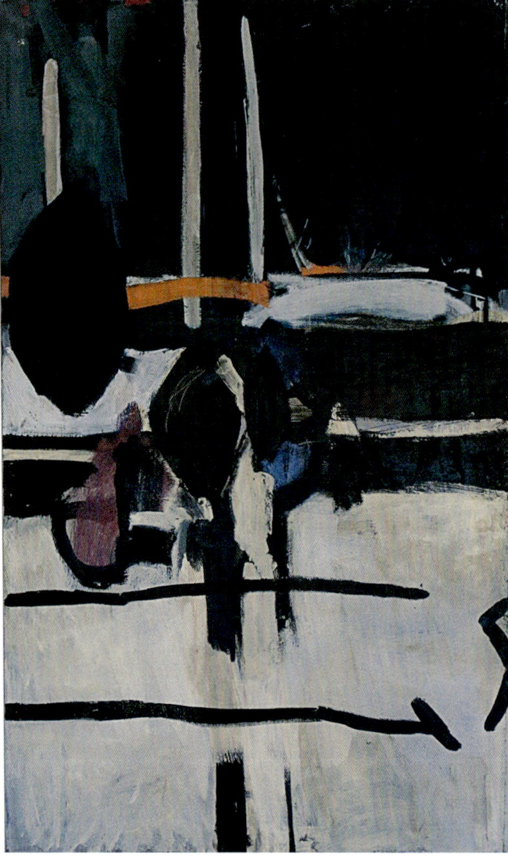
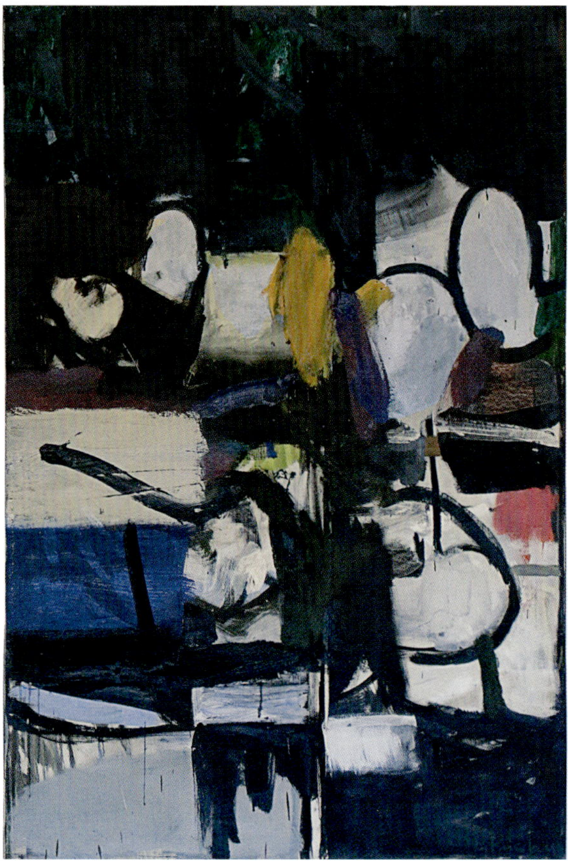

IRVING KRIESBERG, *Trumpets (Triptych)*, 1960
Oil on canvas, H: 50 1/4 inches; panels width: 18 1/2 in., 30 in., 32 1/2 in.; separation between panels: 1/4 in.
Collection of Irving Kriesberg

IRVING KRIESBERG, [1919-]

Born March 13, 1919

Studied 1941: Chicago Art Institute School, BFA; 1941–1944: Escuela Nacional de Artes Plasticas, Mexico City; 1972: New York University, MA (cinema).

Teaching Positions 1955–1961: Parsons School of Design, NYC; 1961–1972: Prat Institute; 1962–1969: Yale University, New Haven, CT; 1969–1972: City University of New York; 1972–1976: State University New York; 1977, 78: Columbia University, NYC.

Selected Solo Exhibitions 1946: Curt Valentine Gallery, NYC; The Art Institute of Chicago, IL; 1953: Museum of Modern Art, NYC; 1954: St. Louis Art Museum, St. Louis, MO; The Detroit Institute of Arts, Detroit, MI; 1962: Graham Gallery, NYC; 1966: Kumar Gallery, Delhi, India; 1967: Yale University, New Haven CT; 1978, 80, 82: Terry Dintenfass, Inc., NYC; 1979: Fairweather–Hardin Gallery, Chicago, IL; 1980, 81: Brandeis University, Waltham, MA; 1980: Everson Museum of Art, Syracuse, NY; Galerie Elizabeth, Chicago, IL; 1981: Fiedler Gallery, Washington, D.C.; 1981, 83: Jack Gallery, NYC; 1982: Washington University St. Louis, MO; Zenith Gallery, Pittsburgh, PA; 1985, 87: Graham Modern Gallery, NYC; 1990: Scheele Gallery, Cleveland, OH; 1992, 94: Katherina Rich Perlow Gallery, NYC; 1996, 2005: Peter Findlay Gallery, NYC; 2005: Lori Bookstein Fine Art, NYC. Retrospective: 1962: Jewish Museum, NYC.

Selected Group Exhibitions 1946: The Art Institute of Chicago, IL; 1952: *New Talent*, Museum of Modern Art, NYC; *Fifteen Americans*, circ., Museum of Modern Art, NYC; 1953: The Detroit Institute of Arts, Detroit, MI; 1954: St. Louis Art Museum, St. Louis, MO; 1968: *Directions I: Options*, circ., Milwaukee Art Center, Milwaukee, WI; 1972: *Ten Independents*, Solomon R. Guggenheim Museum, NYC.

ALFRED LESLIE

I had not set a course to become a realist artist or a figurative painter. But there was a point at which I realized that if my work was to develop and evolve, and if I was to mature as an artist, the figurative ideas could not be ignored, even though following them could seem to imply that I would be turning my back on the twentieth century, turning my back on my abstract achievement. I was not going to simply walk away from everything that I had done before - and I didn't. But I was willing to leave myself open to all the seemingly contradictory impulses that existed in my work, to re-examine where I was as an artist.

Alfred Leslie, Statement; *The evolution of the Grisailles*, from: Alfred Leslie:
The Grisaille paintings, 1962-1967 an interview with Barbara Flynn 1991, p. 55.

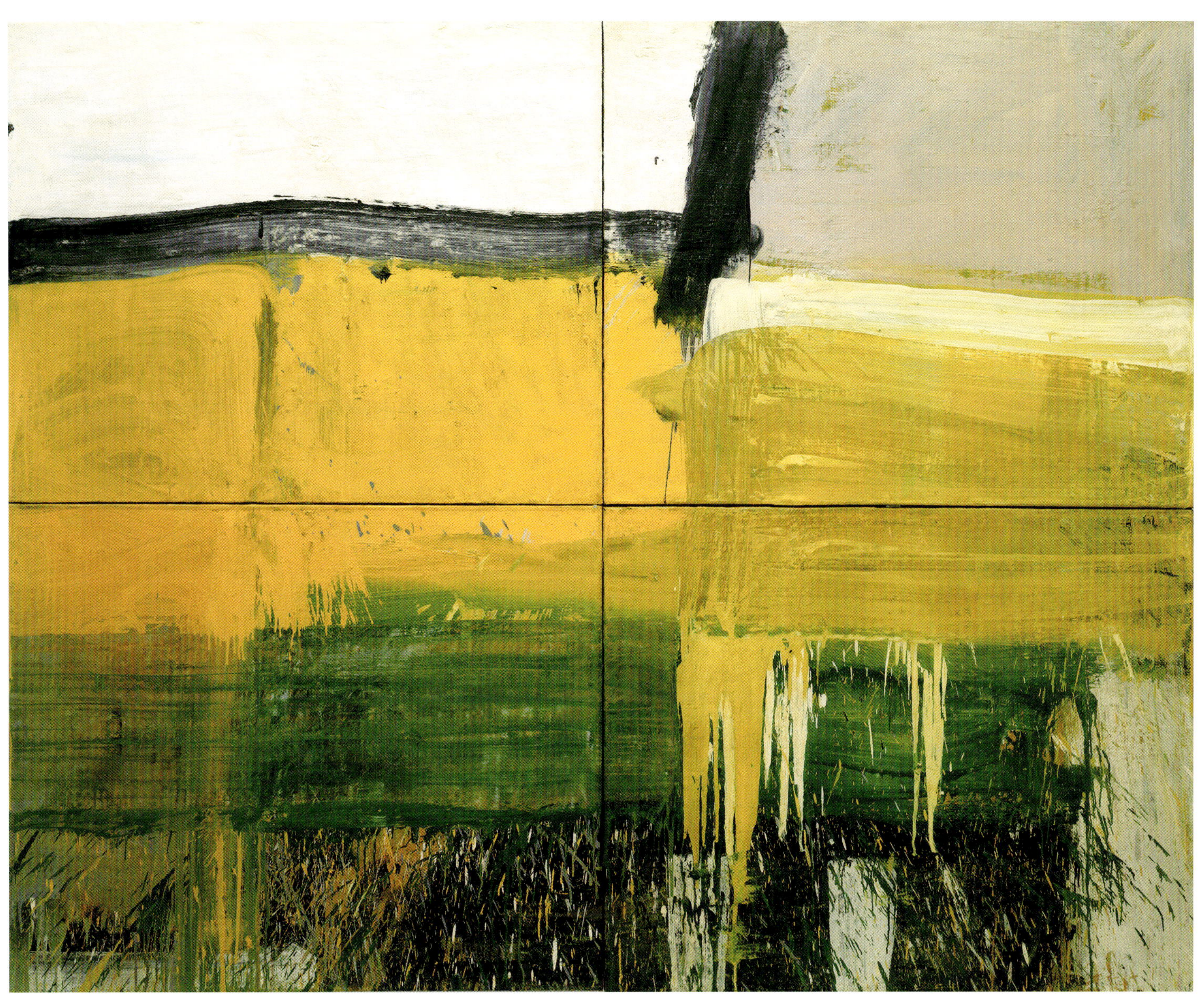

ALFRED LESLIE, *Ornette Coleman*, 1956
Oil on linen, 82 x 100 inches, (208.3 x 254 cm)

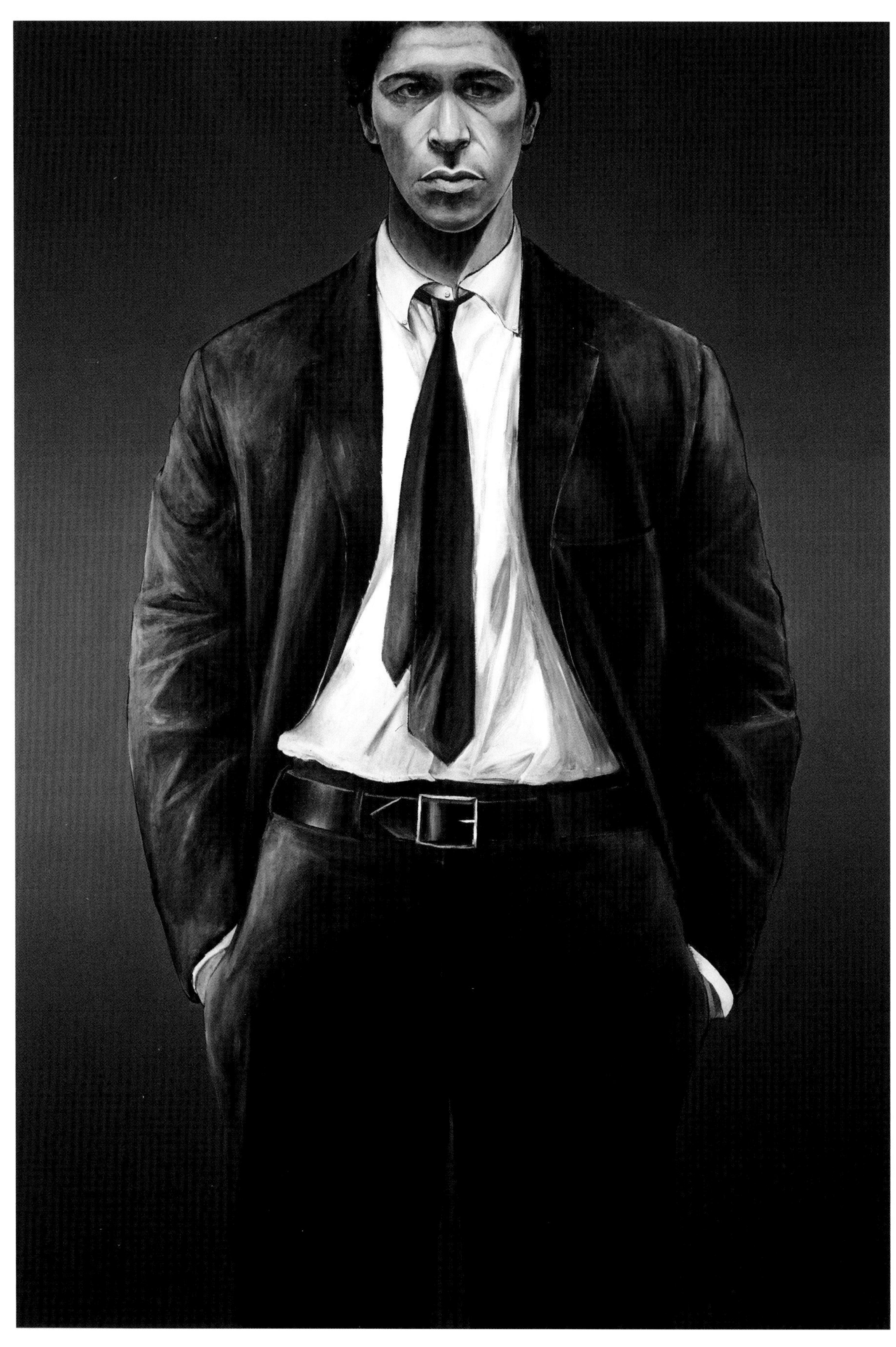

ALFRED LESLIE, *Alfred Leslie*, 1964
Oil on linen, 108 x 72 inches, (274.3 x 182.9 cm)
 Courtesy of Ameringer & Yohe Fine Art, New York.

ALFRED LESLIE, [1927-]

Born October 29, 1927, New York City.

Studied with Tony Smith, William Baziotes, Hale Woodruff, John McPherson in New York University, NYC, 1956-57; also Pratt Institute; and Art Students League, NYC.

Military Service in World War II 1945-46: US Coast Guard.

Teaching Positions 1956–57: Great Neck (N.Y.) Adult Education Program; 1964: San Francisco Art Institute, summer.

Selected One-man Exhibitions (first) 1951 also 1952, 53, 54, 57: Tibor de Nagy Gallery, NYC; 1959, 60: Martha Jackson Gallery, NYC; 1960: Holland-Goldowsky Gallery, Chicago, IL; 1968, 69, 71: Noah Goldowsky; 1975, 78: Allan Frumkin Gallery, NYC; 1977: Allan Frumkin Gallery, Chicago; Youngstown State University; 1978: University of Connecticut; 1986: Texas Gallery, Houston; 1987: Hill Gallery, Birmingham, MI; Compass Rose Gallery, Chicago; Krygier/Landau Gallery, Los Angeles, CA; 1988: The College of Saint Rose, Albany; Boca Raton; 1991, 92: Flynn Gallery, NYC; 1991: St. Louis Art Museum, St. Louis, MO. Retrospective: 1991: University of Hartford, CT; 2007: Ameringer & Yohe Fine Art, NYC.

Selected Group Exhibitions 1951, 53, 55, 56, 57: *9th St*., Show, the first and subsequent 4 *New York Painting and Sculpture Annual*, Stable Gallery, NYC; 1958: Festival of Two Worlds, Spoleto, Italy; *Young Americans*, Musee de'Art Moderne de la Ville de Paris, France; 1959: V São Paulo Biennial; 1960: *Sixty American Painters, 1960*, Walker Art Center, Minneapolis, MN; 1961: Carnegie Institute of Technology, Washington, DC; *Four Americans*, National Museum, Stockholm, Sweden; 1961, 65, 67, 68, 71, 72, 73: *Annuals and Biennials*, Whitney Museum of American Art NYC; 1963: *4 Americans*, Kunsthalle, Basel; 1967: *Recent Figurative Art*, Bennington College, NY; *In Memory of My Feelings: Frank O'Hara*, Museum of Modern Art, NY; 1970: *22 Realists*, Whitney Museum of American Art, NY; 1971: *Contemporary Views of Man*, MIT; 1973: *American Drawings: 1963–1973*, Whitney Museum of American Art; 1974: *The Figure in Recent American Painting*, St. John's University; 1975: *Three Centuries of the American Nude*, New York Cultural Center; *The Figure as Form: American Painting 1930–1975*, Museum of Fine Art, St. Petersburg, FL; 2007: Ameringer & Yohe Fine Art, NYC; 1976: *Venice Biennial; America '76*, circ., US Department of the Interior; 1977: *41st Annual Midyear Show*, Butler Institute of American Art, Youngstown, OH; *Perception of the Spirit in the 20th Century American Art*, Indianapolis Museum of Art; *8 Contemporary American Realists*, Pennsylvania Academy of the Fine Arts, PA; 1980: *The Fifties*, Hirshhorn Museum and Sculpture Garden Smithsonian Institution, Washington, DC; *The Figurative Tradition*, Whitney Museum of American Art, NYC; *Realism/ Photorealism*, Philbrook Art Center, Tulsa, OK; 1981: *Real, Really Real, Super Real*, San Antonio Museum of art, San Antonio, TX; *Contemporary American Realism Since 1960*, Pennsylvania Academy of the Fine Arts, PA; *Amrikanische Malerei, 1930–1980*, Haus der Kunst, Munich; 1983: *American still Life, 1945– 1983*, circ., Contemporary Art Museum, Houston, TX; 1984: *Action/Precision,* circ., Newport Harbor Art Museum, Newport Beach, CA.

CONRAD MARCA-RELLI

Collage forces you to think and clarify your ideas, with regard to both space and volumes. This discipline obliges me to think in terms of forms, outlines, real and imagined spaces, so as not to fall into the temptation of thinking that nature is a reality.

Conrad Marca-Relli, Statement: From Marca-Relli, by Daniel Giralt-Miracle. Published by Ediciones Poligrafa, S.A., 1976, p.25.

...I recall having read one of Picassos' many statements. He had said 'I do not seek, I find.' I had thought a lot about this. I came to the conclusion, that for me the pure joy of painting was in the 'seeking', and not in the 'finding'.

Painting to me was a problem that had a thousand possible solutions. Each painting represented one of the possible solutions. That is why, it did not matter whether the problem was figurative, abstract, or other. Finding the solution is what intrigued me. In a sense the painting was a by–product of the search. It only came to be because of the search, and once I found a solution, I moved on to a different problem. Perhaps what made my work recognizable was the search, and what gave my work a cohesiveness, in spite of different problems was the act of the search that was constant.

Conrad Marca-Relli, Statement: From manuscript: I remember when..., An autobiographical commentary on the abstract expressionist era and the subsequent years, by Conrad Marca–Relli. Manuscript provided by the artist to the editor in 1996.

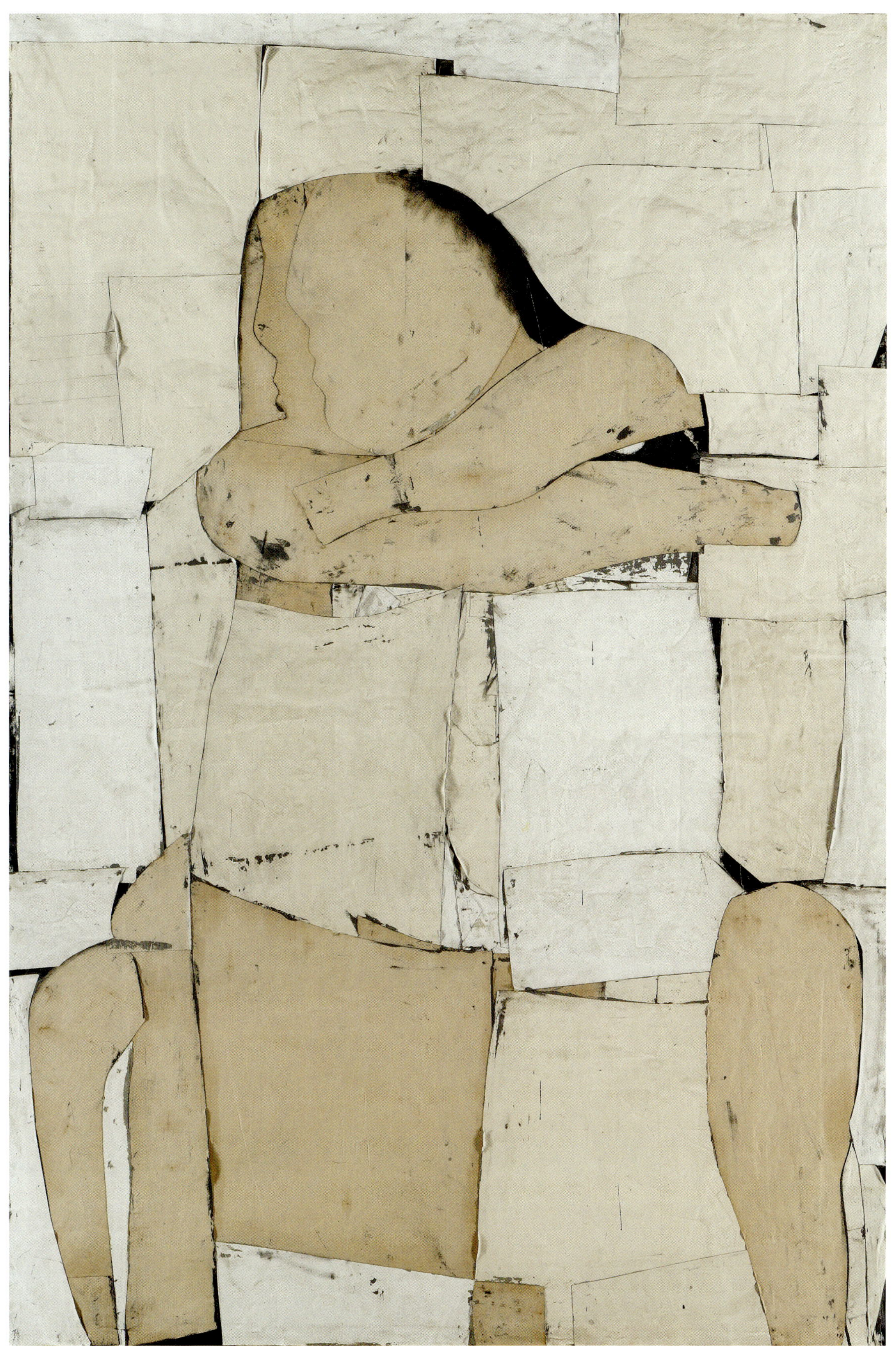

CONRAD MARCA-RELLI, *Seated Figure*, 1953-54
Oil and canvas on linen. 186.1 x 123.2 cm (73 1/4 x 48 1/2 in.)
Mr. and Mrs. Frank G. Logan Purchase Prize Fund, 1954.271, The Art Institute of Chicago.

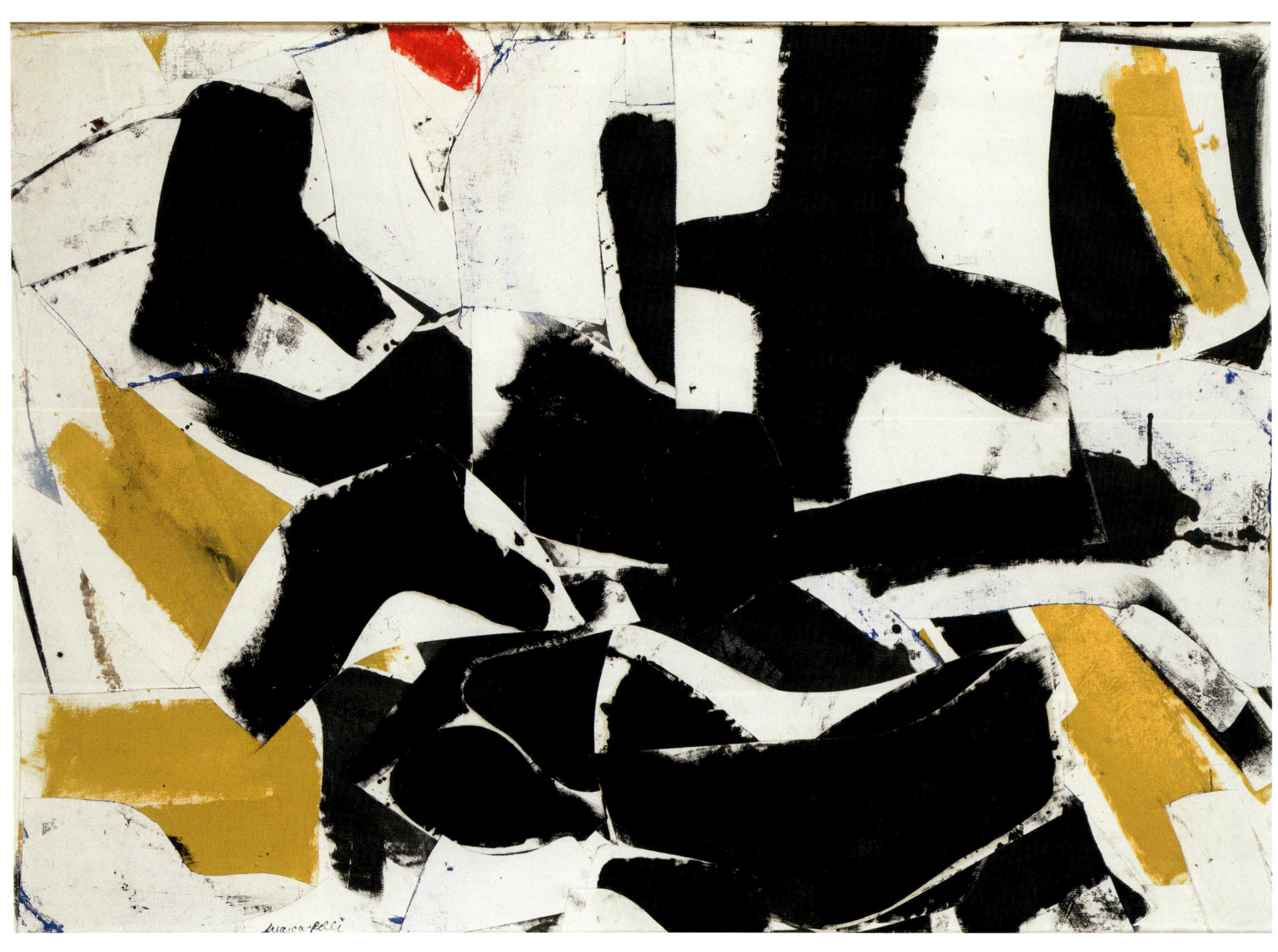

CONRAD MARCA-RELLI, *Junction*, 1958
Collage of painted canvas, 56 x 77 ½ in. (142.24 x 196.85 cm)
Whitney Museum of American Art, New York;
purchase with funds from the Friends of the Whitney Museum of American Art, 59.11

CONRAD MARCA-RELLI, [1913-2000]

Born June 5, 1913, Boston. 1926 settled in New York.
Died August 29, 2000, Parma, Italy.

Studied 1930: Cooper Union. Mostly self taught.

Federal Art Project WPA 1935–1938: Easel and mural painting.

Military Service in World War II 1941–45: US Army.

Teaching Positions 1954-55, 1959-60: Yale University; 1958: University of California, Berkeley; 1966: New College, Sarasota, FL.

Selected Solo Exhibitions 1947, 49, 51: Niveau Gallery, New York; 1953, 55, 56, 58: Stable Gallery, NYC; 1959, 60, 61, 62, 63, 64: Kootz Gallery, NYC; 1967: *Retrospective Exhibition*, Whitney Museum of American Art, NYC; Rose Art Museum, Brandeis University, Waltham, MA, also in 1968; 1968: Albright-Knox Members Gallery, Buffalo, NY; 1970, 75, 79: Marlborough Gallery, NY; Norton Gallery, West Palm Beach, FL; 1971, 78, 79: Fort Lauderdale Museum of Art, CA; Lowe Art Museum, University of Miami, FL; 1974: Marlborough Galeria, Zurich; 1980: *Retrospective*, Ringling Museum, Sarasota, FL; 1985, 86, 87, 89, 91: Marisa del Re Gallery, NYC; 2001: *Conrad Marca-Relli: Canvas Collages*, Joan T. Washburn Gallery, NYC.

Selected Group Exhibitions 1951, 53, 54, 55, 56, 57: The *9th St.* Show and 5 *New York Painting and Sculpture Annuals*, Stable Gallery, NYC; 1953, 55, 56, 57, 59, 61, 63, 64, 65, 66, 67, 69: *Annuals and Biennials*, The Whitney Museum of American Art NYC; 1954, 61, 63: *Annuals*, The Art Institute of Chicago IL; 1955, 58, 61, 64, 68: Carnegie Institute of Technology, Washington, DC; 1959: *Documenta II*, Kassel, Germany, organized by The Museum of Modern Art, NYC; 1960: *60 American Painters*, Walker Art Center, Minneapolis, MN; 1961: *Abstract Expressionists and Imagists*, The Solomon R. Guggenheim Museum, NYC; *Contemporary American Painting and Sculpture*, Krannert Art Museum, University of Illinois, Urbana; 1961–62: *The Art of Assemblage*, circ., Museum of Modern Art, NYC; 1962: *Art Since 1950*, Seattle, World's Fair; 1964: *Between the Fairs, 25 Years of American Art, 1939–1964*, The Whitney Museum of American Art, NYC; 1967: *White House Rotating Exhibition*, Smithsonian Institution, Washington, D.C.; 1968–69: *American Painting, the 1950s*, American Federation of Arts, NYC; 1947–1951: Art Students League, NYC ; 1990: *East Hampton Avant-Garde, A Salute to the Signa Gallery*, Guild Hall Museum, East Hampton, NY; 1994: *Reclaiming Artists of the New York School. Toward a more inclusive view of the 1950s*, Baruch College, City University, NYC.

EZIO MARTINELLI

I see the artist who exists at this moment as rather a small object in an enormous universe whose role is one of making a humble contribution to the mainstream of cultural flow. This means that he respects and adores and venerates as the Chinese did that which is old and he minimizes his own position and tries to contribute however large or small may be the contribution. For myself I venerate all of that which I am forced to call, for the sake of clarity, the past, my own Western Heritage and the even older and brilliant past of the Far East and near East and their multiple cultures. In this way I feel I pay homage to the Titan's, both anonymous and known... I feel awed by the phenomena of nature as my eyes perceive it and my wish would be to transpose some of this awe into my work.

Ezio Martinelli, 1952

Ezio Martinelli, Statement: Provided by Robert Henry Adams Fine Art, Inc. to the editor, November 4, 2008.

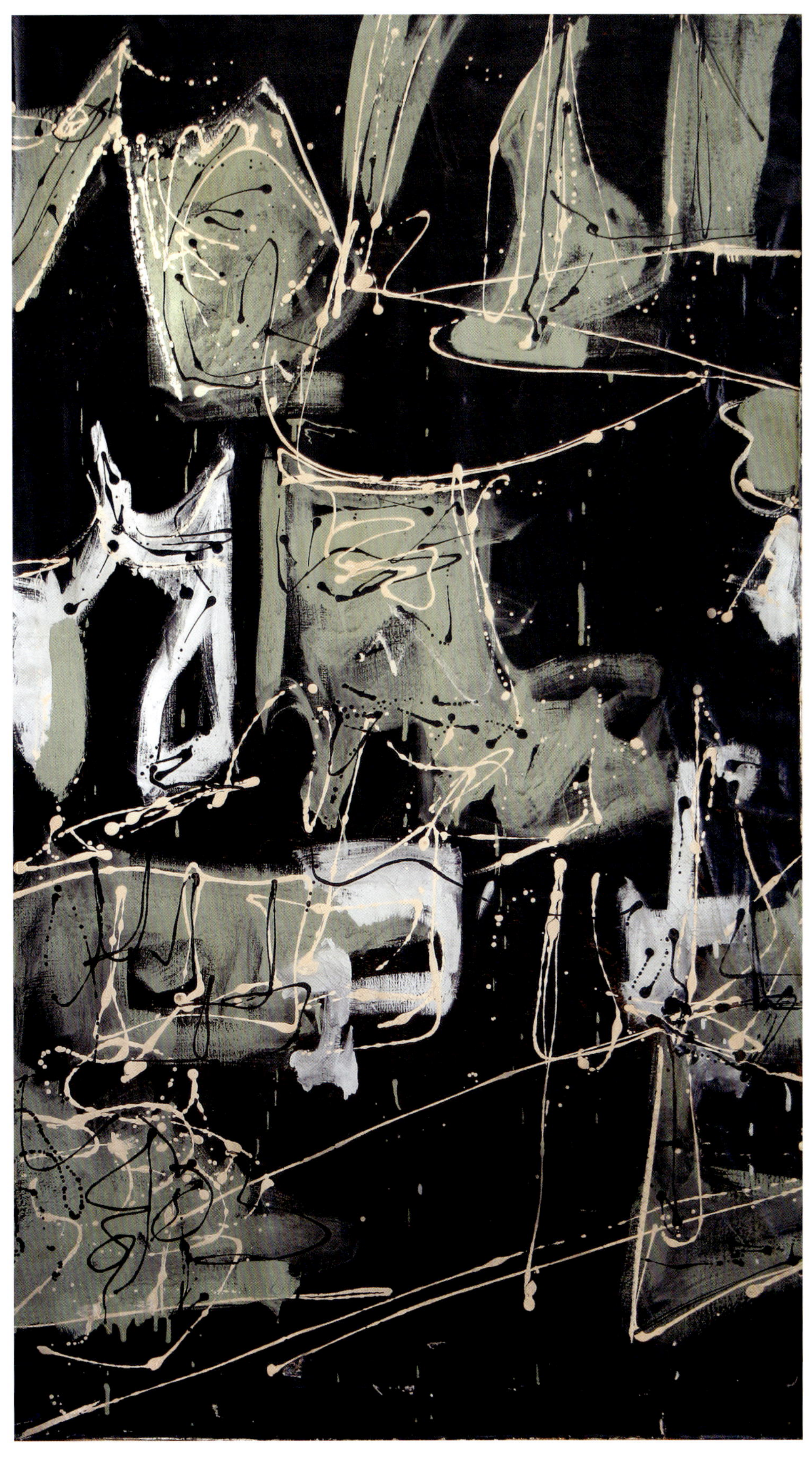

EZIO MARTINELLI, *Untitled (Abstraction)*, 1949
Oil on canvas, 72 x 40 inches
Courtesy of Robert Henry Adams Fine Art, Inc., Chicago, IL

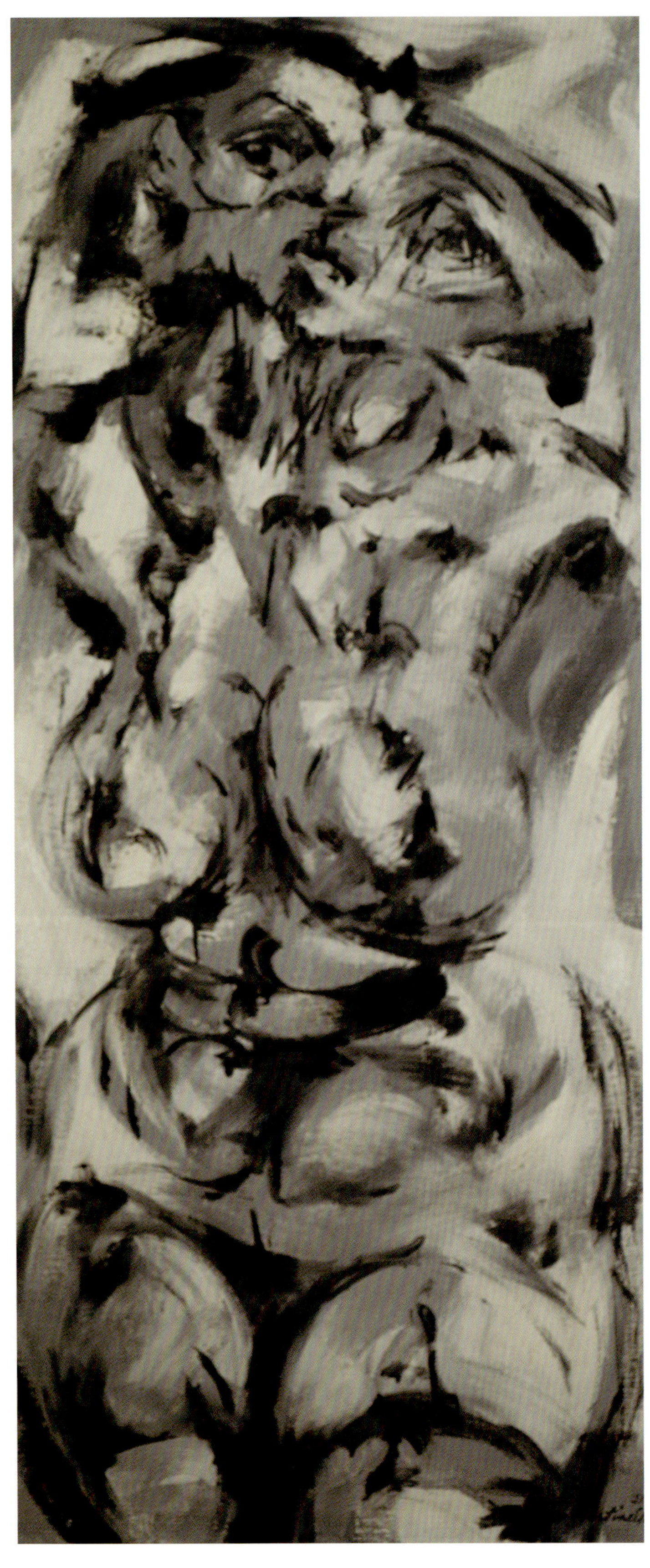

EZIO MARTINELLI, *Grief*, 1951
Oil on canvas, 60 x 25 inches
Private collection
Courtesy of Cincinnati Art Gallery, Cincinnati, OH

EZIO MARTINELLI, [1913-1980]

Born November 27, 1913, West Hoboken, NJ.
Died 1980, upstate New York.

Studied 1931: Academy of Fine Arts, Bologna; 1932-1936: National Academy of Design, NYC (with Leon Kroll & Gifford Beal, drawing with Ivan Olinsky, and sculpture with long-time sculpture teacher, Robert Aiken).

Teaching Positions 1946-1949: Graphic Arts at the Philadelphia Museum School; Pennsylvania School of Industrial Art, PA; 1949-1975: Painting at Sarah Lawrence College, Bronxville, N.Y.; 1954-1957: Parsons School of Design, NYC; 1964-1965: American Academy, Rome, Artist-in-residence; 1969: Sculpture class at Skowhegan School of Painting and Sculpture, ME, summer.

Federal Art Project WPA 1937-1941: easel painter and unit supervisor.

Selected Solo Exhibitions 1943: Philip Regan Gallery, PA; 1946, 47, 52, 55, 57, 59, 64, 66: The Willard Gallery, NYC; 1956, 68: Seattle Art Museum, Seattle, WA; 1956: Weisman Art Museum, Minnesota, MN; 1962: Art Institute of Chicago, IL; 1968: University of Minnesota, MN; Benson Gallery, East Hampton, NY.

Selected Group Exhibitions 1934: Society of Independent Artists, NYC; 1936: Federal Art Project Gallery, NYC; 1939: ACA Gallery, NYC; 1940: Pennsylvania Academy of Fine Art, - annuals; 1941: American Drawing Annual, Albany Institute of Art and History, NY; *20th International Exhibition of Watercolors*, Art Institute of Chicago; Elgin Academy of Fine Art, IL; San Diego Fine Art Society, CA; Denver Art Museum, CO; 1942, 43, 44: Peggy Guggenheim's, *Surrealist-orientated* Art of This Century Gallery, Spring Salon for Younger Artists, NYC; San Francisco Art Association, CA; 1943: Newark Museum of Art, Newark, NJ; 1944: Philadelphia Print Club; 1947: Corcoran Gallery of art, Washington, D.C. – biennial; *International Watercolor Show*, Brooklyn Museum, NYC; *Abstract and Surrealist Art in America*, Art Institute of Chicago; 1947, 58, 67: Pennsylvania Academy of Fine Art, – annuals; 1948, 56, 60, 62, 64, 66: Whitney Museum of American Art, Annuals; 1949: Brooklyn Museum, NY; 1952: *Drawings From Twelve Countries*, Art Institute of Chicago; 1955, 56: *American Watercolors in France*, Paris; 1956: Walker Art Center, Minnesota, MN; American Federation of Arts, NYC; *Monumentality in Modern Sculpture* Contemporary Arts Museum Houston, TX; 1957: *Irons in the Fire: An Exhibition of Metal Sculpture/Contemporary Arts* Museum, Houston, TX; *Eight American Artists – Contemporaries Abroad – Europe Edition*, circ., sponsored by State Department; *Eight American Artists – Contemporaries Abroad – Asian Edition*, circ., sponsored by State Department; *Major Work in Minor Scale*, American Federation of Arts, NYC; 1959: *Carnegie International*, Carnegie International Pittsburgh, PA; Katonah Museum of Art, Katonah, NY; 1959, 66: National Institute of Arts and Letters, NYC; 1960: *Aspect de la Sculpture Americaine*, Galerie Bernard, Paris France; *Business Buys American Art: Third Loan Exhibition by the Friends of the Whitney Museum of American Art*, Whitney Museum of American Art, NYC; 1962: The Architectural League of New York - National Gold Medal Exhibition of the Building Arts; *A Survey of American Sculpture: Late 18th Century to 1962*, The Newark Museum, NJ; 1964: *Westside Artists*, Riverside Museum of Art, NYC; 1965: *Major 19th and 20th Century Drawings*, Gallery of Modern Art, NYC; *White on White*, DeCordova Museum, Lincoln, Nebraska; *The Drawing Society National Exhibition 1965*, American Federation of Art, NYC; 1966: *Made of Iron*, Fine Arts Gallery, University of St. Thomas, Houston, TX; 1971: *Modern Sculptors – Their Drawings,* Watercolors, Storm King Art Center, Storm King, NY.

GEORGE MCNEIL

Spontaneity, like wit, cannot readily be analyzed and explained. How can one indicate how a phrase is turned into an epigram or how dirty color which 'works' may be inserted into an area which calls for luminosity? The way painting spontaneity operates is worth describing, although not psychologically explainable, since it has been singularly important in characterizing much post-1942 painting.

At the outset, two points must be stated. Spontaneity is not a value but rather a means or technique. To say that a painting is "spontaneous" is not to say that it is good or bad; this merely describes how the painting was done. Also, 'spontaneity' will be treated in terms of my own interpretation. For example, perhaps I was asked to write this because others see my work as 'spontaneous'; I see it more as labored, with spontaneity as an occasional lead to greater meaning.

Here is how it works with me. When the hacking begins to slow and finally stop, when conscious building of color masses or extensions of movement, in short, known and sophisticated approaches, ceases to force the painting on, I react by spontaneously striking lines or colors into the dead structure to enliven or resuscitate it. Here intuition works explosively to shake up or dislocate known relations into an unknown which facilitates further re-working. Spontaneous cutting-through or cutting-into negates or should negate consciously processed relating, and helps counter the designing which enfeebles abstract painting. Thus conscious, continued ordering towards expressiveness alternates with spontaneous, subliminal 'destructions' which, enigmatically, are the most constructive steps in painting.

....Both accidental and figured spontaneous statements tend toward massive simplicity, toward singular form: this is one of the most significant aspects of action painting and of spontaneity as its means.

George McNeil, Statement, *It is*. Winter-Spring, 1959, Vol. 3, p.14. A Magazine for Abstract Art, Second Half Publishing Co., NYC.

...Trying to make my paintings come alive pictorially and psychologically is an attempt to celebrate the pulsating vividness of being, mostly joyously but sometimes somberly as well. In both cases I go toward a liberating form, for breaking art experience, for going further. They say that the first eighty years are the hardest, so now I hope for the best: freedom leading to more freedom.

George McNeil, Statement: *From George McNeil Recent Paintings*, catalog, New York Studio School of Drawing, Painting and Sculpture;

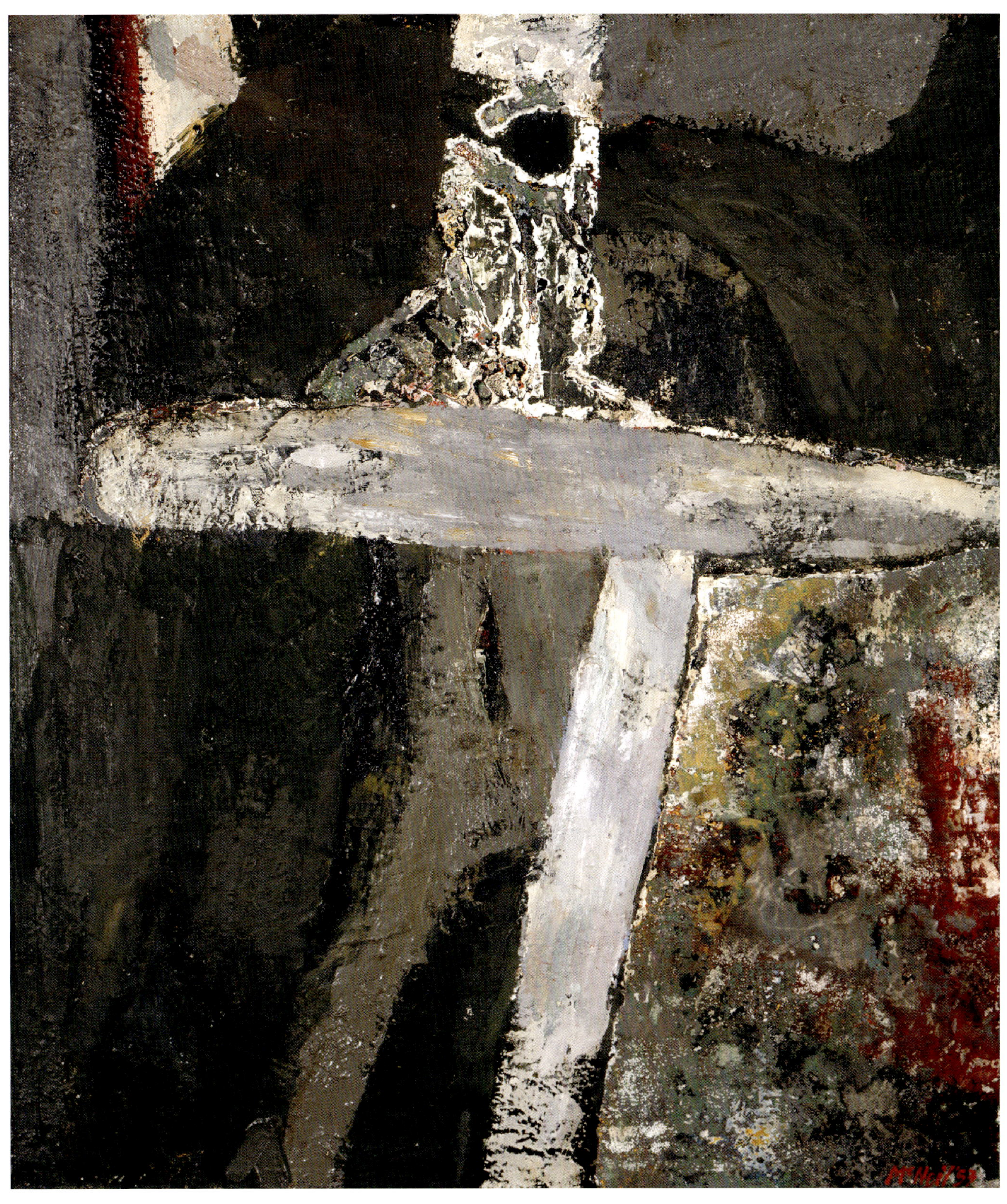

GEORGE MCNEIL, *Essence*, 1953
Oil on panel, 48 x 40 inches, (121.9 x 101.6 cm)
Collection of Helen McNeil

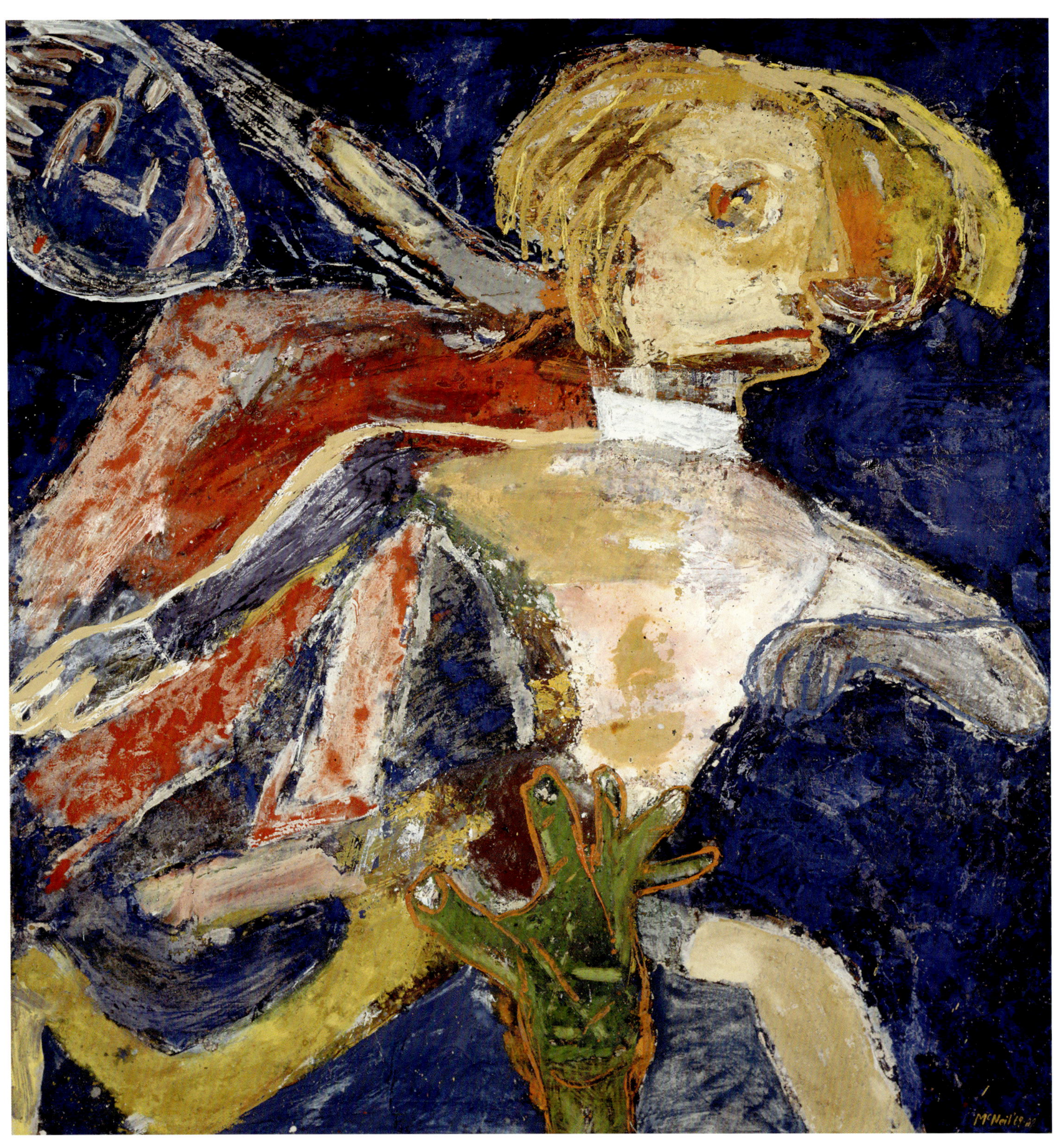

GEORGE McNEIL, *Maenad and Friends*, 1982
Oil on canvas, 78 x 72 inches, (198.1 x 182.9 cm)
Collection of Helen McNeil

GEORGE MCNEIL, [1908-1995]

Born February 22, 1908, New York City.
Died 1995, Brooklyn, NY.

Studied 1927–29: Pratt Institute; 1930–33: Art Students League; 1933–36: Hofmann School of Fine Art; Columbia University, BS, MA, 1943; Ed.D., 1952.

Federal Art Project 1935–40: Designed abstract murals.

Military Service in World War II
1943–46: US Navy.

Teaching Positions 1948–81: Pratt Institute; 1946–1948: University of Wyoming; 1955–56: University of California, Berkeley; 1974: Syracuse University; 1975: Columbia University; 1966–81: New York Studio School.

Selected Solo Exhibitions 1941 (first) Lyceum Gallery, Havana; 1947: Black Mountain College; 1948: University of Wyoming; University of New Mexico; University of Colorado; 1953: Charles Egan Gallery, Boston, MA; 1954: Hendler Gallery, Philadelphia, PA; 1957, 59: Poindexter Gallery, NYC; 1960, 62, 64, 67: The Howard Wise Gallery, NYC; 1961: Nova Gallery, Boston, MA; 1966: University of Texas; Great Jones Gallery, NYC; 1969: Des Moines; 1973: Pratt Institute, Manhattan Center, NYC; 1974: University of California, Santa Crux, CA; 1975: Northern Arizona University; Landmark Gallery, NYC; 1977: Aaron Berman Gallery, NYC; 1979: Terry Dintenfass, Inc., NYC; 1982: Fort Lauderdale; University of Connecticut; 1981, 83, 85: Gruenebaum Gallery, NYC; 1981: Montclair Art Museum, NJ; 1989: University of Hartford, CT; M. Knoedler & Co., NYC; 1991: Hirschl & Adler Modern, NYC.

Selected Group Exhibitions 1936: American Abstract Artists; *New Horizons in American Art*, Museum of Modern Art, NYC; 1939: *New York World's Fair*; 1951, 53, 55, 56, 57: The *9th St*. Show, *4 New York Painting and Sculpture Annuals*, Stable Gallery, NYC; 1951: *Abstract Painting and Sculpture in America*, The Art Institute of Chicago, IL; 1953, 57, 61, 65: *Annuals and Biennials*, Whitney Museum of American Art NYC; 1953, 55, 58: Carnegie Institute of Technology, Washington, DC; 1960: *60 American Painters, 1960*, Walker Art Center, Minneapolis, MN; 1961: *Abstract Expressionists and Imagists*, Solomon R. Guggenheim Museum, NYC; *American Painting*, circ., United States Information Agency, Latin America; 1962: The Pennsylvania Academy of the Fine Arts, PA; 1963–64: *Hans Hofmann and His Students*, circ., Museum of Modern Art, NYC; 1968: *The 1930's*, Whitney Museum of American Art, NYC; 1969: *The New American Painting and Sculpture*, Museum of Modern Art, NYC; 1977: *American Abstract Artists*, University of New Mexico; 1983: *The Painterly Figure*, The Parrish Museum Southampton, NY; 1987: *The Interior Self,* Montclair Art Museum, NJ.

HANS MOLLER

Color means everything to me. The subject is the inspiration, the point of departure to explore color. I have always considered myself abstract but now my works have more figurative references. To me it doesn't matter what I paint but how I paint. I am not interested in what it is, but how it is done.

Hans Moller, Statement: *Works of the Fifties On the occasion of the artist's 90th birthday.* Edited by Torsten Brohen. Book for the Hans Moller Jubilee Exhibition. Düsseldorf, 1995. pp. 13-14.

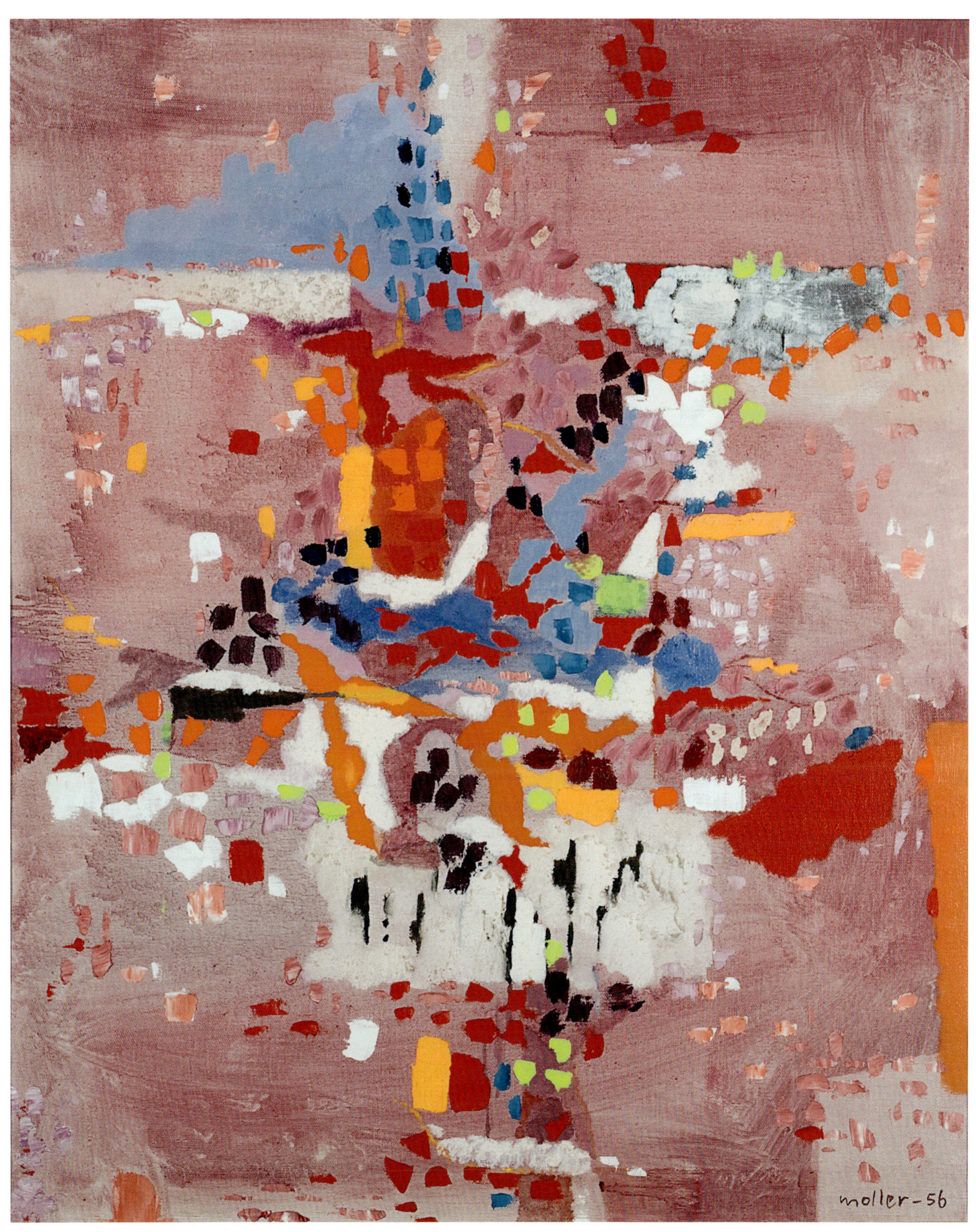

HANS MOLLER, *Cobalt Violet*, 1956
Oil on canvas, 30 x 24 inches, (77 x 61.5 cm); catalogue raisonne no.: 148
Private collection

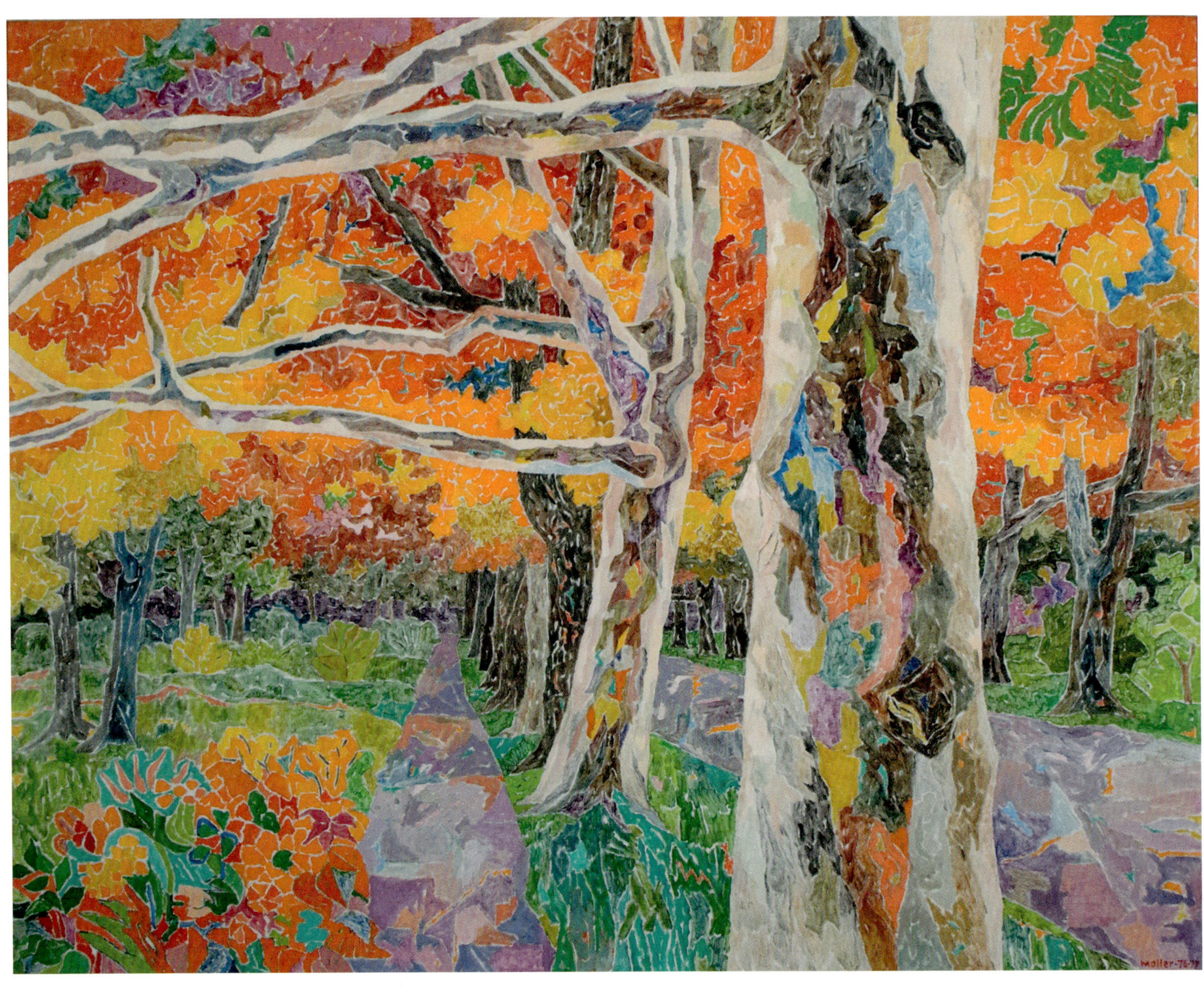

HANS MOLLER, *Autumn-Allen Street*, 1976-77
Oil on canvas, 48 x 60 inches; catalogue raisonne no.: 735
Private collection

HANS MOLLER, [1905-2000]

Born March 20, 1905 in Wuppertal, Germany. **US citizen** 1944.
Died 2000 in Allentown, PA.

Studied 1919–1927: Kunstgewerbeschule Wuppertal-Barmen, Germany; 1927–1928: Academy of Fine Arts, Berlin,

Teaching Positions 1944–1956: Cooper Union. New York City.

Selected Solo Exhibitions 1942, 43: Bonestell Gallery, NY; 1945: Arts Club of Chicago, IL; University of Michigan; 1945, 47, 48, 49, 50: Kleemann Gallery, NY; 1951, 53, 54, 56: Grace Borgenicht Gallery, New York; 1956–1964: *Hans Moller, 1926–1956,* circ., The Olsen Foundation, Inc.; 1957, 60: Fine Art Associates, NY; 1962: Albert Landry Gallery, NY; 1964, 67, 70, 73, 76, 79, 81, 84, 87: Midtown Galleries, NY; 1968: Art Allience, Philadelphia, PA; 1969, 2001: Allentown Art Museum, Allentown, PA; 1970: Norfolk Museum, VA; 1977: Muhlenberg College, Allentown, PA; Lehigh University, Bethlehem, PA; 1978: Hunterdon Art Center, Clinton, NJ; 1980: Northeastern Pennsylvania Art Alliance; 1987: Madison Gallery, Madison, CT; 1993: Baum School of Art, Allentown, PA; 1995: Torsten Broehan Gallery, Dusseldorf, Germany; 2001: Lore Degenstein Gallery, Susquehanna University, Selinsgrove, PA; 2002: Nuriel and Philip Berman Museum of Art, Ursinus College, Collegeville, PA.

Selected Group Exhibitions 1946, 47, 48, 49, 50, 51, 52, 53, 54, 55, 56, 58, 65: *Annual & Biennial Exhibitions*, The Whitney Museum of American Art, NYC; 1950: *American Painting Today*, The Metropolitan Museum of Art, NYC; 1955, 56: *New York Artists' Painting and Sculpture Annuals*, Stable Gallery, NYC; 1958: *Nature in Abstraction*, The Whitney Museum of American Art, New York; 1964: *100 Artists of the 20th Century*, Colby College; 1965, 67, 68, 69: The National Academy of Design, NYC;1966, 1967: Federation of Modern Painters and Sculptors.

JAN MÜLLER

In our age the artist cannot take flight from the rottenness of society to portray just the spirit of man. He has a responsibility toward that stench if any awareness and must try to reach the more social position in his ethical and moral evaluation of life. He should portray life, but as life of possibility not the refuge and well–being stimulated by acrobatics without content. He has to find a way to the closer relationship among things and has to become aware of man's multiple sensitiveness not just tied down to the string of an apron of one thing called purity in our age. But what is purity, perfection or a multitude of ideas? The artist has a responsibility toward that stench and cannot take flight to the Elysian Fields of the preciousness of perfection, the prism of the eye, but has to deal with matter complex. If not coming to the conclusion he must hint and try to portray and achieve the most of his inherent capacity instead of taking refuge into the laws pre–established for him, the prism of the eye of our age. Art is first and foremost content, actually any human manifestation with critical faculty goes away from the therapeutic element of norm...

From a notebook 1956, Jan Müller

Jan Müller, Statement: *New Images of Man by Peter Selz with statements by the artists*, Published by The Museum of Modern Art, New York in collaboration with The Baltimore Museum of Art. p. 106

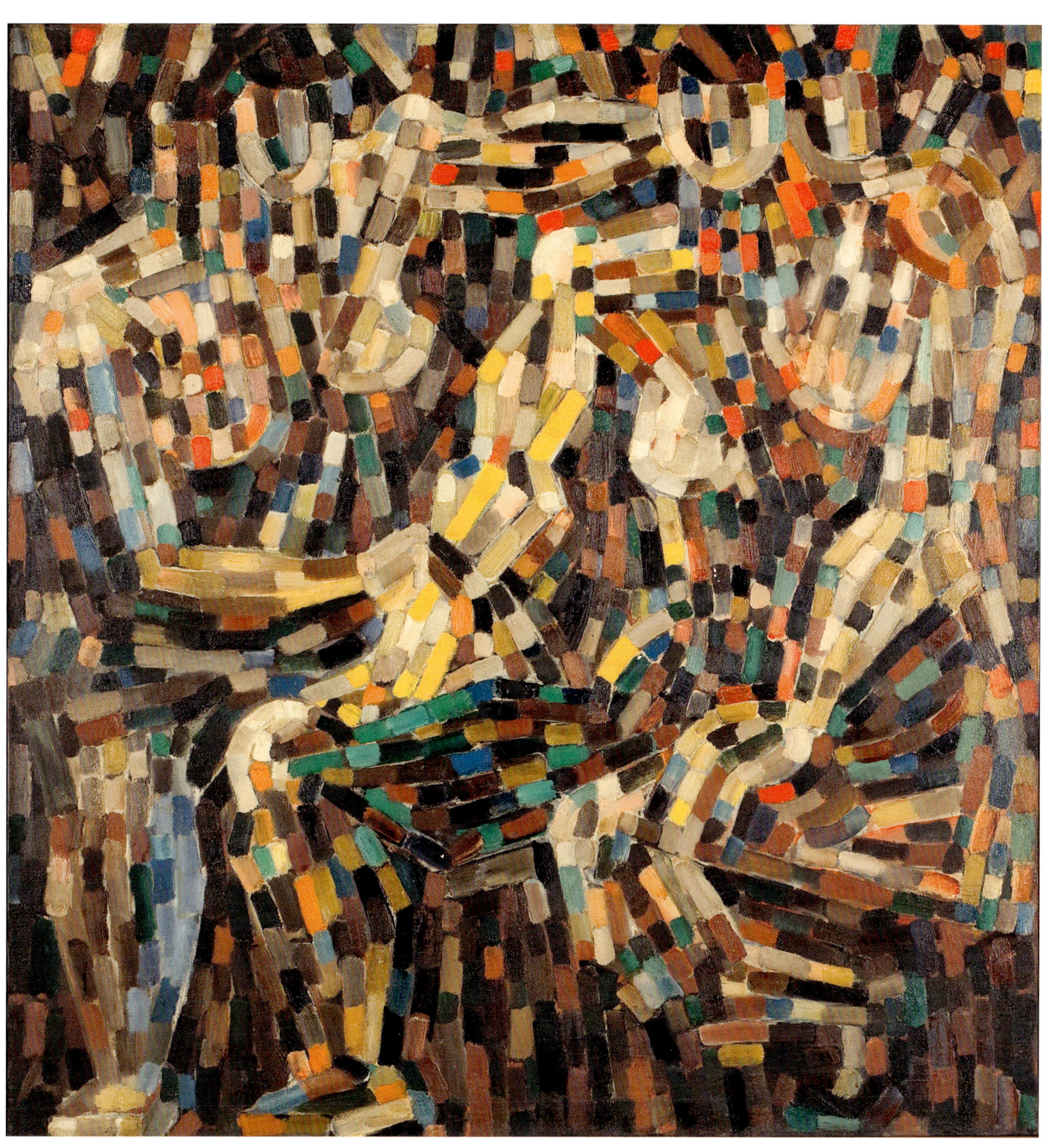

JAN MÜLLER, *Seated Figures*, 1953
Oil on canvas, 54 x 49 1/2 inches (137.2 x 125.7 cm)
Private collection
© Courtesy of Lori Bookstein Fine Art, New York

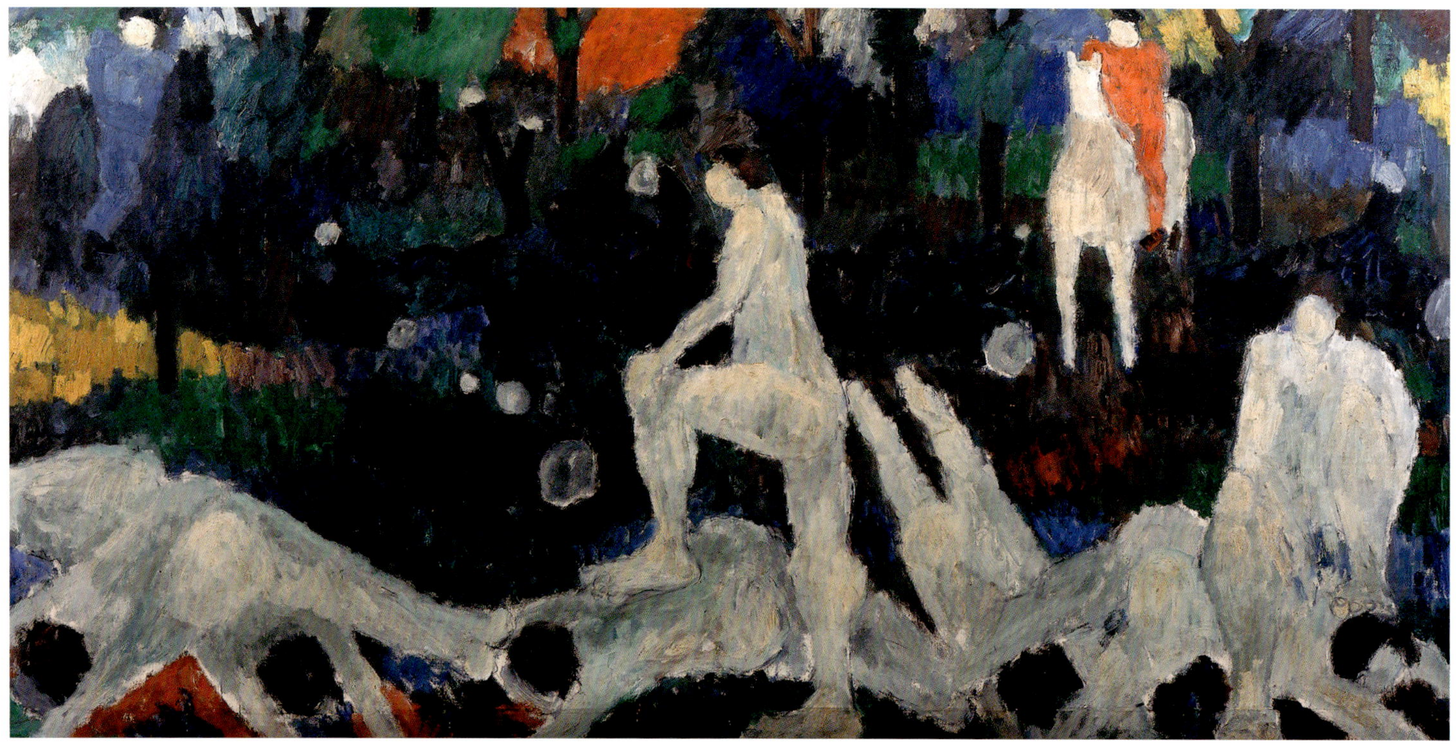

JAN MÜLLER, *Of This Time Of That Place*, 1956
Oil on canvas, 48 x 96 inches (121.9 x 243.8 cm)
Collection of Spanierman Gallery, New York

JAN MÜLLER, [1922-1958]

Born December 27, 1922 in Hamburg, Germany. **To USA** 1941.
Died January 29, 1958, NYC.

Studied 1945–1950: Hans Hofmann School.

Selected Solo Exhibitions 1953, 54, 55, 56, 57, 58: Hansa Gallery, NYC; 1955, 56: Sun Gallery, Provincetown, MA; 1960: University of Minnesota, MN; 1961: Zabriskie Gallery, NYC; 1970, 71, 72: Noah Goldowsky Gallery, NYC. Retrospectives: 1959: Hansa Gallery, NYC; 1962: Solomon R. Guggenheim Museum, NYC 2004; *Jan Müller: The Mosaic Paintings 1952–1955*, Lori Bookstein Fine Art, NYC.

Selected Group Exhibitions 1952: 813 Broadway (Gallery), NYC; 1953: The Art Institute of Chicago, IL; 1955: University of Minnesota, MN; 1955, 56: *New York Painting and Sculpture Annuals*, Stable Gallery, NYC; 1957: *The New York School, Second Generation*, Jewish Museum, NYC; *Young America*, Whitney Museum of American Art, NYC; *Annual*, Whitney Museum of American Art, NYC; 1958: Carnegie Institute of Technology, Pittsburgh, PA; *Festival of Two Worlds*, Spoleto, Italy; 1958, 59: Institute of Contemporary Art, Boston, MA; 1959: *New Images of Man*, Museum of Modern art, NYC; 1960: *The Figure*, circ., American Federation of Arts, NYC; 1962: Venice Bienale; 1999: *Search for the Unicorn: Paintings by Jan Müller and Bob Thompson*, Lori Bookstein Fine Art, NYC.

ROBERT NATHANS

My time is mostly spent alone in front of a canvas hanging on the studio wall. I bring all the stuff I love together into the studio, most of it in my head as well as quite a bit of material stuff saved through years of collecting is thrown about my work space. The radio on with today's news among turps and paint thinner, coffee and bread, tools, toys, photographs, glue, staples, wooden things and paint piled onto paper plates.

I bring all my memories with me as I stand in front of my canvases. Here my intuition comes into play. It will sometimes take me months of working. Then, somewhere in this process of painting and observing, I would inextricably disappear. Unaware of body, time, and space – when I become painting.

It will sometimes take me months of work to feel that a painting is finished. The work goes through many scrapings, washings and new layers of pigments. There feels like a clearly defined natural progression where materials and imagery become my own, be it figurative or abstract, the mark–making is personal.

Almost always, surprisingly I know exactly when a painting is finished. I will not leave off working a piece until it is a perfect moment of imperfection – when paint, with color, texture, and ideas, is a clear and tense passionate representation of life.

R. Nathans, 2008

Robert Nathans, Statement: Letter provided to the editor November 30, 2008

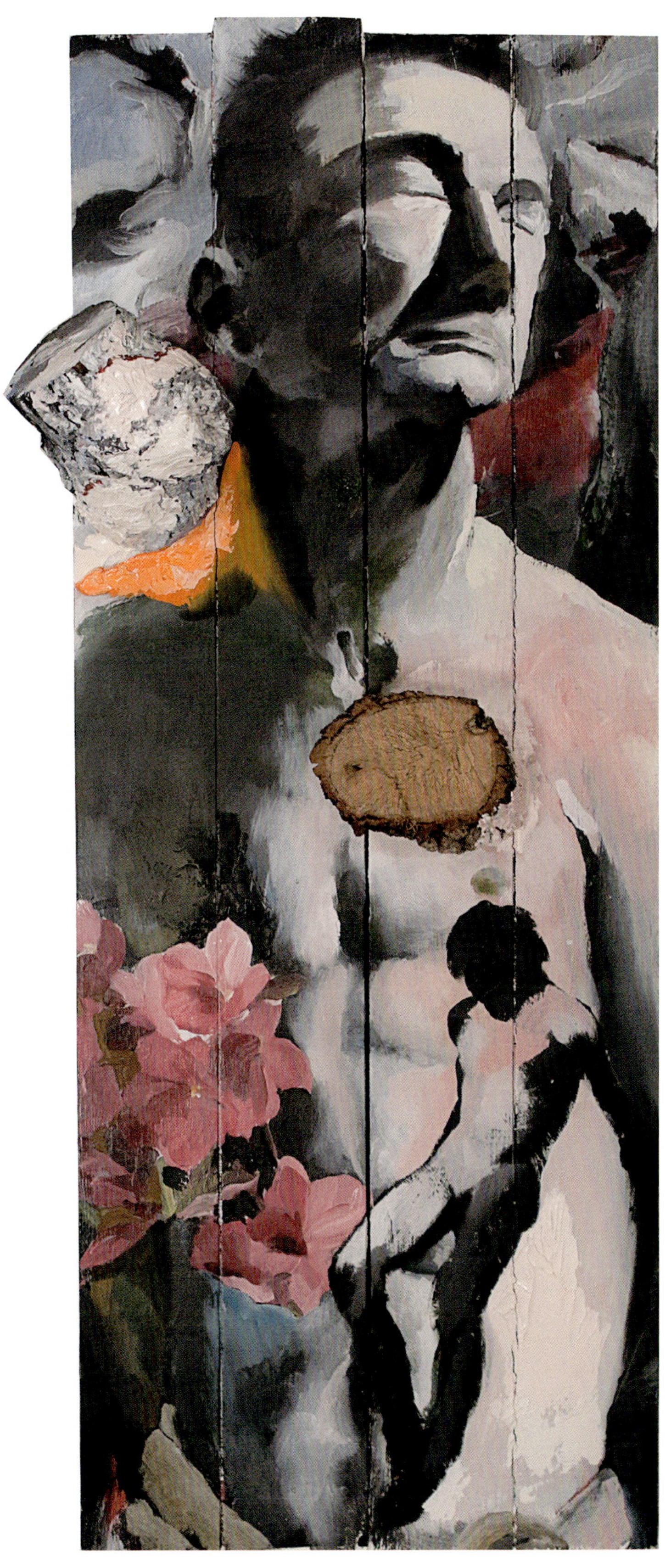

ROBERT NATHANS, *The Destructive Character*, 1986
Oil on wood and tree stumps, 36 x 14 inches
Private collection

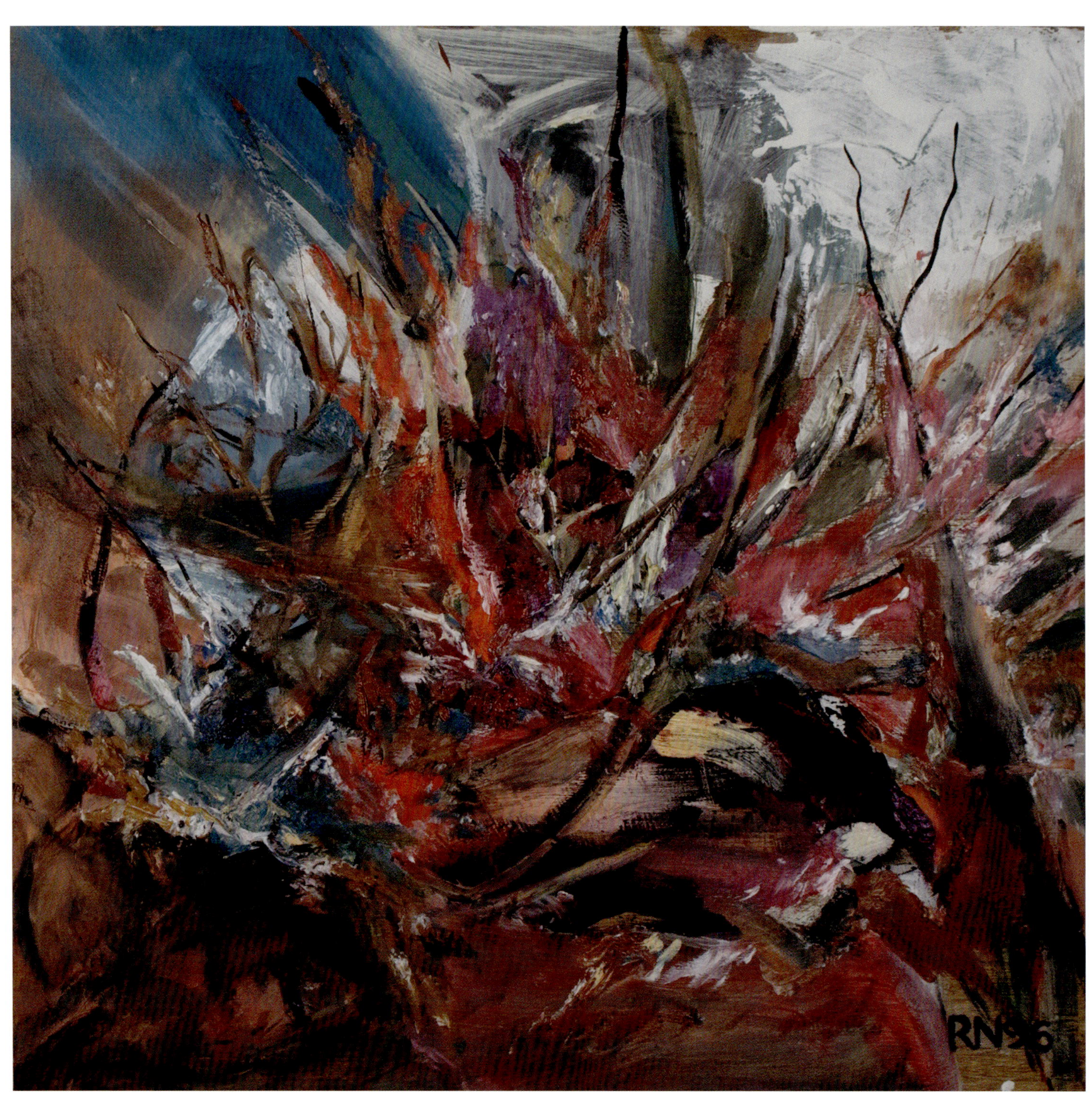

ROBERT NATHANS, *False Friend*, 1996
Oil on wood panel, 24 x 24 inches
Collection of the artist
© Robert Nathans

ROBERT NATHANS, [1955-]

Born December 3, 1955 in Paterson, NJ.

Studied 1969–1971: Art Student's League of New York; 1973–1976: Pratt Institute, Brooklyn, NY; 1980–1981: Art Student's League of New York with Isaac Soyer; 1981–1986: University of South Florida, Tampa, FL (B.A., 1984; M.F.A., painting, 1986).

Teaching Positions 1990: Chautauqua Institute, School of Art, Chautauqua, NY; 1992–1995: Museum of Art Fort Lauderdale, FL; 1992–1995: Art and Culture Center of Hollywood, Hollywood, FL; 1995 – present, Broward College, Fort Lauderdale, FL.

Selected Solo Exhibitions 1986: Teaching Gallery, University of South Florida, Tampa, FL; 1988: *Rob Nathans: Drawings*, Passaic County Community College, Paterson, NJ; 1989: *Rob Nathans: Paintings and Watercolors*, Gaumann Cicchino Gallery, Fort Lauderdale, FL; 1994: *Robert Nathans*: *Paintings*, Artist Grocery Warehouse, Fort Lauderdale, FL; 1999: *Robert Nathans: Drawings*, Nathans Gallery, West Paterson, NJ; 2005: *Paint: Self Portraits and Stuff*, Stonewall Library & Archives, Fort Lauderdale, FL.

Selected Group Exhibitions 1985: *Prospective Show: Inaugural Exhibition*, Florida Center of Contemporary Art, Tampa, FL; *New Work Invitational*, Gallerybor, Ybor City/Tampa, FL; 1986: *Kunst Aus Florida Invitational*, Kultur/Piccolo Galleria, Bergisch Gladbach, Koln, Germany; 1987: *Invitational*, Galerie fur Moderne Kunst, Kissinger Sommer, Bad Kissingen, Germany; *Josette Urso and Robert Nathans Studio Exhibition and Loft Opening*, 139 West 22nd Street, NYC; 1988: *Annual Juried Exhibition*, Fine Arts Museum of Long Island, Hempstead, NY; *National Juried Exhibition*, Viridian Gallery, NYC; 1989: *Winter Exhibition*, Broward Art Guild, Ft. Lauderdale, FL; *Human Image*, Broward Art Guild, Fort Lauderdale, FL; 1990: *Artists Teaching Art: Chautauqua School of Art Faculty Exhibition*, The Michael Rockefeller Gallery, State University of New York, Fredonia, NY; 1993: *Between the Emotion and the Response*, Art Institute of Fort Lauderdale, FL; 1993, 94: *Annual Hortt Memorial Competition and Exhibition*, Museum of Art, Fort Lauderdale, FL; 1996: *1996 Fellowship Recipients: South Florida Cultural Consortium*, Museum of Art, Fort Lauderdale, FL; 1997: *Printmaking*, Common Space Gallery, Art Center South Florida, Miami Beach, FL; 2001: *Selected Works from the Archives*, Stonewall Library & Archives, Fort Lauderdale, FL; 2004: *Adjunct Faculty Exhibition*, Broward College, Davie, FL; 2005: *Visual AIDS: Postcards from the Edge*, Robert Miller Gallery, NYC; 2007: *Community*, Meyerhoefer Gallery, Lake Worth, FL; 2008: *Twisted*, Broward College Fine Arts Gallery, Davie, FL; *The South Florida Cultural Consortium 2008 Fellowship for Visual and Media Artists Exhibition: Thirteen-08*, Museum of Art/Fort Lauderdale, Nova Southeastern University, Fort Lauderdale, FL.

MANUAL NERI

...I did a lot of painting, and the most of it became nonobjective with much color. Then the nonobjective color went right into the sculpture. It was as if everything I had been doing in painting went right into the sculpture, and things began to happen with the figure that really pleased me...

[All] of the painting that I used to do before on canvas—all those ideas came into the figure. What's taking place on the surface of the structure when I move the material around or hack into it is no different from pushing paint around. The color on the surface is a natural extension of the way I have always worked. Color can either destroy a surface or it can accent or draw attention to a certain area....Color is part of what's happening on the surface, and it does not relate to actual, anatomical form.

Manual Neri, Statement: From Butterfield, Jan. Ancient Auras—Expressionist Angst: Sculpture by Manual Neri. Images and Issues (Spring 1981): pp. 38-43.

Jones, Caroline A., Manual Neri: The Figurative Plasters, 13. San Francisco: San Francisco Museum of Modern Art, 1989. Exh.cat. Quoting Jan Butterfield, Ancient Auras—Expressionist Angst: Sculpture by Manuel Neri. Images and Issues (Spring 1981): pp. 41,43.

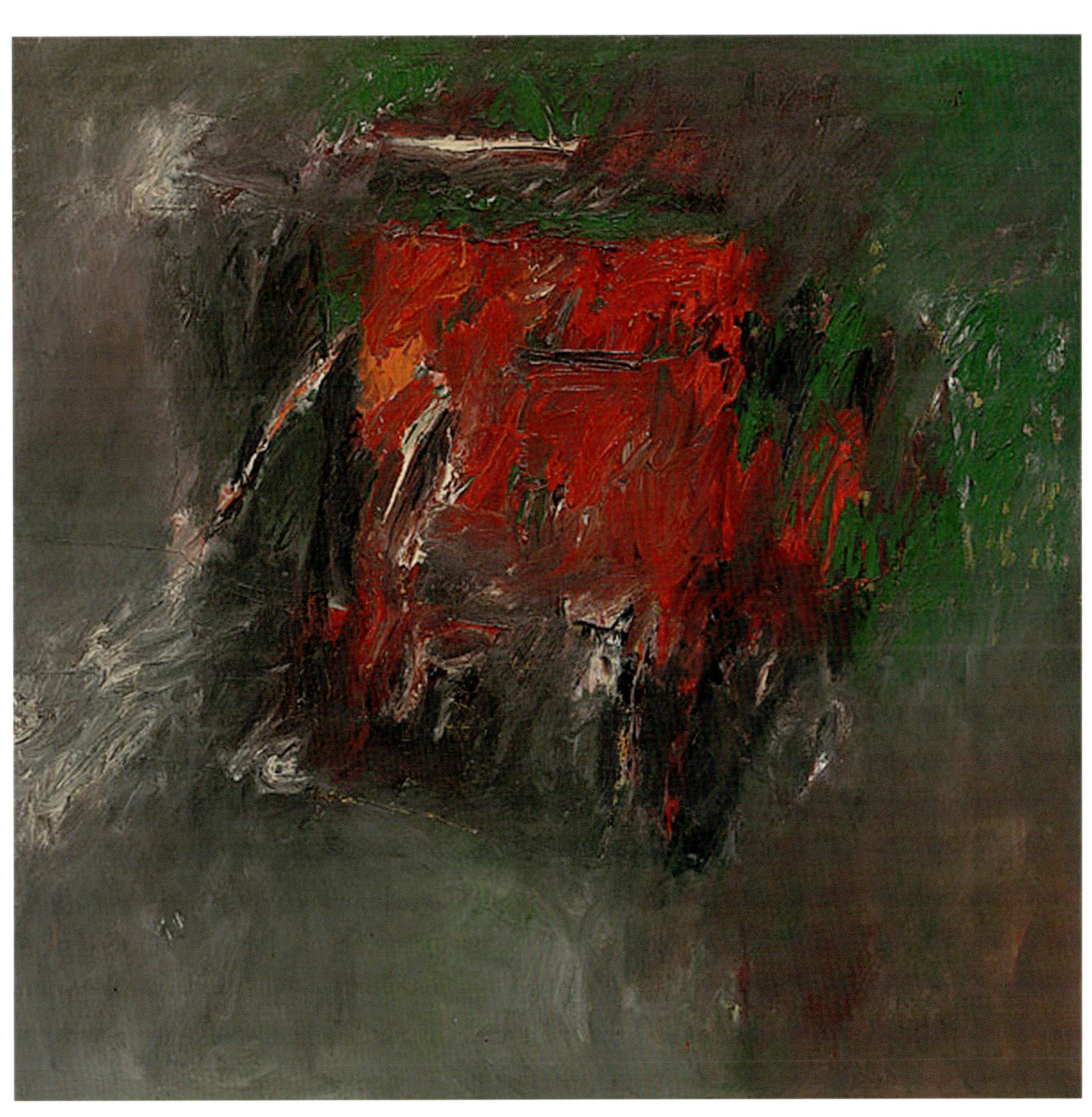

MANUAL NERI, *Windows Series No. 8*, 1959
Oil on canvas 70 x 70 inches
© Manual Neri. Courtesy Hackett-Freedman Gallery, San Francisco, CA

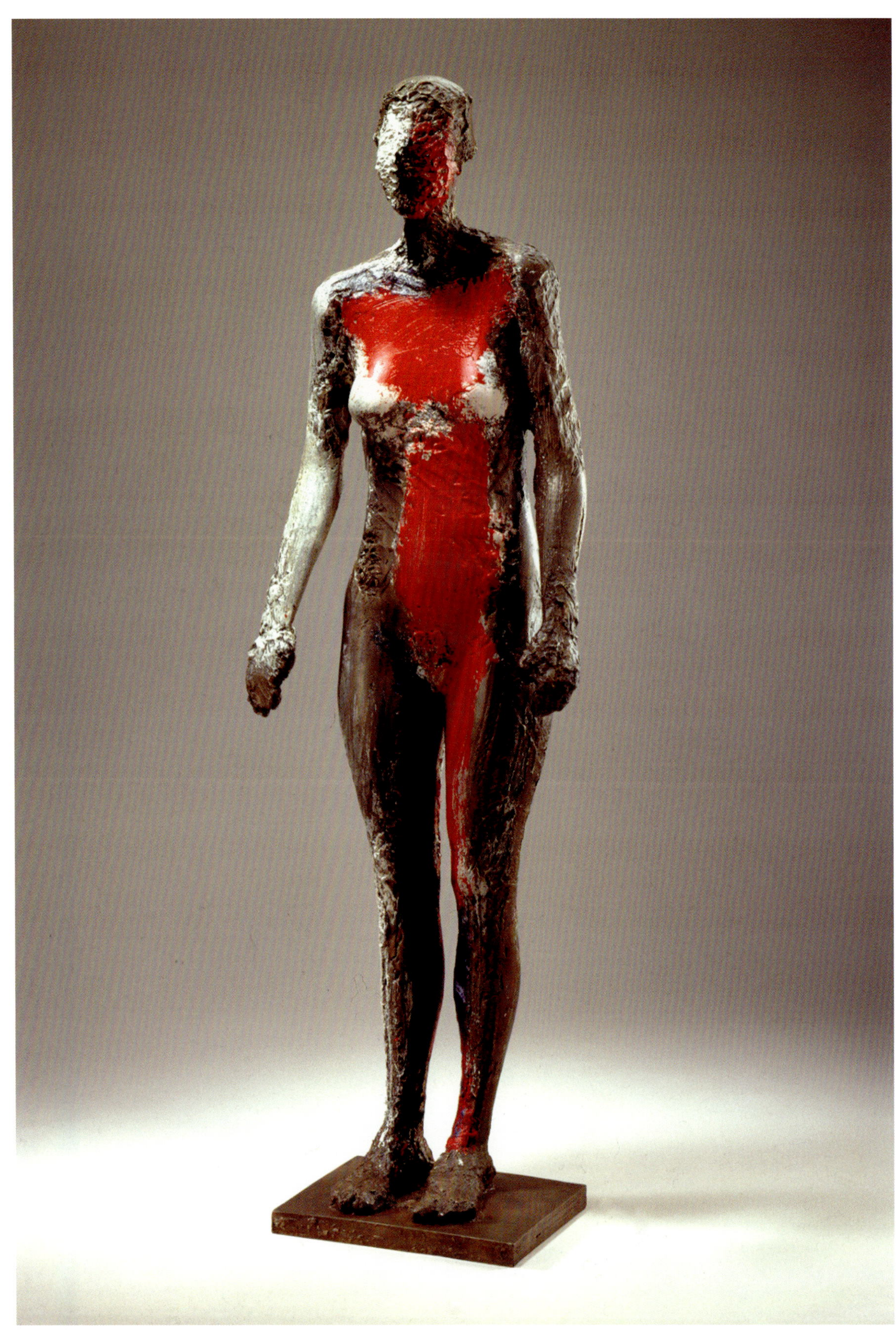

MANUAL NERI, *Catun No. 1*, 1986
bronze sculpture with oil-based enamel, (cast 1/4) 67 x 19 x 12.5 inches

MANUAL NERI, [1930-]

Born April 13, 1930, Sanger, CA.

Studied 1949–1950: San Francisco City College; 1951–1952: University of California, Berkeley, CA; 1952–1957: California School of Arts and Crafts, Oakland, CA; 1957–1959: California School of Fine Arts, San Francisco, CA, with Elmer Bischoff; 1964–1990: University of California, Davis, CA.

Teaching Positions 1959–1964: California School of Fine Arts, San Francisco, CA; 1964: University of California, Davis, CA.

Selected Solo Exhibitions 1957: Six Gallery, San Francisco, CA; 1959: Spatsa Gallery, San Francisco, CA; 1960: Dilexi Gallery, San Francisco, CA; 1963: New Mission Gallery, San Francisco, CA; 1966, 68, 71, 75: Quay Gallery, San Francisco, CA; 1969: Louisiana State University; 1970: Mary's College, Moraga, CA; 1971, 89: San Francisco Museum of Modern Art, San Francisco, CA; 1972: Sacramento State College, CA; 1972: Davis Art Center, Davis, CA; 1974: San Jose State University, CA; 1976: Braunstein Quay Gallery, NYC; 60 Langton St., San Francisco, CA; Oakland Art Museum, CA; 1977, 90: E. B. Crocker Art Gallery, Sacramento, CA; 1979: Gallery Paule Anglim, San Francisco, CA; 1980: Whitman College; Richmond Art Center, CA; Grossmont College; 1981: The Mexican Museum, San Francisco, CA; Seattle Art Museum, WA; 1981, 82, 86, 89, 91: Charles Cowles Gallery, NYC; 1981, 84, 88, 90: John Beggruen Gallery; 1983: Middendorf/Lane Gallery, Washington, D.C.; 1984: California State University, Chico; Galerie Andrè Emmerich, Zurich; Gimpel-Hanover & Middendorf Gallery, Washinton, D.C.; 1985: California State University, Sacramento, CA; 1987: Fay Gold Gallery, Atlanta, GA; Marion Koogler McNay Art Institute, San Antonio, TX; 1988: College of Notre Dame; James Corcoran Gallery, Santa Monica; 1989: University of Nevada; Greg Kucera Gallery, Seattle, WA; 1989, 91: Riva Yares Gallery, Scottsdale, AZ; 1990: Bingham Kurts Gallery, Memphis, TN; Dominican College, San Rafael, Ca; Margulies/Taplin Gallery, Coconut Grove, FL; 1991: University of California, davis, CA; Eve Mannes Gallery, Atlanta, GA.

Selected Group Exhibitions 1955, 57: Oakland Art Museum Annuals; 1959: *Four-man show,* San Francisco Museum of Modern Art, San Francisco, CA; 1962: *The Nude*, California Palace of the Legion of Honor, San Francisco, CA; *Some Points of View*, Stanford University, Palo Alto, CA; 1963: *Sculpture Today*, Oakland Art Museum, CA; 1964: *Current Painting and Sculpture of the Bay Area*, Stanford University, Palo Alto, CA; 1966: *Abstract Expressionist Ceramics*, University of California, Irvine; 1967: *Funk Art*, University of California, Berkeley; 1969: *On Looking Back: Bay Area 1945–1962*, San Francisco Museum of Modern Art, San Francisco, CA; 1970: Whitney Museum of American Art Annual, NYC; 1974: *A Third World Paintig and Sculpture Exhibition*, San Francisco Museum of Modern Art, San Francisco, CA; 1975: *Survey of Sculptural Directions in the Bay Area*, De Anza College; 1976: *California Painting and Sculpture: The Modern Era*, San Francisco Museum of Modern Art, San Francisco, CA; *The Handmade Paper Object*, Santa Barbara Museum of Arts, Santa Barbara CA; 1978: *A Century of Ceramics in the U.S. 1878–1978*, Everson Museum of Art, Syracuse, NY; 1980: *20 American Artists*, San Francisco Museum of Modern Art, San Francisco, CA; 1982: *100 Years of California Sculpture*, Oakland Art Museum, CA; 1984: *Figurative Sculpture: Ten Artists/Two Decades*, California State University, Long Beach, CA; *Drawings: 1974–1984*, The Hirshhorn Museum and Sculpture Garden Smithsonian Institution, Washington, D.C.; *Dilexi: The Dilexi Years, 1958–1970*, Oakland Art Museum, CA; *American Sculpture of Three Decades*, Seattle Art Museum, Seattle, WA; *California Sculpture Show*, circ., University of Southern California; 1985: *Contemporary Bronze: Six in the Figurative Tradition*, circ., University of Nebraska; *Art in the San Francisco Bay Area, 1945–1980*, Oakland Art Museum, CA; 1987: *Figurative Sculpture*, Palm Springs Desert Museum; *Contemporary Hispanic Art in the United States*, circ., Museum of Fine Arts, Houston, TX; 1988: *The Latin American Spirit*, circ., The Bronx Museum, NY; 1989: *Bay Area Figurative Art*, circ., San Francisco Museum of Modern Art, San Francisco, CA.

GEORGE ORTMAN

Talking about my painting I find most difficult. I have done many drawings explaining graphically the meaning of my vocabulary. The painting is my statement.

George Ortman, Statement: From *Contemporary American Painting and Sculpture 1965,* Krannert Art Museum, Champaign, College of Fine and Applied Arts, University of Illinois, Urbana. p. 57

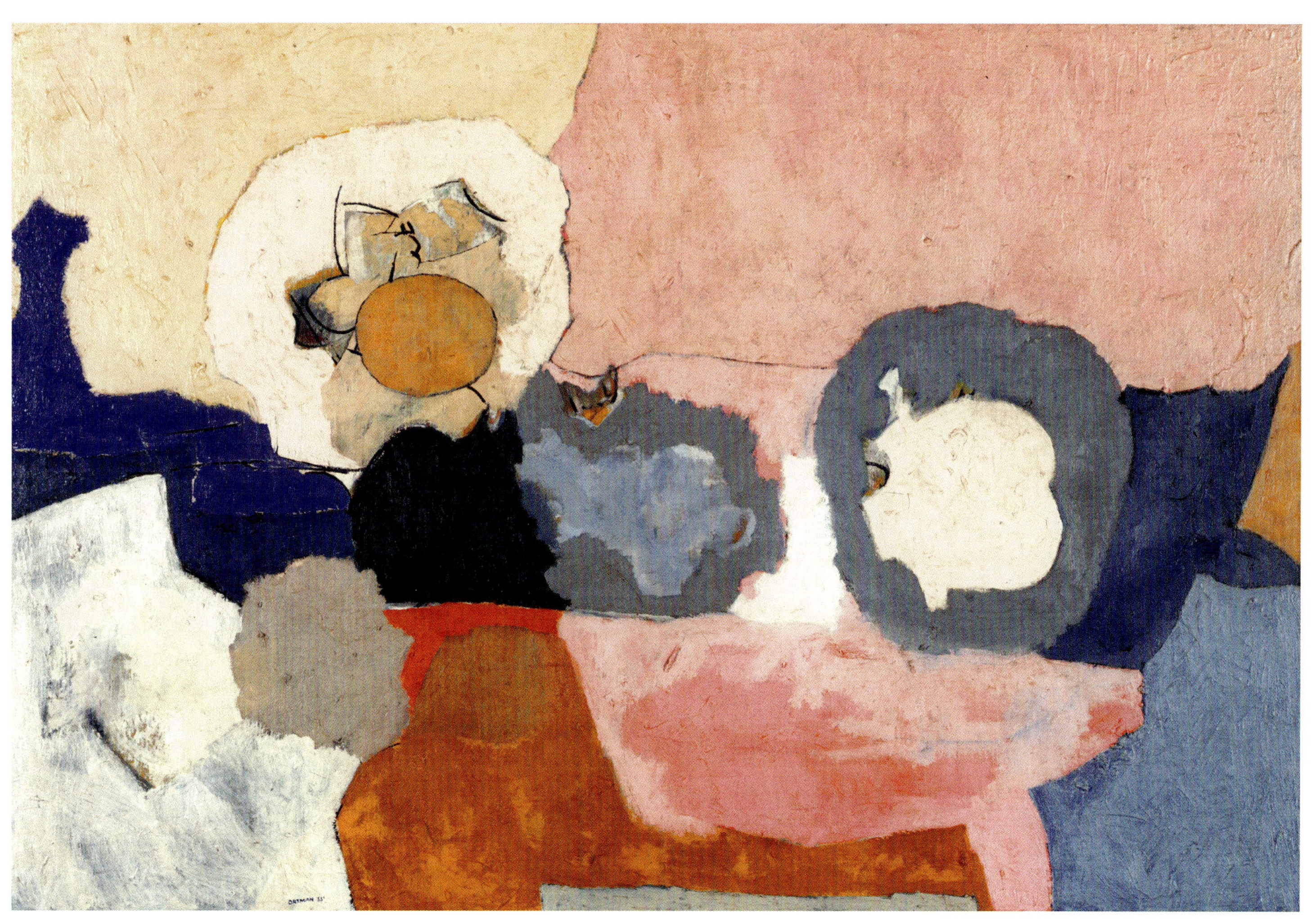

GEORGE ORTMAN, *Landmark*, 1953
Oil on canvas, 32 3/8 x 46 3/8 in. (82.1 x 117.8 cm.)
Smithsonian American Art Museum
Gift of Katharine Sergava Sznycer in honor and loving memory of Bernard W. Sznycer and Andrius Jilinsky 1979.42.1

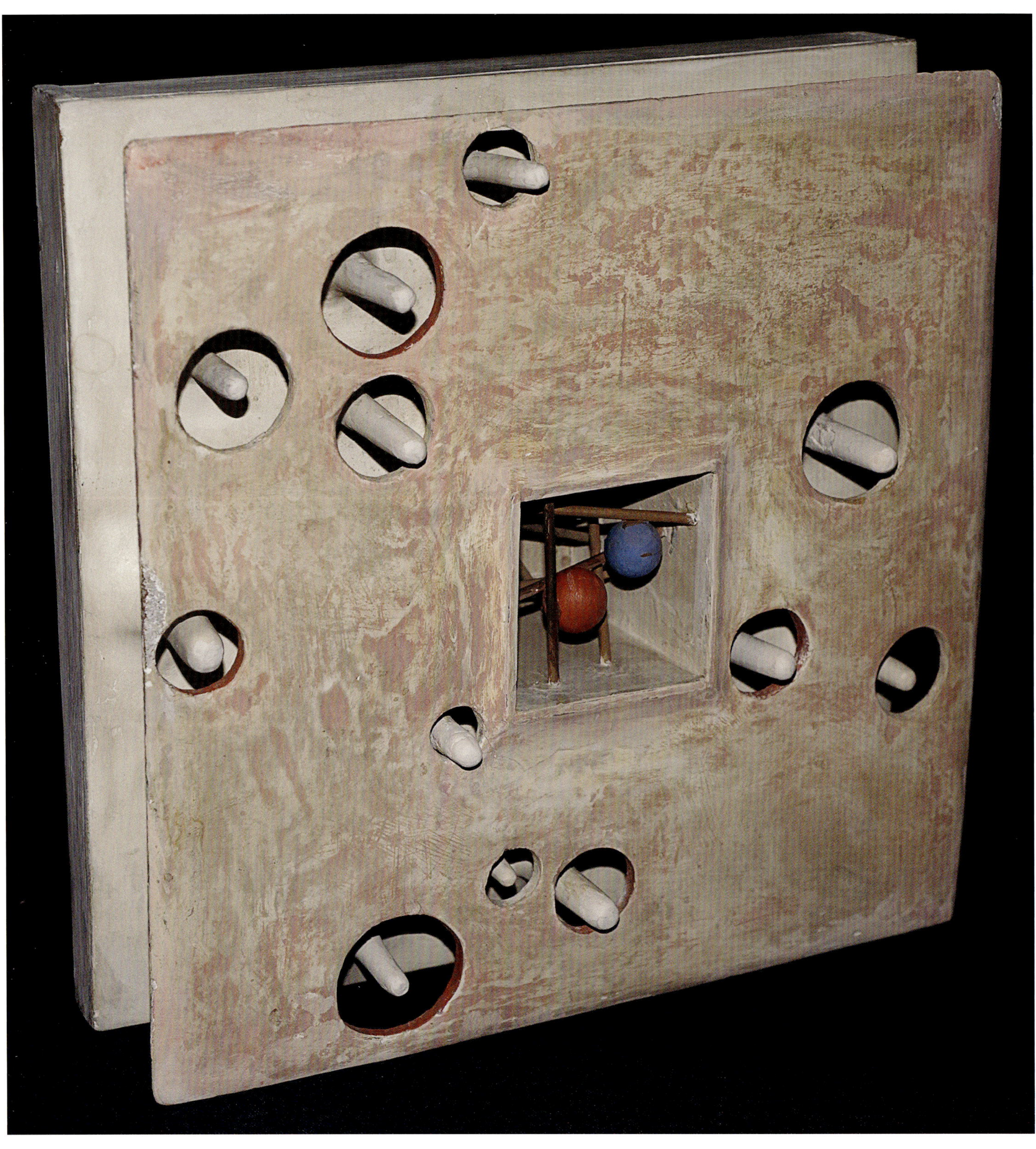

GEORGE ORTMAN, *A Sweet Woman*, 1956
Painted construction ¾ x 11 ¾ inches
Private collection

GEORGE EARL ORTMAN, [1926-]

Born October 17, 1926, Oakland, CA.

Studied 1947–1948: California College of Arts and Crafts; 1949: Atelier 17, NYC with S.W. Hayter; 1950: Academie Andre Lhote, Paris; 1950–1951: Hans Hofmann School.

Teaching Positions 1960–1965: School of Visual Arts, NYC; 1963–1965: New York University, NYC; 1964 summer: Fairleigh Dickinson University, Teaneck, NJ; 1966–1969: Princeton University, NJ; 1969–1970: Honolulu Academy, Havaii; 1970: Cranbrook Academy of Art, Bloomfield Hills, MI.

Selected Solo Exhibitions 1953 (first): Tanager Gallery, NYC; 1956: Wittenborn Gallery, NYC; 1957, 60: Stable Gallery, NYC; 1961,62: The Swetzoff Gallery, Boston, MA; 1962, 63, 64, 67, 69: Howard Wise Gallery, NYC; 1962: Fairleigh Dickinson University, Teaneck, NJ; 1964: David Mirvish Gallery; 1965: Container Corp. of America; The Walker Art Center, Minneapolis, MN; 1966: Milwaukee Art Center, WI; Dallas Museum of Fine Arts, Dallas, TX; Akron Art Institute, Akron, OH; Portland Museum of Art, Portland, ME; Harcus-Krakow Gallery, Chicago, IL; David Stuart Gallery; 1967: University of Chicago, IL; 1967–1969: Galeria Van der Voort; 1967: Princeton University, NJ; 1968: Temple University, Philadelphia, PA; 1969: Middlebury College, VT; 1970: Reed College, Portland OR; 1970, 81: Cranbrook, CO; 1971: J.L. Hudson Art Gallery, Detroit, MI; Indianapolis Museum of Art, IN; 1972: Western Michigan University; Gimpel & Weitzenhoffer, Ltd.; 1976: Gertrude Kasle Gallery, Detroit, MI. Retrospectives: 1963: Fairleigh Dickinson University, Teaneck, NJ; 1965: The Walker Art Center, Minneapolis, MN; 1967: Princeton University, NJ; 1991: Indianapolis Museum of Art, IN.

Selected Group Exhibitions 1950: Salon du Mai, Pris, France; 1952: San Francisco Museum of Modern Art Annual, CA; 1960: *New Media-New Forms I*, Martha Jackson Gallery, NYC; *Young America*, Whitney Museum of American Art, NYC; 1960, 64, 67, 70: Carnegie, PA; 1961, 62: The Art Institute of Chicago, IL; 1962: *Geometric Abstraction in America*, circ., Whitney Museum of American Art, NYC; Seattle World's Fair, WA; 1963–1964: *Hans Hofmann and His Students*, circ., The Museum of Modern Art, NYC; 1963: Stedelijk Mueum, Amsterdam, Holland; *Toward a New Abstraction*, Jewish Museum, NYC; *Direction—Painting USA*, San Francisco Museum of Modern Art, CA; 1962–1967: circ., Whitney Museum of American Art Annuals, NYC; 1963–1964: *Contemporary Wall Sculpture, circ.*, American Federation of Arts, NYC; 1964: *Decade of New Talent*, circ., American Federation of Arts, NYC; 1965: International Biennial Exhibition of Paintings, Tokyo; *A Decade of American Drawings*, Whitney Museum of American Art; University of Illinois; 1966: *Art of the US 1670–1966*, Whitney Museum of American Art; 1971: *Holograms*, Finch College, NYC.

FELIX PASILIS

They want a statement!
My mind went blank.

For me it was a 'muddle'. Could I swim to the distant shore and paddle the 'Artistic' puddle with my single neurotic oar? A search for strings to knit my 'Ego' Soul.

I stand somewhere now; maybe close; to the 'Illustraradi' and their feet of gold.

Felix Pasilis, Statement: Letter to the editor September 26, 2008.

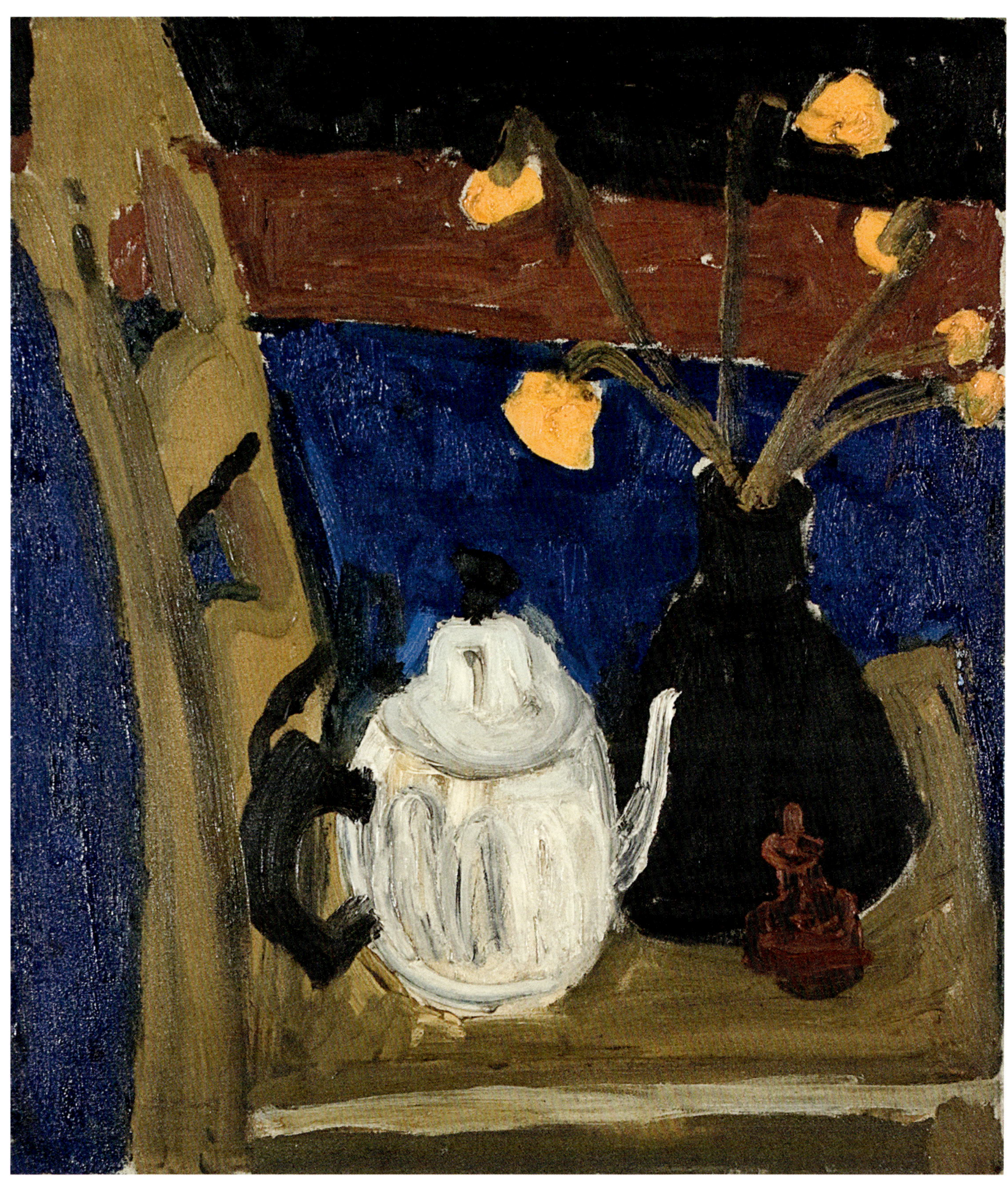

FELIX PASILIS, *Untitled*, c. 1953
Oil on canvas 28 1/8 x 24 1/8
Private collection
© Felix Pasilis

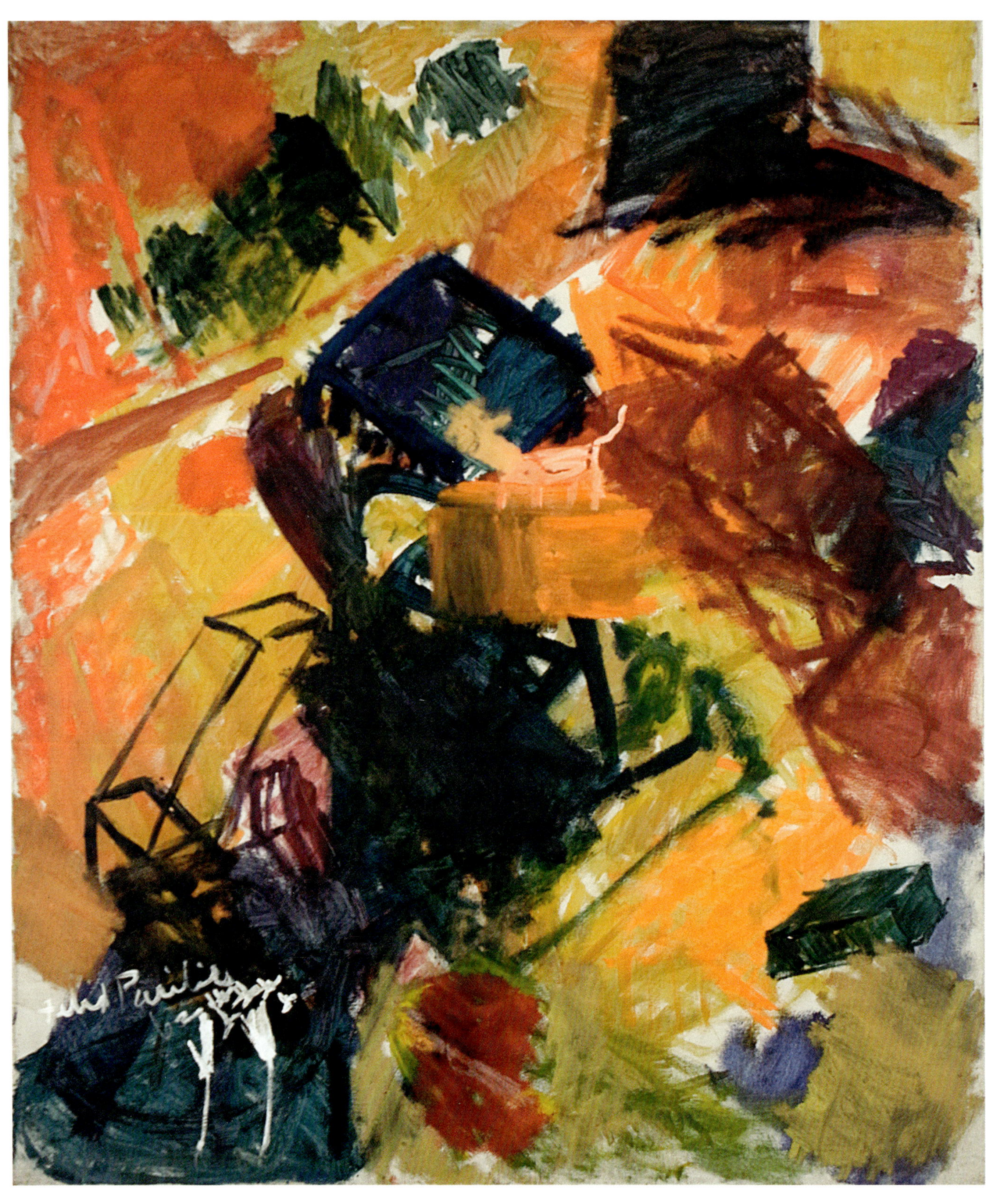

FELIX PASILIS, *Untitled*, 1962
Oil on canvas 49 3/8 x 41 1/8 inches
Private collection

FELIX PASILIS, [1922 -]

Born August 1922, Batvia IL.

Studied 1946-1948: American University, Washington, D.C. studied drawing, painting and composition under William Calfee; 1949-1952: Hans Hofmann School.

Military Service in World War II 1940-1945: Army Air Corps., attaining the rank of Master Sargent.

Selected Solo Exhibitions 1953: Hansa Gallery, NYC; 1954: 1954, 55: Urban Gallery, NYC; 1956: Tibor de Nagy Gallery, NYC; 1956: Bernard Ganymede Gallery, NYC; 1957: Zabriskie Gallery, NYC; 1959: Marino Art Gallery, NYC; 1961: Green Gsllery, NYC; 1962: R.J Gallery; 1963: The Greer Gallery, NYC; 1966: Great Jones Gallery, NYC.

Selected Group Exhibitions 1951: 813 Broadway Gallery, NYC; 1952: Tanager Gallery, NYC; 1953: Hansa Gallery, NYC; 1953, 54, 55, 56, 57: *New York Painting and Sculpture Annuals*, Stable Gallery, NYC; 1955, 58, 61: *Carnegie International*; Pittsburgh, PA; 1955: *21 Young Americans*, Stable Gallery, NYC; 1957: *The New York School, Second Generation*, Jewish Museum, NYC; 1959: Staten Island, Richard Brown Baker Collection; 1961: Yale University.

ROLAND PETERSEN

[This} painting is typical of the approach that has interested me for the past few years. The picnic set in deep space offers ample opportunity for me to explore the human figure singly and in groups. I am especially interested in integrating figures, still life material and landscape by means of light—especially the brilliant sunlight of the Sacramento Valley. I am attempting to create a somewhat surrealistic aura through the use of quiet impersonal figures placed in a deep landscape.

Much of my past work has been done in the so–called Abstract and Non–objective concepts. From my experience, the main differences between the non–representational (abstract and non–objective) and the representational (figurative) lie in the ideas which the artists wish to convey. I have found that the non–representational or strictly formal approaches are limiting and somewhat stark.

At the present, there is a strong figurative movement in American painting, stemming from the abstract and non–objective. The result is a vital and perspective approach to representational subject matter.

For the past six years, I have been using the human figure, singly and in groups, as subject matter for my oil paintings. The landscape is a setting for these figures has been a more recent introduction.

Roland Petersen, Statement: From *Eleventh Exhibition of Contemporary American Painting and Sculpture 1963*, College of Fine and Applied Arts, University of Illinois, Urbana, March 3 through April 7, 1963. p.183

I am attempting to integrate figures and landscape by means of light. The unification of a painting through light passages allows me much freedom of color and form. The placement of the figures is meant to create an atmosphere of tranquility and spaciousness. The somewhat surrealistic effect of passive figures in deep space suggest a universality which interests me. I have found this approach a natural evolution from my periods of abstract and non–objective painting.

Roland Petersen, Statement: From *Contemporary American Painting and Sculpture 1961*, College of Fine and Applied Arts, University of Illinois, Urbana, February 26 through April 2, 1961. p.122

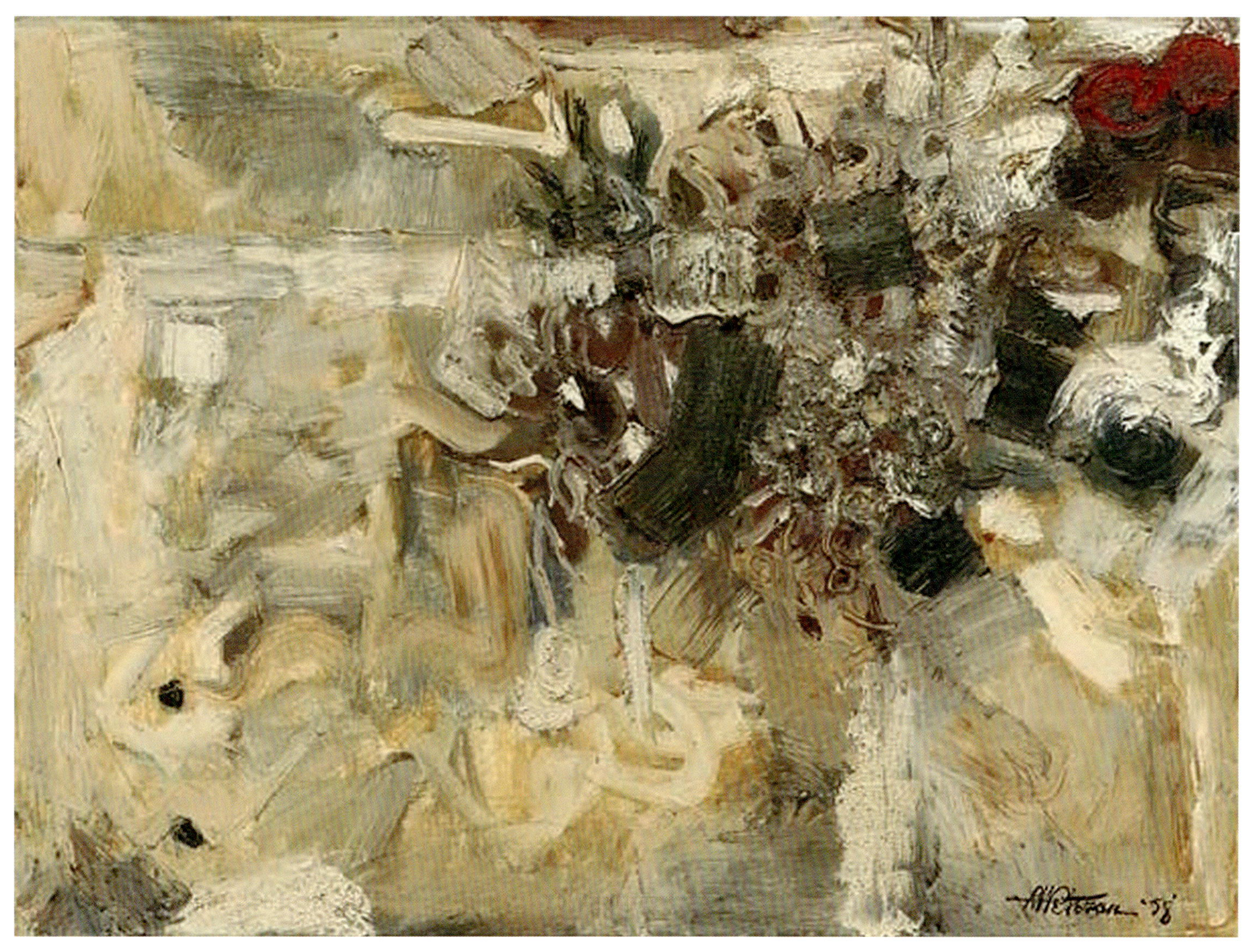

ROLAND PETERSEN, *Untitled*, 1958
Oil on canvas, 29 x 38 1/2 inches
 Courtesy Hackett-Freedman Gallery, San Francisco, CA

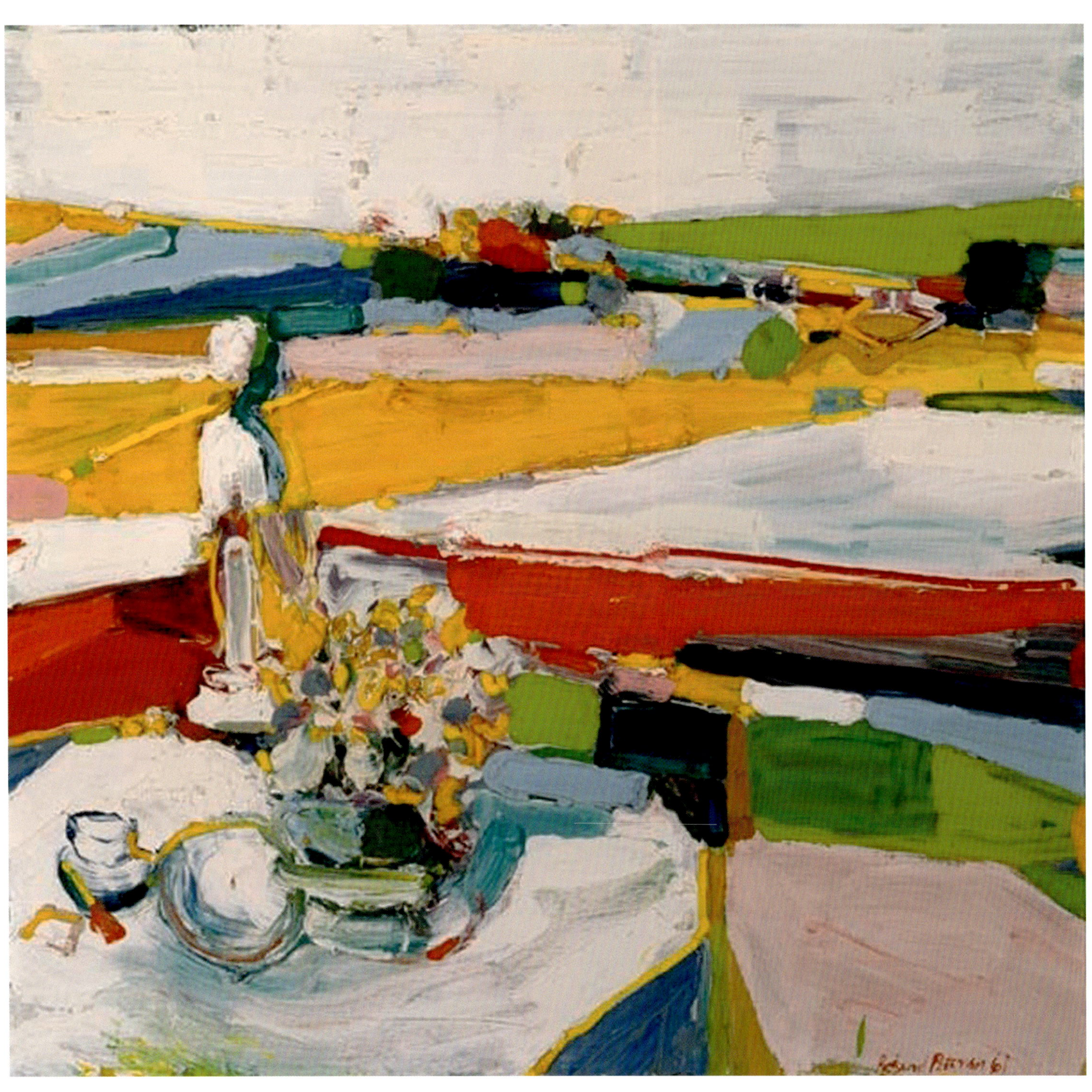

ROLAND PETERSEN, *Girl with Flowers*, 1961
Oil on canvas, 36 x 37 1/4 inches

ROLAND CONRAD PETERSEN, [1926-]

Born March 31, 1926, Endelave, Horsens, Denmark. **To USA** 1928.

Military Service World War II
1943–1945: US Navy.

Studied 1949 AB, AM, 1950: With Glenn Wessels, Chiura Obata, Erle Loran, John Haley, Worth Ryder, James McGray, University of the Pacific and University of California; 1950–1951: Hans Hofmann School; 1950: Atelier 17, Paris; 1963, 1970: with S. W. Hayter, Paris; 1954: California School of Fine Arts.

Teaching Position 1952–1956: Washington State University; 1956–1991: University of California, Davis.

Selected Solo Exhibitions 1954: (first) Oakland Art Museum, Oakland, CA; 1954, 55, 57: Spokane Art Center of Washington State University; 1954: Boise (Idaho) Art Association; 1961: Esther Robles Gallery, Los Angeles, CA; City Library, Sacramento, CA; California Palace; 1962: Gump's Gallery; 1963, 65, 67: Staempfly Gallery, NYC; 1966: E. B. Crocker Art Gallery, Sacramento, CA; Chico State College; 1966, 69, 72, 73, 75, 76: Adele Bednarz Gallery; 1968: M. H. de Young Memorial Museum, San Francisco, CA; 1968–1969: Western Association of Art Museum Directors, circ.; 1972: Phoenix Art Museum, Phoenix, AZ; 1973: Santa Barbara Museum of Art, Santa Barbara, CA; 1974: Whitman College, Walla Walla, WA; 1975: Solano Community College, Solano, CA; 1976: University of California, Davis, CA; 1976: American River College, Scramento, CA; 1977: College of Siskyous, CA; Artists Cooperative Gallery, Sacramento, CA; 1978: California State College, Stanislaus, CA; Shasta College Redding, CA; 1979: Brubacher Gallery, Sarasota, FL; 1980: University of Nevada, NV; University of Reading, England; 1981, 84: Davis Art Center, CA; 1981: The Print Mint, Chicago, IL; 1981, 82, 83, 84, 85: Forick Gallery; 1982: Rara Avis Gallery, Sacramento, CA; University Club Chicago, IL; 1983: Cunningham Memorial Art Gallery, Bakersfield, CA; 1984, 85: Art Works, Fair Oaks, CA; 1984: Smith-Anderson Gallery, Palo Alto, CA; Sacramento State Capital, CA; 1991: Harcourts Modern and Contemporary Art, San Francisco, CA.
Retrospectives: 1966: *15 years, 1950–65*, Chico College, CA; 1968: *5 years, 1963–1968*, M. H. de Young Memorial Museum, San Francisco, CA;1976: Washington State University, Pullman, WA; 1978: University of California, Davis, CA.

Selected Group Exhibition 1961: *Pacific Profile*, Norton Simon Museum, Pasadena, CA; Poindexter Gallery, NYC; 1961, 63, 69: University of Illinois, IL; 1962: Santa Barbara Museum of Art, CA; 1964: Carnegie Institute of Technology, Pittsburgh, PA; 1965: *Annual* The Art Institute of Chicago, IL; 1966: *American Painting, Virginia Museum of Fine Arts*, Richmond, VA; 1968: *Humanist Tradition*, New School for Social Research, NYC; 1975: *California Landscape*, Oakland Art Museum, Oakland, CA; 1977: *Atelier 17*, University of Wisconsin, Madison, WI.

JACKSON POLLOCK

I don't care for "abstract expressionism" . . . and it's certainly not "nonobjective," and not "nonrepresentational" either. I'm very representational some of the time, and a little all of the time. But when you're painting out of your unconscious, figures are bound to emerge. We're all of us influenced by Freud, I guess. I've been a jungian for a long time . . . painting is a state of being . . . . Painting is self-discovery. Every good artist paints what he is.

Jackson Pollock, Statement: from *Conversation with Artists*, published by Selden Rodman, New York, 1957. Reproduced in Jackson Pollock, by Francis V. O'Connor. Museum of Modern Art, New York, 1967, p. 73.

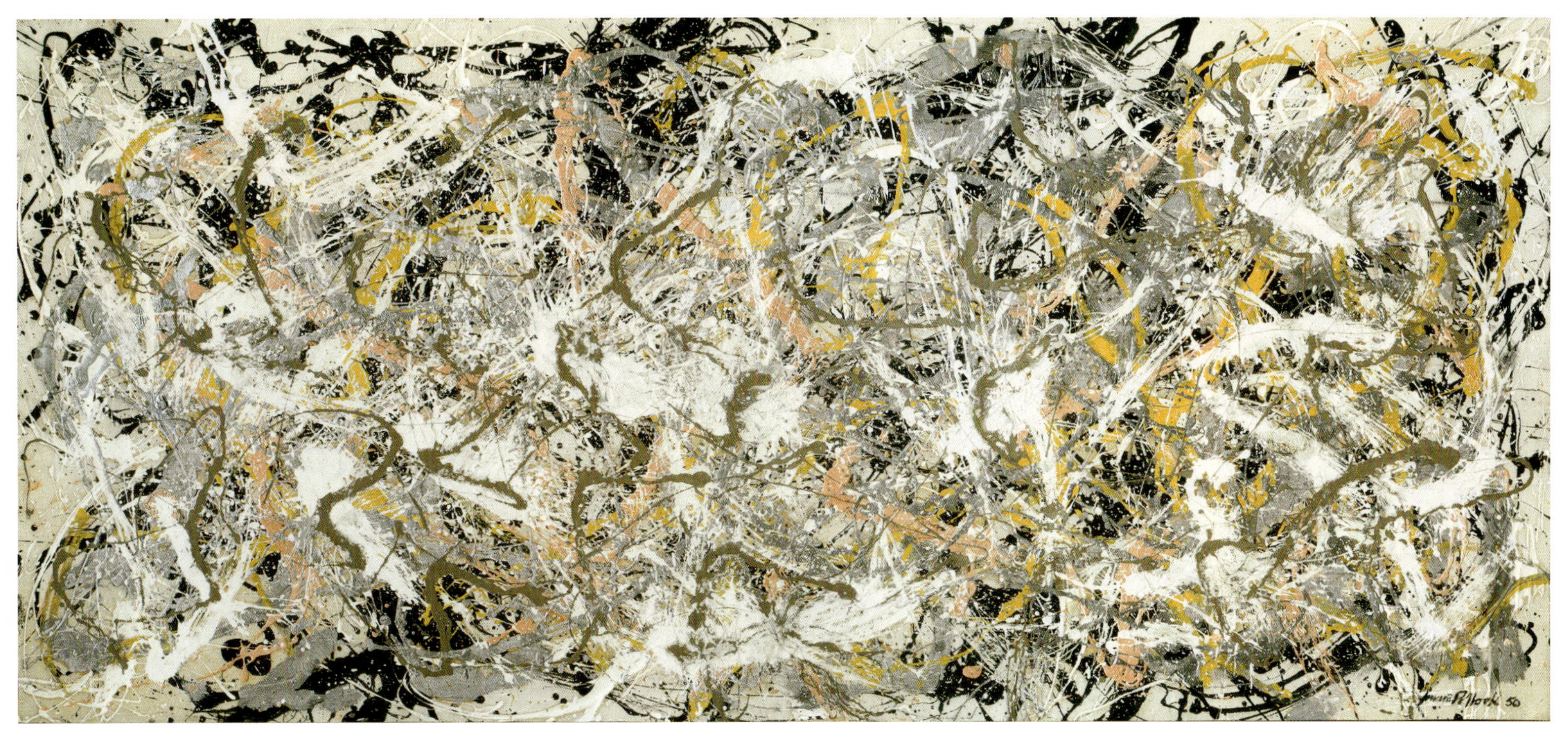

JACKSON POLLOCK, *Number 27, 1950*, 1950
Oil on canvas, 49 x 106 in. (124.46 x 269.24 cm)
Whitney Museum of American Art, New York; purchase, 53.12

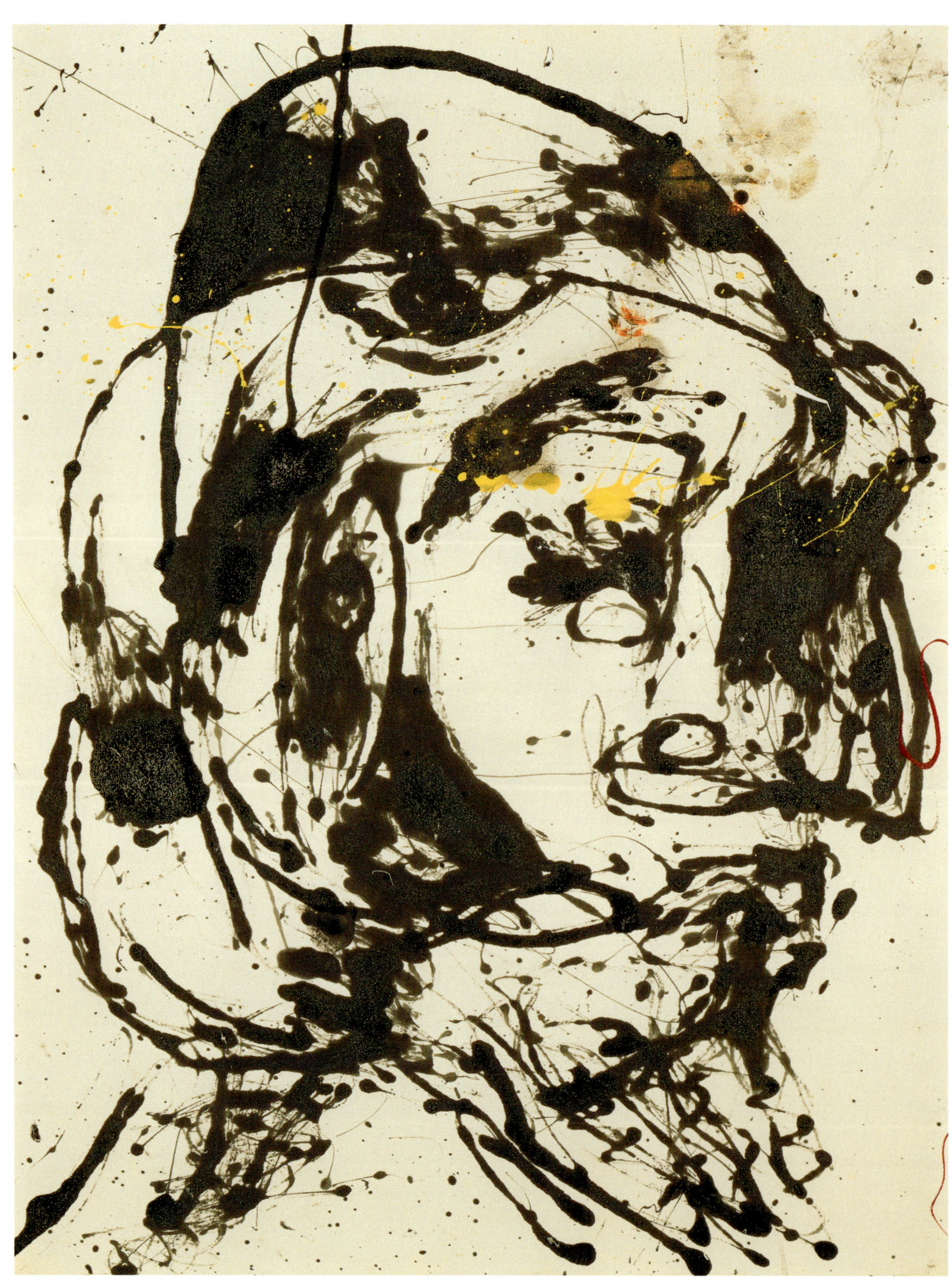

JACKSON POLLOCK, *Number 7*, 1952
Enamel and oil on canvas, 53 1/8 x 40 inches (134.9 x 101.6 cm)
The Metropolitan Museum of Art
Purchase, Emilio Azcarraga Gift, in honor of William S. Lieberman, 1987 (1987.92)

JACKSON POLLOCK, [1912-1956]

Born January 28, 1912, Cody, WY.
Died August 11, 1956, East Hampton, NY.

Studied Art Students League, NYC: 1930–33, with Thomas Hart Benton.

Federal Art Project (WPA) 1935-1943: Easel painting.

Selected Solo Exhibitions 1943 (first) 45, 46, 47: Art of This Century, NYC; 1948–1951, 83: Betty Parsons Gallery, NYC; 1945, 51: Arts Club of Chicago; 1950: Museo Civico Correr, Venice; Galleria d'Arte del Naviglio, Milan; 1952: Galerie Paul Facchetti; 1952, 54, 55, 57: Sidney Janis Gallery; 1953: Zurich; 1957: IV São Paulo Biennial; 1962: Marlborough Gallena d'Arte, Rome; 1964, 69: Marlborough Gerson Gallery, Inc., NYC; 1965: Marlborough Fine Art Ltd., London; 1970: The Whitney Museum of American Art; 1977: Berry-Hill Galleries, NYC; 1978: Yale University; 1979: American Cultural Center, Paris; 1979: Musee d'Art Moderne de la Ville de Paris, France; 1987, 92: Jason McCoy Inc., NYC; 1989: Anthony D'Offay Gallery, London. Retrospective: 1956, 67, 80, 99: Museum of Modern Art, NY; 1981: Guild Hall Museum, NY; 1982: Centre National D'Art et de Culture Georges Pompidou, Centre Beaubourg, Paris.

Selected Group Exhibitions 1949: *Jackson Pollock/William Gear,* Betty Parsons Gallery, NYC; 1946–1954: *Annuals and Biennials*, The Whitney Museum of American Art, NYC; 1948, 50, 56: XXIV, XXV, and XXVIII Venice Biennials; 1951, 54: *9th St.*, Show, the first and one subsequent *New York Painting and Sculpture Annual*, Stable Gallery, NYC; 1951: I São Paulo Biennial; 1952: *Fifteen Americans*, circ., Museum of Modern Art, NYC; *American Vanguard*, Galerie de France, Paris; 1953–55: *12 Modern American Painters and Sculptors*, circ., Europe, Museum of Modern Art, NYC; 1954–55: *The New Decade*, Whitney Museum of American Art, NYC; 1957: *75 Paintings from The Solomon R. Guggenheim Museum*, circ., Europe; 1987: *Abstract Expressionism: The Critical Development*, Albright-Knox Art Gallery, Buffalo, NY.

JEANNE AMELIE SILLS REYNAL

Today in America, the emphasis in art is upon the individual adventure.

But this freedom is not touched upon by craftsmen in the art of mosaic. With the exception of Gaudi, no one has adventured in the fragmentation of stones.

Gaudi was fortunate to find among the Barcelonan artisans helpers equal to his humor. With their help, he used simple crockery to create a milky light in the Catalonian day.

Owning much to so many, I have worked to rediscover in terms of our times the primary meaning and real poetry in the art of mosaic - light. By means of a technique available to all, permitting an immediacy of expression lost since the Renaissance, the palimpsest, or third hand, is buried.

I affirm that the art of mosaic can rise from the pavement where Ghirlandaio placed it. The end result must and will be judged on its quality. Mosaic, to be real, must be individual, coherent and luminous-the reality fresh and frightening, like every original.

Jeanne Reynal, Statement: Provided to the editor by the estate of Jeanne Reynal. November 4, 2008.

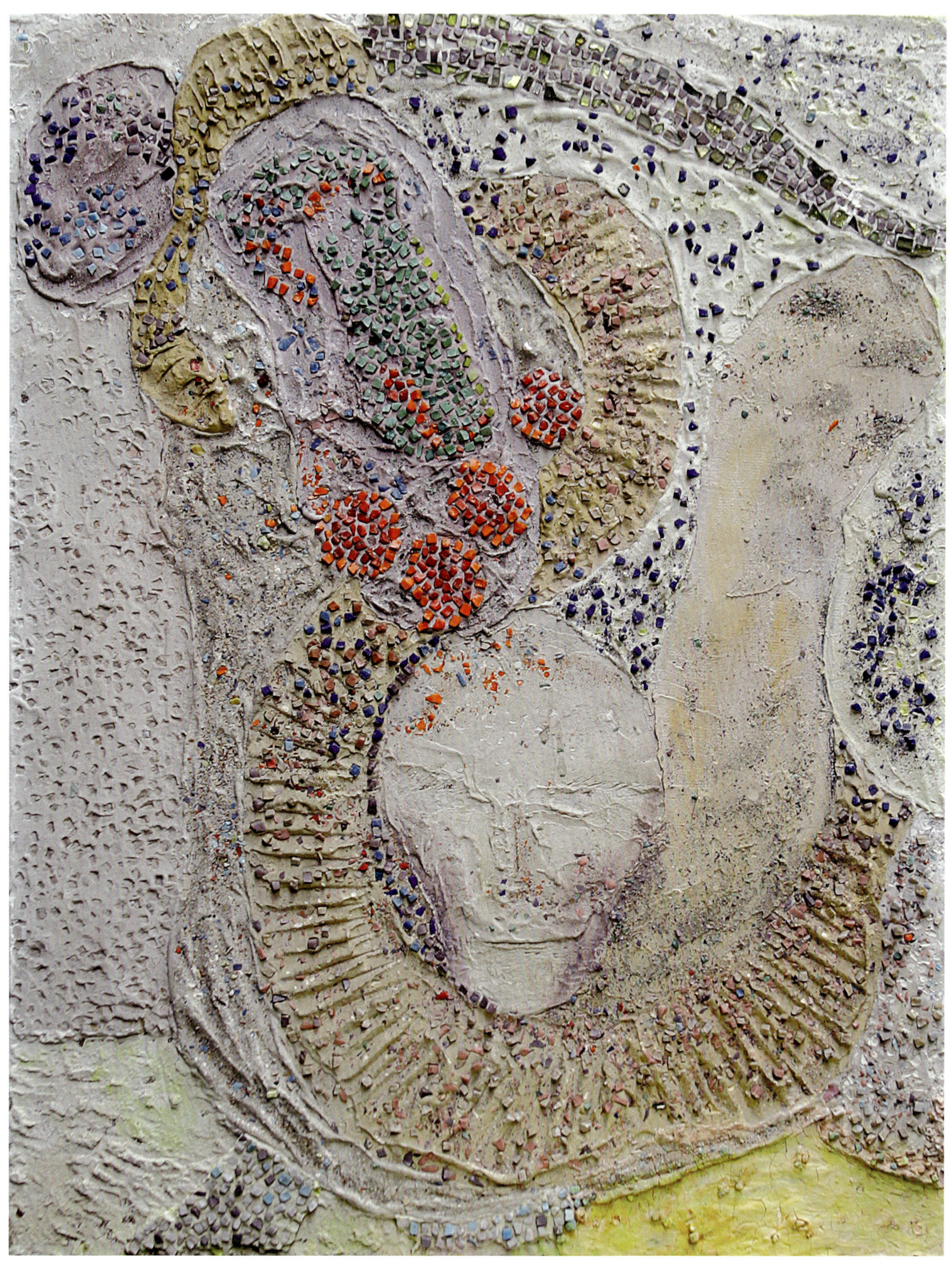

JEANNE REYNAL, *Untitled*, 1958
Cement with mosaic, 29 x 22 inches
Private collection

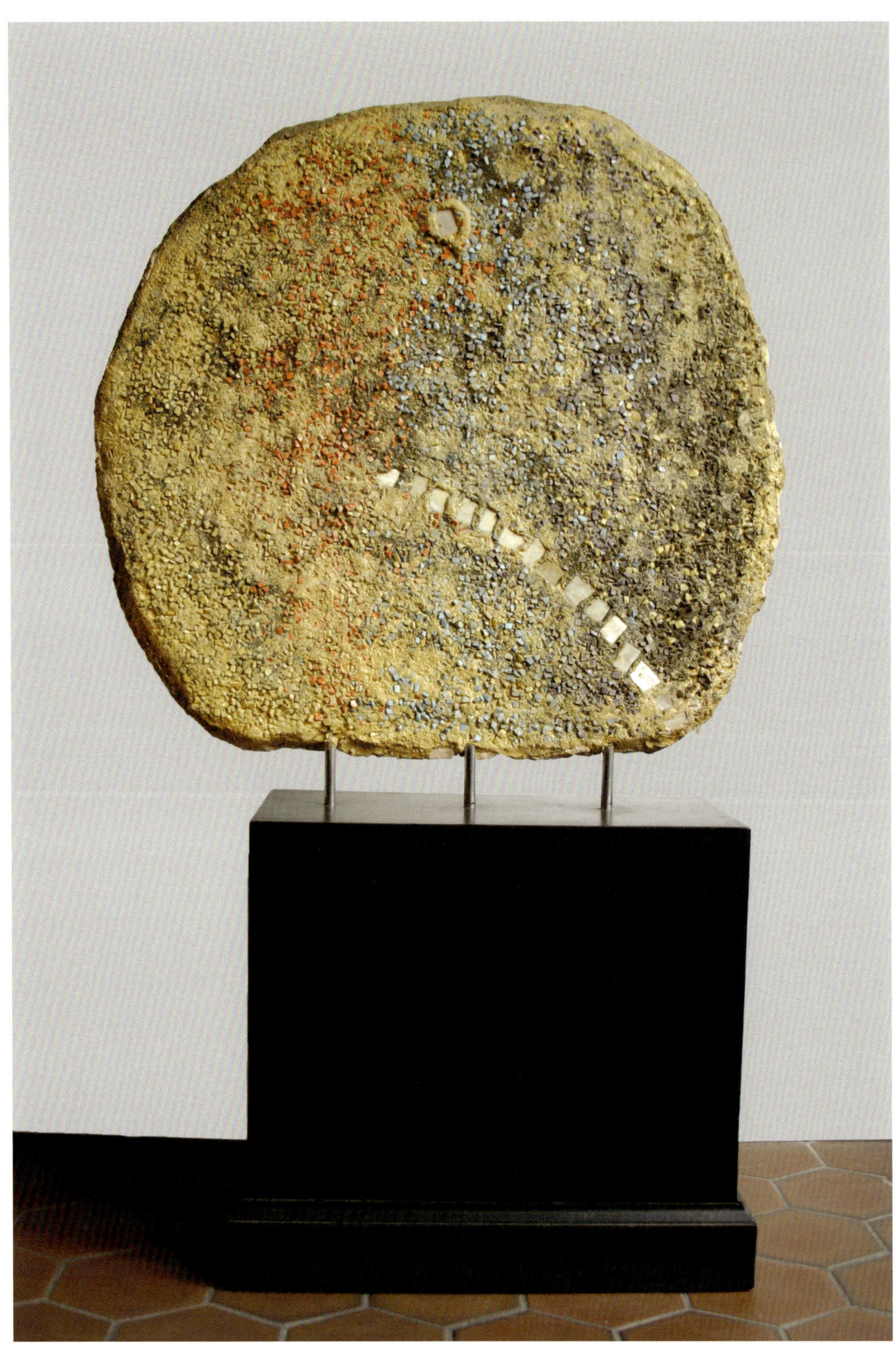

JEANNE REYNAL, *Sphere*, c. 1950s
Cement with mosaic, Diameter: 29 inches
Collection of Anita Shapolsky Gallery, New York

JEANNE AMELIE SILLS REYNAL, [1903-1983]

Born 1903, White Plains, NY.
Died 1983, New York City.

Studied 1930–38: Apprentice in the atelier of Boris Anrep in Paris; Worked with him on Bank of England and Greek Church of London commissions.

Teaching Positions 1964: Dord Fitz Gallery, Amarillo, Texas;
1969: Notre Dame University, Indiana.

Selected Solo Exhibitions 1940: Walker Gallery, Los Angeles, CA; 1943: Arts Club, Chicago, IL; 1959: *One-man exhibition, Section Eleven* (Annex of Betty Parsons Gallery), NYC; 1961: Exhibition *Outdoor View*, Millbrook, New York (Sidney Wolfson); 1961: Loeb Student Center, New York University, NY; 1964 P.V. I. Gallery, NY.

Selected Group Exhibitions 1942–46: *Annual Shows*, San Francisco Museum of Art, San Francisco, CA; 1944: *Sixty-fourth Annual Exhibition*, San Francisco Museum of Art, CA; 1945: *Sixty-fifth Annual Exhibition*, San Francisco Museum of Art, CA; 1945 *Blood Flames*, Iolas Gallery, NYC; 1947: *Exhibition Le Surrealisme en 1947*, Paris, France; 1951, 52, 53, 54, 55, 56, 57: *Whitney Museum of American Art Annuals and Biennials*, Whitney Museum of American Art, NYC; 1951: *Abstract Painting and Sculpture in America*, The Museum of Modern Art, NYC; 1953: Florence, Italy; 1957: Mills College of Education, Oakland, CA; 1960: *16 Women Artists,* Dord Fitz Gallery, Amarillo, TX; 1962: *Seattle World's Fair*, Seattle, WA; 2006: *Encore*, Sidney Mishkin Gallery, Baruch College, The City University of New York; 2006: *Encore* Anita Shapolsky Gallery, NYC; 2008: *Art Couple - Jeanne Reynal & Thomas Sills* Anita Shapolsky Gallery, NYC.

JAMES ROSATI

I honestly believe that every man has a problem. He has a point of departure, but that point of departure is not what makes his work important. What really makes it important is the personality he's been able to project into his work. ...the total personality. When you use the word "design," are you talking about it in the sense of putting whatever you're doing in the highest order that is possible?...

And in that conscious state you have a plan by which you are going to determine the result. That's the kind of thing we're not involved in. There are other states when the work actually takes over, when you stand as a handmaiden to the work: then the work dictates what you are going to do rather than you dictating.

James Rosati, Waldorf Panel, 1. "The Spontaneous and Design," *It Is.* 6 Autumn 1965, NYC. A Magazine for Abstract Art, Second Half Publishing Co., Inc. 1965.

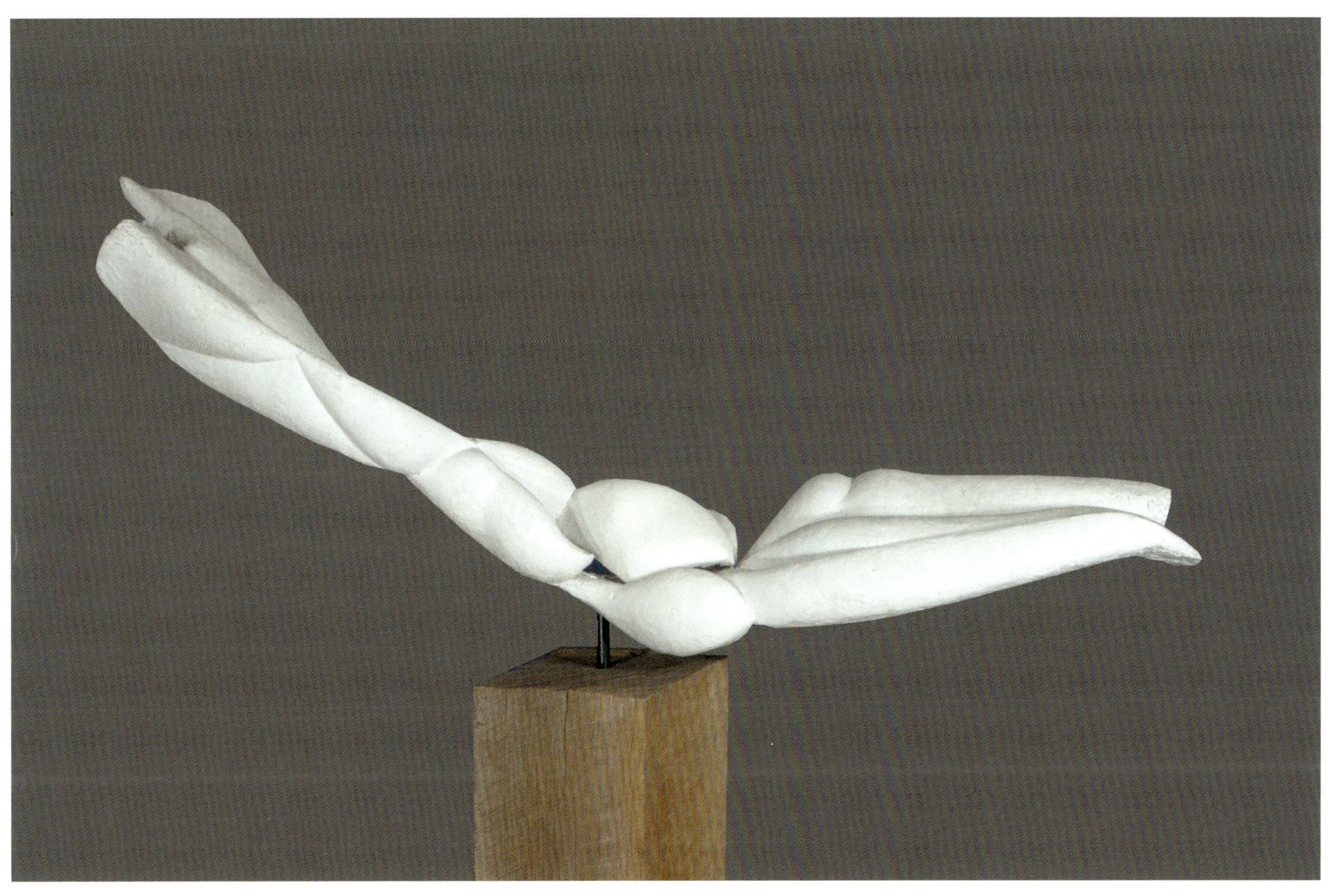

JAMES ROSATI, *Flying Figure*, 1952
Plaster, wire mesh and metal with wood base, 23 x 48 x 10 inches
Private collection

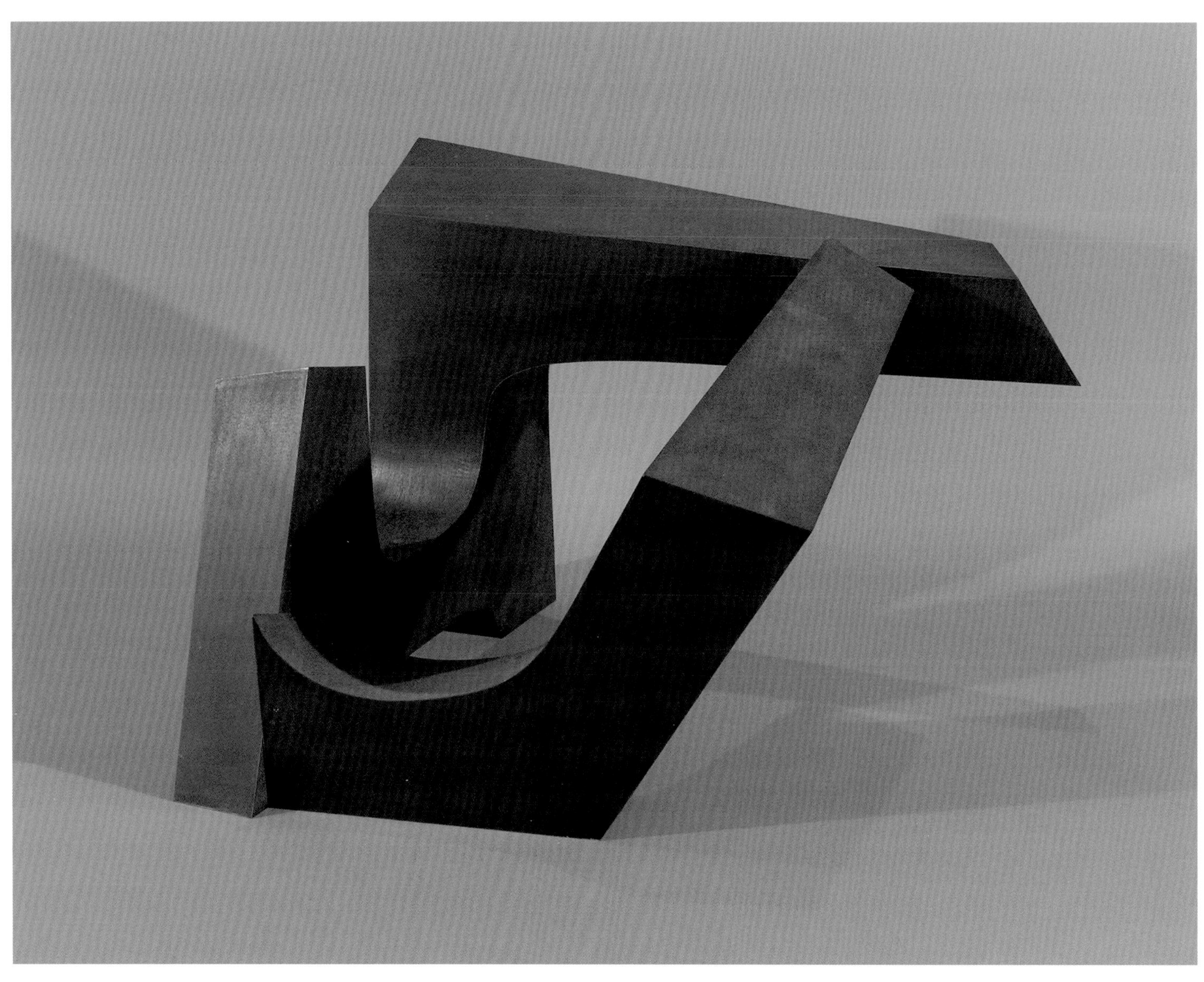

JAMES ROSATI, *Untitled (Two Forms)*, 1987 - 88
Steel, Ed. 3, 21 x 27 x 28 inches

JAMES ROSATI, [1912-1988]

Born 1912, Washington, PA. In 1943 came to New York where he resided the rest of his life.
Died 1988 in New York.

Federal Art Project (WPA) 1938: Sculptor.

Teaching Positions 1960–73: Cooper Union; Pratt Institute; Yale University; 1977–79: University of Pennsylvania; 1960–73: Dartmouth College.

Selected Solo Exhibitions 1954 (first) The Peridot Gallery, NYC; 1959, 62: Otto Gerson Gallery, NYC; 1963: Dartmouth College; 1968: Colgate University; 1969: Brandeis University; 1970: Albright-Knox Art Gallery, Buffalo, NY; Yale U., 1970; Marlborough Gallery, Inc., NYC, 1970, 77, 81; Gibbes Art Gallery, Charleston, SC, 1981.

Selected Group Exhibitions 1951, 1953–1957: The *9th St.*, Exhibition, the first *New York Painting and Sculpture Annual* and subsequent 5 Annuals, Stable Gallery, NYC; 1956: *Painters & Sculptors on 10th Street*, Tanager Gallery, NYC; 1952, 53, 54, 60, 62, 64, 66, 68: Art *Annuals & Biennials*, Whitney Museum of American NYC; 1958, 61, 64: Carnegie Institute of Technology, Washington, D.C; 1960: Claude Bernard, Paris; *Contemporary Sculpture*, American Federation of Artists; 1961: *International Outdoor Sculpture Exhibitions*, Otterlo, Holland; 1961, 62: Art Institute of Chicago; 1962: Seattle World's Fair; *Festival of Two Worlds*, Spoleto; 1963: *International Sculpture Exhibition*, Battersea Park, London; 1964–65: New York World's Fair; 1966: *I Flint Invitational*, Flint Institute of Arts, MI; 1967: Colby College; 1967–68: Museum of Contemporary Crafts, circ.; 1969: *Sculpture of the 60s*, Grand Rapids, MI; 1970: *American Sculpture*, University of Nebraska; *The Partial Figure in Modern Sculpture*, Baltimore Museum of Art, Baltimore, MD; 1971: *Biennial* Middleheim, Antwerp; 1974: *Monumenta*, Newport, RI; 1975: *Artist and Fabricator*, University of Massachusetts; 1976: *The American Salon des refuses*, Stamford Museum, Stamford, CT; 1979: *l'Art Vivant Aux Etats Unis*, Foundation Maeght, Paris.

RICHARDS RUBEN

Art is the electricity of humanity touched and passed through generations.

Each act the drawer/painter directs to their selected working surface is a positive action whether in mark or erase...all acts contained in the total mass of the work.
The actual content of the drawing/painting, the touching into visibility is the nature of its meaning, often far-a-field from what is depicted independent of style or school or subject.

A painting describes nothing so much as it describes itself.

I wonder if writers are ever asked to paint an analysis of their writings the way painters are asked to write about their paintings?

Richards Ruben, Statement: From the artist's journal provided by Gail Diven Ruben to the editor.

What is painting, what is art? To me a religion, a philosophy, a way of life, and the constant search for the means of expressing it.

Richards Ruben, Statement: From the University of Illinois exhibition catalog, *Contemporary American Painting*, Sunday, March 2, through Sunday April 13, 1952. College of Fine and Applied Arts, Urbana, IL. p. 228

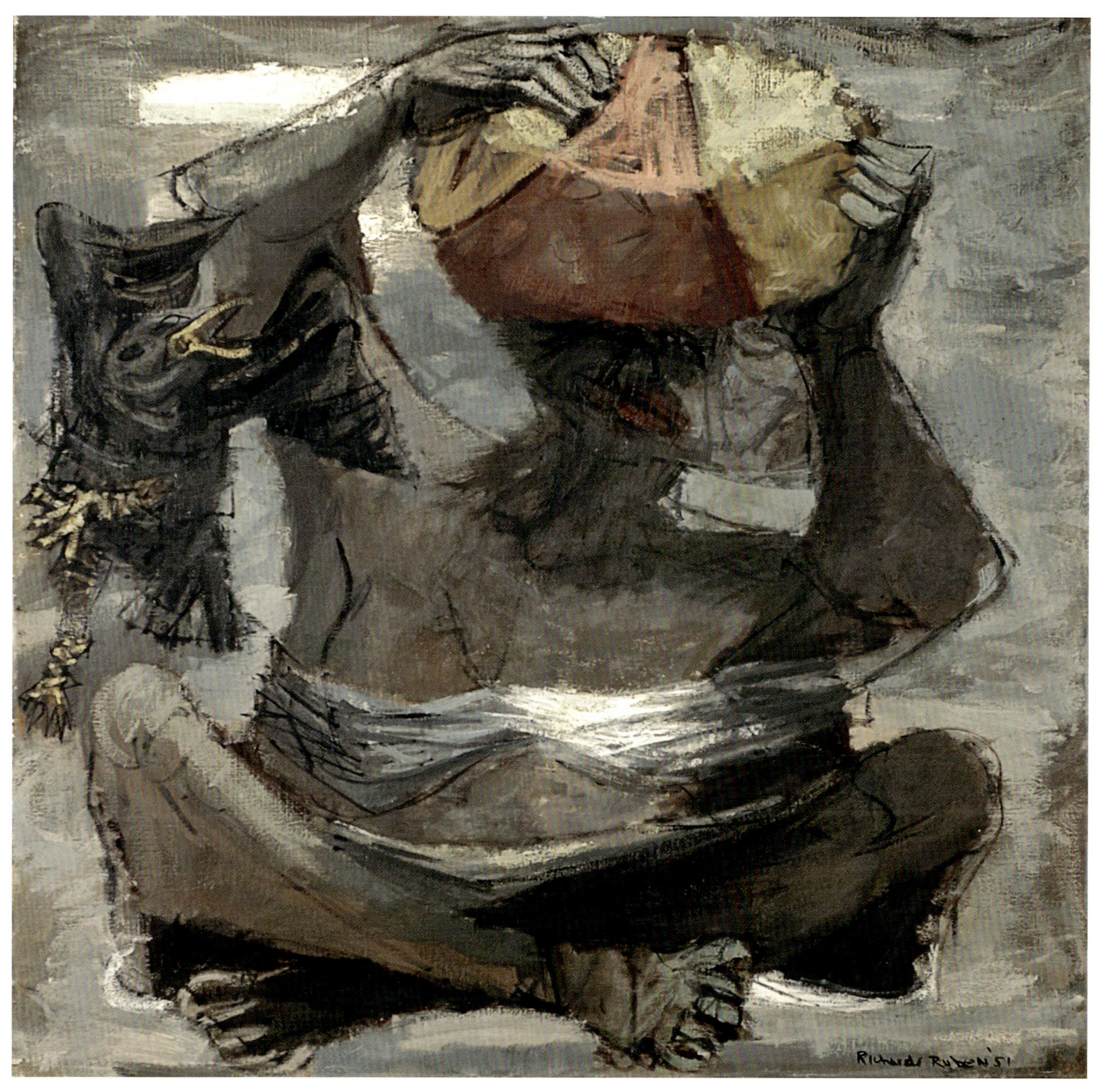

RICHARDS RUBEN, *Ball and Bird*, 1951
Oil on canvas, 40 x 36 inches
Private collection

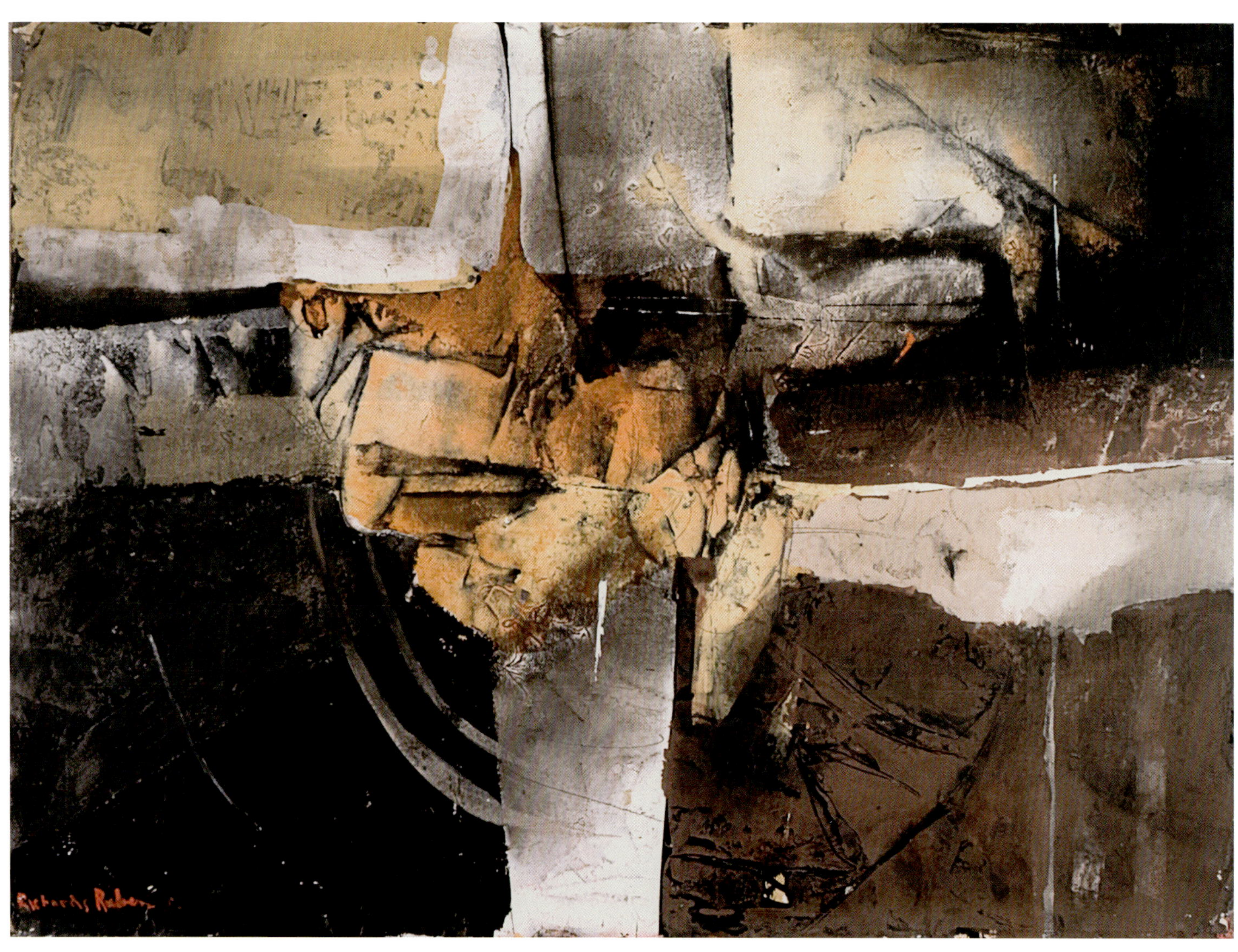

RICHARDS RUBEN, *Summer Solstice*, 1956
Watercolor on board, 21 x 29 1/2 inches
Private collection
© Estate of Richards Ruben. Courtesy of Anita Shapolsky Gallery, New York

RICHARDS RUBEN, [1925-1998]

Born November 29,1925, Los Angeles, CA.
Died 1998 in Venice, Italy.

Studied 1944-46: Chouinard Art Institute, Los Angeles, CA.

Military Service in World War II 1942–44: US Army.

Teaching Positions 1947–48: San Bernardino Valley College, CA; 1948–49, 46–47: Arts and Crafts Center, Pittsburgh, PA;1949–54: Pasadena Art Center, CA; 1954–61: Chouinard Art Institute, Los Angeles, CA; 1956: Pasadena Art Museum, CA; 1958: University of California, Los Angeles, CA; 1958–62: Claremont Graduate School, Claremont, CA; 1958–62: Pomona College; 1962–65: Cooper Union, New York, NY; 1964: Santa Barbara Museum of Art, CA;1965: University of Southern California, Los Angeles, CA; 1967–71, 1982–98: Pratt Institute, Brooklyn NY; also 1984, 87–98: Pratt in Venice Italy; 1966–69: Columbia University, New York, NY; 1963–72, 1974–76: New York University, New York,NY; 1976: Drew University, Madison NJ.

Selected Solo Exhibitions 1952, 54: Felix Landau Gallery, Los Angeles, CA; 1954, 55, 61: Pasadena Museum of Art, CA; 1957: Oakland/AM; 1958: Paul Kantor Gallery, Beverly Hills, CA; Grand Central Moderns, NYC; 1960, 61, 63: Ferus Gallery, Los Angeles, CA; 1961: California Palace of the Legion of Honor, San Francisco, CA; 1962, 64, 69: Poindexter Gallery, NYC; 1970: San Francisco Museum of Modern Art, CA; 1974, 76: Cornell University, Ithaca, NY; 1977: Peter Rose Gallery, NYC; Neuberger Museum of Art, State University of New York at Purchase; 1979: Ericson Gallery, NYC; 1981: Harm Bouckaert Gallery, NYC; Race Gallery, Philadelphia; 1984: Baruch College, NYC; 1986–2001: Anita Shapolsky Gallery, NYC; 1992, 94: Ball State University Art Gallery, Muncie, IN. Retrospective: *40 years Retrospective Exhibition*, circ., Mills College, Oakland CA.

Selected Group Exhibitions 1948, 53, 55, 57, 68: Los Angeles County Museum of Art, CA; 1952, 56: University of Illinois, Urbana; 1953: Corcoran Gallery, Washington, D.C.; 1953, 57, 59: Pennsylvania Academy of Fine Arts, Philadelphia, PA; 1954: *Younger American Painters*, Solomon R. Guggenheim Museum, NY; 1955: Sao Paulo 3rd Biennial, Brazil; Carnegie (Pittsburgh International), PA; 1955, 58: Santa Barbara Museum of Art, CA; 1957, 59: Brooklyn Museum, NY; 1959: 1st Paris Biennial, Paris, France; 1962–63: *Fifty California Artists*, Whitney Museum of American Art, NY; 1963: *Arte de America y Espana,* El Retiro Parquet, Madrid; Whitney Museum of American Art, Biennial, NY; 1966: University of Texas, Austin, TX; 1975: Drew University Art Gallery Madison, NJ; New Port Harbor Museum of Art, New Port Beach, CA; 1976: San Francisco Museum of Art, Bi-Centennial, CA; 1980: Gallerie Ressle, Stockholm, Sweden; 1984: Louise Ross Gallery, NYC; 1986: *American Abstractions: Four Currents,* Lewis Meisel Gallery, New York, NY; 1986, 89, 90, 94, 95, 96: Anita Shapolsky Gallery, New York, NY; 1987: *Eight New York Artists,* Cornell University, Ithaca, NY; 1999: *Radical Past: Contemporary Art & Music in Pasadena, 1960–1974,* Norton Simon Museum of Art, Pasadena, CA; 2001: *Abstract Expressionism: Then and Now,* Hofstra Museum, Hempstead, NY; *Chouinard a Living Legacy,* Oceanside Museum of Art, CA.

JOAN SAVO

I paint almost every day — three or four hours...I paint over canvases that are failures, sometimes. I am not satisfied if it just doesn't have a certain vitality or strength. Sometimes it lacks humor: it gets too serious. Then I have to destroy it or introduce some new element into it.

...Some of the abstract things I work on are mostly pure color. They are very large. Those are really Zen paintings.

...There's something wonderful and mobile about people. Photographers get this. I think. I don't use any models, so when I make a figure, I'm hoping for a universal figure.

Joan Savo, Statement: From *Zen and the Art of Joan Savo*, by Sheila E. Toner. Art & The Artist. Monterey Life, p. 65

I think one painting suggests the next. There might be something in one painting that I would like to enlarge upon in the next. I begin working in terms of light and dark, warm and cool. then I keep working up until the colors react or oppose one another a certain way, the composition having been established from the beginning. When painting, I feel like Zoot Sims sounds playing jazz, with a free, soaring emotion and large reckless tangents nesting in the stream of action. And because I am working on many levels of consciousness, there are moments of extreme concentration on a line I am traveling unhesitatingly across the canvas and times when I drop everything and step back to see where I've been.

Joan Savo, 1978

Joan Savo, Statement: From *Zen and the Art of Joan Savo*, by Sheila E. Toner. Provided by Buff Germaine Savo

Visualizing, rather then working from the model, provides me a sustaining theme with fewer limitations and more possibilities in defining the human form. And to express the attitude of the figure, as displayed in his gesture or posture, is of more interest to me then to portray the image. My choice of the figure as subject matter possibly has something to do with my interest of the human scene. I have a concern for man in his existential aspect. While coping with the phantasmagoria of his world of trifling urgencies he maintains remarkable stature. I see this nobility presented in his 'epiphanies.' Colin Wilson, in his book, The strength to Dream, describes 'epiphanies' as 'moments observed by an artist in which the soul of the commonest object seems to us radiant.'

Joan Savo

Joan Savo, Statement: From Gallery de Silva announcement for: New Painting by Joan Savo, March 8- april 3, 1965

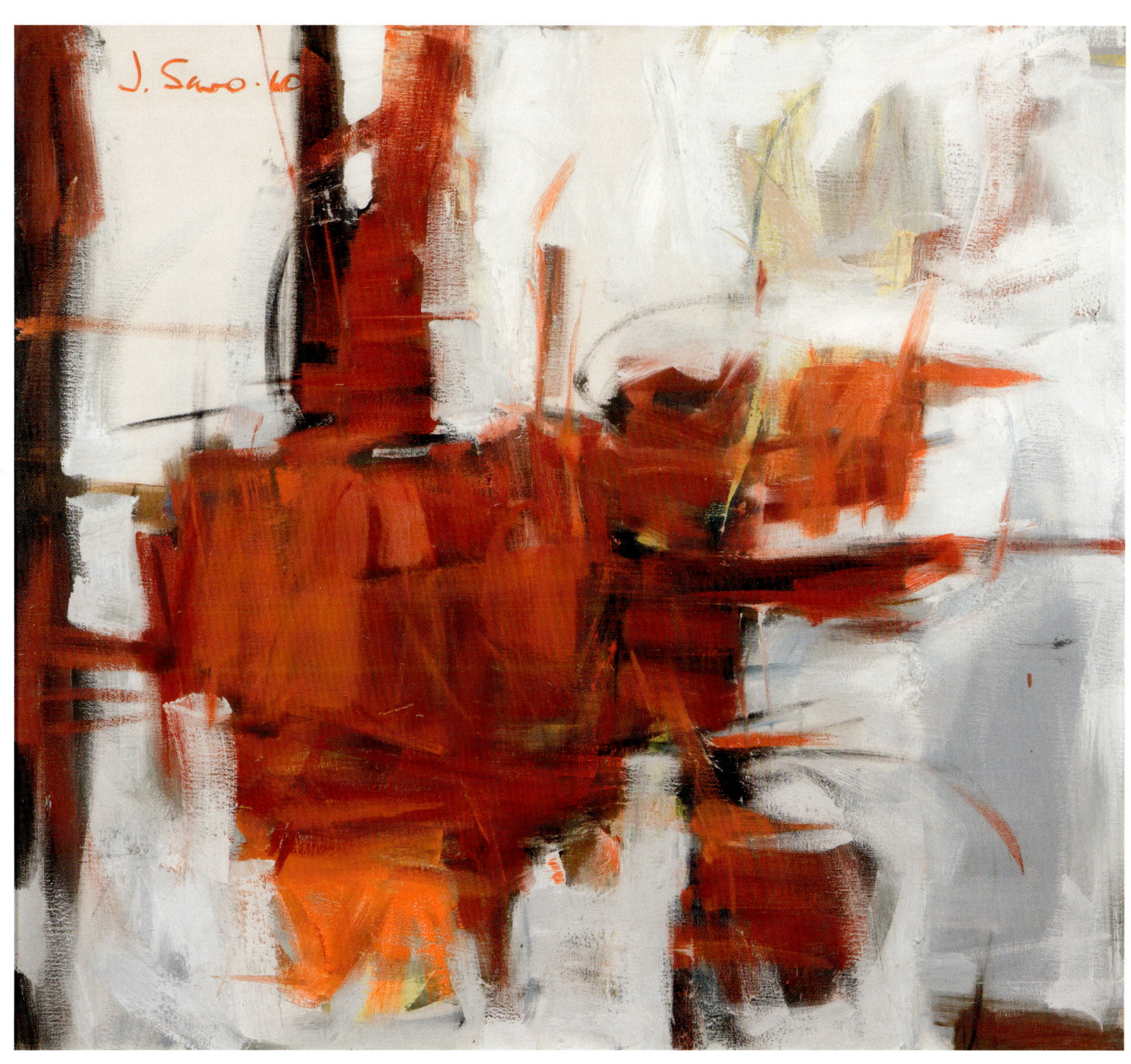

JOAN SAVO, *Red Abstract*, c. 1960
Oil on canvas, 46 x 50 inches
Collection of John & Katherine Simpson

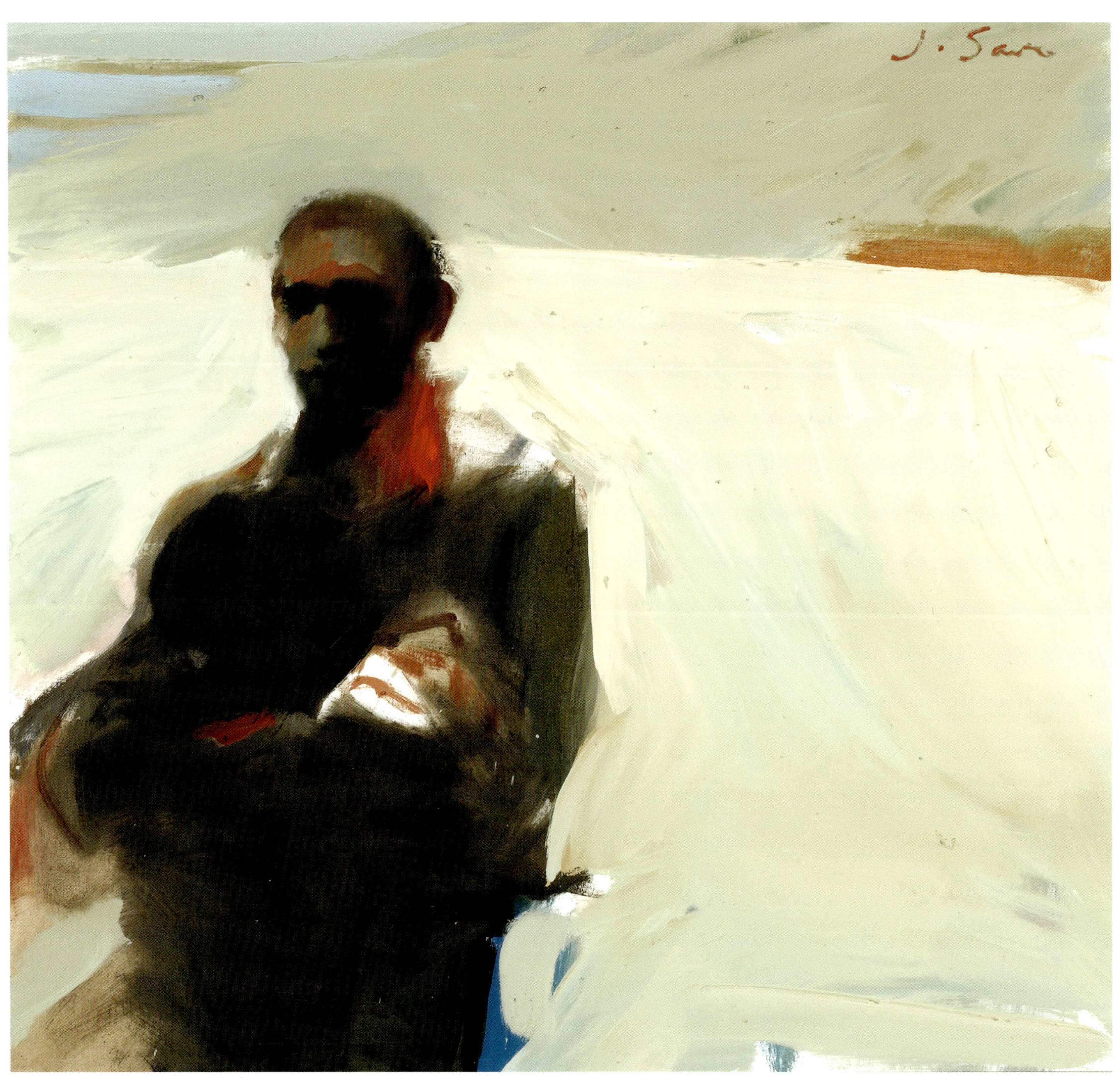

JOAN SAVO, *The Visible Man*, 1964
Oil on canvas, 36 x 38 inches,
Collection of Westbrook Galleries, Carmel, CA

JOAN SAVO, [1918-1992]

Born 1918 in Portland, OR.
Died 1992 in Pacific Grove, CA.

Selected Solo Exhibitions 1959, 60: Telegraph Hill Gallery, San Francisco, CA; 1959, 61: Coffee Gallery, San Francisco, CA; 1960: City Lights Bookshop, San Francisco, CA; San Francisco University, CA; Threadoare Square Gallery, Pacific Grove CA; 1961: Cannery Row Gallery, Monterey, CA; 1961, 67: Ring's Gallery, Monterey, CA; 1962, 63, 65: Hollis Gallery Fine Art, San Francisco, CA; Gamble Galleries, Monterey, CA; 1963: Tunnel Gallery, San Francisco, CA; 1963, 64, 74: Robert Pyle Gallery, Morro Bay, CA; 1964, 65, 67, 69: Gallery De Silva, Santa Barbara, CA; 1964: California Palace Of The Legion Of Honor, San Francisco, CA; Grove Gallery, Pacific Grove, CA; 1967: Seaside City Hall Inaugural Show, Seaside, CA; 1970, 74, 75: Pacific Grove Art Center; Pacific Grove, CA; 1977: Cafe Balthazar, Pacific Grove, CA; 1978: *Retrospective: 1959–1978*, Fresno Art Center, Fresno, CA; 1979: Monterey Conference Center, CA; Seventeenth St. Gallery, Pacific Grove, CA; 1980: Monterey Museum of Art, Monterey, CA; 1981: Robert Louis Stevenson School, Pebble Beach, CA; 1982, 88: Pacific Grove Art Center, Pacific Grove, CA; 1984: *Inaugural Exhibition*, Site 311 Gallery, Pacific Grove, CA; 1985: Victor Fisher Galleries, Oakland, CA; 1988: Carmel Art Association, Carmel, CA; 1991: Claypoole–Freese Gallery, Pacific Grove, CA.

Selected Group Exhibitions 1959: Sausalito Gallery, Sausalito, CA; *San Francisco Art Festival*, CA; 1959, 60: *Monterey County Fair*, Monterey, CA; 1959, 60, 63, 64: *Monterey Jazz Festival*, CA; 1960: *79th Annual*, Museum of Modern Art, San Francisco, CA; Tolosa Gallery (Two) San Luis Obispo, CA; Cannery Row Gallery (Two), Monterey, CA; *Carmel Valley Invitational*, CA; Gallery De Tours, Carmel, CA; 1960, 62: *Jack London Art Festival*, Oakland, CA; 1961: Brunn Gallery, San Francisco, CA; 1963: *Richmond Annual,* Richmond, CA; *Eight Figurative Painters*, Bolles Gallery, San Francisco, CA; *Contemporary Arts,* Berkeley, CA; *Cabrillo Arts/Festival*, Cabrillo College, CA; 1963, 64, 65, 66: American Federation of Art, Carmel, CA; 1964: *Fifth Winter Invitational*, Palace Of The Legion Of Honor, San Francisco, CA; *Walnut Creek Annual; The Small Format*, Hollis Galleries, San Francisco, CA; *Variation on a Theme–Paintings of Women*, Gallery de Silva, Santa Barbara, CA; 1965: *The New Group: Ten Monterey Peninsula Painters*, Thunderbird Bookshop, Carmel Valley, CA; San Jose Art Center, San Jose, CA; *Square Foot Paintings, Drawings, San Francisco Art Institute Members' Exhibition*; 1966, 69: Crocker Art Gallery, Sacramento, CA; *Newport Beach Collectors' Show*, Newport Beach, CA; *Salinas Art Festival*, Monterey, CA; 1967: Stanford University, Palo Alto, CA; *Inaugural Show*, Seaside City Hall Art Gallery, CA; 1968: *Inaugural Exhibition*, Trutton Gallery, San Francisco, CA; 1970, 73, 88, 89: Pacific Grove Art Center; 1970: *Toys of the Artist*, circ., Civic Arts Gallery of Walnut Creek, CA; *Northern California Arts Annual*, Sacramento, CA; *Inaugural Exhibition*, Pacific Grove Art Center, Pacific Grove, CA; 1974, 75, 77: *Monterey County Art Annual*, Monterey Museum, CA; 1976: *Surface and Image*, Walnut Creek Arts Center, Walnut Creek, CA; 1977: *Three Decades Of American Art,* Santa Barbara Museum, CA; 1980: *Award Exhibitions: Joan Savo and Elizabeth Tracy*, Monterey Peninsula Museum of Art, Monterey, CA; *Introductions*, Source Gallery, San Francisco, CA; 1981: *Painters and Printmakers*, Brookhouse Gallery, Orinda, CA; 1982: *Twelfth Night: Holiday Exhibition*, Source Gallery, San Francisco, CA; 1983: *Monterey County Art Competitive Winners, 1966–1981*, Monterey Peninsula Museum of Art, Monterey, CA; 1984: *Legacy*, Pacific Grove Art Center, Pacific Grove, CA; 1985: *Monterey Museum Women Show*, Monterey Peninsula Museum of Art, Monterey, CA; 1986: *Works on Paper: Contemporary Concerns*, Shasta College Art Gallery, Reading, CA; *A Survey of Contemporary California Artists*, Site 311 Gallery, Pacific Grove CA; *Passages: A Survey of California Women Artists, 1945 to the Present*, Fresno Art Center and Museum, Fresno, CA; 1987: *Third Annual Member Exhibition*, Monterey Peninsula Art Foundation, Pacific Grove, CA; 1988: *The Carmel Art Association Today*, Carmel Art Association, Carmel, CA; 1989: *Art Against Aids–San Francisco*, San Francisco, CA; 1990: *Monterey Collects: Black and White,* (Graphic Art), Monterey Museum of Art, Monterey, CA.

ETHEL SCHWABACHER

Having acquired a background ... my struggle has been to find for myself a rhythm in style which would be the rhythm of a living thing. My efforts [are] to introduce into our world of vision something which is neither optical nor mechanical nor intellectual — psychological, but rather poetical and relying largely on intuitive awareness. It is my hope that in some small measure I may have succeeded in these attempt.

Ethel Schwabacher, Statement: Excerpts from the announcement of her solo exhibition in 1947 at the Passedoit Gallery in New York City.

There are paintings possibly not properly to be categorized as art. They do not rely in any sense on the beauty of form of the single figures in them, nor do they rely on beauty of composition, or on gradations of color. They do not rely on most of the usual constants of art but speak rather of personal experience at a very deep level. They are true in this sense. Not technically but psychologically.

Ethel Schwabacher, Statement: Excerpts from Ethel Schwabacher Journal, *Hungry for Light* edited by Brenda Webster and Judith Johnson. Indiana University Press, 1993. February 8, 1979, p. 195.

...Painting had to have a base in sensuality. The task was to let sensuality expand and then to bring it under the control of the mind for purposes of making the finished painting sufficiently abstract. This was a possible goal. It was not a question of eliminating a whole portion of the responsive personality but of bringing about a new kind of classicism.

Ethel Schwabacher, Statement: Excerpts from Ethel Schwabacher Journal, *Hungry for Light* edited by Brenda Webster and Judith Johnson. Indiana University Press, 1993. May 29, 1979, p. 205.

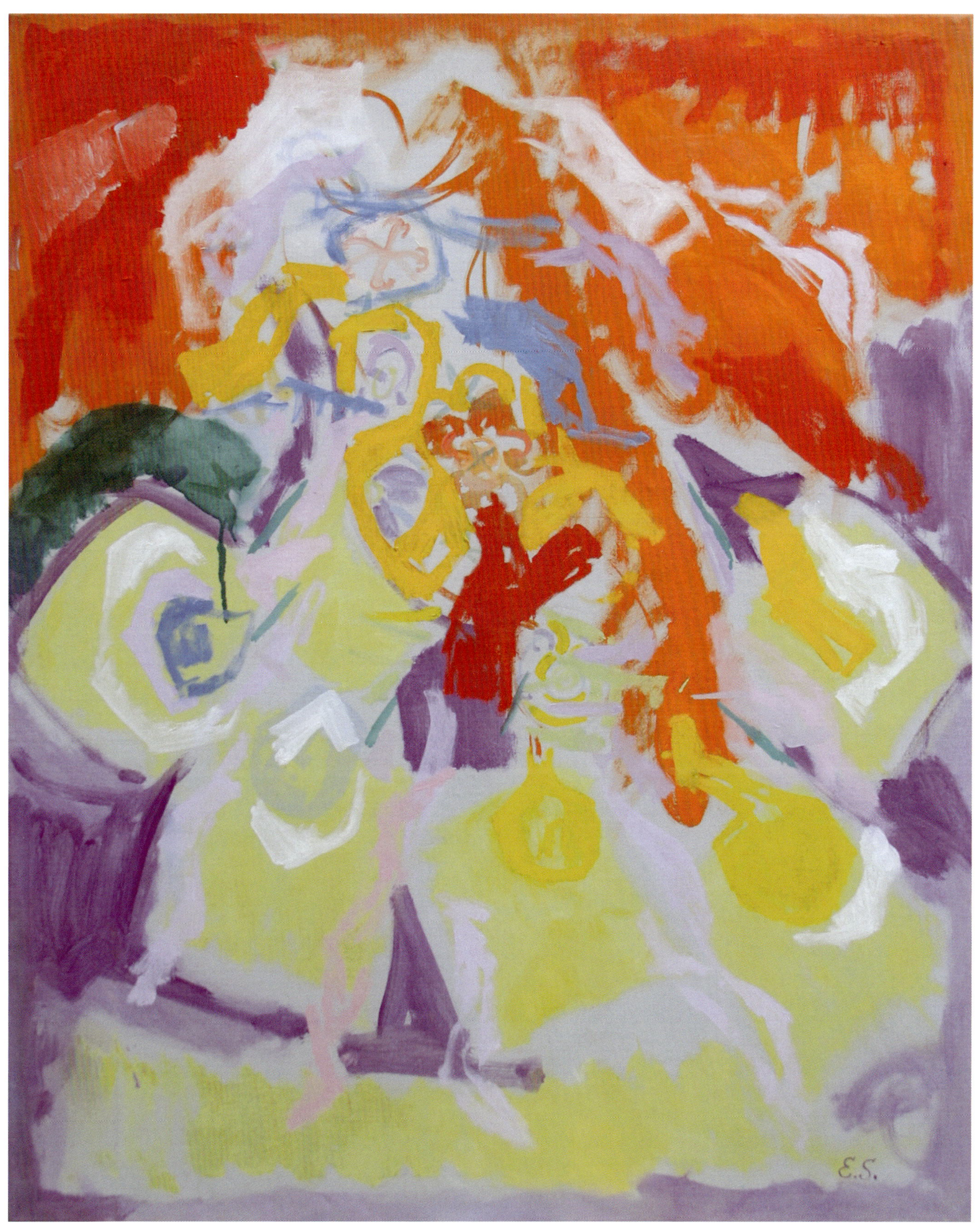

ETHEL SCHWABACHER, *Untitled*, Seasons and Days Series, 1955
Oil on canvas 40 x 32 inches
Collection of Anita Shapolsky

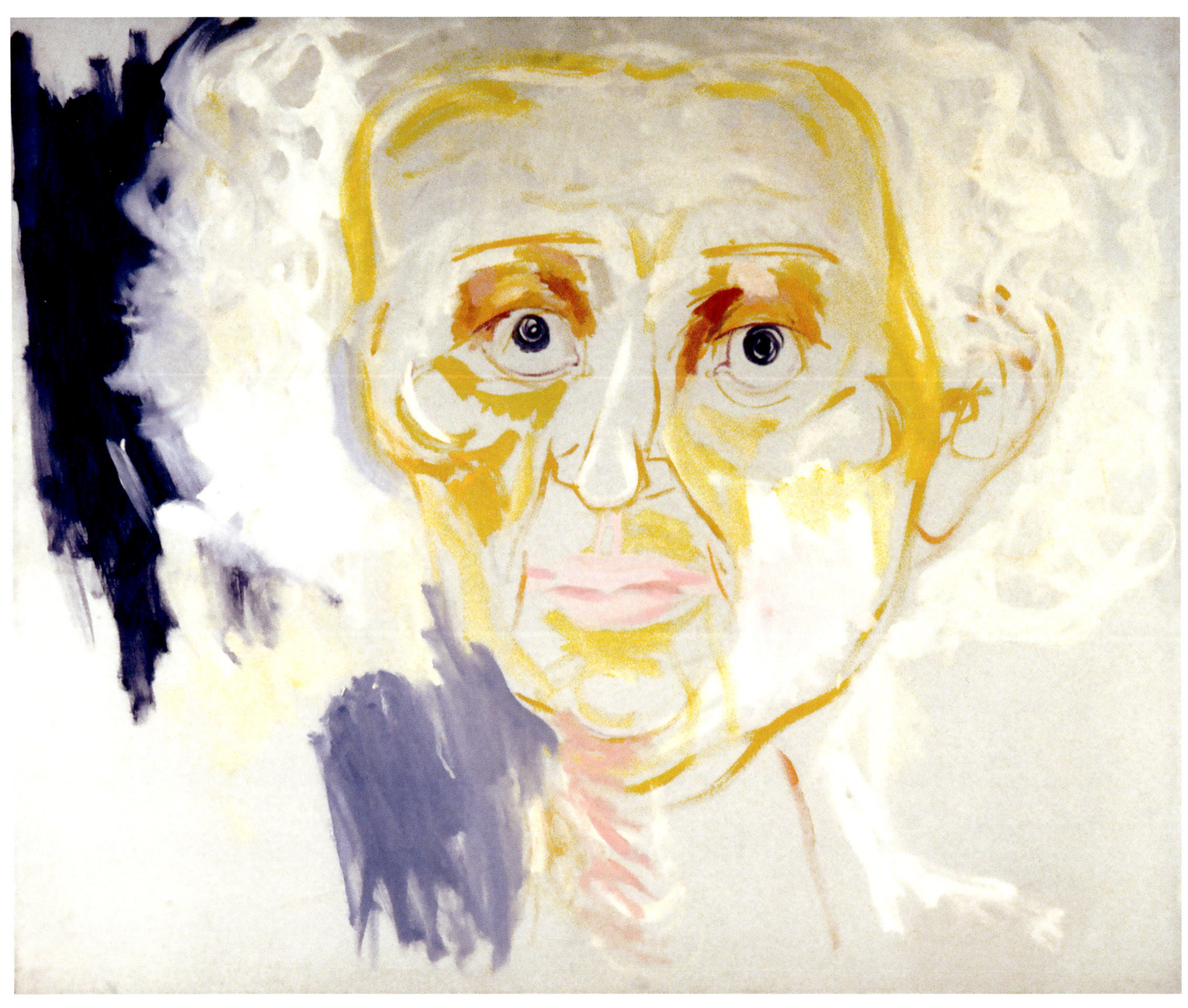

ETHEL SCHWABACHER, *Portrait of Mina*, 1964
Oil on canvas, 35 x 42 inches
Collection of the Estate of Ethel Scwabacher

ETHEL SCHWABACHER, [1903-1984]

Born 1903, New York, NY.
Died 1984, New York, NY.

Studied 1920: National Academy of Design, New York, sculpture; 1921: Study with Brenda Putnam, Sculpture; 1923: Art Students League, New York, drawing; 1927: Starts to paint, studying with Max Weber; 1928–1934: Independent study in Europe; 1934–1936: Studies with Arshile Gorky.

Selected Solo Exhibitions 1947: Passedoit Gallery, New York, NY; 1953, 56, 57, 60, 62: Betty Parsons Gallery, New York, NY; 1955: Women's City Club, New York, NY; 1964: Greenross Gallery, New York, NY; 1972: Gallery 219, State University of New York, Buffalo, NY; 1976: Bodley Gallery, New York, NY; 1987: *Retrospective*, circ., Zimmerli Art Museum, Rutgers University, New Brunswick, NJ, 1988: Mills College Art Gallery, Oakland, CA and State University of New York, Albany, NY; 1987, 89, 93: Gallery Schlesinger, New York, NY; 1988: 871 Fine Arts, San Francisco, CA.

Selected Group Exhibitions 1947, 49, 51, 52, 55, 56, 57, 58, 61, 63: Whitney Museum of American Art, New York, NY; 1947: Passedoit Gallery, New York, NY; 1953, 54, 55, 56, 57, 58, 59, 60, 61, 62, 63: Betty Parsons Gallery, New York, NY; 1954: *149th Annual Exhibitions of Painting and Sculpture*, Pennsylvania Academy of Fine Arts, Philadelphia, PA; *10 Women Artists*, Riverside Museum, NY; *Works from the Permanent Collection*, Whitney Museum of American Art, New York, NY; 1959: *26th Biennial Exhibition of Contemporary American Painting, 1959*, Corcoran Gallery of Art, Washington, D.C.; *Recent Acquisitions*, Whitney Museum of American Art, New York, NY; 1960: *60 American Painters: Abstract Expressionists of the Fifties*, Walker Art Center, Minneapolis, MN; 1961: *International Watercolor Exhibition*, Brooklyn Museum, Brooklyn, NY; *Thirtieth Anniversary Exhibition*, Whitney Museum of American Art, New York, NY; 1967: *Twentieth Century Works from the Permanent Collection*, Whitney Museum of American Art, New York, NY; 1970: *Women in the Permanent Collection*, Whitney Museum of American Art, New York, NY; 1977: *The Sacred Image in Traditional and Contemporary Art, East and West*, Museum of Religious Art, Cathedral Church of St. John the Divine, New York, NY; 1989: *American Women Artists: The 20th Century*, circ., Knoxville Museum of Art, TN; *Abstract Expressionism: Other Dimensions*, Zimmerli Art Museum, Rutgers University, New Brunswick, NJ; 1994: *Reclaiming Artists of the New York School: Toward a More Inclusive view of the 1950s*, Sidney Mishkin Gallery, Baruch College, NY; 1997: *Women and Abstract Expressionism: Painting and Sculpture, 1945–1959*, circ., Sidney Mishkin Gallery, Baruch College, NY; 1993, 97, 98, 2000, 02, 05, 06, 07: Anita Shapolsky Gallery, New York, NY.

GEORGE SPAVENTA

I came upon situations in life that have a symbolic character, a meaning larger than their actuality. The moments are so intense and total that I have to make sculpture of them, sculpture which is biographical and ought to be dated. They seem to be mere events at which I am present, but I guess I choose them, too. Still there's not too much of a choice, since I have no wish to find them; they happen. I don't go around looking for trouble, and yet these experiences often lead me out of sculpture to realms of danger — fantastic, literal, psychic danger.

George Spaventa
ART NEWS, September, 1961

George Spaventa, Statement: *From A Tribute to George Spaventa, January 5 — February 2*, 1980, catalog. Gruenebaum Gallery, Ltd. p.3

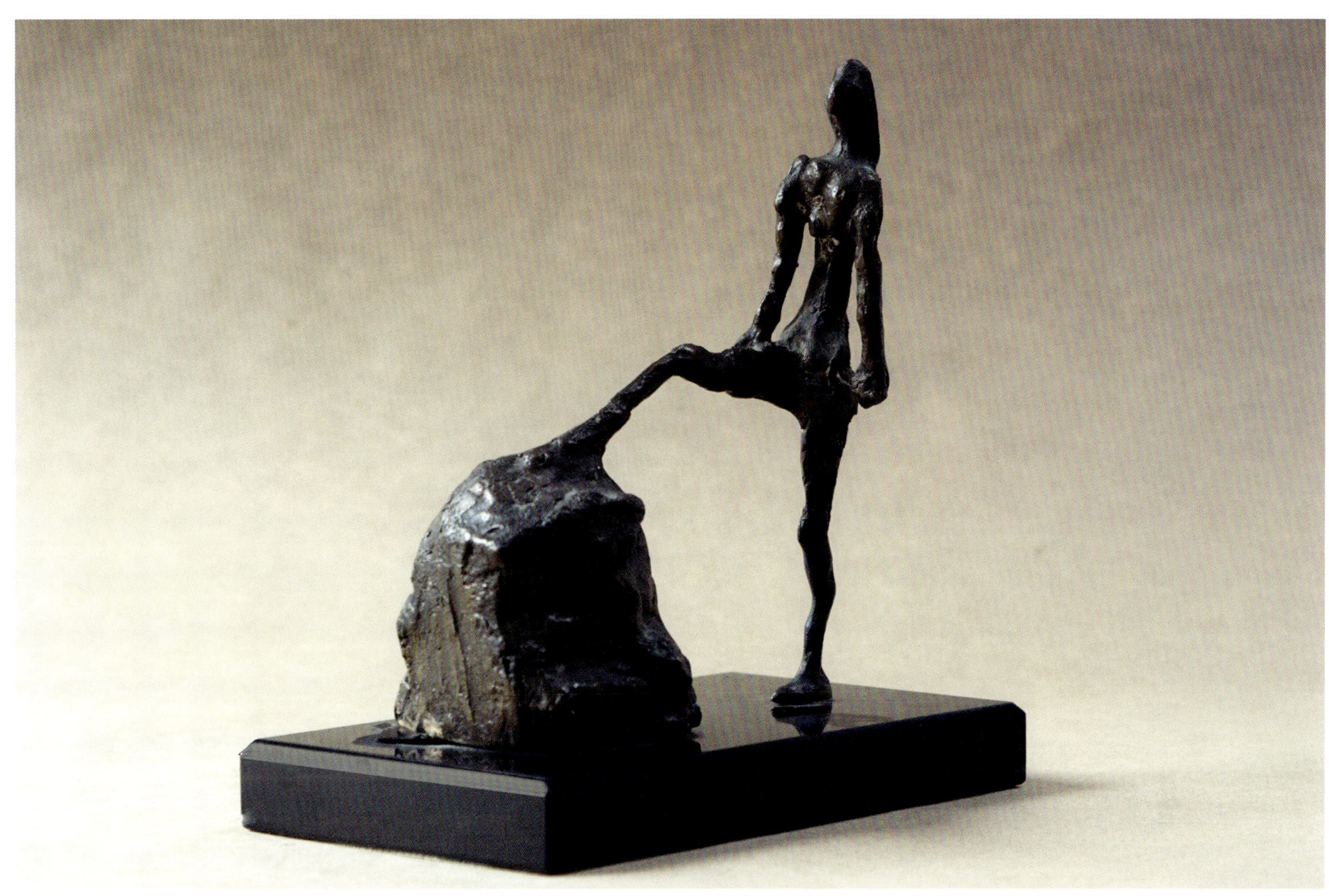

GEORGE SPAVENTA, *Standing Figure*, 1962
Bronze, edition 2/6, H.: 7 1/4 inches
Private collection

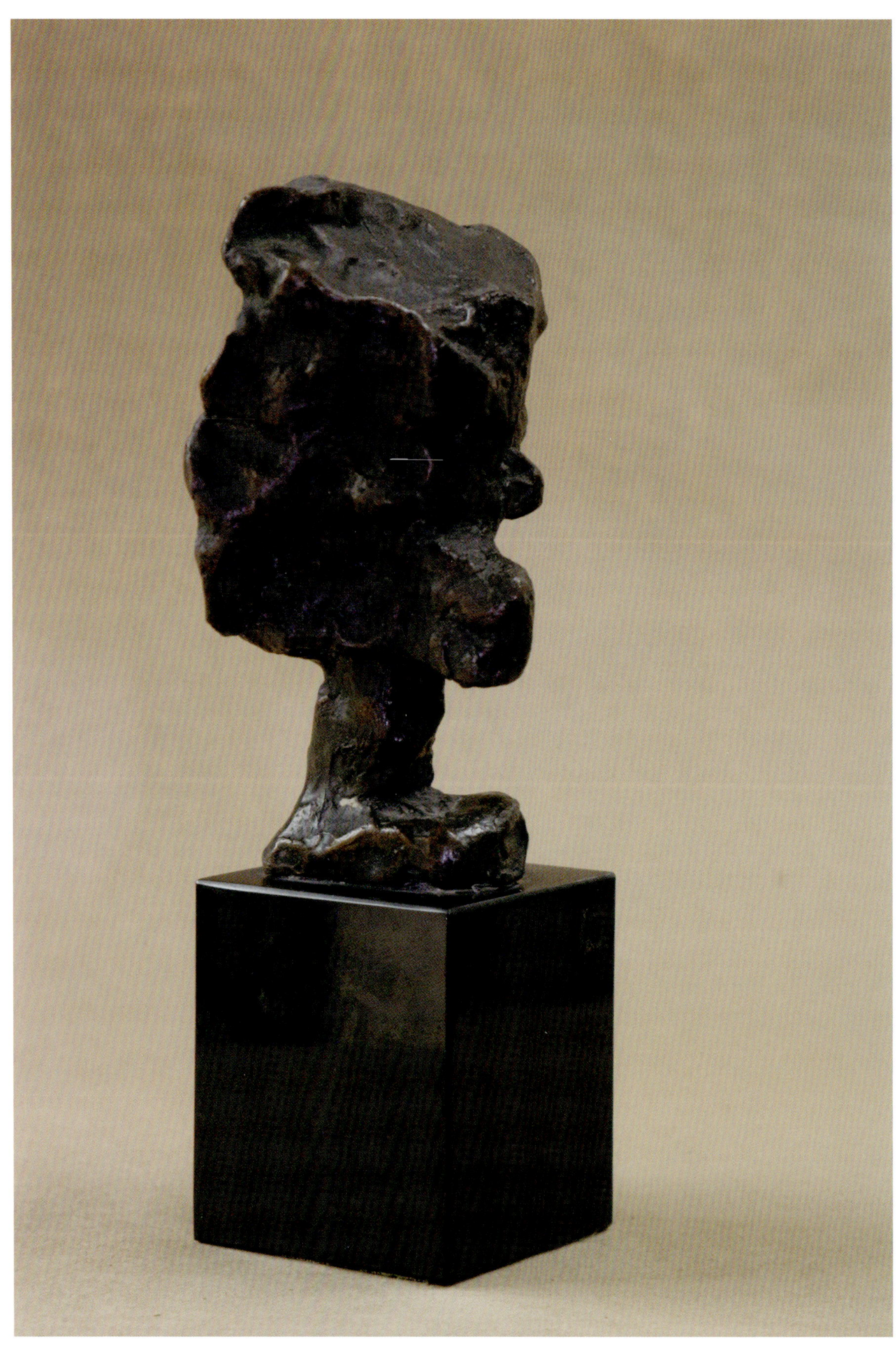

GEORGE SPAVENTA, *Grotesque Head*, 1962
Bronze, edition 4/6, H.: 7 inches
Private collection

GEORGE SPAVENTA, [1918-1978]

Born 1918 in New York City.
Died 1978 in New York City.

Studied Leonardo Da Vinci School of Art; Beaux-Arts Institute of Design; 1947-1950: Acadèmie de la Grande Chaumière with Ossip Zadkin under the G.I. Bill; Visited Brancusi in his studio and met Giacometti.

Military Service in World War II 1942–1945

Teaching Positions 1964–1978: New York Studio School, NYC; 1968: Skowhegan School Painting & Sculpture; 1969: Maryland Institute of Art.

Selected Solo Exhibitions 1962: (first) B.C. Holland Gallery, Chicago, IL; 1964–70: Poindexter Gallery, NYC.

Selected Group Exhibitions 1948 Salon de Mai, Paris, France; 1955: *Sculpture at Tanager*, Tanager Gallery, NYC; 1955, 56, 57: *New York Painting and Sculpture Annuals*, Stable Gallery, NYC; 1956: *Painters and Sculptors on Tenth Street*, Tanager Gallery, NYC; 1957: *May Salon*, Camino Gallery, NYC; 1958: *The 1958 Pittsburgh International Exhibition of Painting and Sculpture*, Carnegie Institute; Poindexter Gallery, NYC; *Annual Summer Exhibition*, Spoleto, Italy; 1959: *Recent Sculpture U.S.A.*, Museum of Modern Art, NYC; 1960: *Aspects of American Sculpture*, Galerie Claude Bernard, Paris, France; 1961: *The 1961 Pittsburgh International Exhibition of Painting and Sculpture*, Carnegie Institute; *Heads*, Great Jones Gallery, NYC; *The Private Myth,* Tanager Gallery, NYC; *American Exhibition*, Art Institute of Chicago, IL; 1962, 66: *The Whitney Annuals*, Whitney Museum of American Art, NYC;1964: *Four American Sculptors*, Museum of Modern Art, NYC; 1974: *Works on Paper I*, Ciba–Geigy Corporation, Summit Art Center, Summit, NJ; 1976: Landmark Gallery, NYC; *Works on Paper II*, Wichita Falls Museum and Art Center, Wichita Falls, TX; 1977: Noho Gallery, NYC; *Works on Paper III*, Neuberger Museum College at Purchase, Purchase, NY, State University of New York; 1978: *Memorial Exhibition*, New York Studio School of Painting and Sculpture, NYC; 1980: *Memorial Exhibition, A Tribute to George Spaventa*, Gruenebaum Gallery, NYC.

NORA SPEYER

The heart of my paintings is its expressive power, not the descriptive tradition. Abstract expressionism gave me this opportunity.

Nora Speyer, Statement: Provided to the editor on October 12, 2008.

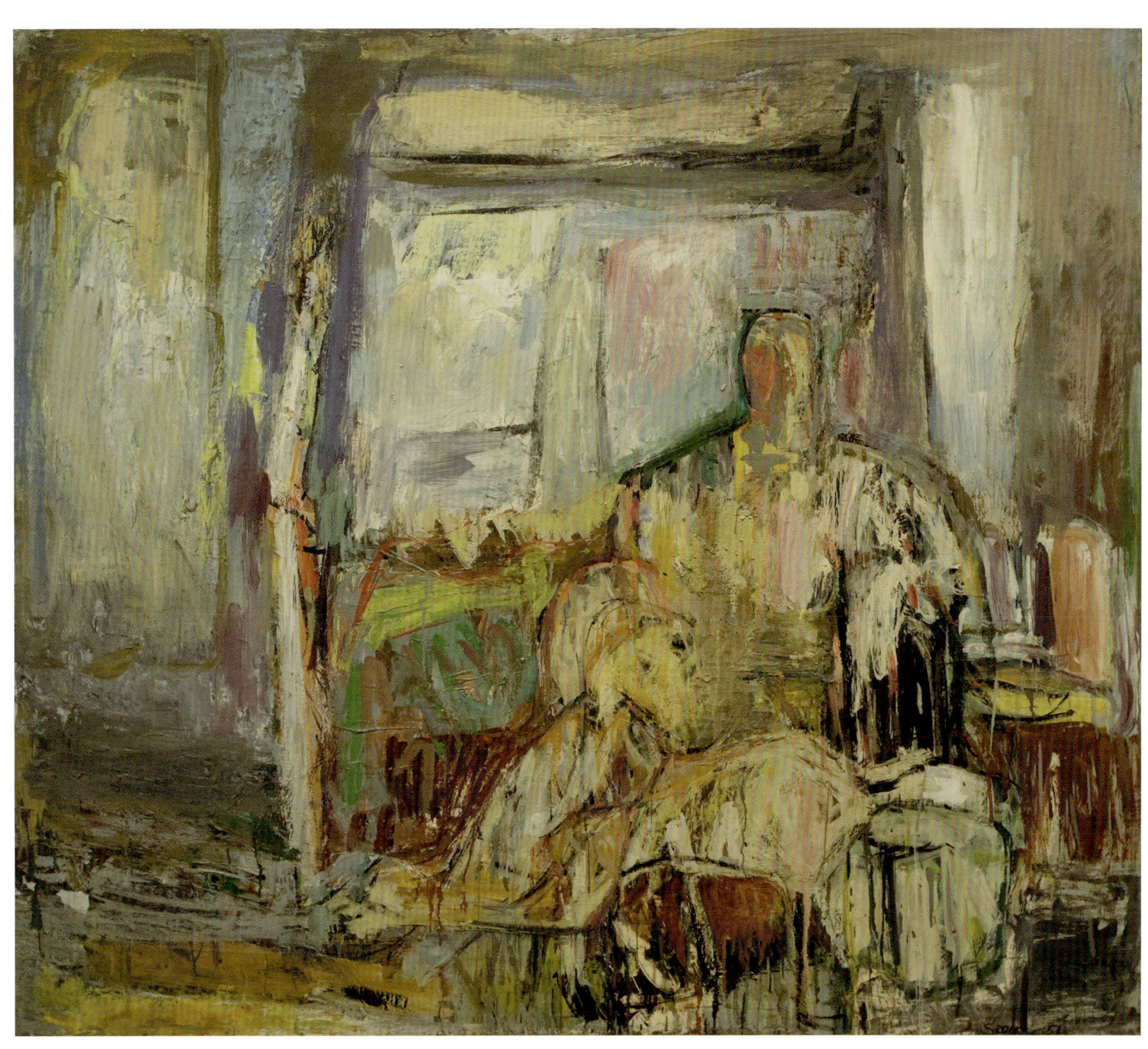

NORA SPEYER, *Studio*, 1958
Oil on canvas, 50 x 60 inches
Collection of the artist

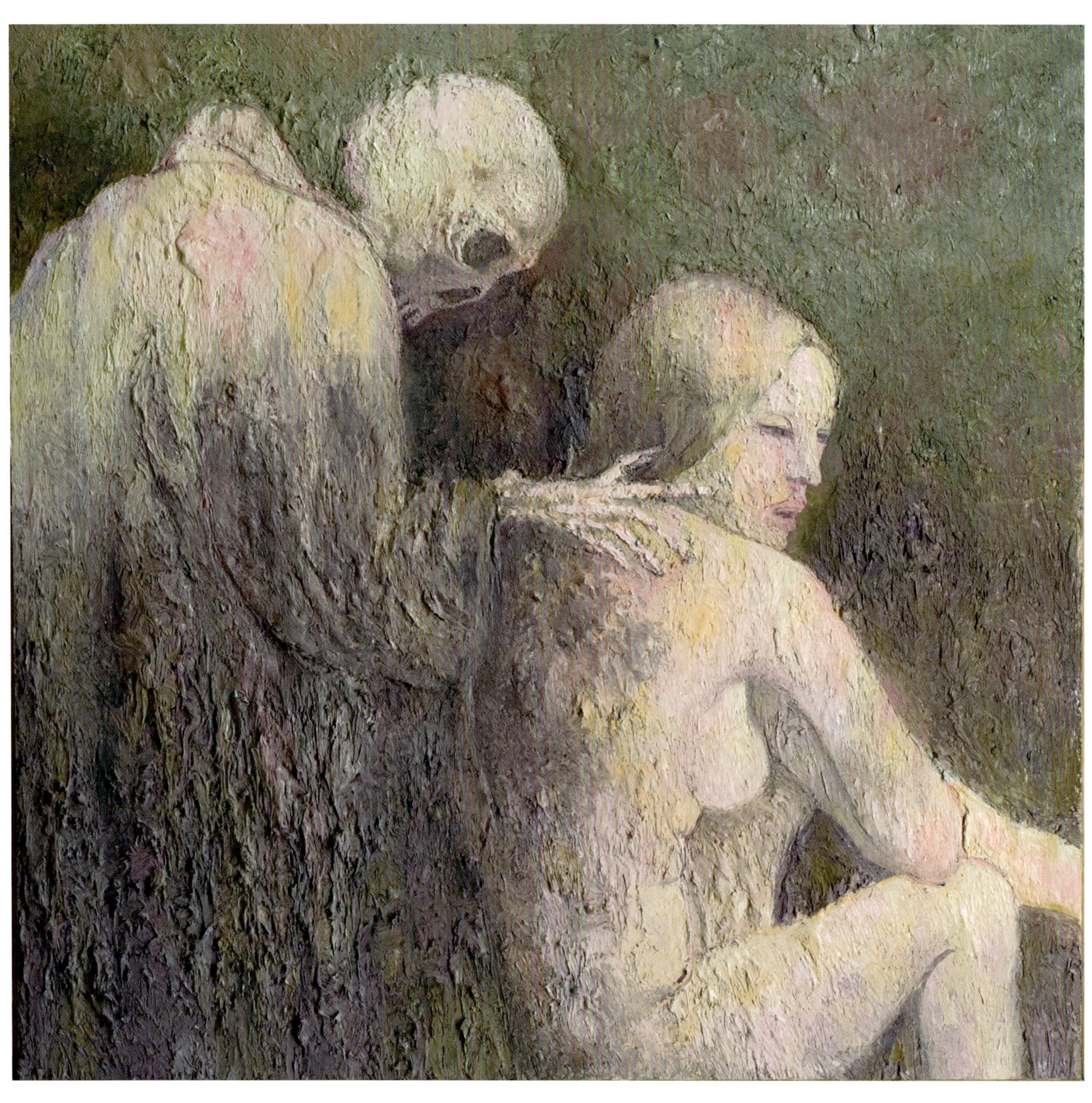

NORA SPEYER, *Death and The Maiden III*, 2003
Oil on canvas, 50 x 50 inches
Collection of the artist

NORA SPEYER, [1923-]

Born November 24, 1923, Pittsburgh, PA.

Studied 1940-1943: Tyler School of Fine Arts, Temple University, PA.

Selected Solo Exhibitions 1954: Zena Gallery Woodstock, NY; 1957: Tanager Gallery, NYC; 1959: Galerie Faccheti, Paris, France; 1962: Stable Gallery, NYC; 1966: Poindexter Gallery, NYC; 1970, 74, 89, 96, 2001: Galerie Darthea Speyer, Paris, France; 1970, 72: Terza Karlis Gallery, Provincetown, MA; 1973, 75, 78, 80, 82: Landmark Gallery, NYC; 1978, 80, 82, 85, 87, 88, 91, 94, 96: Long Point Gallery, Provincetown, MA; 1980: William & Mary College, Williamsburgh, VA; Pennsylvania State University, PA; 1983: Gross McCleaf Gallery, Philadelphia, PA; Brownson Art Gallery, Manhattanville College, Purchase, NY; 1984: Maurice M. Pine Library, Fairlawn, NJ; 1987: Ingber Gallery, NYC; 1994: Concept Art Gallery, Pittsburgh, PA; 1996: *Collage Drawings,* Denis Bibro Fine Art, NYC; 1998: *Trees and Flowers*, Denis Bibro Fine Art, NYC; 2000: *Dream Sequence*, Denis Bibro Fine Art, NYC; 2002: *Landscapes*, Denis Bibro Fine Art, NYC; Provincetown Art Association and Museum, Provincetown, MA; 2004: *Landscape*, Cherry Stone Gallery, Wellfleet, MA.

Selected Group Exhibitions 1954: *New Talent Exhibition*, Museum of Modern Art, NYC; 1956, 57: *New York Painting and Sculpture Annuals,* Stable Gallery, NYC; 1956: *Four Young Americans*, Poindexter Gallery, NYC; 1958: *Carnegie International*, Carnegie Institute, Pittsburgh, PA; *Group of the Galerie Facchetti*, Liverkusen Museum, Germany; 1965: *Two Artists*, Bradford College, Bradford, MA; 1967, 68: Terza Karlis Gallery, Provincetown, MA; 1968: *The Obsessive Image, 1960–1968*, Institute of Contemporary Art, London, England; 1969: *Certain Figure Trends Since the War*, Musèe d'Art, Saint–Etienne, France; *L'Oeil Ecoute Festival*, Avignon, France; *Salon de Mai*, Museum of Modern Art, Paris; 1972: Philadelphia Civic Center, Philadelphia, PA; 1973: *Visual R & D at Corporations. Collection, University of Texas, Austin; IX artists*, Fordham University, New York; Four Artists, Landmark Gallery, NYC; 1974: *Woman's Work*, Museum of Philadelphia Civic Center, PA; 1975: *Works by Women*, Kresge Art Center, Michigan State University, Lansing, MI; 1977: *Ten Artists*, Landmark Gallery, NYC; *Art on Paper,* Weatherspoon Art Gallery, Greensboro, North Carolina; 1978: Butler Art Institute of American Art, Youngstown, OH; 1981: *14 Provincetown Artists*, Weatherspoon Art Gallery, Greensboro, North Carolina; *Realist Drawing*, Gross McCleaf Gallery, Philadelphia, PA; 1982: *A Gray Day*, Long Point Gallery, Provincetown, MA; 1982–1983: *Five Contemporary Artists*, Allentown Art Museum, Allentown PA; 1984: *La Part des Femmes dans L'Art Contemporain*, Galerie Municipale, Vitry sur Seine; *Emotional Impact, New York School, Figurative Expressionism,* circ., in five museums, by the Art Museum Association of America, San Francisco, CA; *Images and Imagery*, Pace University, Art Gallery, New York; Juried exhibition, Academy of Design, New York, Prize in Drawing; 1985: *Male Nude, Women Regard Men*, Hudson Center Galleries, New York; *Survival of the Fittest II*, Ingber Gallery, New York; 1987: *The Flower*, Southern Allegheny Museum of Art, Loretto, PA; 1991: *Sixth Annual Art in the Garden*, Cape Museum of Fine Arts, Dennis, MA; 1992, 93, 98, 2000: National Academy of Design, NYC; 1993: *Long Point Gallery Artists*, Stuart Levy Gallery, NYC; 1994–1997: *Relatively Speaking: Mothers and Daughters in Art*, circ., Sweetbriar College, VA; 1994, 95, 97: Galerie Dartheia Speyer, Paris; 1996: Emily Lane Gallery, Hofstra Museum, Hempstead, NY; 1998: *A Tribute to Long Point*, Cape Museum of Fine Arts, Dennis, MA; 2003: Cherry Stone Gallery, Wellfleet, MA.

JACK TWORKOV

Just as there is no self except in relation to other selves so there is no artist except in relation to other artists. The problem of identity for me is to work out my relation to the artists and art of my immediate environment. This is impossible unless one arrives at some fundamental ideas of value – at some concept of man and an idea of what a life is.

–Journal, January 9, 1954.

My hope is to confront the picture without a ready technique or a prepared attitude – a condition which is nevertheless never completely attainable; to have no program and, necessarily then, no preconceived style. To paint no Tworkovs. It does not mean I can face the canvas with empty head and an empty heart. In such an event I go to sleep. Does one not need to put limits around oneself to keep from being overwhelmed by the stream of art? The fashioned person is already limited enough – the hope is to be fashioned by the work. The task of the painting is to discover and squeeze out, from all the forces streaming through it, all that is not necessary. Such impurities as remain are finally present to lend coherence to the process.

–Catalogue for Stable Gallery Exhibition, April, 1957.

Art is thought to be a search for order. But art is also a search to transcend our human limitations. Artists are trying to express things in our life that are real but cannot be expressed by ordered arrangement. Also art may very well be aimed at our discomfort and hence disorder. Whenever we become too smug, too limited in our ideas and values, art comes to upset us. It causes us sometimes acute discomfort for a time but we should come out of it to a new plane of ideas and values.

–Journal, c. 1958

Jack Tworkov, Statements: From the forthcoming publication: *The Extreme of the Middle; Writings of Jack Tworkov*, edited by Mira Shor. New Haven and London. Yale University Press, 2009.

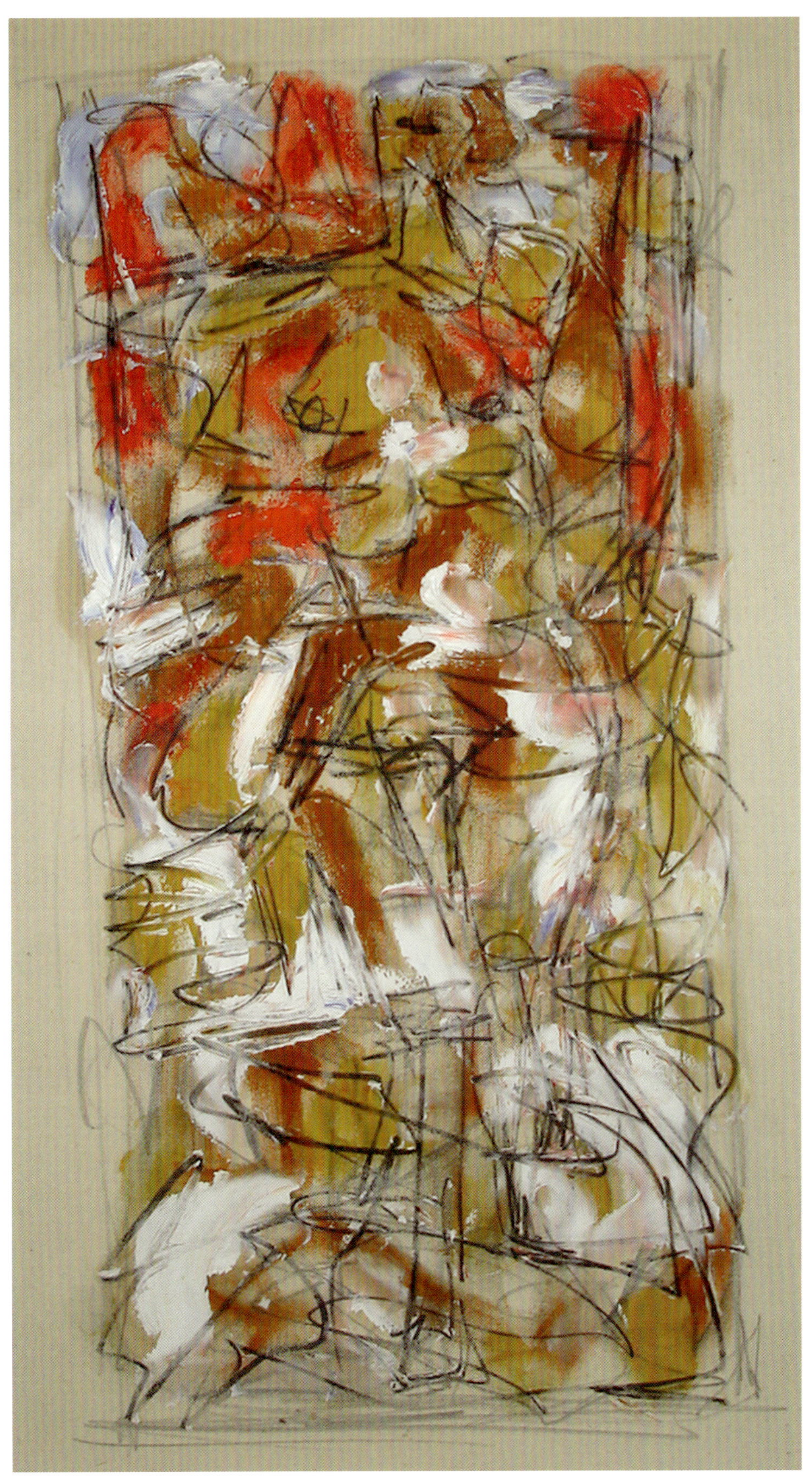

JACK TWORKOV, *Study for Athene*, c.1948
Oil and graphite on paper, 13 7/8 x 11 inches (sheet size)

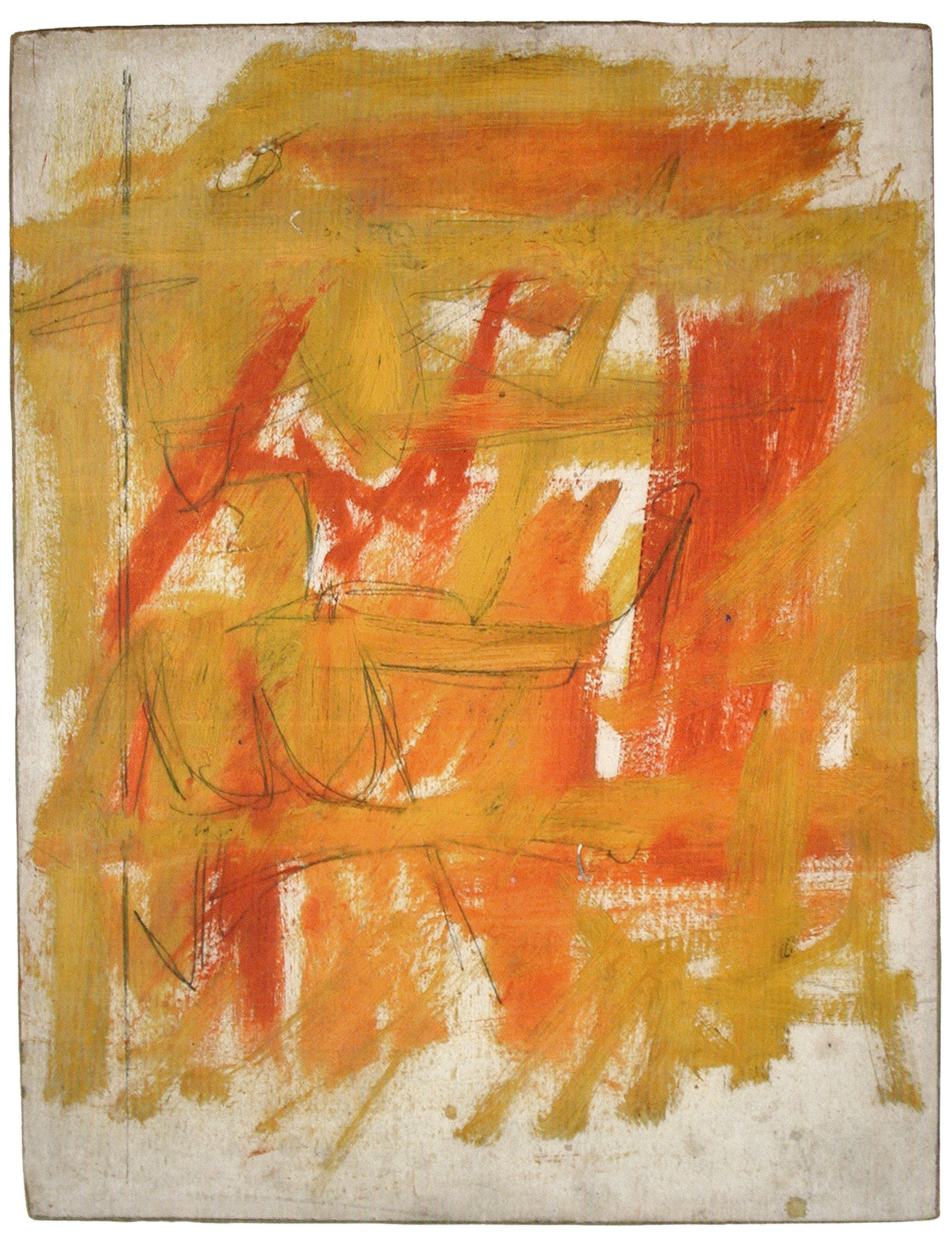

JACK TWORKOV, *Study for Watergame*, c.1955
Oil and graphite on Masonite, 16 x 12 ½ inches
© Estate of Jack Tworkov. Courtesy of Mitchell-Innes & Nash, New York

JACK TWORKOV, [1900-1982]

Born August 15, 1900, Biala, Poland.
To USA 1913. **USA Citizen** 1928.
Died September 4, 1982, Provincetown, MA.

Studied 1920–23: Columbia University; 1923–25: National Academy of Design, with Ivan Olinsky, Charles Hawthorne; 1924–25: privately with Ross Moffett; 1925–26: Art Students League, NYC with Guy Pène Du Bois, Boardman Robinson.

Federal Art Project (WPA) 1935–41: Easel painting.

Military Service in World War II 1942–45: tool designer.

Teaching Positions 1931: Fieldston School, NYC; 1948–55: Queens College; 1948–51: American University; 1952 summer: Black Mountain College; 1955–58: Pratt Institute; 1963–69: Yale University;1970–72, 76: Copper Union, NYC; 1972: American Academy, Rome; 1973: Dartmouth College; Columbia University; 1974: Royal College of Art, London; 1976: University of California.

Selected Solo Exhibitions 1939: (first) ACA Gallery; 1947,49, 52, 54: Charles Egan Gallery, NYC; 1948: Baltimore Museum of Art, Baltimore, MD; 1954: University of Mississippi, Oxford, MS; 1957: Walker Art Center, Minneapolis, MN; The Jefferson Place Gallery, Washington, D.C.; 1957, 58, 59: The Stable Gallery, NYC; 1960, 63: Holland-Goldowsky Gallery, Chicago, IL; 1961: Newcomb College Art Gallery, Tulane University, New Orleans; 1961, 63: Leo Castelli, Inc., NY; 1963: Yale University, New Haven, CT; 1964 circ., 1971: The Whitney Museum of American Art, NY; 1964, 66, 69, 71, 73: Gertrude Kasle Gallery, NYC; 1966: Merida Gallery, Louisville, KY; 1968: Dana Creative Arts Center, Colgate University, Hamilton, NY; 1973: Dartmouth College; 1974: Portland (Ore.) Center for the Visual Arts; Reed College; Denver Art Museum; Harcus Krakow Rosen Sonnabend; 1974, 75, 77, 82, 83, 85, 87: Nancy Hoffman Gallery, NYC; 1975: Ohio State University; Youngstown State University; Contemporary Art Center, Cincinati, OH; New Gallery, Cleveland; 1977: University of California, Santa Barbara; 1979: Third Eye Center, Glasgow, circ.; 1980: Rhode Island School of Design; 1981: Middlebury College; 1982: Solomon R. Guggenheim Museum; 1983: American Academy and Institute of Arts and Letters; Provincetown (MA) Art Association; 1987: Pennsylvania Academy of Fine Arts, circ.; 1990, 91, 92, 95: André Emmerich Gallery, NYC; 2000, 02, 07: Mitchell Innes & Nash, New York.

Selected Group Exhibitions 1951, 53, 54, 57: The *9th St.* Show, the first and subsequent 3 Annuals, *New York Painting and Sculpture Annuals* Stable Gallery, NYC; 1958-59: *The New American Painting*, Museum of Modern Art, NY; 1960: *60 American Painters, 1960*, The Walker Art Center, Minneapolis, MN; 1961: *Abstract Expressionists and Imagists*, Solomon R. Guggenheim Museum, NYC; University of Illinois; 1961–63: *Abstract American Drawings and Watercolors*, Museum of Modern Art, circ., Latin America; 1962: Seattle World's Fair; 1962–67: *ART: USA: Now*, circ.; 1951, 53, 55, 56, 57, 59, 61, 62, 65, 67, 72, 73, 81: *Whitney Museum of American Art Annuals and Biennials*, NY; 1963: Corcoran Gallery of Art, Washington, D.C.; 1969: *The New American Painting and Sculpture*, Museum of Modern Art; 1974: *l2 American Painters*, Virginia Museum of Fine Arts; *Five Americans*, Santa Barbara Museum of Arts; University of Illinois; 1975: *100 Years*, Art Students League, NYC; 1976: *The Golden Door: Artist Immigrants of America, 1876–1976*, Hirshhorn Museum and Sculpture Garden Smithsonian Institution, Washington, D.C.; 1978: *Drawing the Line*, The Montclair Art Museum, NJ; *Seventies Painting*, Philadelphia College of Art; *A Century of Master Drawings*, Creighton University; 1981, 83: American Academy and Institute of Arts and Letters; 1987: *Painting Since World War II*, Solomon R. Guggenheim Museum, NY; 1998: *Twentieth Century American Drawing*, Arkansas Arts Center, Little Rock; 1999: *Made in USA: 1940–1970*, Centre Cultural de la Fundacio, Barcelona, Spain; 2007: *Abstract Expressionism and Other Modern Works: The Muriel Kallis Steinberg Newman Collection*, Metropolitan Museum of Art, NY; 2008: *Abstract Expressionism: A World Elsewhere*, Haunch of Venison, NY.

HANS VAN DE BOVENKAMP

The studio is my playground, my laboratory, my sanctuary, where I practice and experiment with sculptural ideas. There the confluence of thought, intuition, experience and inspiration percolate, constantly being in the present moment, between the conscious and the unconscious. I observe ballet for composition and listen to music as a form of drawing in space.

I am busy establishing a personal style or mythology, not what sculpture IS, but what IT DOES to the onlooker through symbolism. And so the "play" continues.

Hans Van de Bovenkamp

Hans Van de Bovenkamp, Statement: Excerpts from a letter provided to the editor. November 12, 2008.

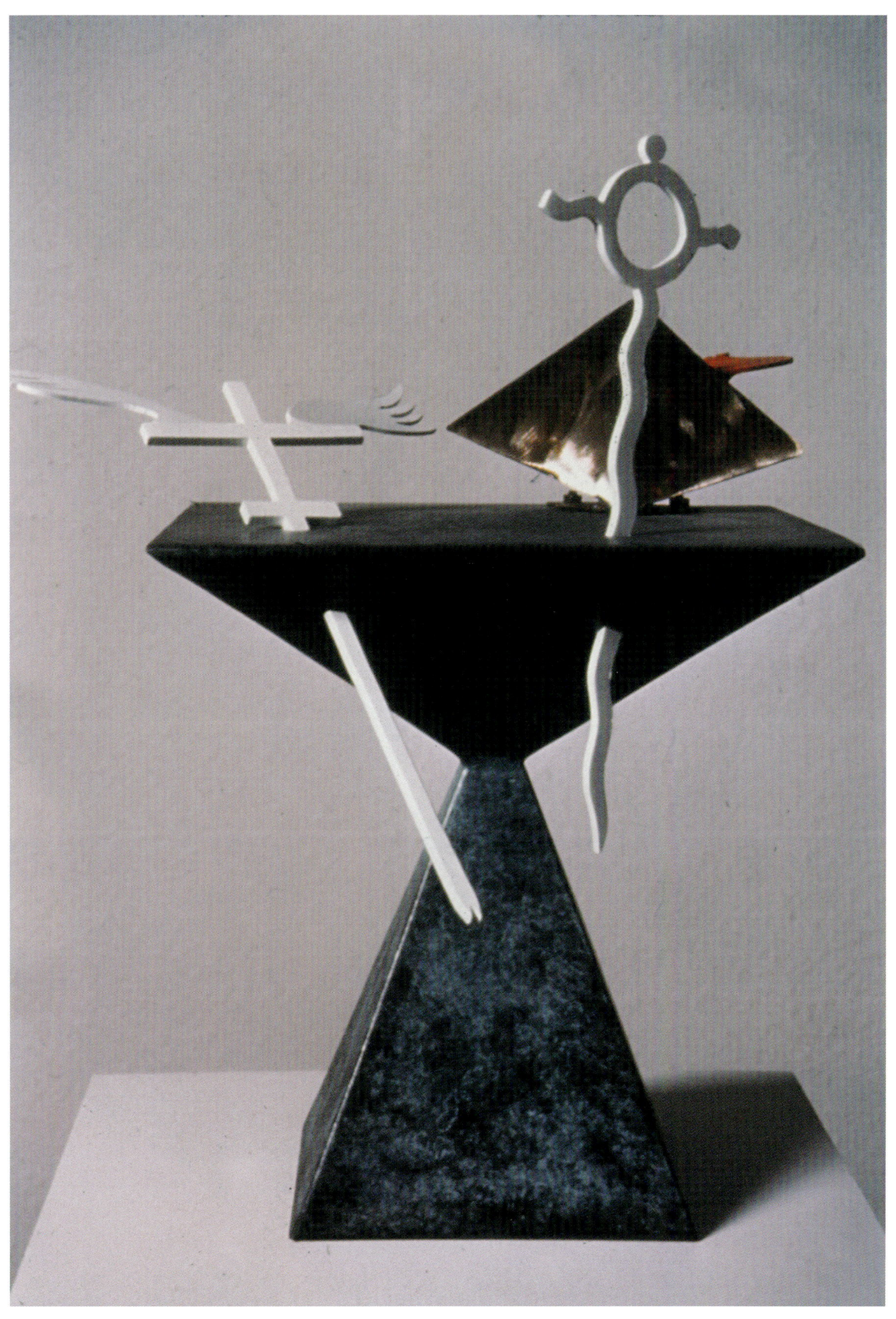

HANS VAN DE BOVENKAMP, *Offering (table still life)*, 1979
Bronze & Painted Aluminum 59 x 48 x 24 inches
Collection of the artist

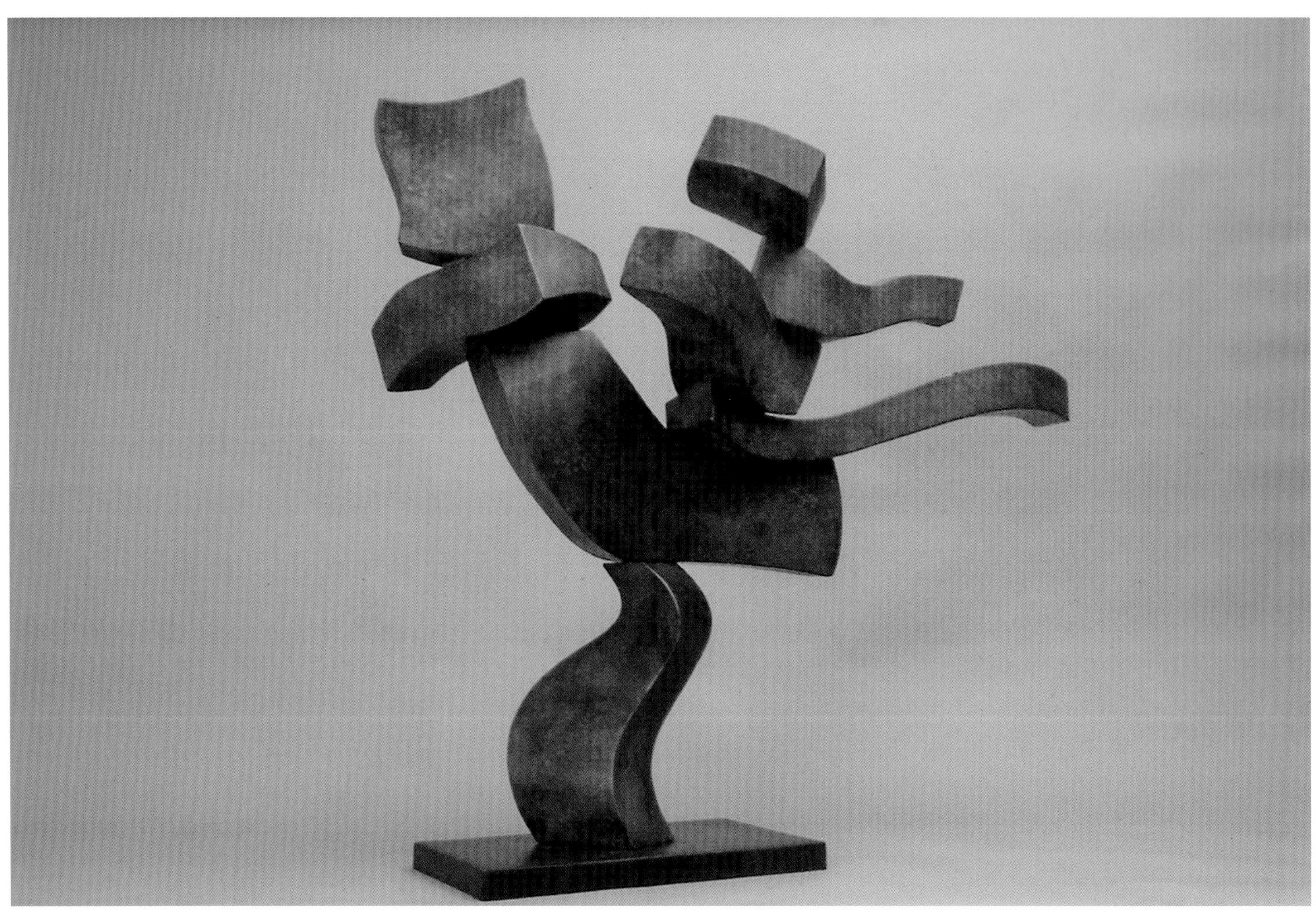

HANS VAN DE BOVENKAMP, *Pas de Deux*, 2001
Bronze, 49 x 26 x 13 inches
Collection of Mr & Mrs. Barney Millens

HANS VAN DE BOVENKAMP, [1938-]

Born 1938 in Garderen, Holland.
To USA 1958 **USA citizen** 1975.

Studied 1958: School of Architecture, Amsterdam, Holland 1958-61: University of Michigan, Ann Arbor, Ml (BS Science & Design).

Selected Solo Exhibitions 1961: University of Michigan, Ann Arbor, Ml; 1963, 81: Tiffany's NYC; 1963: New York University, NYC; 1965: Glassboro State Collage, Glassboro, NJ; 1968: 10 Downtown, NYC; 1970: Jacksonville Children's Museum, Jacksonville, FL; 1971: Hall's Art Gallery, Kansas City, MO; 1972: Serra Gallery, Rome, Italy; 1976: Gallery El Muro, Caracas, Venezuela; Arnot Art Museum, Elmira, NY; Brooklyn Borough Hall, NY; 1979: Sculpture Center, NYC; 1981: University of Missouri, Columbia, MO; 1983: Arras Gallery, NYC; 1985, 87: Joy Moos Gallery, Miami, FL; 1989: Kleinert Arts Center, Woodstock, NY; Lowe Gallery, Atlanta, GA; 1990: Nina Owen Ltd., Chicago, IL; 1992: Shidoni Contemporary Gallery, Tesuque, NM; 1993: Elaine Benson Gallery, Bridgehampton, NY; 1994: Dietrich Contemporary Arts, NYC; Quietude Gallery, East Brunswick, NJ; 1996: Michener Museum, Doylestown, PA; Felissimo, NYC; 2003: Sagaponack Sculpture Fields, Sagaponack, NY; Bernarducci Meisel Gallery, NYC; Louis K. Meisel Gallery, NYC; 2005–06: *Grounds for Sculpture*, Hamilton, NJ; 2006: Danubiana Meulensteen Museum, Bratislava, Slovakia; 2007: Auberge du Soleil, Napa, CA; Gary Nader Fine Art, Miami, FL; Goldman Warehouse, Miami, FL; Sculpturesite Gallery, San Francisco, CA; Yellow Bird Gallery, Newburgh, NY.

Selected Group Exhibitions 1964: Contemporary Arts Museum, Houston, TX; 1968: Colgate University, NY; Stamford Museum, Stamford, CT; Loeb Student Center, New York University, NYC; 1969: New York Sculptors Guild, Bryant Park, NYC; 1969, 78: Medici–Berenson Gallery, Miami, FL; 1969–2004: Elaine Benson Gallery, Bridgehampton, NY; 1970: University of Connecticut, Storrs, CT; 1973: Metz & Co., Amsterdam, Holland; 1973–76: Storm King Art Center, Cornwall, NY; 1976: American Institute of Arts & Letters, NYC; Wellfleet Art Gallery, Cape Cod, MA; 1977: National Academy of Design, NYC; 1977–78: Temple University, Philadelphia, PA; 1978: PS1 Contemporary Art Center, Long Island City, NY; Nassau County Art Museum, NY; The United States Mission, NYC; Harkness House Gallery, NYC; Nassau County Museum of Art, Roslyn Harbor, NY; 1980: Gallery Hawaii, Honolulu, Hawaii; Artists Representing Environmental Art (AREA), Washington, D.C.; 1980–8: Arras Gallery, NYC; 1981: New York Botanical Gardens, NYC; 1982: Oakland Museum, Oakland, CA; Dutch Embassy, Philadelphia, PA; 1984: Molly Barnes Gallery, Los Angeles, CA; Snugg Harbor Museum, Sculptors Guild, Staten Island, NY; 1985: Atelier Amei Oberli, Zürich, Switzerland; 1985–86: Kouros Gallery, NYC; 1986: Ann Norton Sculpture Garden, West Palm Beach, FL; 1988: *Chicago Art Fair*, Navy Pier, Chicago, IL; 1984–89: Shulman Park, White Plains, NY: 1987–89: Nina Owen Limited, Chicago, IL; 1990: The New East Side Sculpture Walk, Chicago, IL; 1992: Omega Institute, Rhinebeck, NY; 1982–1993: Bologna–Landi Gallery, East Hampton, NY; 1993–94: Couturier Gallery, Los Angeles, CA; 1994: Cavalier Gallery, Stamford, CT; 1990–96: Lowe Gallery, Atlanta, GA; Camino Real, Boca Raton, FL; 1996: Stamford Museum, Stamford, CT; 1999: *Grounds for Sculpture*, Hamilton, NJ; 1998–2000: Rondout Sculpture Biennial, Kingston, NY; 2000–04: City of Ft. Lauderdale, Ft. Lauderdale, FL; 2002: Albright College Center for the Arts, Reading, PA; 2003: Guild Hall Museum, East Hampton, NY; David Floria Gallery, Aspen CO; 2003–04: ACA Gallery, Santa Fe, NM; 1994–2004: Cavalier Gallery, Greenwich, CT; 2005: Hillwood Art Museum, Brookville, NY; Sculpturesite Gallery, San Francisco, CA; 2006: Westchester Sculptor's Guild, White Plains, NY; Camino Real Gallery, Boca Raton, FL; 2007: Pratt Institute, NY; *40 Years of Central Park*, Lincoln Center , New York, NY; 2008: *Sculpture Walk,* Gettysburg, PA; *ArtHamptons*, Bridgehampton, NY; Spanierman Gallery, East Hampton, NY.

JANE WILSON

I would say that painting is a meditative practice...Artistic practice is work -- it's very focused and rigorous -- and yet at the same time, doing it, you somehow get beyond immediate distractions, into something inner, deep and important...the under-self.

My landscapes are not painted on-site or from photographs. They come out of my mind...out of my bones, really. I seek to capture what it feels like to be there, on a strip of land or sand. I move into a kind of recall about season, climate, time of day.

The painting I do is the only way I have to catch something that is constantly changing. To capture experience. Light has a physical presence, but at the same time it's fused into this magnetic experience of sky which is totally elusive. So there's a metaphorical element to this practice -- the constant challenge of trying to capture something that can't be captured. I love how the sky is constantly changing, how it's so complicated. Changing color, changing humidity, changing light, changing winds, changing temperature. It's really too much to deal with! And yet, at the same time, I find the experience vital and elating.

I'm fascinated by moments of absolute stillness, those moments when we are just hypnotized by stillness. What I'm aiming for are moments of strong sensation -- moments of total physical experience of landscape, when the weather just reaches out and sucks you in. And the challenge of trying to trigger those moments with pigments of ground-up earth. When you think about it, it's really very mysterious.

Jane Wilson

Jane wilson, Statement: From artist's statement created from an interview provided by Sandy Paci from the DC More Gallery, New York.

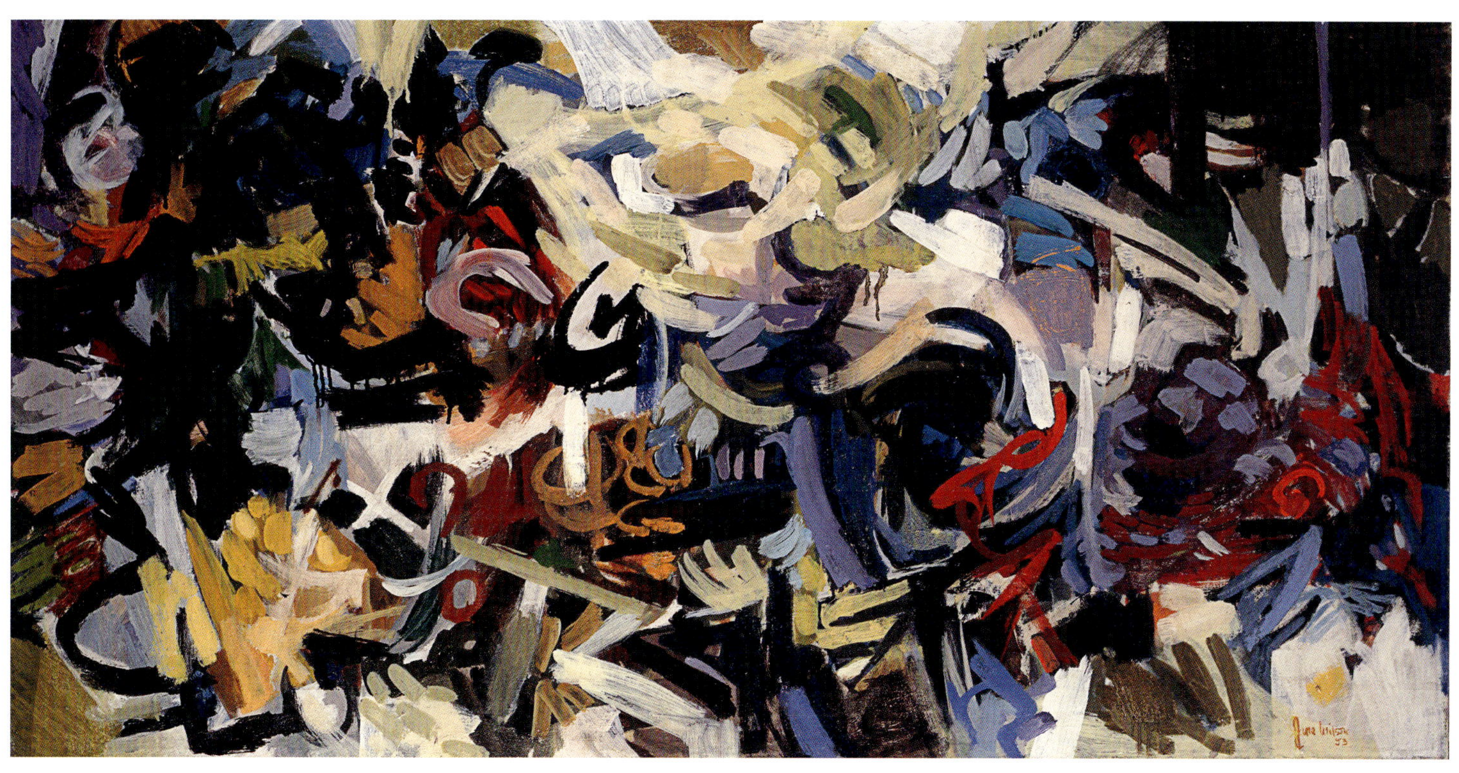

JANE WILSON, *Carnival*, 1953
Oil on canvas, 25 1/2 X 50 INCHES

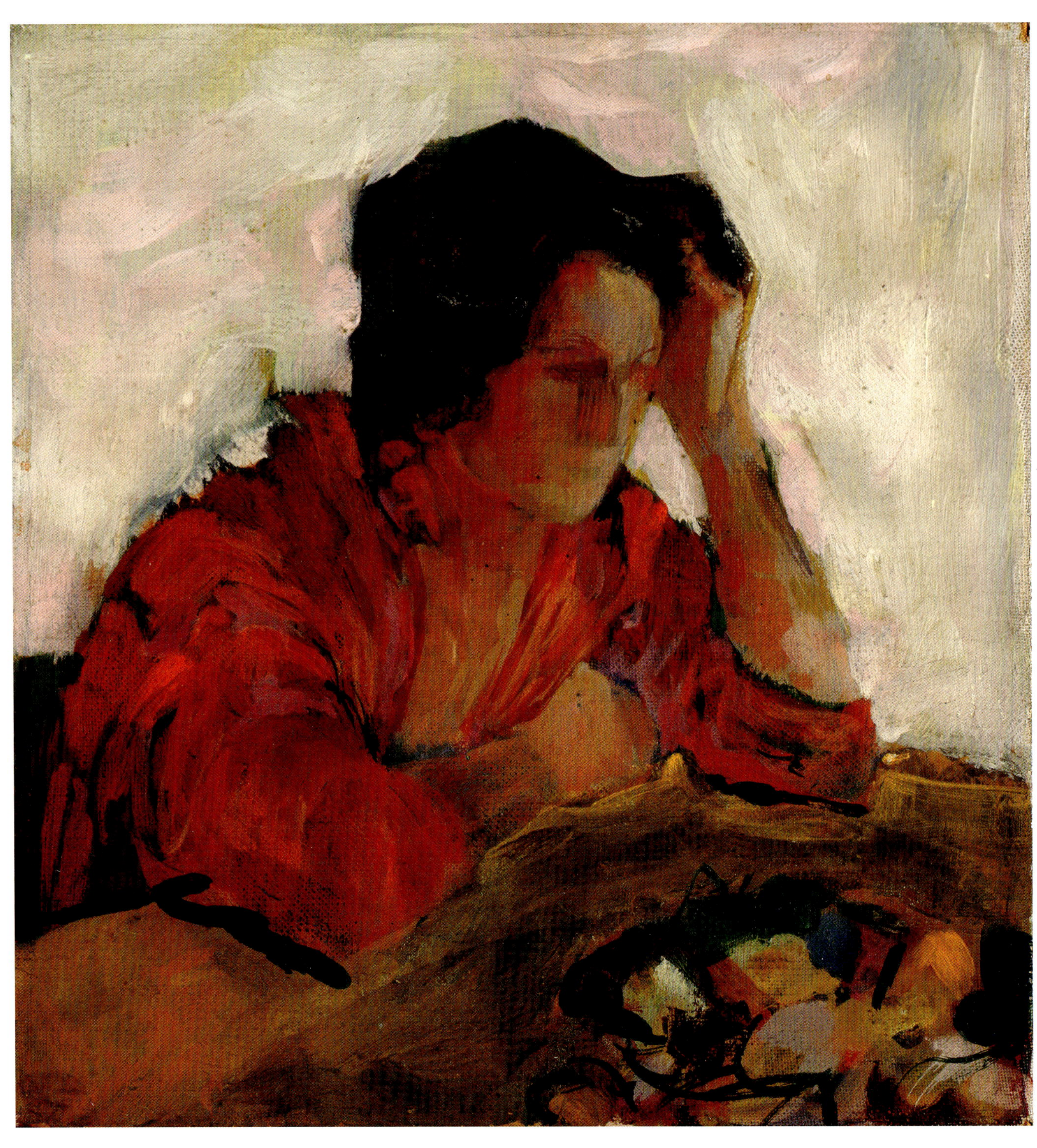

JANE WILSON, *Red Robe*, 1957
Oil on canvas, 10 x 9 inches

JANE WILSON, [1924-]

Born April 29, 1924, Seymour, Iowa.

Studied 1945: B.A., University of Iowa, Iowa City, IA; 1947: M.A., University of Iowa, Iowa City, IA.

Teaching Positions 1947–1949: State University of Iowa; 1967–1969: Pratt Institute; 1971–1983: Parsons School of Design, NYC; 1974: University of Iowa. 1975, 1986–1988: Columbia University; 1977–1978: Cooper Union; and privately.

Selected Solo Exhibitions 1951: St. John's College, Annapolis, MD; 1953, 55, 57: Hansa Gallery, NYC; 1958, 59: Ester Stuttman Gallery, NYC; 1960–1966: Tibor de Nagy Gallery, NYC; 1963: Gump's Gallery, NYC; 1963, 64: Esther Baer Gallery, Santa Barbara; 1968, 69, 71, 73, 75: Graham Gallery, NYC; 1978, 81, 84, 85, 88, 90, 91, 93, 95, 97: Fischbach Gallery, NYC; 1971: Bowling Green State University; 1974: Benson Gallery, East Hampton, NY; 1976: Westark Community College; 1979: Sordoni Art Gallery, Wilkes-Barre; Washington Public Library; 1980: Munson–Williams–Proctor Institute, Utica, NY; 1982: Cornell University, Ithaca, NY; 1988: Compass Rose Gallery, Chicago, IL; Bachalier Cardonsky, Kent, CT; 1989: Watkins Gallery, American University, Washington, D.C.; Benton Gallery, Southampton, NY; 1990: University of Virginia; Earl McGrath Gallery, Los Angeles, CA; 1991: Jaffe-Friede and Strauss Galleries, Dartmouth College, Hanover, NH; 1992: Earl McGrath Gallery, Los Angeles, CA; 1993: Arnot Art Museum, Elmira, NY; 1996: The Parrish Art Museum, Southampton, NY; Glenn Horowitz Bookseller, Inc., East Hampton, NY; 1999, 2001, 03, 04, 07: DC Moore Gallery, New York, NY; 2001: Heckscher Museum of Art, Huntington, NY; 2006, 08: The Drawing Room, East Hampton, NY.

Selected Group Exhibitions 1946: The Art Institute of Chicago, IL; 1953, 54, 55: *New York Painting and Sculpture Annuals*, Stable Gallery, NYC; 1957–1959: *New Talent*, circ., Museum of Modern Art, NY; 1961, 65, 67: *Whitney Annuals and Biennials*, Whitney Museum of American Art, NY; 1963: American Federation of Artists, circ.; 1964–1965: MIT; Corcoran, New York World's Fair; 1970: *The New Landscape,* Heckscher Museum, Huntington, NY; 1972: *The Realist Revival*, New York Cultural Center; 1974: *New Images*, Queens Museum, NY; 1978: *American Realists*, William and Mary College; 1980: *The Fifties: Aspects of Painting in New York*, Hirshhorn Museum and Sculpture Garden, Smithsonian Institution, Washington, D.C.; 1981: *Next to Nature*, The National Academy of Design, NYC; 1983: *American Still Life, 1945–1983*, Contemporary Arts Museum, Houston, TX; 1984: *The First Eight Years*, The Artists' Choice Museum, NYC; 1986: *Contemporary Romantic Landscape Painting*, Loch Haven Art Center; *The Homecoming Exhibition*, University of Northern Iowa; 1987, 89, 91, 92: *Annual Exhibitions*, National Academy of Design, NYC; 1987: *Still Life Painting*, University of Massachusetts; 1988: *Drawing on the East End, 1940–1988*, The Parrish Museum, Southampton, NY; *Art on Paper*, University of North Carolina; 1989: *American Art Today*, Florida International University; *At the Water's Edge*, circ., Tampa Museum of Art, Tampa, FL; 1990: *The 1950s at the Tibor de Nagy Gallery*, Brooklyn College, NY; 1991: *The Artist in the Garden*, National Academy of Design, NYC; *Exhibition of Works by Newly Elected Members and Recipients of Awards*, American Academy of Arts and Letters, New York, NY; *Exquisite and Sublime*, New Jersey Center for Visual Arts, Summit, NJ; *American Realism & Figurative Art: 1952–1991*, circ., organized by John Arthur and the Japan Association of Art Museums; *On Tabletop and Wall: The Art of the American Still Life*, Pennsylvania Academy of the Fine Arts, Philadelphia, PA; 1992: *New Viewpoints: Contemporary American Women Realists*, Consular Residence, Universal Exposition, Seville, Spain, developed by The National Museum of Women in the Arts, Washington, D.C.; 1993: *Contemporary Realist Watercolor,* Sewall Art Gallery, Rice University, Houston, TX; *The Collection: Porters Circle*, Parrish Art Museum, Southampton, NY; 1995: *10 + 10*, New York Studio School of Painting and Sculpture, New York, NY; 1998, 2002, 03, 04, 08: DC Moore Gallery, New York, NY; 1999: *Looking at the Visual: Art as Object, Art as Experience*, Marsh Art Gallery, University of Richmond, VA; 2005: *Artist and Nature in Eastern Long Island 1940 to 2005*, Spanierman Gallery, East Hampton, NY.

PAUL WONNER

From Cubism, there is a hangover of the conviction that somehow, whatever the three–dimensional space, the two–dimensional surface ought to be recognized, not necessarily as an intimate relationship, but rather as a speaking acquaintance.
...I think a painting has to be some kind of translation of psychological experience.

Paul Wonner, Statement: From *Bay Area Figurative Art, 1950–1965*, catalogue by Caroline A. Jones, San Francisco Museum of Modern Art, University of California Press. p. 88

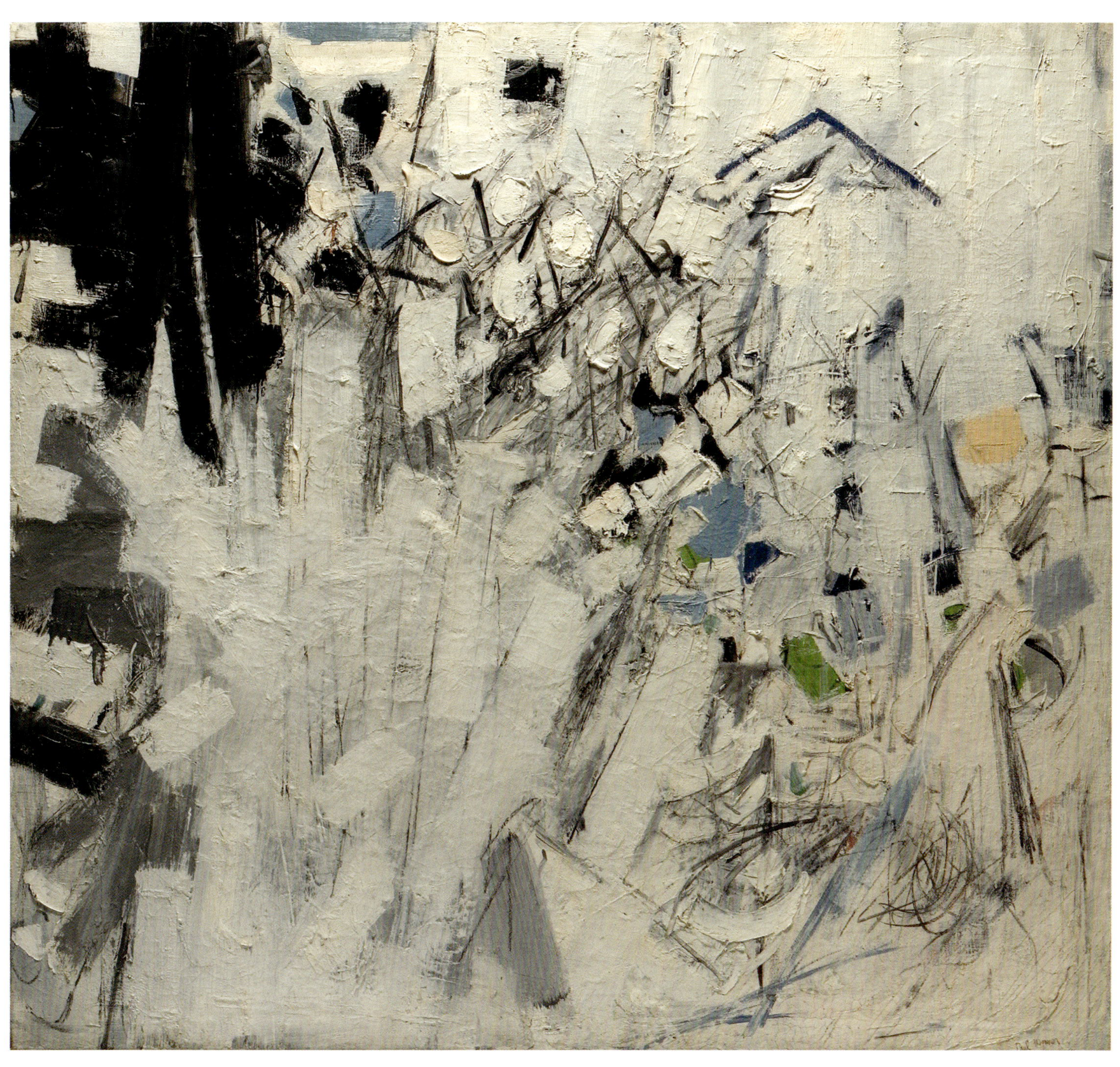

PAUL WONNER, *Abstract Landscape #2*, 1955
Oil on canvas, 45 x 48 inches
Crocker Art Museum, promised gift of George Y. and LaVona J. Blair

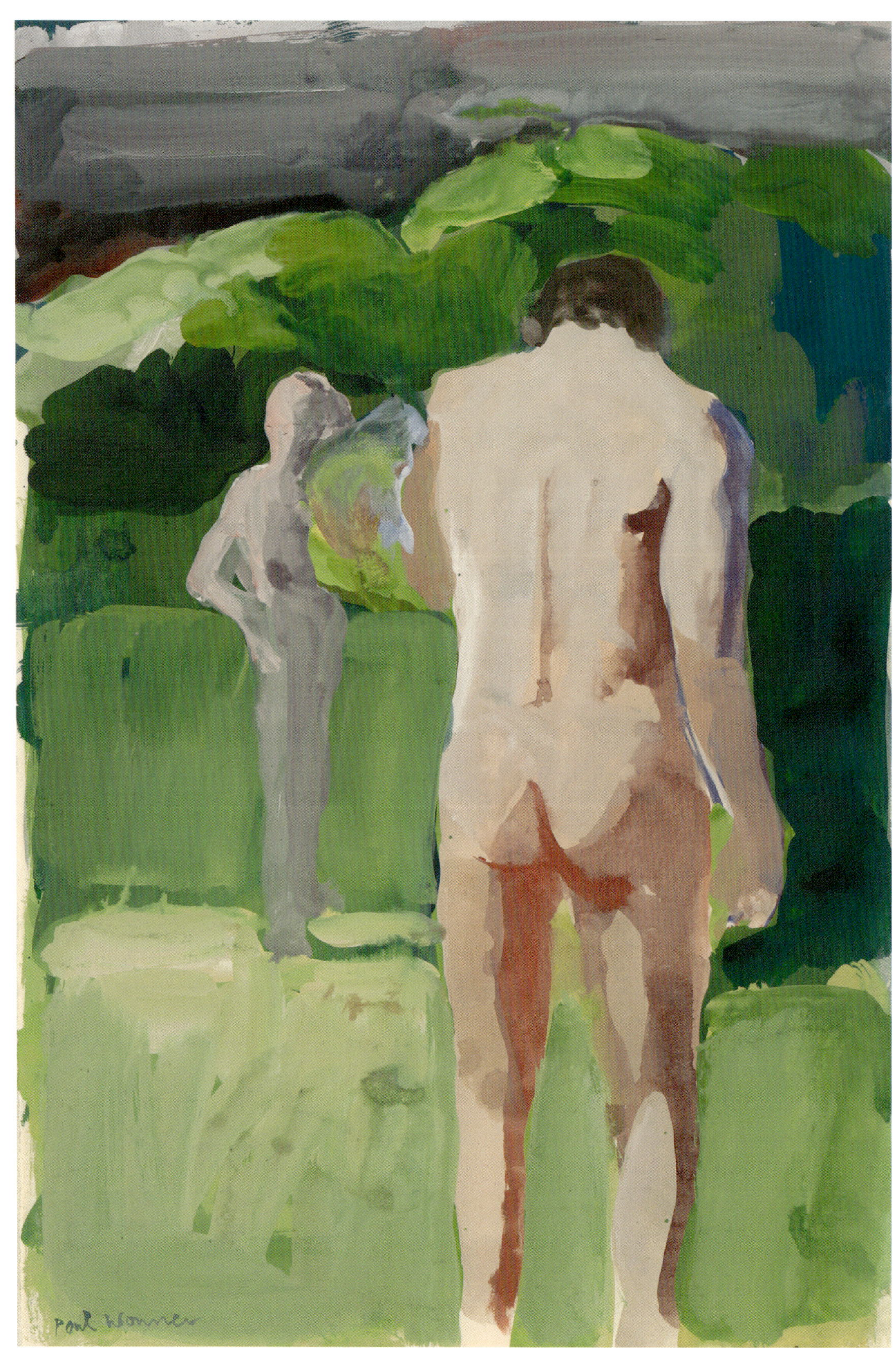

PAUL WONNER, *Figures in Sunlight*, c. 1960s
Acrylic on paper, 18 x 12 inches
Image courtesy Hackett-Freedman Gallery, San Francisco, CA

PAUL WONNER, [1920-2008]

Born 1920, Tucson, AZ.
Died April 23, 2008 in San Francisco, CA.

Studied 1942: California College of Arts and Crafts, B.A., Oakland, CA; 1947: Art Students League of New York; 1952: University of California Berkeley, B.A., 1953: M.A., Berkeley, CA.

Selected Solo Exhibitions 1956: M.H. de Young Memorial Museum, San Francisco, CA; San Francisco Art Association Gallery, California School of Fine Arts; 1959, 60, 62, 63, 64: Felix Landau Gallery, Los Angeles, CA; 1960: Santa Barbara Museum of Art, CA; 1962: California Palace of the Legion of Honor, San Francisco, CA; 1962, 64: Poindexter Gallery, NY; 1965: *Watercolors, 1963–1964*, Waddington Galleries, London, England; Marion Koogler McNay Art Institute, San Antonio, TX; 1975: The Art Galleries, California State University, Long Beach, CA.

Selected Group Exhibitions 1950, 52, 53, 54, 58, 59, 60, 61: *Annual Exhibitions of the San Francisco Art Association*, San Francisco Museum of Art, CA; 1954: *Younger American Painters*,circ., Solomon R. Guggenheim Museum, NY; *Western Painters' Annual Exhibition*, Oakland Art Museum, CA; *Fourth Annual Oil and Sculpture Exhibition*, Richmond Art Center, CA; 1955: *Art in the Twentieth Century*, San Francisco Museum of Art, CA; *III Bienal,* Museu de Arte Moderna, São Paulo, Brazil; *Vanguard 1955*, Walker Art Center, Minneaapolis, MN; *Fifth Annual Painting and Sculpture exhibition*, Richmond Art Center, CA; 1956: *Pacific Coast Art: United States' Representation at the Third Biennial of São Paulo*, circ., San Francisco Museum of Art, CA; 1957: *Contemporary Bay Area Figurative Painting*, circ., Oakland Art Museum, CA; 1958: *Artist Members' Exhibition*, California Palace of the Legion of Honor, San Francisco, CA; *The 1958 Pittsburgh International Exhibition of Contemporary Painting and Sculpture*, Carnegie Institute, Pittsburgh, PA; 1959: *Art U.S.A.* New York Coliseum; *1959 Annual Exhibition of Contemporary American Painting*, Whitney Museum of American Art, NY; 1960: *Winter International Exhibition*, California Palace of the Legion of Honor, San Francisco, CA; *Third Pacific Coast Biennial*, Santa Barbara Museum of Art, CA; *East–West*, Zabriskie Gallery, New York; 1961: *1961 Northern California Painters' Annual*, Oakland art Museum, CA; 1961, 63, 65: *Contemporary American Painting and Sculpture*, Krannert Art Museum, University of Illinois, Champaign; 1962: *Treasures from East Bay Collections*, Oakland Art Museum, CA; 1963: *Artists West of the Mississippi: The Realistic Image*, Colorado Springs Fine Arts Center, CO; 1964: *Sixty–Sevens Annual american Exhibition: Directions in Contemporary Painting and Sculpture*, The Art Institute of Chicago, IL; *Seven California Painters*, Staempfli Gallery, New York; *The 1964 Pittsburgh International Exhibition of Contemporary Painting and Sculpture*, The Carnegie Institute, Pittsburgh, PA; 1965: *Selections from the Work of California Artists*, Witte Memorial Museum, San Antonio, TX; 1972: *Surrealism is Alive and Well in the West*, Baxter art Gallery, California Institute of Technology, Pasadena, CA;

JACK ZAJAC

I used the figure primarily until 1952; then came a series of seascapes and birds in flight. In 1954 the human figure returned with as series of drawings of people in anticipation of death, its occurrence, and in resurrection.

To have a message or an emotional stimulation soaked up by an uncertainty of the Artist's tool — color — shape — form — which are the punctuation of his message, is a discouraging thing. This is the kind of anemia I'm trying to eliminate.

Jack Zajac Statement: From Thirty American Painters and Sculptors Under Thirty Five; *YOUNG AMERICA 1957*. Whitney Museum of American Art, NYC.

Jack Zajac Statement: From the *University of Illinois Exhibition of Contemporary American Painting*, Sunday, March 2, through Sunday, April 13, 1952. College of Fine and Applied Arts, Urbana, p. 241

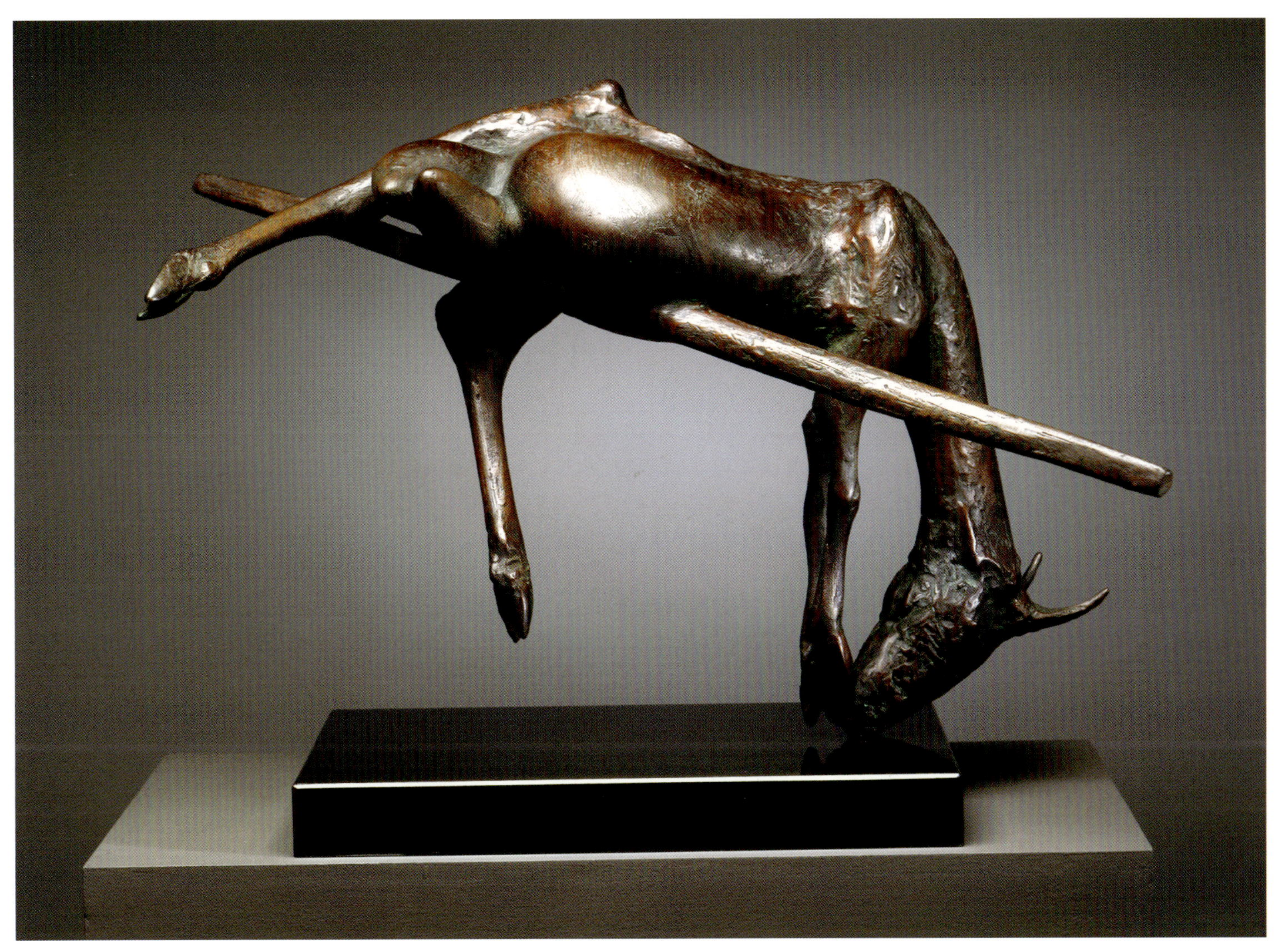

JACK ZAJAC, *Easter Goat I*, 1959
Bronze, 19 x 30 x 10 inches
Collection of The Museum of Modern Art, New York

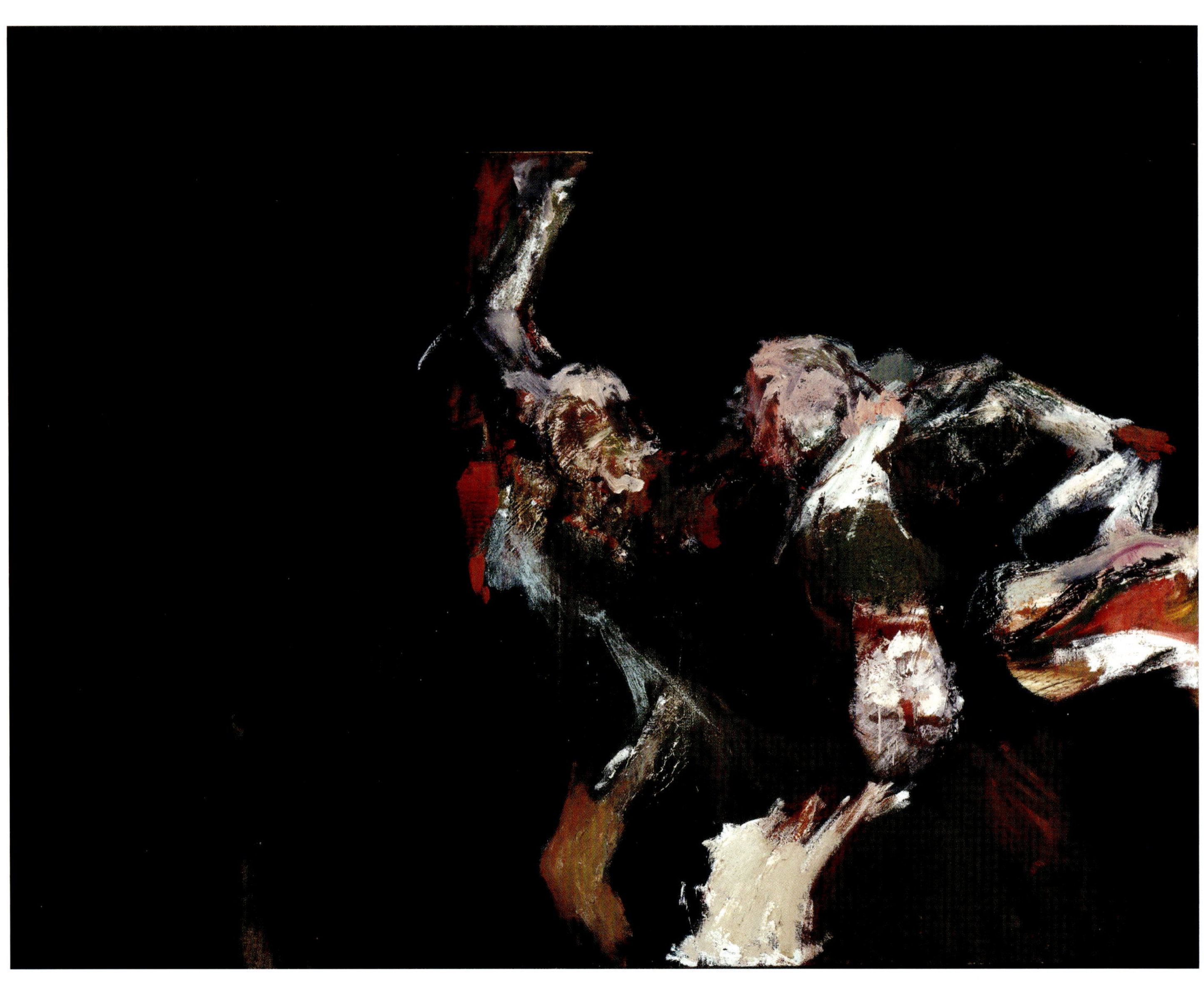

JACK ZAJAC, *Journey*, 1961
Oil on canvas, 40 x 60 inches
Collection of the artist

JACK ZAJAC, [1929-]

Born December 13, 1929 Youngstown, Ohio

Studied 1949–1953: Scripps College, Special Classes, Claremont, CA.

Selected Solo Exhibitions 1951, 53, 54, 56, 58, 60, 62, 64, 67, 69: Felix Landau Gallery; 1951: Pasadena Art Museum; 1953: Santa Barbara Museum of Art; 1955: Scripps College, Claremont, CA; 1955, 61: Schneider Gallery, Rome; 1956: John Young Gallery, Honolulu, HI; 1957: Il Segno, Rome; 1960: Downtown Gallery, New York, NY; 1960, 63: Devorah Sherman Gallery, Chicago, IL; 1960: Roland, Browse and Delbanco, London, England; 1967: Gallery Marcus, Laguna Beach, CA; 1961: Bolles Gallery, San Francisco, CA; 1963: Mills College, Oakland, CA; California Palace of the Legion of Honor, San Francisco, CA; Galleria Pogliani, Rome; 1965: Newport Pavilion Gallery, Balboa, CA; 1966, 68: Landau-Alan Gallery, New York, NY; 1968: Alpha Gallery, Boston, MA; 1970: Fairweather Hardin Gallery, Chicago, IL; 1971, 74, 78, 83: Forum Gallery, New York, NY; 1972, 76: Margherita Gallery, Rome, Italy; 1973, 75, 77: Jodi Scully Gallery, Los Angeles, CA; 1973: L'Obelisco Gallery, Rome, Italy; 1976: Maitani Gallery, Orvieto, Italy; 1989: Jan Turner Gallery, Los Angeles, CA; 1974, 77: James Willis Gallery, San Francisco, CA; 1977: Zara Gallery, San Jose, CA; 1979, 83: Mekler Gallery, Los Angeles, CA; 1980: Cedar Street Gallery, Santa Cruz, CA; 1983, 87: *Bound Goats, Santa Cruz Series*, Forum Gallery, NY; 1984, 87: Stephen Wirtz Gallery, San Francisco, CA; 1990: Jan Turner, Gallery, Los Angeles, CA. Selected retrospectives: 1953, 75: Santa Barbara Museum of Art, Santa Barbara, CA; 1968: The Galleries of Temple University, Tyler School of Art in Rome; 1970: Jaffe-Friede Gallery, Dartmouth College; 1977: Palm Springs Desert Museum, Palm Desert, CA; 1978: California State University, Los Angeles, CA; 1981: Fresno Arts Center, Fresno, CA; 1984: El Paso Museum of Art, El Paso, TX; 1990: Oakland Museum, Oakland, CA.

Selected Group Exhibitions 1950: *Artists You Should Know*, Los Angeles Art Association; 1951: Pennsylvania Academy; 1952: University of Illinois; 1955: Sao Paulo Biennale; Carnegie International; 1956: *New Talent, U.S.A., Recent Drawings U.S.A.*, Museum of Modern Art, New York; 1957: *Young America*, Whitney Museum of American Art, NYC; 1958: Festival of Two Worlds, Spoleto, Italy; *Ten Americans Living Abroad*, University of Wisconsin; 1957, 59: Santa Barbara Museum Biennial; 1959, 60: Los Angeles County Museum Annual; 1959: Whitney Museum Annual; *63rd American Exhibition*, Art Institute of Chicago; *Recent Sculpture, U.S.A.*, Museum of Modern Art, New York; 1960: *Liturgical Art*, Arts Club of Chicago; American Sculpture, Galerie Claude Bernard, Paris, France; American Academy in Rome Annual; 1961: *Drawings by Sculptors*, Smithsonian Institution, Washington, D.C; 1962: *Modern Sculpture from the Joseph H. Hirshhorn Collection*, Solomon R. Guggenheim Museum, NYC; *American Painters Today*, circ., Whitney Museum, Los Angeles County Museum and twenty others; *Fifty California Artists*, Whitney Museum of American Art; *Some Directions in Modern Sculpture*, Providence Art Club, Providence, RI; *American Painting 1962*, Virginia Museum of Fine Art, Richmond, VA; *Recent Painting U.S.A.: The Figure*, Museum of Modern Art, NYC; 1962-1963: *The Artist's Environment: The West Coast*, Amon Carter Museum Fort Worth, TX; U.C.L.A. Art Galleries; Oakland Art Museum, Oakland, CA; 1963: *Chadwick, Moore, Zajac: Small Works*, M. Knoedler & Co., NYC.

KARL ZERBE

[All modern artists have] the desire to give to the object a functional beyond its naturalistic aspect to free it from its accidental surroundings, to develop and organize it within the frame of the picture into an emotional potential. In other words, the object is elevated to a symbol.

Karl Zerbe, Statement: From Karl Zerbe, *Expressionism and Symbolism*, Art Panorama (January- February, 1945). p.12

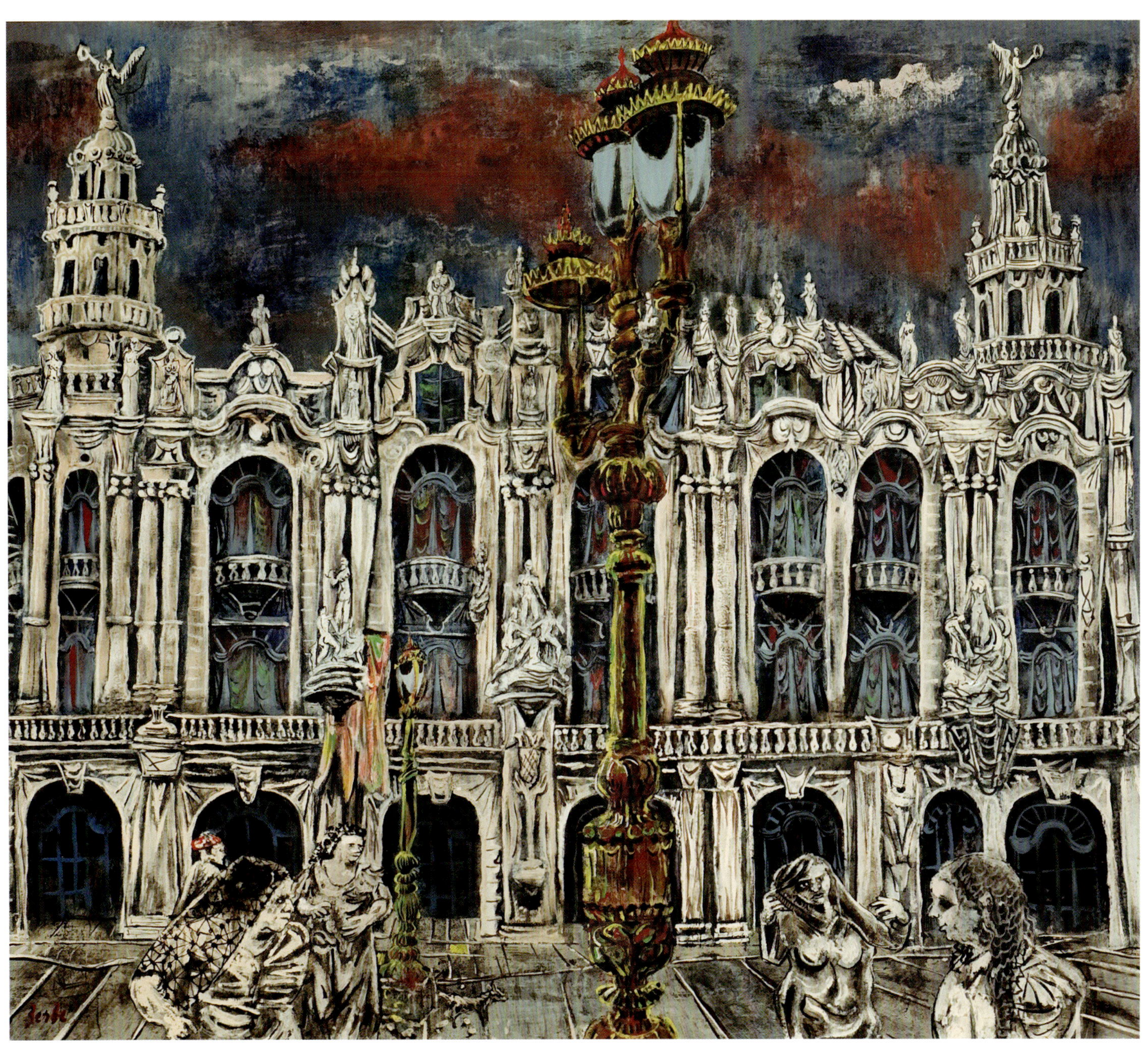

KARL ZERBE, *Spanish Facade*, 1947
Encaustic, 40 x 36 inches
Private collection

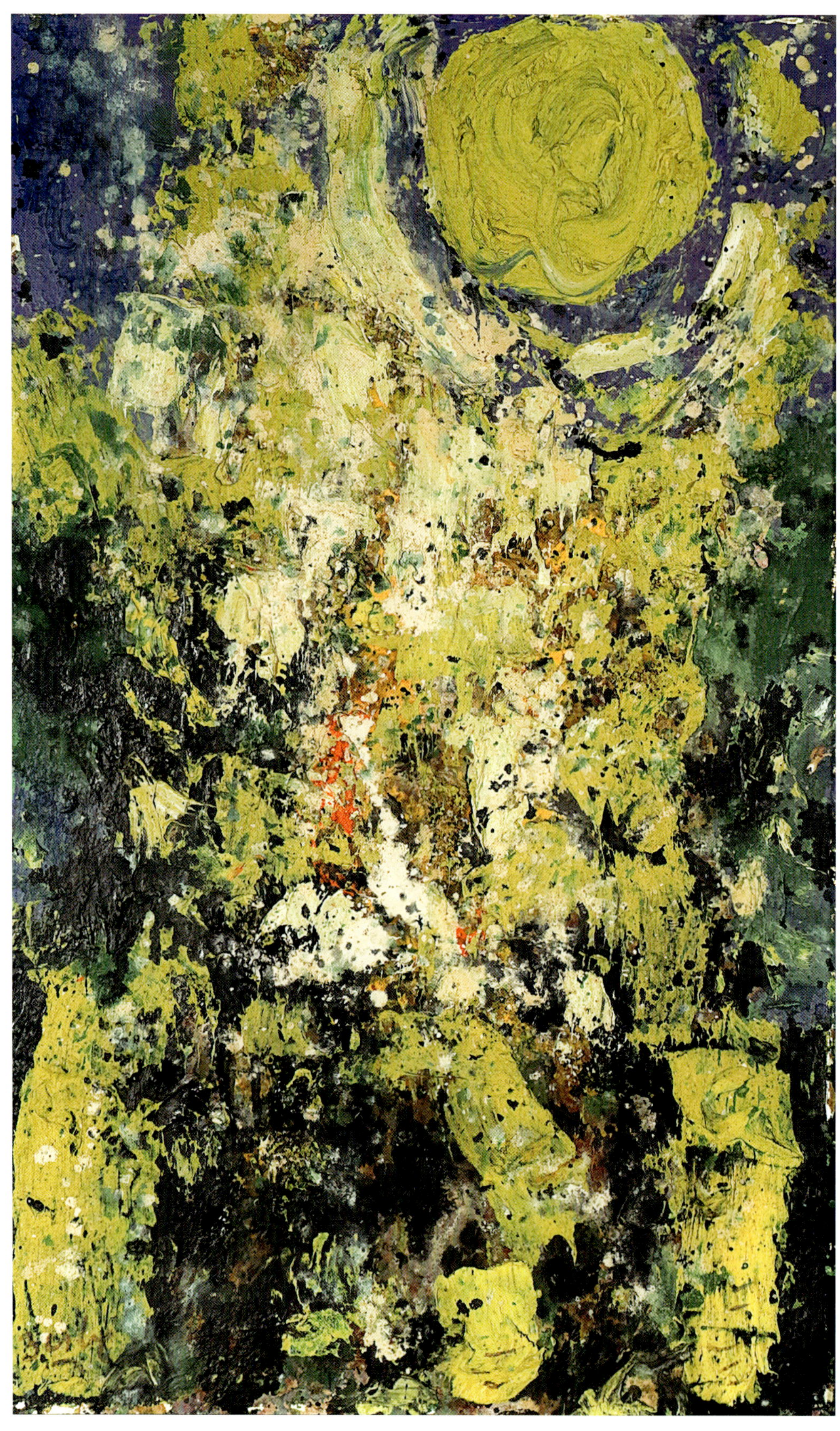

KARL ZERBE, *Growth*, 1960
Acrylic on canvas, 20 x 14 inches
Private collection

KARL ZERBE, [1903-1972]

Born September 16, 1903, Berlin, Germany. **USA citizen** 1939.
Died November 28, 1972, Tallahassee, FL.

Studied 1920: Technische Hochschule, Friedberg; 1921–1923: Debschitz School, Munich, with Josef Eberz.

Teaching Positions 1935-1937: Fine Arts Guild, Cambridge, MA; 1937–1955: Boston Museum School, Boston, MA; 1954-1972: Florida State University.

Selected Solo Exhibitions 1922: (first) Gallery Gurlitt, Berlin, Germany; 1934, 35, 36, 37: Marie Sterner Gallery, NYC; 1936, 38, 39, 40: Grace Horne Galleries, Boston, MA; 1941: Vose Gallery, Boston, MA; Buchholz Gallery, NYC; 1943: Mount Holyoke College; 1943, 47: Berkshire Atheneum, Pittsfield, MA; 1943, 46, 48, 51, 52: The Downtown Gallery, NYC; 1945, 46: The Art Institute of Chicago, IL; 1946: The Detroit Institute of Arts, Detroit, MI; 1948, 49: Philadelphia Art Alliance, PA; 1948, 55, 66: Boris Mirski Gallery, Boston, MA; 1950: Munson–Williams–Proctor Institute, Utica, NY; 1954: The Alan Gallery, NYC; 1958: John and Mable Ringling Museum of Art, Sarasota, FL; 1958, 59, 60, 64, 70: Nordness Galleries; 1962: Whitney Museum of American Art (two man), NYC; Florida State University; 1963: St. Armands Gallery, FL; James David Galley, Miami, FL; Mickelson's Gallery, Washington, D.C.; 1964: Glassboro State, College; 1965: University of Tampa, FL; 1966: Kovler Gallery. Retrospectives: 1951–1952: Institute of Contemporary Art, circ., Boston, MA; 1961–1962: American Federation of Arts, circ., NYC.

Selected Group Exhibitions 1937, 38, 39: Art Institute of Chicago, IL; 1938: Museum of Modern Art, NYC; 1939: *Golden State Exposition*, Golden Gate and San Francisco/Oakland Bay bridges, San Francisco, CA; 1941, 42, 43, 44, 45, 46, 47, 48, 49, 50, 51, 52, 53, 55, 56, 57, 58, 63: *The Whitney Annuals and Biennials*, Whitney Museum of American Art, NYC; 1948: *3rd Annual Exhibition*, California Palace of the Legion of Honor, San Francisco, CA.

INDEX OF NAMES